FOUNDATIONS of HUMAN RESOURCE DEVELOPMENT

Richard A. Swanson
Elwood F. Holton III

BERRETT-KOEHLER PUBLISHERS, INC.
San Francisco

Copyright © 2001 by Richard A. Swanson and Elwood F. Holton III

Berrett-Koehler Publishers, Inc.

235 Montgomery Street, Suite 650
San Francisco, CA 94104-2916
Tel: (415) 288-0260   Fax: (415) 362-2512   www.bkconnection.com

ORDERING INFORMATION

Quantity sales. Special discounts are available on quantity purchases by corporations, associations, and others. For details, contact the "Special Sales Department" at the Berrett-Koehler address above.

Individual sales. Berrett-Koehler publications are available through most bookstores. They can also be ordered direct from Berrett-Koehler: Tel: (800) 929-2929; Fax: (802) 864-7626; www.bkconnection.com

Orders for college textbook/course adoption use. Please contact Berrett-Koehler: Tel: (800) 929-2929; Fax: (802) 864-7626.

Orders by U.S. trade bookstores and wholesalers. Please contact Publishers Group West, 1700 Fourth Street, Berkeley, CA 94710. Tel: (510) 528-1444; Fax (510) 528-3444.

Production Management: Michael Bass & Associates

Printed in the United States of America

   Printed on acid-free and recycled paper that is composed of 80% recovered fiber, including 30% post consumer waste.

Library of Congress Cataloging-in-Publication Data

Swanson, Richard A., 1942-
   Foundations of human resource development / Richard A. Swanson, Elwood F. Holton, III.
     p. cm.
   Includes bibliographical references and index.
   ISBN 1-57675-075-2
     1. Employees—Training of. 2. Personnel management. 3. Manpower planning.
   4. Human capital. I. Holton, Ed, 1957- II. Title.

HF5549.5.T7 S883 2001
658.3—dc21   2001035602

First Edition

   06   05   04   03   02   10   9   8   7   6   5   4   3   2

Dedicated to the

ACADEMY OF HUMAN RESOURCE DEVELOPMENT

and its vision of leading the profession through research.

Brief Contents

Contents

PART FIVE
Unleashing Human Expertise through Organization Development   257

PART SIX
Human Resource Development in the 21st Century   333

List of Figures

Preface

Human resource development (HRD) is a very large field of practice and a relatively young academic discipline. Furthermore, HRD is deeply concerned about the dynamic issues of individual and organizational change. Such a profession is in need of a complete and thoughtful foundational text. That is the purpose of this book.

The intention is that this foundation book will serve the needs of both practitioners and academics for the purpose of adding clarity to their professional journeys. While we have a personal preference as to the purpose and primary means of doing HRD work, the attempt has been to provide a fair review of the range of major views that exist in the profession.

This is not a principles-of-practice book. Many books in HRD outline their version of "best practices" but do not probe more deeply to the underlying foundations of practice. This book does the opposite. For the most part, we define the underlying foundations while providing an overview of practice. Readers who seek a deeper understanding of core models that undergird best practice; who seek to understand the history and philosophies in HRD; who want to think more deeply about learning, performance, and change; and who prefer to be reflective about their practice rather than blindly follow the latest formulas will find this book a refreshing and thoughtful explication of the field.

Because the discipline of HRD is so young, there has been little work to define the foundations of the field. Our struggle with this book has been to draw boundaries without building walls. For us this book continues the conversation about the foundations of the field. In a discipline as young as HRD, a consensus about foundations will be a work in progress for many years.

This book is directed toward several audiences. First, it is designed for university courses in HRD. We argue that every HRD academic program needs a course that teaches the foundations of the field. Second, HRD researchers will find the book thought-provoking and useful as a guide to core research issues. Third, it is written for reflective practitioners who actively seek to lead the field as it grows and matures. Finally, almost every practitioner will find parts of the book that will add depth to their practice.

The seventeen chapters of the book are organized into six parts. The first part, "Introduction to Human Resource Development," establishes a basic understanding as to what HRD is, the general HRD model and process it relies on to do its work, and the history of HRD. Part Two, "Theory and Philosophy in Human Resource Development," provides the critical theoretical and philosophical foundations of HRD. Both of these perspectives have generally been missing among HRD professionals and are believed to be essential for understanding and advancing the field. The third part is titled "Perspectives of Human Resource Development," and it explicates the learning and performance paradigms of HRD and associated models within each. An attempt is made in this section to clarify the learning-performance perspectives and their logical connection.

The next part, "Developing Human Expertise through Personnel Training and Development," captures the essence of the personnel training and development component of HRD as well as the nature of human expertise. Illustrations of personnel training and development practice that exist in host organizations are presented along with variations in core thinking, processes, interventions, and tools. Part Five, "Unleashing Human Expertise through Organization Development," describes the essence of the organization development component of HRD as well as the nature of the change process. This section presents examples of organization development as well as variations in core thinking, processes, interventions, and tools.

The sixth and final part is titled "Human Resource Development in the Twenty-first Century" and serves as a springboard into the future based on best practices and identification of the twenty-first-century challenges to HRD. Major issues for HRD—strategic roles of HRD, accountability in HRD, and the globalization and technology challenges to HRD—are carefully explained.

Our sincere thanks go to the many HRD scholars throughout the world and their good work. They have made this book possible. We especially thank several of our colleagues for allowing us to include portions of their work in this book as well as for their critical review of the full manuscript: Richard W. Herling (chapter 10), Sharon S. Naquin (chapter 16), Wendy E. A. Ruona (chapter 5), Richard J. Torraco (chapters 5 and 15), and Karen E. Watkins (chapter 4). Additional critical reviews were provided by K. Peter Kuchinke, Susan A. Lynham, and Michael J. Marquardt. Our organizational partners also deserve recognition. We are grateful for the support we receive from the Academy of Human Resource Development, Berrett-Koehler Publishers, Louisiana State University, and the University of Minnesota.

Richard A. Swanson
Elwood F. Holton III

Introduction to Human Resource Development

This first section establishes a basic understanding as to what HRD is, the basics of HRD that it relies on to do its work, and the history of HRD.

CHAPTERS

HRD as a Professional Field of Practice

CHAPTER OUTLINE
Purpose of HRD
Definition of HRD
Origins of HRD
HRD Context
HRD Core Beliefs
HRD as a Discipline and a Professional Field of Practice
Conclusion
Reflection Questions

Human resource development (HRD) is a relatively young academic discipline but an old well-established field of practice. The idea of human beings purposefully developing, in anticipation of being able to improve conditions, seems almost part of human nature. HRD theory and practice are deeply rooted in this developing and advancing perspective.

This first chapter serves to highlight briefly the purpose, definition, origins, context, and core beliefs of HRD. These highlights are meant to provide an initial understanding of HRD and an advanced organizer for the book. The chapters that follow fully explore the depth and range of thinking within the theory and practice of HRD.

PURPOSE OF HRD

HRD is about adult human beings functioning in productive systems. The purpose of HRD is to focus on the resource that humans bring to the success equation—both personal success and organizational success. The two core threads of HRD are (1) individual and organizational learning and (2) individual and organizational performance (Ruona, 2000; Watkins & Marsick, 1996; Swanson, 1996a). Some view learning and performance as alternatives or rivals, while most see them as partners in a formula for success. Thus, assessment of HRD successes or results can be categorized into the domains of learning and performance. In all cases the intent is improvement.

DEFINITION OF HRD

HRD has numerous definitions. Throughout the book, we will continue to reflect on alternative views of HRD to allow readers an exposure to the range of thinking in the profession. The definition we choose to support is as follows:

HRD is a process for developing and unleashing human expertise through organization development and personnel training and development for the purpose of improving performance.

It is useful to recognize that alternative definitions of HRD have been presented over the years. For example, a recent definition took an inclusive international perspective of HRD that finds HRD functioning as an agent of societal and national development, not just focused on organizations. It reads as follows: "Human Resource Development is any process or activity that, either initially or over the long term, has the potential to develop adults' work-based knowledge, expertise, productivity, and satisfaction, whether for personal or group/team gain, or for the benefit of an organization, community, nation, or, ultimately, the whole of humanity" (McLean & McLean, 2000). Figure 1.1 provides a historical summary of the HRD definitions found in the literature through 1998 (Weinberger, 1998).

Figure 1.1　Human Resource Development Definition Summary

AUTHOR	DEFINITION	KEY COMPONENTS	UNDERLYING THEORIES
Nadler (1970)	"HRD is a series of organized activities conducted within a specified time and designed to produce behavioral change" (p. 3).	Behavioral change; adult learning	Psychological
Craig (1976)	"HRD focus is on the central goal of developing human potential in every aspect of lifelong learning."	Human performance	Philosophical; psychological

AUTHOR	DEFINITION	KEY COMPONENTS	UNDERLYING THEORIES
Jones (1981)	"HRD is a systematic expansion of people's work-related abilities, focused on the attainment of both organization and personal goals" (p. 188).	Performance, organizational, and personal goals	Philosophical; system; psychological; economic
McLagan (1983)	"Training and development is identifying, assessing and—through planned learning—helping develop the key competencies which enable individuals to perform current or future jobs" (p. 25).	Training and development	Psychological
Chalofsky and Lincoln (1983)	Discipline of HRD is the study of how individuals and groups in organizations change through learning.	Adult learning	Psychological
Nadler and Wiggs (1986)	"HRD is a comprehensive learning system for the release of the organization's human potentials—a system that includes both vicarious (classroom, medi-ated, simulated) learning experiences and experiential, on-the-job experiences that are keyed to the organization's reason for survival" (p. 5).	Formal and informal adult learning; performance	System; economic; psychological
Swanson (1987)	HRD is a process of improv-ing an organization's per-formance through the capabilities of its personnel. HRD includes activities deal-ing with work design, aptitude, expertise, and motivation.	Organizational performance	Economic; psychological; philosophical; system
Jacobs (1988)	Human performance technology is the develop-ment of human performance systems and the manage-ment of the resulting systems, using a systems approach to achieve organi-zational and individual goals.	Organizational and individual performance	System

(Continued)

Figure 1.1 Continued

AUTHOR	DEFINITION	KEY COMPONENTS	UNDERLYING THEORIES
R. Smith (1988)	"HRD consists of programs and activities, direct and indirect, instructional and/or individual that positively affect the development of the individual and the productivity and profit of the organization" (p. 1).	Training and development; organizational performance	Economic; system; psychological
McLagan (1989)	"HRD is the integrated use of training and development, career development and organizational development to improve individual and organizational effectiveness" (p. 7).	Training and development; career development; organizational development	Psychological; system; economic
Watkins (1989)	"HRD is the field of study and practice responsible for the fostering of a long-term, work-related learning capacity at the individual, group and organizational level of organizations. As such, it includes—but is not limited to—training, career development and organizational development" (p. 427).	Learning capacity training and development; career development; organizational development	Psychological; system; economic; performance
Gilley and England (1989)	"HRD is organized learning activities arranged within an organization to improve performance and/or personal growth for the purpose of improving the job, the individual and/or the organization" (p. 5).	Learning activities; performance improvement	Psychological; system; economic; performance
Nadler and Nadler (1989)	"HRD is organized learning experiences provided by employees within a specified period of time to bring about the possibility of performance improvement and/or personal growth" (p. 6).	Learning; performance improvement	Performance psychological

AUTHOR	DEFINITION	KEY COMPONENTS	UNDERLYING THEORIES
D. Smith (1990)	"HRD is the process of determining the optimum methods of developing and improving the human resources of an organization and the systematic improvement of the performance and productivity of employees through training, education and development and leadership for the mutual attainment of organizational and personal goals" (p. 16).	Performance improvement	Performance system; psychological; economic
Chalofsky (1992)	"HRD is the study and practice of increasing the learning capacity of individuals, groups, collectives and organizations through the development and application of learning-based interventions for the purpose of optimizing human and organizational growth and effectiveness" (p. 179).	Learning capacity; performance improvement	System; psychological; human performance
Marquardt and Engel (1993)	HRD skills include developing a learning climate, designing training programs, transmitting information and experience, assessing results, providing career counseling, creating organizational change, and adapting learning materials.	Learning climate; performance improvement	Psychological; human performance
Marsick and Watkins (1994)	"HRD as a combination of training, career development, and organizational development offers the theoretical integration need to envision a learning organization, but it must also be positioned to act strategically throughout the organization" (p. 355).	Training and development; career development; organizational development; learning organization	Human performance; organizational performance; system; economic; psychological

(Continued)

Figure 1.1   Continued

AUTHOR	DEFINITION	KEY COMPONENTS	UNDERLYING THEORIES
Swanson (1995)	"HRD is a process of developing and unleashing human expertise through organization development and personnel training and development for the purpose of improving performance" (p. 208).	Training and development and Organization development; performance improvement at the organization, work process, and individuals levels	System; psychological; economic

Source: Weinberger (1998, pp. 77–79). Used with permission.

You can think of HRD in more than one way. Our preferred definition of HRD describes HRD as a process. Using the process perspective, HRD can be thought of as both a system and a journey. This perspective does not inform us as to who does HRD or where it resides in the organization. At the definitional level, it is useful to think about HRD as a process and specifically as a process open to engaging different people at different times and to locating HRD in different places inside and outside the host organization.

Another way to talk about HRD is to refer to it as a department, function, and job. It can be thought of as an HRD department or division in a particular organization with people working as HRD managers, HRD specialists, and so forth. Furthermore, these people work in HRD spaces called HRD centers, training rooms, retreat centers, and corporate universities. HRD can also be identified in terms of the context and content it supports—for example, insurance sales training and insurance sales organization development. Even with these department, function job, and physical space titles, HRD can also be defined as a process.

We have identified two major realms of focus within HRD. One is organization development (OD); the other is personnel training and development (T&D). As implied by their names, OD primarily focuses at the organization level and connects with individuals, while T&D primarily focuses on individuals and connects with the organization. The realms of career development, quality, and performance improvement are important extensions of HRD theory and practice.

ORIGINS OF HRD

It is easy to logically connect the origins of HRD to the history of humankind and the training required to survive or advance. While HRD is a relatively new term, training—the largest component of HRD—can be tracked back through evolution of the human race. Chapter 3 on the field's history provides the long-range view of the profession. For now, it is important to recognize the massive development effort that took place in the United States during World War II as the origin of contemporary HRD. Under the name of the "Training within Industry" project (Dooley, 1945), this massive development effort gave birth to systematic (1) performance-based training, (2) improvement of work processes, and (3) the improvement of human relations in the workplace—contemporary HRD.

HRD CONTEXT

The context in which HRD functions is almost always within a host organization. The organization can be a corporation, business, industry, government agency, or a nonprofit organization—large or small. The host organization is a system having a mission with mission-driven goals and outputs. In an international context, the host organization for HRD can be a nation. This strategic investment in HRD at the nation level can range from maintaining high-level national workforce competitiveness to fundamental elevation of a nation from poverty and disarray.

The host organization may also be a multinational or global organization with operations in many continents and many nations. Such complex organizations can both affect the structure of HRD and be the focus of HRD work. HRD has traditionally been sensitive to culture within an organization and between organizations. Making the transition to global issues has been relatively easy for HRD.

HRD can be thought of as a subsystem that functions within the larger host system for the purpose of advancing, supporting, harmonizing, and, at times, leading the host system. Take, for example, a company that produces and sells cars to customers. Responsible HRD would be ever vigilant to this primary focus of the company and see itself as supporting, shaping, or leading the various elements of the complex automobile organizational system in which it functions. Much more will be said about this contextual reality of HRD in the following chapters. For now, it is important to think about the great variations in how HRD fits into any one organization as well as the variation among the many types of organizations that exist in society. This complexity is compounded by the cultural differences from region to region and nation to nation in which HRD functions. It is an interesting and exciting profession!

HRD CORE BELIEFS

HRD professionals, functioning as individuals or workgroups, rarely reveal their core beliefs. This is not to say that they do not have core beliefs. The reality is that most HRD professionals are busy, action-oriented people who have not taken the time to articulate their beliefs. Yet, almost all decisions and actions on the part of HRD professionals are fundamentally influenced by subconscious core beliefs.

The idea of core beliefs will be discussed in a number of places throughout this book. We will reveal for now one set of HRD core beliefs and a brief interpretation of each for the purpose of providing an initial understanding of what motivates and frames the HRD profession.

1. *Organizations are human-made entities that rely on human expertise to establish and achieve their goals.* This belief acknowledges that organizations are changeable and vulnerable. Organizations have been created by humankind and can soar or crumble, and HRD is intricately connected to the fate of any organization

2. *Human expertise is developed and maximized through HRD processes and should be done for the mutual long- and/or short-term benefits of the sponsoring organization and the individuals involved.* HRD professionals have powerful tools available to get others to think, accept, and act. The ethical concern is that these tools not been used for exploitation but rather for the benefit of all.

3. *HRD professionals are advocates of individual/group, work process, and organizational integrity.* HRD professionals typically have a very privileged position of accessing information that transcends the boundaries and levels of individuals, groups, work processes, and the organization. Getting rich information and seeing things that others may not have a chance to see also carries a responsibility. At times harmony is required, and at other times the blunt truth is required.

Gilley and Maycunich (2000, pp. 79–89) have set forth a set of principles that guide the HRD. They contend that effective HRD practice

- integrates eclectic theoretical disciplines;
- is based on satisfying stakeholders' needs and expectations;
- is responsive but responsible;
- uses evaluation as a continuous improvement process;
- is designed to improve organization effectiveness;
- relies on relationship mapping to enhance operational efficiency;
- is linked to the organization's strategic business goals and objectives;
- is based on partnerships;
- is results oriented;
- assumes credibility as essential;
- utilizes strategic planning to help the organization integrate vision, mission, strategy, and practice;
- relies on the analysis process to identify priorities;

- is based on purposeful and meaningful measurement; and
- promotes diversity and equity in the workplace.

Most sets of principles are based on core beliefs that may or may not be made explicit. The pressures for stating principles of practice are greater than for stating overarching core beliefs. Both have a place and deserve serious attention by the profession.

HRD AS A DISCIPLINE AND A PROFESSIONAL FIELD OF PRACTICE

The HRD profession is large and widely recognized. As with any applied field that exists in a large number and variety of organizations, HRD can take on a variety of names and roles. This can be confusing to those outside the profession and even sometimes confusing to those in the profession. We take the position that this variation is not always bad. We see this book, and HRD, embracing the thinking underlying

- training,
- training and development,
- employee development,
- technical training,
- management development,
- executive and leadership development,
- human performance technology,
- organization development, and
- organizational learning.

Thus, practitioners who work in HRD may have varying titles such as manager of management development, organization development specialist, and director of technical training.

In addition, HRD roles can span the organization such as the chief learning officer, director of organizational effectiveness, or director of executive development. They can also fit within a subunit such as manager of sales training, HRD coordinator (at a particular company location), or bank teller training specialist. Furthermore, a very large contingent in organizations is doing HRD work as part of their non-HRD jobs. For these people, HRD work is part of their larger job. It is almost impossible to calculate the total organizational commitment to HRD. Reports of chief executive officers leading executive development programs and shipping clerks doing on-the-job training of new employees are commonplace. Efforts at analyzing the total financial commitment to HRD have been elusive.

Estimates in the United States have led enormous financial numbers spent annually to conceptual comparisons. For example, it is estimated that the money spent on HRD in the workplace each year exceeds all the money spent on public education—kindergarten through universities—in the same time period. By any assessment, HRD is a huge profession with a huge annual expenditure.

We also see HRD as overlapping with the theory and practice underlying other closely linked domains, including the following:

- Career development
- Organizational and process effectiveness
- Performance improvement
- Strategic organizational planning
- Human resource management (HRM)
- Human resources (HR)

Probably the most apparent connection is with human resources (HR). HR can be conceived of as having two major components—HRD and HRM. As an umbrella term, HR is often confused with HRM. Thus, many HR departments are actually limited to HRM goals and activities such as hiring, compensation, and personnel compliance issues. Even when HRD and HRM are managed under the HR title, their relative foci tend to be fairly discrete.

CONCLUSION

The practice of HRD is dominated by positive intentions for improving the expertise and performance of individuals, work groups, work processes, and the overall organization. Most observers suggest that HRD evokes common sense thinking and actions. This perspective has good and bad consequences. One good consequence is the ease with which people are willing to contribute and participate in HRD processes. One bad consequence is that many of the people working in the field have little more than common sense to rely on.

The ultimate importance of this book is to reveal the underlying thinking and supporting evidence that allow HRD professionals to accept and apply sound theories and tools confidently. Such a foundation has the potential of ridding the profession of frivolous and invalid armchair theories and faddish practices. Foundational HRD theory and practices are the focus of this book.

REFLECTION QUESTIONS

1. Identify a definition of HRD presented in this chapter that makes the most sense to you and explain why.

2. Identify a definition of HRD presented in this chapter that makes the least sense to you and explain why.
3. What would you consider to be part of HRD and not part of HRD? Why?
4. Of the three HRD core beliefs presented in this chapter, which one is closest to your beliefs? Why?
5. Based on the ideas presented in this chapter, what is it about HRD that interests you the most?

Basics of HRD

CHAPTER OUTLINE
Points of Agreement
   Goal of Improvement
   Problem Orientation
   Systems Thinking
HRD Worldview
   HRD and Its Environment
   Learner Perspective
   Organizational Perspective
   Global Context
HRD Process
   Process Phases of HRD
   Interplay between the Phases of the HRD Process
Threats to a Systematic Approach
   Turning the HRD Process into an Event
   The Rate of Change
   Characteristics of the Key Players
Ethics and Integrity Standards
   Standards
Conclusion
Reflection Questions

There is no one way to view HRD or to go about the work of HRD. In this chapter we will present some of the basic HRD underpinnings as a further orientation to HRD. The selection of HRD basics in this chapter is meant to illustrate, not to be exhaustive. Like chapter 1, this Chapter provides a basic framework for understanding HRD. You should be prepared to expand on the thoughts in this chapter as you progress through the book. For now these basics help to orient readers who are new to HRD and serve to refresh the thinking of those already familiar with the profession.

POINTS OF AGREEMENT

As with any field of theory and practice, there are rival views and intense debates as to the importance of rival views or those differences. Pointing out differences is important. Even more important is to point out the agreements. It is the agreements that provide the solid core of HRD theory and practice. In contrast, the differences create the tension required for serious reflection and growth among scholars and reflective practitioners.

HRD is an evolving discipline, which makes for exciting debates within the profession. It is important for those engaging in and listening to these debates not to lose sight of their points of agreement. Three overriding points of agreement include the goal of improvement, a problem orientation, and systems thinking.

Goal of Improvement

The idea of improvement overarches almost all HRD definitions, models, and practices. To improve means "to raise to a more desirable or more excellent quality or condition; make better" (*American Heritage Dictionary,* 1993, p. 684). The improvement ideas of making positive change, attaining expertise, developing excellent quality, and making things better are central to HRD. This core goal of *improvement* is possibly the single most important idea in the profession and the core motivator of HRD professionals.

The HRD profession is focused on making things better and creating an improved future state. Examples include everything from helping individuals learn and master new content to helping organizations determine their strategic direction. There is a core debate among HRD professionals as to the purpose of HRD being either learning or performance. For example, Krempl and Pace (2001) contend that HRD "goals should clearly link to business outcomes" (p. 55), while Bierema (1996) states that "valuing development only if it contributes to productivity is a view point that has perpetuated the mechanistic model of the past three hundred years" (p. 24). It is interesting to listen more closely to each side and to discover that learning is seen as an avenue to performance and that performance requires learning. In both cases there is the overarching concern for improvement.

Problem Orientation

HRD is problem oriented. A problem can be thought of as "a situation, matter, or person that presents perplexity or difficulty" (*American Heritage Dictionary,* 1993, p. 1090). It is these perplexing or difficult situations, matters, and people that justify HRD and ignite the HRD process. In that HRD professionals see themselves as constructive and positive agents, some do not want to talk about their work in the language of problems. Essentially, their view is that there is a present state and a future desirable state, and the gap between is the *opportunity* (or problem).

At times HRD professionals know more about the present state than the desired future state, and at other times they know more about the desired future state than the actual present state. HRD critics often say that HRD practitioners know more about what needs to be done than they know about either the present or desired states. Other critics would say that many HRD people are more interested in their programs and activities than in the requirements of their host organization. These criticisms are summarized as "having a solution in search of problem" and "a program with no evidence of results."

With all the various tools and techniques reported in the HRD literature, each having its own jargon, it is useful to think generally about HRD as a problem-defining and problem-solving process. HRD professionals have numerous strategies for defining the problem and even more strategies for going about solving the problem (techniques for making things better). A core idea within HRD is to think of it being focused on problems for the purpose of improvement. (More positive terms to use would be *opportunity* or *requirements*—as in improvement opportunities or improvement requirements.)

Systems Thinking

HRD professionals talk about systems views and systems thinking. They think this way about themselves and the organizations they serve. Systems thinking is basic to HRD theory and practice. It is described as "a conceptual framework, a body of knowledge and tools that have been developed over the past fifty years to make full patterns clearer, and to help us see how to change them effectively" (Senge, 1990, p. 7). Systems thinking is an outgrowth of system theory. General system theory was first described by Boulding (1956) and Bertalanffy (1962) with a clear *antimechanistic* view of the world and the full acknowledgment that all systems are ultimately *open systems*—not closed systems.

The basic system theory model includes the (1) inputs, (2) processes, and (3) outputs of a system as well as a feedback loop. Furthermore, basic system theory acknowledges that the system is influenced by its larger surrounding system or environment (see Figure 2.1).

This is referred to as an *open system* or a system that is capable of being influenced by forces external to the system under focus. These systems ideas provide the basis for many practical HRD tools used for identifying improvement problems (opportunities) and for taking action.

Systems thinking allows HRD to view itself as a system and to view its host or sponsoring organizations as a system. When HRD professionals think of HRD as a system, they generally talk about HRD being a subsystem within a larger or-

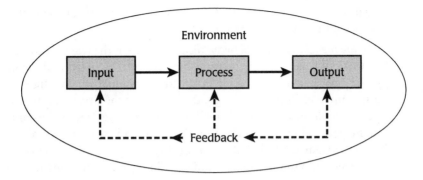

Figure 2.1   Basic Systems Model

ganizational system. Organizational analysis experts sometimes refer to subsystems as *processes*, and thus HRD is more often discussed as a process than a system. This is not meant to be confusing—most people simply see that a systems view and a process view are almost the same. What can be said is that when people talk about a systems view, they are usually thinking more broadly and more generally than when they talk about a process view. There is a point when system and process views overlap.

Basic system theory—the root of systems thinking—informs us that there are initial and fundamental requirements to engage in systems thinking and analysis about systems (and processes). Just being able to respond to the following three questions in actual organizational and HRD work situations represents a fundamental application of systems thinking in practice.

1. *What is the name and purpose of the system?* What systems are called and their purposes are often points of great departure from one person to another. By naming the system, people can first agree as to what system they are talking about. It is very interesting to have intelligent and experienced people in a room begin to talk about a situation only to find out that the unnamed system some are talking about differs from the system others are talking about. Furthermore, differing perspectives on the purpose of the system are almost always under contention until they are made explicit.

2. *What are the parts or elements of the system?* This question throws another elementary but essential challenge to a systems thinker. We find that people with a singular or limited worldview only see the world through that lens. Examples we have seen are production people not seeing the customer; salespeople not seeing production; new-technology people only seeing technology as the system rather than the larger system of people, processes, and outputs; and legal people seeing the system as conflictual in nature versus harmonious. With these limited views, indi-

viduals will be drawn to limited perceptions of the parts or elements of the system that may not match reality.

3. *What are the relationships between the parts?* Here is the real magic of system theory—analyzing the relationships between the parts and the impact of those relationships. Even HRD experts wonder whether they ever get it complete. Quite frankly, good analysts are the first to admit their own shortcomings. Yet, their belief is that in the struggle to understand a system, you end up with a better and more complete understanding of that system. An analysis of the relationship between parts forces one to dive deeper into understanding and explaining a system—why it works and why it is not working. The simple analogy of putting enormous pressure on an employee to find out whether he or she can, in fact, perform a task illustrates the point. If the person can then perform the task, expertise is not the missing piece. Thus, the idea that people are not performing tasks well, and therefore training is needed, is unacceptable until more is known. Workers may know how to perform the task well but choose not to for many reasons. You probably could name several from your own personal experience. There are numerous reasons in any system why things happen and do not happen. Figuring these out requires more than superficial analysis or metaphoric analogy. System theory is basic.

HRD WORLDVIEWS

The good news is that HRD professionals almost always have a view of the world. The bad news is that they rarely articulate it and systematically operationalize it for themselves, their colleagues, and their clients. Years ago, Zemke and Kerlinger (1982, pp. 17–25) implored HRD professionals to have general mental models for the purpose of being able to figure out the complexity and context surrounding HRD work.

HRD and Its Environment

Figure 2.2 contains a worldview of HRD in context of the organization and environment. This holistic model positions HRD as a five-phase system or process paralleling the other processes in the organization. The organizational system and the processes within each have their inputs, work processes, and outputs. The environment in which organizational system functions is also identified and illustrated. The organizational system is seen to have its unique mission and strategy, organization structure, technology, and human resources. The larger environment is characterized by its economic, political, and cultural forces. As expected, this is an open system where the influence of any component can slide up and down the levels of this model—from the global economy down to the na-

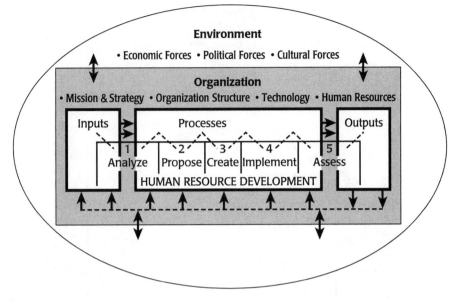

Figure 2.2   HRD in Context of the Organization and Environment

ture of an executive development program sponsored by a particular HRD department in a specific company.

Learner Perspective

Other worldviews that gain support in HRD include a view of the organization as a productive enterprise and individuals as learners and contributors. Figure 2.3 stems from the original work of Malcolm Knowles, who is considered to be the father of adult learning or *andragogy*. This worldview of andragogy in practice places adult learning principles into the context of adult life through the perspectives of (1) individual–situation differences and (2) the goals-purposes for learning. In Figure 2.3 you see the six adult learning principles enveloped by these contextual issues that impact learning. The worldview related to the adult learner is concerned with the learning process within the context of the learning purpose and situation (Knowles, Holton, & Swanson, 1998).

Organizational Perspective

The organizational worldview perspective is represented here by the work of Rummler and Brache (1995). In their matrix of Nine Performance Variables, the dominance of the organization and its need to perform are acknowledged (see Figure 2.4). Included are three performance levels: organization, work process, and individual performance. This worldview argues for the organization that

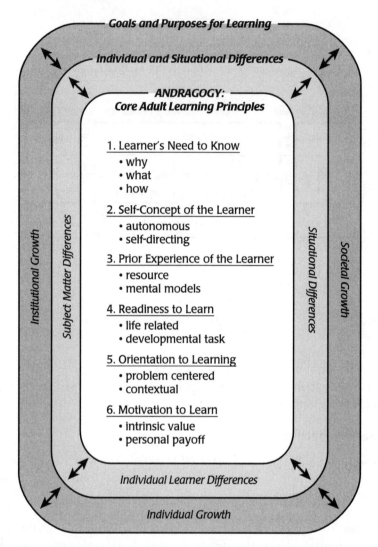

Figure 2.3 Andragogy in Practice (*Source:* Knowles, Swanson, & Holton, 1998.)

reaches to the individual, while the learner perspective has the individual dominating and reaching to the organization. The organization performance view takes the general stance that good people are working in bad systems. For example, the quality improvement expert, W. Edwards Deming, estimated that 90 percent of the problems that might be blamed on individuals in the workplace were a result of having them working in bad processes or systems. He fundamentally believed in human beings and their capacity to learn and perform. His goal was to focus on the system structure and processes that got in the way of learning and performance.

THE THREE PERFORMANCE NEEDS

		Goals	Design	Management
	Organization Level	Organization Goals	Organization Design	Organization Management
THE THREE LEVELS OF PERFORMANCE	Process Level	Process Goals	Process Design	Process Management
	Job/Performer Level	Job Goals	Job Design	Job Management

Figure 2.4   Nine Performance Variables (*Source:* Rummler & Brache, 1995. Used with permission.)

Global Context

The global context in which we all function has fundamentally changed. Political, economic, and cultural forces have shifted in the last decade and continue to shift. The outer rim of concerns for most HRD professionals—those things that happened far away in other nations—are now part of standard considerations. HRD fortunately has had a tradition of cultural sensitivity as it has worked from region to region and from one work group to another, resulting in a demand for HRD expertise in the globalization process.

McLean and McLean (2001) have hypothesized that HRD is an important factor in the inevitable move to globalization. They note that while globalization is not new, its present demands are so intense that it fundamentally changes the way and rate at which change occurs. Globalization "enables the world to reach into individuals, corporations, and nation-states farther, faster, deeper, and cheaper than ever before" (Freidman, 2000, p. 9). One framework for HRD to use in dealing with globalization is to adopt the following new mindsets (Rhinesmith, 1995):

1. Gather global trends on learning, related technology, training, and organization development to improve the competitive edge.

2. Think and work through contradictory needs resulting from paradoxes and confrontations in a complex global world.

3. View the organization as a process rather than a structure.

4. Increase ability to work with people having various abilities, experiences, and cultures.

5. Manage continuous change and uncertainty.

6. Seek lifelong learning and organizational improvement on numerous fronts.

Our overall message in presenting these several worldviews is that every HRD professional should have a worldview that allows him or her to think through situations time and time again. Conceptual worldview models help HRD professionals gain clarity from the complex situations they face.

Thus far we have discussed basic ideas that influence HRD. Each of these basic ideas assists in understanding the challenges HRD faces and the strategies it takes in facing those challenges. The ideas include

- improvement as a goal of HRD,
- problem orientation of HRD,
- systems thinking in HRD,
- worldviews for HRD, and
- global context.

HRD PROCESS

Based on the basic ideas in the prior section, it is rational to think of HRD as a purposeful process or system. Thus, the general consensus regards HRD as a process. In addition to being thought of as a process, HRD is viewed as an organizational function, a department, and a job.

Our position is that the dominant view should be of HRD as a process. Moreover, the views of HRD as a function, department, and job are less important contextual variations.

When HRD is viewed as a process and is thought of in terms of inputs, processes, outputs, and feedback, potential contributors and partners are not excluded. In that HRD needs to engage others in the organization to support and carry out portions of HRD work, it is best to have the process view as the dominant view.

Most often, HRD is talked about as a process and not a system. Within HRD there are specialized terms to describe its process elements. These elements are most commonly called *phases*.

Process Phases of HRD

We have defined HRD as a process that is essentially a problem-defining and problem-solving method. HRD and its subsets of personnel training and development (T&D) and organization development (OD) can be portrayed as five-phase processes. Variations in the wording for the HRD, T&D, and OD process phases capture the common thread and varying terminology. Here are all three variations:

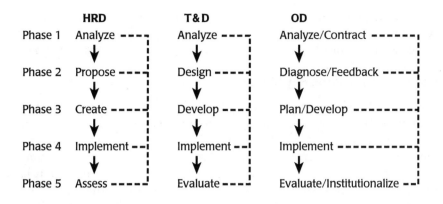

Interplay between the Phases of the HRD Process

The process phase view suggests that they are major stages in the HRD process and that each phase has an important relationship crucial to achieving the desired outcomes. One of the biggest professional problems facing HRD practitioners is in honoring all phases. Studies of HRD practice reveal shortcomings at the analysis and assessment/evaluation phases. These are the two most strategic phases of the HRD process. The disturbing shortcomings are compounded because relationships between the phases rely on the analysis phase for direction and substance. Furthermore, organizational commitment to HRD is dependent on positive performance results reported at the assessment/evaluation phase (Kusy, 1984; Mattson, 2001).

THREATS TO A SYSTEMATIC APPROACH

Davis and Davis (1998) tell us that "the HRD movement, on its way to becoming a serious profession, can no longer afford an atheoretical approach" (p. 41). Even so, there are serious threats to theoretically sound and systematic HRD. Three of the threats are discussed here briefly.

Turning the HRD Process into an Event

This is an ever-present threat to a systematic approach to HRD. The actual time that people get together within the HRD process can become the focal point, with the real reason for getting together being lost. Obsessions with fun-filled training and hearing everybody's full opinion on a matter can become an end unto itself rather than a means to an end. An irrational concern for participant satisfaction can also fuel the possibility of undermining the process.

The Rate of Change

The familiar saying "The faster I go, the behinder I get" haunts most HRD practitioners. The intensity of the rate of change requires more from HRD, which then can threaten to undermine a systematic HRD process. Not enough time? It is very tempting to eliminate the assessment or cut back on the up-front analysis and go with your off-the-head analysis or to bypass the final assessment phase.

Characteristics of the Key Players

Sleezer (1991) informs us of the strengths and liabilities of the critical characteristics of the HRD professional, the client/decision maker, and the host organization in impacting the HRD process. These characteristics influence the thoroughness and integrity of the overall process—for the good or detriment. For example, an analyst overly focused on human relationships may ignore hard organizational performance data. When the characteristics of the key players are ignored and not managed properly, the integrity of the HRD process will likely erode. Responsibly engaging multiple stakeholders and multiple sources of data in the HRD process is essential to good practice and requires careful attention.

ETHICS AND INTEGRITY STANDARDS

Being in the business of defining and solving problems associated with people in dynamic organizations is challenging work. While opportunities exist for improvements, HRD as a discipline calls upon multiple theories in a manner unique to its own purposes. HRD is focused on personnel training and development and organization development to improve processes and enhance the learning and performance of individuals, organizations, communities, and society.

HRD professionals are individuals engaged in HRD-related practice, research, consulting, and instruction/facilitation/teaching. They strive to create a body of research-based knowledge and to apply that knowledge to HRD in various organizational, community, and societal settings while functioning as professors, researchers, organization development consultants, trainers, managers, and leaders.

The Academy of Human Resource Development (AHRD) has produced *Standards on Ethics and Integrity* (AHRD, 1999) to provide guidance for HRD professionals engaged in practice, research, consulting, teaching, and facilitation. Although these principles are aspirational in nature, they provide standards of conduct and set forth a common set of values. Adherence to these standards builds further definition and clarification of HRD as a profession. The primary goal of the AHRD standards is to define more clearly a holistic balance among individuals, groups, organizations, communities, and societies whenever conflicting needs arise. Case studies connected to the ethics and integrity standards have also been produced to assist in the interpretation of the standards (Aragon & Hatcher, 2001).

To ensure this balance, these standards identify a common set of values upon which HRD professionals build their professional and research work. In addition, the standards clarify both the general principles and the decision rules that cover most situations encountered by HRD professionals. They have as their primary goal the welfare and protection of the individuals, groups, and organizations with whom HRD professionals work.

In providing both the universal principles and limited decision rules to cover many situations encountered by HRD professionals, this document is intended to be generic and not a comprehensive, problem-solving, or procedural document. Specific statements and solutions for special HRD-related situations will emerge from the development of case studies appended to this standard. Each professional's personal experience as well as his or her individual and cultural values should be used to interpret, apply, and supplement the principles and rules set forth in these pages.

Standards

The content outline for the standards follow. A full standards document is available on the AHRD Web site (www.ahrd.org).

TABLE OF CONTENTS FOR THE AHRD STANDARDS ON ETHICS AND INTEGRITY

Preface
Purpose
General Principles
    Competence, Integrity, Professional Responsibility
    Respect for People's Rights and Dignity
Concern for Others' Welfare
    Social Responsibility
Standards
    General Standards
        Boundaries of Competence; Maintenance of Expertise; Basis for Research and Professional Judgments; Description of HRD Professionals' Work; Respecting Others; Nondiscrimination; Exploitative Relationships; Misuse of HRD Professionals' Work; Multiple Relationships; Consultations and Referrals; Third Party Request for Services; Delegation to and Supervision of Subordinates; Documentation of Professional and Research Work; Records and Data; Fees and Financial Arrangements; Accuracy in Reports to Payers and Funding Sources; Referrals and Fees
    Research and Evaluation
        Research and Evaluation in Professional Context; Data Collection Responsibility; Compliance with Law and Standards; Institutional Approval; Informed Consent; Incentives to Participants; Deception in Research; Interpretation and Explanation of Research and Evaluation Results.
    Advertising and Other Public Statements
        Definition of Public Statements by Others; Avoidance of False or Deceptive Statements; Media Presentations
    Publication of Work
        Reporting of Research and Evaluation of Results; Plagiarism; Publication Credit; Duplicate Publication of Data; Release of Data; Professional Reviewers; Ownership of Intellectual Property

Privacy and Confidentiality
Discussions of the Limits of Confidentiality; Protection of Confidentiality; Maintenance and Ownership of Records; Disclosures; Consultations; Confidential Information in Databases; Use of Confidential Information for Didactic or Other Purposes
Teaching and Facilitating
Design, Development, Implementation, and Evaluation of Programs; Descriptions of Programs; Accuracy, Objectivity, and Professionalism in Programs; Limitation on Training and Instruction; Assessment of Performance
Resolution of Ethical Issues and Violations
Familiarity with Ethics; Informal Resolution of Ethical Violations; Conflicting Pressure with Organizational Demands; Improper Complaints

CONCLUSION

To be effective over time, it is essential to have a worldview model for thinking about how HRD fits into the milieu of an organization and society. It is also essential to have a process view of how HRD works and connects with other processes. Taking the five-phase process view of HRD, the HRD profession has traditionally been stronger in its middle creation and implementation phases and has been working hard at mastering the analysis and assessment phases at each end of the process. In pursuit of problems, improvements, and systematic practice, HRD professionals struggle to maintain high standards of ethics and integrity.

REFLECTION QUESTIONS

1. What is the relationship among the improvement, problem orientation, and systems thinking within the HRD profession?
2. Identify and explain something about systems thinking in the chapter that is new to you.
3. What, if any, is the logical connection between the figures presented in this chapter?
4. Explain how your own general worldview(s) fits with the HRD in the context of the organization and environment worldview.
5. Why are integrity and ethics important to HRD?

History of Human Resource Development

The history of human resource development reveals that education, training, and organization development of all sorts are largely the products of social and economic conditions. Scott's (1914) early characterization of education is still meaningful: "education is the attempt of a civilization to perpetuate what it believes to be most vital in itself" (p. 73).

Personnel training and development has a unique role in the history of the human resource development (HRD) profession. As you will read in this chapter, training—in the form of parent–child, master–apprentice workplace learning models—has existed throughout all recorded history of the human race. The history of HRD helps the reader understand (1) the origins of the HRD profession,

(2) the major developments and events, and (3) the reason why the profession is as it now exists.

THE BEGINNINGS: SURVIVAL THROUGH LABOR AND LEARNING

Human experience and the nature of human resource development have passed through many stages since the beginning of the human journey. Training in its most simple form was found among our most primitive ancestors. The development of humans was driven exclusively by the need to survive. When learning first involved the making of simple tools from wood, stone, and fibers, primitive humans knew still nothing about the productive use of fire and of metals. Harnessing these elements would become critical to further development of the human race

The context of primitive education was limited to the family or tribe, and education was a science, such as it was known at the time—informal and often-chaotic activity. It occurred through unconscious imitation of the head of a family or group, usually the father. Even as recently as the early twentieth century, Monroe (1907) points out, "the father, then, becomes the one who trains the younger generation in the formal conduct of life—in the proper way of doing things" (p. 8). Yet despite its informality, an essential feature of education was apparent even in this most primitive form—"the fitting of the child to his physical and social environment through the appropriation of the experience of previous generations" (Monroe, 1907, p. 1).

The Use of Tools and Mutual Cooperation

Eventually humans gained the ability to control fire for the cooking of food, the smelting of metals, and the making of simple mechanical and agricultural tools. This allowed people to engage in crafts and undertake domestic activities that were previously impossible without basic tools. It also led to a true division of labor wherein some pursued weaving, others became carpenters, still others became stone masons, and so on.

For the first time, people began to rely on tools and on each other to meet their needs. Indeed, humankind's progress through the ages has been inextricably linked to the development of practical tools and securing the bonds of mutual cooperation necessary for survival. With the development of tools and bonds of mutual cooperation came a new form of education—one characterized by conscious imitation rather than the unconscious imitation of earlier education (Bennett, 1926). The transfer of skill from one person to another now became a conscious process. Learning occurred through deliberate imitation of examples provided by one who had achieved mastery of a particular skill. Yet, education followed no theory or system and had not yet become a rational process. Those seeking a skill simply copied a model over and over until it could be precisely reproduced. Despite some advancement, the training of one person by another was still a quite primitive process.

Especially during humankind's early history, we are reminded that modest intellectual development came almost exclusively through efforts to adapt to a harsh physical and social environment. As Davidson (1900) states, "Human culture advances in proportion as men husband their powers by the use of implements, and by union for mutual help. Such husbandry requires higher and higher education" (p. 25). As the history written here reveals, the education and training needed for human progress was painfully slow in developing.

100 B.C.–300 A.D.: THE INFLUENCE OF THE GREEKS AND ROMANS

The key Roman legacy has been their ingenuity in creating the institutions needed to carry out political and social agendas. Although Roman education did not have the persistent influence of Greek contributions to education (e.g., the Socratic method of inquiry), the Roman educational infrastructure and organization of schools continued well after the conquest and fall of the Roman Empire.

The Greek Disdain for Menial Work

The legacy of "the golden age of Greece" has been a philosophy of education that, unlike any culture since that of ancient Greece, is most consistent with the present notion of a liberal education. Indeed, the Greeks were the first to see education as providing an opportunity for individual development (Moore, 1936).

The Greek conception of education included many dimensions vital to individual development that are still valued today. Human inquiry into all phases of life—nature, man, the supernatural—was an important dimension of Greek education that is today often considered the pursuit of knowledge for its own sake. The moral dimension of education, which emphasized the ethical rights and responsibilities of individuals, first found expression during the Greek era. In addition, aesthetic education and education's role as an agent of culturation and citizenship were first proposed by the Greeks. Above all, the Greeks viewed education as a vehicle for individual development and personal achievement. Through education, the Greeks sought to gain the capabilities of using and even profiting by their talents.

Despite this perspective, the Greeks did not hold the same generous view of training in the trades and mechanical arts (Bennett, 1926). They felt disdain toward what were seen as menial occupations such as farming, cattle raising, shoemaking, smithing, and tool making. Socrates is credited with providing some reasons for this contempt for handwork. He wrote of these trades as ruining the bodies of those who work at them, having gloomy and distasteful working conditions, allowing little time for leisure, and providing no development of the mind or soul (Moore, 1936). With this attitude toward manual labor, it is not surprising that training in manual arts had no place in the education of Greek youth of the upper classes. Yet training in manual arts was not completely shunned by the Greeks, for it was through an enduring system of apprenticeship among the lower classes that skills were developed in construction, manufacturing, agriculture, and other areas that were instrumental in the historic accomplishments of Greek civilization. Although not held in high esteem by the Greek upper classes, apprenticeship training clearly had an important role in the development of ancient Greece.

It is difficult to overstate the influence of the Greek era on the subsequent development of the philosophy and methods of education. It is remarkable that the present notion of education as a means for personal and intellectual development had its roots so long ago.

In light of this rich legacy, it seems almost trivial to note that the Greeks could not develop the infrastructure or institutions to allow a majority of their citizens to become educated. Most ancient Greeks did not have their freedom, and only the small minority of Greeks who were free could participate in education. A belief in the importance of education and personal development ironically coexisted with the reality of slavery.

The Pragmatic View of the Romans

The Romans adopted Greek ideals but went further by integrating them into Roman life through the establishment of laws and institutions. Unlike the standards of excellence and harmony held by the Greeks, the Romans were a more practical people whose judgments were based on usefulness and effectiveness. Although their influence on education was not nearly as profound as that of the Greeks, the Romans provide an example of how laws and political infrastructure can be used to achieve long-term social, economic, and cultural change.

The great Roman achievements in public works, architecture, and the construction of roads and aqueducts is well known, yet there is little evidence that the handwork and mechanical arts required for these accomplishments were valued by the Romans. Like the Greeks, the Romans relied on laborers and tradesmen to develop the infrastructure of their empire, despite the fact that manual skills were never held in high esteem. Romans acquired these skills through family apprenticeship. An important duty of Roman fathers was the development of practical skills and trades in their children.

The Roman Empire, like others that reached a period of great success, eventually began to decline. Roman life became more corrupt as lethargy and materialism replaced the virility and strength of character associated with early Rome. Roman education became artificial and drained of the vitality it once had. Even before the invasion of Rome by barbarians from the north, education provided by the early Christian Church was gradually replacing Roman education in both substance and spirit. The influence of Christianity on the purposes and methods of education was to continue to grow throughout the Middle Ages.

300–1300 A.D.: THE MIDDLE AGES

The goals and methods of training continued to be influenced by the many developments that occurred during an extended period in history known as the Middle Ages. Barlow (1967) characterizes the period spanned by the Middle Ages in the following way: "The so-called Middle Ages account for approximately a thousand years of history between ancient and modern. Beginning in the early 300's and extending into the early 1300's, the period is divided into two nearly equal parts. The turning point between the early and later Middle Ages is marked at 800, when Charlemagne was crowned Holy Roman Emperor" (p. 18).

The influence of Christianity permeated medieval life. Although successive imperial decrees during the fourth century made Christianity the official religion of the Roman Empire, for all practical purposes institutional control of the people had already passed to the Church. In the wake of the decadent Romans and barbarous Goths and Vandals, there was a great need for the structure and moral discipline that Christianity offered. The Church also embraced the lower classes, which had been neglected by the pagan society of Rome and the elitist culture of Greece.

Greco-Roman culture and education were methodically displaced by the training and rituals of Christianity: Training in Church dogma and spiritual consciousness replaced Greek aesthetic and intellectual ideals and rigid moral training and discipline were substituted for Roman materialism. Under the dominance of Christianity, the education of that era received a completely new character.

Monastic School Influence

An important element of Christian discipline and teaching is the spiritual value of one's own labor. This view was exemplified by the fervor and discipline of early Christian monastic life. As the intellectual landscape became more barren in the Middle Ages, the burden of academic learning and preserving the classics fell almost completely to Christian monasteries.

The Christian value of labor and the role of the monastery as guardian of academic learning combined to provide an environment conducive to the advancement of manual labor and training in manual and mechanical arts. As monasteries were intended to be separate from the secular world and as self-sufficient as possible, they operated many small-scale agricultural and industrial functions needed to maintain an independent existence such as gardens, mills, bakeries, and various shops for construction and maintenance. Monks and prelates skilled in these trades directed monastery operations and provided the necessary training in agriculture, practical arts and crafts, and various building and mechanical skills (Bennett, 1926). Practical learning, such as it was at that time, was a central part of monastic life.

Monasteries were also the center of intellectual life and preserver of literature and art throughout the Middle Ages. All who participated in monastic life were taught basic reading and writing skills. In addition, monks worked tirelessly at writing manuscripts, producing and preserving books, and developing their skills in the arts of painting, music, and sculpture. As the skills of writing and bookmaking were held in high esteem, academic and artistic training were also an important part of monastic life.

Outside the monasteries participation in skilled labor was also the principal means of learning new skills and improving one's economic position. As crafts and trades became more differentiated and specialized, apprenticeship continued to emerge as the dominant mode of transmitting practical and technical expertise from one person to another.

The Apprenticeship Method

Apprenticeship has been a basic and persistent influence on the development of workplace and is probably the most important nonschool institution around which training has grown. With roots in the very beginning of recorded history, apprenticeship training from parent to child and master to apprentice has been the enduring of all methods for transferring knowledge and skill. Bennett (1926) observes that up until the nineteenth century a great majority of people, even those from the more progressive nations, received no formal schooling, and what education they acquired was through some form of apprenticeship. This also included the professions such as law and medicine.

Davis (1978) characterizes apprenticeship as a system for preparing the young to become expert workers. The three stages of apprenticeship—apprentice, journeyman, and master—varied in length and in sophistication of expertise developed. One began training as an apprentice for a period of about seven years under direction of a master, one who had achieved the highest level of expertise at a particular vocation. The master was expected to provide apprentices not only with occupational training but also with the same moral, religious, and civic instruction that he would give his own child. The master gradually would impart all of the "mysteries" of his craft—the generally not-so-mysterious rules, recipes, and methods of applying basic arts and sciences to the craft—to apprentices over the course of their apprenticeship. As a journeyman who had achieved the basic skills and understandings of his craft, one could begin working as a day laborer, start to earn a fixed wage, and, if mutually agreeable, work with other masters of the craft. After another period of several years developing his skills as a journeyman, one may have mastered the competencies expected of the craft or present a masterpiece to demonstrate his skills and achieve the level of master. A master craftsman could set up his own business, take on apprentices, and provide instruction in the vocation.

Organization of Merchant and Craft Guilds

One of the most characteristic features of medieval life in the latter half of the Middle Ages was the organization of merchant and craft guilds. These associations were formed among those with common interests for mutual protection and benefit. Craftsmen and artisans organized themselves by occupation to protect themselves from substandard workmanship and low wages and selling prices. Working hours were strictly regulated, and quality standards for products and workmanship were established. Some guilds even prescribed the tools and methods a guild member must use to perform their trade.

By the fourteenth century, most guilds had begun offering education to members and their children in addition to the apprenticeships by which one initially earned membership in the guild. Guild-sponsored educational activities were of two kinds: elementary education provided by clergymen for the children of guild members, and an apprenticeship indenture system for the sons of guild journeymen. These were provided both as benefits to members and to further the interests and influence of the guilds. The first craft guild for which a written record exists is the Candlemakers' guild of Paris in 1061 (Barlow, 1967).

As guilds maintained strict standards for the skills needed to gain membership, they were forerunners of the craft unions of today that still require a prescribed level of competence for membership. Like the guilds, today's craft unions also regulate the quantity and quality of work, restrict the number of new apprentices, and closely monitor wages and prices.

By the close of the thirteenth century, a restless individualism was awakening the intellectual dormancy of the Middle Ages. The unity of medieval thought was broken by rebellion against medieval discipline, the revival of classical learning, and revolt against the Catholic Church known as the Protestant Reformation. In addition, two developments facilitated the intellectual revival of the Renaissance and eventually brought education within the reach of more than just the rich: the use of the vernacular in writing and the invention of printing. Latin had long been the dominant language of learning and religion, even though the great masses of people did not understand it. Even minor progress in bringing reading and writing skills to more people could not take place until this language barrier had been penetrated. In the fourteenth century, books began to appear in languages more people could understand with the appearance of works such as Dante's *The Divine Comedy* and Bocaccio's *Decameron*. Shortly thereafter, in about 1450, the printing of books from type was invented. Prior to this, books had to be meticulously copied by hand from manuscripts, a process that inhibited the widespread availability of books and other printed materials. Yet despite these advances, the Renaissance was a great revival of learning for the few with wealth and education. It would still be centuries before more people could begin to enjoy the benefits of education and personal development. The most common type of training at this time continued in roughly the same form it had always been—the father–son or master–apprentice system.

1400–1800 A.D.: THE RENAISSANCE

The Renaissance heralded a new era of scientific and philosophical thinking. A continuous stream of social, political, and scientific advances began to appear as great minds struggled with the practical and philosophical problems of the day.

Several figures had a profound impact on historical developments, including advancements in education and training, during and after the Renaissance. Four such influential figures were Martin Luther, John Locke, Jean-Jacques Rousseau, and Johan Pestalozzi. The influences of these men are examined in this history because each has made an important and uniquely different contribution to the development of technical training. In addition, each of these figures comes from a somewhat different time during the period of the thirteenth through eighteenth centuries. This allows us to trace a rough chronology of educational developments as they affected technical training during this period.

Secular Education for Girls and Boys

In addition to the criticism Martin Luther (1483–1546) directed at the Roman Catholic Church that catalyzed the Protestant Reformation, he was also critical of the education given in monastic and ecclesiastical schools. Luther, an Augustinian monk and professor of theology at the University of Wittenburg, abhorred the rigid discipline and harsh restrictions of church education, which he described as "monkish tyranny." Consequently, he proposed that religion and the church should no longer dominate education. He felt that education should embrace both religious and secular domains and that educational reform should come through the power of the state, although existing institutional structures for delivering education developed through the centuries by the church should continue to be used.

Luther's vision of education included a remarkable notion for that period—that education be given all people, not just the rich, and be available to girls as well as boys! His view of education was much broader than what could be provided by the schools of his time. Education should go beyond religious training and emphasize the classics, mathematics, logic, music, and history and science.

Sensory Learning

John Locke (1632–1704) possessed a broad range of intellectual interests and wrote a number of important works on the many subjects in which he had expertise. He studied philosophy at Oxford and later received a degree in medicine, which he practiced for a short time. He became a Fellow of the Royal Society of

London and eventually developed a theory of education that combined practical and moral training with intellectual training. He also produced some of the most influential works on political thought ever written (Ebenstein, 1969). Yet it is his two works on the philosophy and methods of education that have had a lasting effect on the development of technical training.

In his "Essay Concerning Human Understanding," Locke formulated his theory of knowledge, emphasizing experience and the perception of the senses as important bases of knowledge. Later known as *empiricism,* this epistemology shaped Locke's ideas on what should constitute an ideal education. Locke's *Some Thoughts on Education* was written as a series of letters to a friend who had requested Locke's advice on the education of his son. This important series of writings specifically laid out the purposes of education, how problems in educating the young should be overcome, and, of significance to the development of technical training, what components of education should provided. Locke firmly believed that education should address the development of logical thinking and preparation for practical life. Consequently, he wrote that an education should include the learning of one or more manual trades, as well as physical, moral, and intellectual training. In addition to learning the skill of drawing, Locke particularly approved of woodworking and gardening as ways in which the young could benefit from a broader, experiential education than could be gained from books alone. Although these were novel ideas at the time, Locke's generous view of the philosophy and substance of education can still be seen in the educational methods of Western nations.

Experience, the Best Teacher

The visionary ideas about education of Jean-Jacques Rousseau (1712–1778) appear to have grown out of his own life. In his earlier years, the restless, self-indulgent Rousseau moved from one work experience to another far more than was acceptable for the time. He was an engraver's apprentice, a lackey, a musician, a seminary student, a clerk, a private tutor, a music copier, and the author of a prize-winning thesis written for the Academy of Dijon on "Whether the progress of the sciences and of letters has tended to corrupt or elevate morals." The later experience demonstrated his brilliant yet quite controversial ideas on the failures of contemporary social progress. His ideas on the values and moral principles that should guide the state and its obligations to the people found full expression in the *Social Contract,* Rousseau's major political treatise that was the ideological basis for the French Revolution and an important influence on our own Declaration of Independence.

Quite possibly through the circumstances of his own life, Rousseau firmly believed that experience is the best teacher and that education must be formed around the active experience of the young. Rousseau's ideas for how education should evolve from a rigid, book-bound process to a more natural, spontaneous experience are found in his delightful and eloquent Emile, named for the child of

Rousseau's imagination whose education and development Rousseau traces from birth to marriage. In explaining Emile's adolescent development in a section of the work entitled "The Choice of a Trade," Rousseau states:

> [S]how him the mutual dependence of men, avoid the moral aspects and direct his attention to industry and the mechanical arts that make themselves useful to each other. As you take him from one workshop to another, never let him see any kind of work without putting his hands to it, and never let him leave till he knows perfectly the reason for all that he has observed. With that in view, set him an example by working yourself in the different occupations. To make him a master, become an apprentice. You can be sure that he will learn more by one hour of manual labor than he will retain from a whole day's verbal instructions. (Boyd, 1962, p. 86)

Rousseau clearly valued handwork and the mechanical arts as a central component of the education of the young. Yet it is significant to note that as the passage cited indicates, Rousseau would have Emile learn a trade not so much for its practical use as for its value in acquiring a broader and more meaningful education. Rousseau's recognition of the value of technical training in educating youth marked the beginning of a new era in education and an important contribution to the development of technical training.

Manual Training

With the contributions to education of Johan Heinrich Pestalozzi (1746–1827) came further movement from the old education of the simple acquisition of knowledge to the evolving notion of education as organic development. For the spirit and energy of his work, and the importance of the educational principles he proposed, Pestalozzi has been called the "father of manual training." Pestalozzi came from a family of modest means and self-admittedly was of no more than average intellectual ability. Yet his contributions not only set a new course for education and technical training in Europe but were among the strongest influences on the development of education and training in the emerging American colonies as well.

Pestalozzi concerned himself with the nature of education as a whole, and his ideas spanned the conceptual spectrum from educational theory and philosophy, to institutional settings best suited to education to techniques for teaching skills. According to Bennett (1926), Pestalozzi's broad conception of education and training grew naturally out of a number of factors: (1) his intense desire to improve the conditions of the poor and of children in his native Switzerland; (2) his firm belief that such improvement must come through education if it was to be permanent; (3) his opinion that school should be closely connected with, and prepare one for life in the home, rather than leading one away from it; (4) his interest in the natural, experiential education of Rousseau; (5) his successful use of manual labor, tools, and objects as means for teaching traditional school subjects;

and (6) his belief that engaging children in manual labor for the primary purpose of their development might also be used to pay for their education. Through practices in the schools he established, Pestalozzi demonstrated that the subject matter of education should be part of the immediate environment of the learner and used to develop their sense perceptions and formation of judgments. Pestalozzi's methods demanded the analysis of subject matter into its component parts and the use of inductive learning methods by proceeding from simple to complex elements as the way of achieving mastery of the whole.

In his writing, Pestalozzi (1898) states, "There are two ways of instructing; either we go from words to things or from things to words. Mine is the second method." This simple yet powerful truth is at the core of Pestalozzi's work, which has had such an important effect on the development of technical training. Pestalozzi's important contributions to education and training were carried forward by other influential figures such as von Fellenberg, Herbart, and Froebel.

APPRENTICESHIP IN COLONIAL AMERICA

As the United States developed, apprenticeship training served a critical role in advancing individuals and the economy.

European Influence

The Europeans who came to settle North America were people of piety and culture who had reaped the fruits of the Renaissance and Reformation and who respected the importance of education. As apprenticeship was the dominant educational institution of the time, as it had been for centuries, the early colonists in America brought apprenticeship with them in much the same form as it existed in the mother country of England. But, as Seybolt (1917) points out, because there were no guild or craft organizations in the colonies through which apprenticeships could be established, the scope of apprenticeships became broader and were administered by municipal authorities. Although apprenticeships were eventually to become displaced by a system of schooling in the wake of the industrial revolution, early Americans expanded the role of apprenticeship as the dominant method of culturation and training of those who would build the new nation.

The English laws that provided for the apprenticeship of poor children were primarily enacted to insure the safety and physical welfare of the poor and only secondarily as a means of instruction. As early as 1641 colonial authorities broadened the scope of apprenticeship to emphasize its educational purpose. The colonists wished to make apprenticeship available to all children whose education might be neglected, not just the poor. This reliance of the colonists on apprenticeship was particularly important because of the strong value placed by the colonists on the merits of "one's own labor." Not only did they feel that teaching young people practical skills and trades would be profitable to the community; they also held Puritan beliefs in the virtue of industry and the "sin of idleness." The Massachusetts Bay Colony consequently enacted a comprehensive apprenticeship law for all children that required training in skills needed for a "calling" and the development of the "ability to read and understand the principles of religion and the capital laws of the country" (Seybolt, 1917, p. 37).

Shortly thereafter, in 1647, the beginning of what was to become the American public school system first appeared. Early Americans realized that all parents and guardians were not able to teach reading and writing, despite the requirement that all children be given this elementary education. As a result, the General Court of Massachusetts ordered that every town of fifty or more homes recruit a teacher from their district and be responsible for paying the teacher's wages. Thus began the system of free public schools in the United States.

Early Leaders

Among early American leaders who influenced the development of American education, Horace Mann (1796–1859) should be singularly distinguished. Davidson (1898) writes, "[T]the first man who fully understood the needs of the nation, and undertook to meet them in large, practical ways, was Horace Mann, to whom American culture owes more than to any other person. He was exactly the influence needed by the nation in her hour of spiritual awakening" (p. 246). Mann recognized the needs of the poor and uneducated of the new nation and saw the important role of education in alleviating them. In addition, he possessed the vision to formulate a broad plan for a new system of education and had the persistence and energy to see it carried out. Indeed, as head of the Massachusetts Board of Education and later as a U.S. congressman, Mann worked tirelessly to establish a system of education that met the needs of the people and the nation.

His belief that education should develop one's intellectual and practical skills furthered the advancement of practical and technical training in the new world. He felt that "education should be a preparation for life, domestic, economic, social, and not merely the acquisition of curious learning, elegant scholarship, or showy accomplishments. Its end should be the attainment of moral and social personality" (Davidson, 1900, p. 251).

After visiting the schools of Europe in 1843, Mann issued his famous *Seventh Annual Report,* which become the basis of school reform in Massachusetts. Later, in a report to the School Committee of Boston, he emphasized the development of practical skills, especially drawing, in school curricula (Bennett, 1926). Indeed, as part of his contribution to the American educational system during our early history, Mann also positively influenced the integration of practical and vocational training within general education.

THE INDUSTRIAL ERA

As America left behind its colonial beginnings and entered the eighteenth century, it slowly shifted from an agrarian to an industrial economy. Like other developed Western nations at the time, the United States underwent a traumatic yet invigorating transition in the workplace from a period of almost total reliance on manual processes to an era of continuing industrialization. Unlike in the European nations that had shaped its development, however, America's shift to an industrial economy was accompanied by a permanent decline in apprenticeship training. Apprenticeship was displaced by a number of public and private institutions for work-related training that became the basis for many of the training arrangements we use today. In this section, we examine the development of technical education and training in America as it struggled to become an industrialized nation.

The Decline of Apprenticeship

Well before the onset of the industrial era in the later part of the nineteenth century, the system of apprenticeship training that had served the nation so well in earlier times was showing signs of weakness. Even before the appearance of factories, the close interaction between master and apprentice was eroding as apprenticeship became more entrepreneurial and less pedagogical. The responsibility for training apprentices was more frequently being turned over to journeymen, and rather than the one-to-one learning relationship modeled after earlier father–son apprenticeships, the number of apprentices in a single shop could be as high as ten or more. As early apprenticeships in this country were administered by local authorities and were not under the strict regulation of craft and merchant guilds as they were in England, apprenticeships were gradually losing the developmental purpose for which they had been established and were becoming more exploitative of apprentices.

Eventually, however, the decline of apprenticeship became quite pronounced as the industrial advances of the later nineteenth century created a new demand for workers trained in a different way. As early as the middle of the eighteenth century, new machinery and other inventions of the emerging industrial era began to bring about remarkable changes in how work was performed. These changes were particularly apparent in the textile industry at that time, in which processes performed manually at home were slowly moved to early "manufactories" that housed new, automated looms and other inventions for textiles manufacturing. Similar innovations were occurring in other industries such as printing, agriculture, and furniture manufacturing.

Although not as readily forthcoming, new ways were needed for training workers for the industrial era. Apprenticeship was unsuited for the more automated work in the evolving factory system. In addition, it was simply unable to keep pace with the growing demand for industrial workers. The important changes in the workplace brought by the industrial revolution required corresponding changes in the preparation of workers.

Training and Corporation Schools

During colonial times, free public schools for elementary education had been established. Secondary schools were established after the founding of the nation's first publicly supported high school in Boston in 1821. Yet means had not yet been devised for providing technical and industrial education for the many who were needed to work in the nation's expanding industries. Providing technical training in the schools along with general and academic courses was an obvious option, but this was not seriously pursued until the late 1800s.

Although still separate from the growing system of public education, a few private manual training schools were established throughout this period that were to have lasting effects on the development of technical training. During the eighteenth century, mechanics and tradesmen formed technical societies for the purpose of mutual assistance and economic advancement modeled after the trade associations of England. A result of these associations was the establishment of "mechanics institutes," which provided formal training in mechanical arts, as well as instruction in reading, English, mathematics, and other subjects. A mechanics' institute was founded in New York City as early as 1820, and a few years later, the Franklin Institute in Philadelphia and Ohio Mechanics' Institute in Cincinnati were established. These facilities had libraries for apprentices and most offered education to the children of mechanics. Although only a small number were established, mechanics' institutes were the earliest examples in the United States of institutions that formally offered both technical and general education. They served as an important example for the later development of private manual training schools and positively influenced public perceptions of manual work and the technical training it required.

Corporation schools were the first programs of formal instruction to be sponsored by businesses held on company premises for their employees (Beatty, 1918). This precursor of today's company-based training function was first developed in the railroad industry in 1905 as a way of improving the performance and efficiency of those who worked in railroad maintenance shops. Prior to this time, similar training for machinists was first offered in the evening at R. Hoe and Company, a New York City manufacturer of printing presses (Bennett, 1926). Apprenticeship training in the trades that companies had previously relied on for trained workers was inadequate for current skill and production demands. Corporation schools—or factory schools, as they were also called—provided technical training in the skills and trades needed in a particular industry and included instruction in mathematics, mechanical and freehand drawing, and other practical skills needed by workers. The concept of corporation schools caught on quickly as similar schools were established by Westinghouse, Baldwin Locomotive, General Electric, International Harvester, Ford, Goodyear, and National Cash Register around the turn of the twentieth century.

Public Education and Training

Although privately sponsored programs for providing training to workers had been successful, opposition to the integration of job training within the public schools had developed among conservative educators who felt that such an approach would lead to lower academic standards. They felt that moral training and instruction in the basic subjects would provide the best preparation for the world beyond school. Education for work had no place in the public schools.

On the other hand, criticism of the general curriculum of the public schools was growing because it was seen as failing to reflect the life for which it was supposed to be preparing youth. Much of what was learned from books in the classroom had little applicability to the world beyond. Education needed more relevance. This could be provided by offering work-related training along with general education in public schools.

The struggle over what should constitute the proper education of youth, and to what degree technical education should become the responsibility of the schools, was not limited to just this country. England, France, and Russia were also dealing with changes brought on by industrialization. All three countries had achieved some progress in improving their educational systems. After studying the Russian system for providing technical training, American proponents of offering manual training in the schools came to the basic and surprising realization that principles involved in manual skills could simply be put on the same educational plane as other school subjects (Bennett, 1937).

The School of Mechanical Arts was created at the Massachusetts Institute of Technology in 1876. The Manual Training School of St. Louis was quite successful and was quickly copied in both its administration and curriculum in Chicago. Although these schools were privately funded, they demonstrated that such schools could be successfully established. Support for this training was growing, and public funding for manual training schools would soon follow.

The first high school for manual training fully supported at public expense was founded in Baltimore in 1884. In the following year, a second school supported as part of the public school system opened in Philadelphia and a third in Toledo. Although these schools were physically separate from the general high schools, the actual integration of manual training courses into general high school curricula was also beginning to occur. By 1884, manual training courses and general academic courses were being offered in the same public high schools in Cleveland, Boston, Minneapolis, and other cities (Bennett, 1937).

The Chautauqua Movement

In the middle of the industrial era was a more holistic educational movement. It started in 1874 at the First Chautauqua Assembly held on Lake Chautauqua, New York. Funded by an Ohio industrialist Lewis Miller and led by Dr. John H. Vincent, a Methodist minister, the assembly called for broadening the education of adults under the mantra of education, recreation, and inspiration (Snyder, 1985). Permanent and traveling Chautauquas spread throughout the nation. The New York Chautauqua remains a lively intellectual community and is one about twelve operating in the United States. While adult educators rightfully look to the Chautauqua movement as important in its history, it is interesting to note the connection between this movement and the outreach mission of the land grant universities in the United States as the nation matured and moved westward. After two years in the first Chautauqua, Vincent went on to establish the Chautauqua of the Great Lakes in Lakeside, Ohio, and then became president of the University of Minnesota, a land grant university.

The Role of Government in Training

Early support for technical training and vocational education came from state legislatures. The success and growth of early private manual training schools permanently established these technical training schools as important sources of skilled workers. In addition, demands of manufacturers, labor leaders, and the general public for more of this instruction and more skilled workers increased. Responding to these increasingly vocal and better organized constituencies, state legislatures funded technical training curricula within public education in schools in Massachusetts, Ohio, Pennsylvania, and in other states. Shortly after 1900, Massachusetts, long a leader in promoting practical and technical training, established independent schools for industrial and technical training, funded these schools with state money equal to half of local expenditures, and allowed administration of these schools through a commission of vocational education that was established independently of the state board of education.

Similar innovations supporting the advancement of technical training both within and outside public education occurred thereafter in other states. State legislation promoting vocational and technical education became more common as interest spread from the industrial states of the East to the Midwest, and later to the South and far West. The greatest initiative for state legislation supporting the development of vocational and technical education came from the Morrill Act of 1862 signed by Abraham Lincoln. Also called the Land Grant Act of 1862, this legislation provided a comprehensive and far-reaching scheme of public endowment of higher education that was to bring higher education within the reach of the average citizen, not just the wealthy, for the first time. It established programs of training at the college level in agricultural education, industrial and trade education, and home economics education, and it did much to clarify the image of this type of technical training in the eyes of the public.

Another major step forward in establishing technical training as a component of public education was the enactment of the Smith–Hughes Act in 1917. It provided for a permanent, annual appropriation of $7 million for programs of industrial, agricultural, home economics, and teacher training within public education. The legislation was carefully crafted to strike balances among three sets of vested interests: (1) management and labor—with each seeking to regulate vocational training in order to control this important source of skilled labor; (2) educators who felt there should be more integration between practical and academic education and those who felt there should not be integration; and (3) among those supporting vocational education, those who felt this should occur through public institutions and those seeking to keep vocational education out of the public schools. The Smith–Hughes Act seems to have balanced these competing interests quite well, for, as Bennett (1937) states, "The law passed was probably the best compromise that could have been obtained at the time" (p. 550). Since the Smith–Hughes Act, three subsequent federal laws enacted between 1929 and 1936 authorized further increases in spending on vocational education.

As America entered the twentieth century and the industrialization of its economy continued, innovations occurred in work design that fundamentally transformed the nature of work: *scientific management* and the introduction of *mass production methods.* Scientific management grew from work originated in the early eighteenth century by Charles Babbage (Davis & Taylor, 1972), which was further refined and popularized by Frederick Taylor.

Scientific management is based on two straightforward principles: break complex tasks down into simple rote tasks that can be performed with machine-like efficiency, and control the large number of workers needed for production with a hierarchical management structure (Taylor, 1912). This elegant concept of production efficiency was first implemented in manufacturing after the turn of the twentieth century, and it was soon adopted and developed into a complete system for "mass production" by Henry Ford. The mass production system required a cadre of engineers, planners, schedulers, supervisors, maintenance personnel, and quality inspectors to keep operations running smoothly and to prevent costly production delays. Direct-line workers performed simple repetitious tasks and depended on a large number of similarly specialized support staff to troubleshoot and control the production process. This approach to production permeated the industrial sectors of the economy and was responsible for our nation's dominance of the world market for manufactured goods during the middle part of the twentieth century.

TWENTIETH-CENTURY INFLUENCES

Several important influences on the development of technical training emerged in the half century surrounding America's involvement in the two world wars. These include the training demands placed on our educational system by the wars themselves and the changes that resulted, the rise of the American labor movement during this period, and the impact of the technological innovations initiated during and after our war involvement. In this section we examine each of these important influences on the development of technical training.

The Early 1900s

The early 1900s marked a clear shift toward the idea that other entities would need to offer work-related training. As described earlier, "corporation schools" were sponsored as early as 1905 and ensured their employees were equipped with the skills necessary to perform (Swanson & Torraco, 1995).

A parallel development was the increasing importance of vocational training and schools. By the early 1900s, vocational education had become increasingly extensive. Professional associations were founded to promote the vocational education consciousness (Steinmetz, 1976). These included the National Society for the Promotion of Industrial Education in 1906 (later to be named the National Society for Vocational Education), the National Vocational Guidance Association in 1913, and the Vocational Association of the Midwest in 1914. During this time, these associations were central in furthering the interests of vocational education and, most notably, in obtaining the governmental money for vocational training—beginning with the Smith–Hughes Act of 1917.

Early in their history, vocational associations were grappling with a divisive issue. Two distinct camps could be identified within many vocational associations—one composed of mostly educators and one composed of men and women from industry. In 1913, Alvin E. Dodd, then assistant secretary of the National Society for Promotion of Industrial Education, found that his philosophy about vocational education was more aligned with those associated with industry rather than the educators.

At a meeting in 1913, Dodd found that his desire for a different approach was shared by Channing R. Dooley, of Standard Oil, and J. Walter Dietz, of Western Electric. The National Association of Corporation Schools was formed to focus more on business issues and training needs. This organization increasingly focused on needs of personnel, merged with the Industrial Relations Association of America in 1920, and finally became the American Management Association in 1923. In this evolution, we see that present-day HRD emerged directly from this stream of increasing training consciousness born out of vocational education and its development.

The World Wars

The trauma of the first and second world wars, and the rise of the American labor movement during these periods, provided ample opportunity for training and its leaders to emerge and become central in America's development.

World War I

Just four years after the founding of the National Association of Corporation Schools and at the onset of World War I, Dooley was appointed director of the War Department Committee for Education and Special Training. His job was to develop materials for colleges to fill the army's needs for over one hundred trades.

Also in 1917, Charles A. Allen was appointed head of the Emergency Fleet Corporation of United States Shipping Board, and Michael J. Kane became his assistant. When the war began, there was a desperate need to build ships quickly. The workforce needed to be expanded tenfold and trained immediately by supervisors at the shipyards. In response, Allen and Kane pioneered and ordered the now famous four-step method of training (discussed later).

World War II

The four men mentioned previously—Dooley, Dietz, Allen, and Kane—along with Glenn Gardiner and Bill Conover, used their wartime experiences to fundamentally shape the history of training when, preceding and during World War II, the War Manpower Commission established the Training within Industry (TWI) Service, naming Dooley as its leader.

Training had begun to wane during the Depression years of the 1930s when companies' budgets were tightened. Industrial education was primarily focused on developing skills in the unemployed to improve their personal welfare. Suddenly, World War II demanded fast mobilization of resources and exorbitant wartime production. Although the war found many people willing to work after the distress of the Depression, there was once again a significant need for training. TWI's objectives were to help contractors produce efficiently with lower costs and higher quality. Dooley (1945) wrote in a retrospective of the 1940–1945 effort that TWI "is known for the results of its programs—Job Instruction, Job Methods, Job Relations, and Program Development—which have, we believe, permanently become part of American industrial operations as accepted tools of management" (p. xi).

Indeed, TWI is known for its simple and elegant way of training incredible amounts of people. Each program had a system to support it: limited steps, key words, subpoints, documentation/work methods, and supporting training so as to obtain certification (Swanson & Torraco, 1995). Its four programs have fostered three key contemporary elements of HRD: performance, quality, and human relations.

TWI and Performance   The philosophy undergirding the TWI Service was a clear distinction between education and training. Dooley (1945) stated, "Education is for rounding-out of the individual and the good of society; it is general, provides background, increases understanding. Training is for the good of plant production—it is a way to solve production problems through people; it is specific and helps people to acquire skill through the use of what they learned" (p. 17). The programs of TWI were closely linked to organizational performance. TWI started with performance at the organizational and process levels and ended with performance at the same levels (Swanson & Torraco, 1995). The primary measure of success was whether a TWI program helped production, efficiency, and cost-effectiveness.

The Job Instruction Training Program (JIT) was created for first- and second-line supervisors who would train most employees. The focus of the program was to teach supervisors how to break down jobs into steps and how to instruct using a derivative of the four-step process introduced during World War I. Another program, the Job Safety Program (JST), was implemented to address the crucial need for employees to be safe in the new, unfamiliar industrial environment.

TWI and Quality   TWI also pioneered when it addressed quality issues impeding performance. Two programs are notable. First, the Job Methods Training Program (JMT) provided a specific method for teaching employees how to address production and quality problems constructively. It encouraged employees to question details of job break-downs and develop and apply new methods that work better.

Second, TWI partnered with General Motors in 1942 to create the Program Development Method (PDM) (Swanson & Torraco, 1995, p. 33). This program introduced a four-step process designed to teach employees how to address quality problems and implement improvements. The four steps were as follows:

1. Spot a production problem.
2. Develop a specific plan.
3. Get the plan into action
4. Check results.

This 1942 method is strikingly similar to the "plan-do-study-check-act cycle" that Edward Deming (1993) brought to the forefront in Japan during the 1950s and in America some thirty years later. Moreover, these core quality principles introduced by TWI still provide a basis from which many in HRD implement their analyses and work.

TWI and Human Relations   The TWI Service was also one of the first to address human relations issues as important aspects of production success. The Job Relations Training Program (JRT) trained supervisors how to establish good relations with their employees. JRT laid important groundwork for the burgeoning of organization development in companies during the 1950s. Clearly, the TWI effort quickly went beyond training and is seen by many as the origin of contemporary HRD as well as a springboard for the human relations perspective of the organization development component of HRD. Much of the original TWI report has recently been republished for the profession under the title *Origins of Contemporary Human Resource Development* (Swanson, 2001).

EVOLUTION OF THE ORGANIZATION DEVELOPMENT COMPONENT OF HRD

Much of the philosophy and methods of organization development (OD) were honed and began to affect people and work environments during the years between 1940 and the 1960. Many parallel developments occurred, including (1) a shift to the human resources school of thought, (2) the growth of laboratory training, (3) the use of survey research and feedback, (4) an increased use of action research (problem solving) techniques, (5) an acknowledgment of sociotechnical systems and quality of work life, and (6) a new emphasis on strategic change.

Shift to the Human Relations School of Thought

From the 1940s to the early 1950s, the primary way to think about and organize work and work environments was based on the human relations model. Developed mostly in response to serious concerns about the viability of traditional and bureaucratic organizations, the human relations model attempted to move away from these classical assumptions and focused more heavily on individuals' identities, their needs, and how to facilitate stronger interpersonal communication and relationships. Leaders of the human relations school of thought included Chester Bernard, Mary Parker Follett, and Frederick Roethlisberger and Elton Mayo, who led the now famous Hawthorne experiments (Conrad, 1994).

By the mid- to late 1950s, it became increasingly clear that the human relations model had not effectively impacted work environments. The human relations school of thought (Rothwell, Sullivan, & McLean, 1995) emerged to address some of its shortcomings. The human resources model was firmly rooted in humanism, "the key values of which include a firm belief in human rationality, human perfectibility through learning, and the importance of self-awareness" (Rothwell et al., 1995, p. 17). Other core roots included (1) applied social science, which increasingly recognized the complexities of individuals and (2) economics, which began to recognize that individuals were as valuable as other capital such as land, machinery, and supplies.

Leaders of humanism included Carl Rogers, who pioneered client-centered consulting; Abraham Maslow, who developed the needs hierarchy; Cyril Houle and Malcolm Knowles, who focused on adult learners; and Douglas McGregor, who developed the theory of X and Y leaders. These men each added to new assumptions of management thought:

- Work is meaningful.
- Workers are motivated by meaningful, mutually set goals and participation.
- Workers should be increasingly self-directed and this self-control will improve efficiency and work satisfaction.
- Managers are most effective when coaching, working to develop untapped potential, and creating an environment where potential can be fully utilized.

These assumptions are still the guideposts of current thinking in organizational development and HRD.

Laboratory Training

Laboratory training, or the T-group, provided an early emphasis on group process and interactions. T-groups were unstructured, small-group sessions in which participants shared experiences and learned from their interactions. The first recorded T-group implementation took place under the auspices of the New

Britain Workshop in 1946 under direction of leaders such as Kurt Lewin, Kenneth Benne, Leland Bradford, and Ronald Lippit. These individuals are most well known for their involvement in the founding of the National Training Laboratories (NTL) for applied behavioral science.

T-groups were first used in industry in 1953 and 1954 when Douglas McGregor and Richard Beckhard took T-groups out of the context of individual development and applied them within the context of an organization. This effort at Union Carbide focused on the team as the unit of development and, interestingly enough, aimed to address the problem of training transfer—an early indication that T&D and OD were closely tied.

Survey Research and Feedback

Attitude surveys and data feedback have become important tools in OD. In 1947, they were just in their infancy as Rensis Likert pioneered the concept of survey-guided development. This process entailed measuring the attitudes of employees, providing feedback to participants, and stimulating joint planning for improvement. The first climate survey was at Detroit Edison in 1948 and was used to measure management and employee attitudes. The data were fed back using a technique that Likert called an "interlocking chain of conferences"—starting at the highest level of management and flowing to successively lower levels.

Likert's work was grounded in, and resulted in, a guiding philosophy of organizational systems. Ultimately, he believed that any system could be categorized based on feedback data into one of four types: exploitative-authoritarian, benevolent-authoritative, consultative, and participative. He advocated the creation of a participative organization based on the use of influence, intrinsic rewards, and two-way communication (Rothwell et al., 1995).

Action Research (Problem-Solving) Techniques

Action research (actually a problem-solving technique rather than a research method), now acknowledged as the core method of OD, originated out of the work of social scientists John Collier, Kurt Lewin, and William Whyte in the late 1940s. Their theory asserted that problem solving must be closely linked to action if organizational members were to use it to manage change. Harwood Manufacturing Company was the site of one of the first such studies led by Lewin and his students. Other contributors to furthering thinking behind action research included Lester Coch, John French, and Edith Hamilton. Ultimately, the cyclical nature of the action research problem solving method is still viable—requiring data collection, analysis, planning and implementation, evaluation.

Tavistock Sociotechnical Systems and Quality of Work Life

Also during the late 1940s to early 1950s, the Tavistock Clinic in Great Britain, known for its work in family therapy, transferred its methods to the organizational setting. Tavistock researchers conducted a work redesign experiment for coal mining teams experiencing difficulties after the introduction of new technologies. The key learning of their initial experiments was a new focus on social subsystems and people—people whose needs must be tended to during times of change.

In the 1950s, Eric Trist and his colleagues at Tavistock extended the idea of sociotechnical systems and undertook projects related to productivity and quality of work life. Their approach increasingly examined both the technical and human sides of organizations and how they interrelated (Cummings & Worley, 1993). The trend to develop interventions that more effectively integrated technology and people spread throughout Europe and to the United States during the 1960s, where the approach tended to be more eclectic and became increasingly popular.

Strategic Change

Since 1960, much of the evolution of OD has focused on increasing the effectiveness of strategic change. Richard Beckhard's use of open-systems planning was one of the first applications of strategic change methods. He proposed that an organization's demand and response systems could be described and analyzed, the gaps reduced, and performance improved. This work represents a shift in OD away from a sole focus on the individual and the supporting assumption that OD is completely mediated through individuals to a more holistic and open systems view of organizations. This shift continues to this day and is evidenced in key learnings stemming from strategic change work including the importance of leadership support, multilevel involvement, and the criticality of alignment between organizational strategy, structure, culture, and systems.

Transformation of Contemporary Work Organizations

Organizations, large and small, public or private, in a range of industry sectors, have been the primary twenty-first-century mediums through which work is accomplished. The structure of contemporary work organizations has changed in fundamental ways in 1980s and 1990s as a result of the globalization of the economy and information technology. Organizations are becoming flatter and less hierarchical in efforts to reduce bureaucracy, manage costs, and be more responsive to their markets. Organizations or equivalent subsystems have become smaller and leaner as managers eliminate work inefficiencies and duplication of effort.

A consequence of these emerging flatter, "downsized" systems is the need for major shifts in the distribution of work tasks and roles among workers and the need for fundamental organization development. In a workplace once modeled on narrow job definitions and a wide range of functional specialists, today's workplace is often characterized by increasingly sophisticated work methods and the presence of relatively fewer workers. Narrow job definitions are giving way to broader responsibilities and a greater interdependence among workers. Jobs are being eliminated, combined, and reconfigured as organizations fundamentally rethink the ways in which work should be done. As organizational and job structures change, training for those who operate within these structures must change.

The Evolving Nature of Work

The nature of contemporary work has changed. Organization development efforts under way in organizations to reduce costs, integrate technology and work (not just to think of labor-saving technology), and expedite communication with customers and suppliers not only eliminate jobs throughout the organization but also increase the sophistication of work for those who remain. Today's workers increasingly need to understand work operations as a whole, rather than what used to be their specific tasks within it. Monitoring and maintaining the work system have become in today's workplace what operating a single machine had been for mass production work. Today's workers have to make sense of what is happening in the workplace based on abstract rather than physical cues. According to Zuboff (1988), this transformation of work involves the development of "intellective" rather than "action-centered" skills. Gone are the days when problem solving meant making a telephone call to management or the maintenance department.

In addition, flatter organizational structures require employees at the shop floor level to exercise more authority over a wider variety of tasks. They can no longer rely on management for planning and scheduling as these duties are being integrated into production jobs themselves. Today's work requires an increasingly holistic perspective of the organizational mission, strategy, and structure along with attention to the demands of both internal and external customers. Once the mainstay of traditional forms of work, procedural thinking has become subordinate to systems thinking for all workers, not just managers.

Clearly, an important factor underlying the changing nature of contemporary work is a perceptible shortening of the half-life of knowledge. New knowledge drives the evolution of new work systems and technologies. The half-life of knowledge in technology-intensive fields such as engineering and health care is now less than four years. Conservatively, this means that the relevant expertise of an engineer completing training today will erode by fifty percent in just four years. The half-life of knowledge is not much longer in most of the other business, professional, and technical fields on which organizations rely for their expertise. The profound influence this constant turnover in knowledge has on the nature of work and the way work is accomplished is all too obvious to those who must continually update their work knowledge and skills.

Advanced technology, leaner organizational structures, and an environment of fewer resources and ever-changing demands of customers and government are powerful factors that are reshaping organizations and fundamentally changing the nature of work.

MANAGEMENT AND LEADERSHIP DEVELOPMENT IN THE UNITED STATES

Histories of HRD have largely focused on organization development and personnel training and development aimed at hourly and supervisory workers, while mostly ignoring management and leadership development (Miller, 1996; Nadler & Nadler, 1989; Knowles, 1977; Ruona & Swanson, 1998; Swanson & Torraco, 1995; Steinmetz, 1976).

A number of specialty areas of HRD have developed over the years as separate entities and have been spurred by unique and independent forces. Management and leadership development (MLD) is one such entity. Managers making decisions about MLD of other managers is worthy of separate consideration. Beyond MLD, other HRD arenas with unique histories are also of interest. Examples include career roles (e.g., nursing and general practice within medicine) and bodies of knowledge (e.g., computer science). Each has its own HRD history.

It is only in modern times that mainstream human resource development and MLD have converged. Consequently, there has been little systematic attempt to study the history of MLD. This section identifies the major periods or eras in MLD history.

When studying MLD, it is difficult to divorce the higher education component from the more traditional HRD components since there are important interactions between them. The whole system of MLD providers include higher education, university-based MLD, corporate-based training and development programs, association activity, private training, and others. MLD programs are designed for all levels of management, including what is often called executive development, but excludes supervisory development. Supervisory development is generally considered to be targeted at persons supervising hourly or nonprofessional-level employees.

Management and leadership development can be thought of as any educational or developmental activity specifically designed to foster the professional growth and capability of persons in or being prepared for management and executive roles in organizations. First, it includes both formal educational activities and on-the-job type programs. As will be seen, the concept of MLD has changed significantly through the years but included primarily more informal activities, though systematically planned and designed, in the early years. MLD is more than just classroom activity, and we must include all aspects of it.

Setting the Stage: American Business in the 1800s

American business prior to 1870 showed little resemblance to business after 1900 and certainly not to business today. America was primarily an agrarian society characterized by very local markets, small owner-operated companies that were largely labor- instead of capital-intensive. Highly trained personnel were not needed because business was not very complicated. America was also largely rural, with only 11 percent of the population living in urban areas in 1840 (Chandler, 1959).

Early commercial schools bore little resemblance to management and leadership development, yet they were an important first step. Prior to this, business was taught through the apprenticeship method. The founders of these schools believed that commercial subjects could be taught better and more efficiently by using a systematic classroom method than the old apprenticeship method. This was a major innovation and laid the foundation for the modern business school.

By 1900, the U.S. economy had been completely transformed. Many more firms were involved in making goods for industrial purposes than consumer goods. Most industries had become dominated by a few large firms. The nation had changed from a business to an industrial economy (Chandler, 1959).

A key outcome was that business began to need managers, at least in the modem sense of the word. As business became large, they also became bureaucratic and decisions were made in large, hierarchical structures. This great new organization—the large corporation—required careful coordination and needed people who could do that. Large companies also created lots of specialized jobs unlike the craft-oriented small businesses. Specialists required managers to direct their activity. But there were no models or theories to guide companies in learning how to run these huge organizations. The profession of management was born and the need for MLD began.

The first formal business schools were formed in this period. The first school of business was formed in 1881 at the University of Pennsylvania with a grant from Joseph Wharton. Other schools followed at the University of California in 1898, and New York University and the University of Wisconsin in 1900. These schools recognized two key things: formal training was needed for business, and technical training was not enough. While there was not much agreement on curricula, they did realize that a breadth of outlook was needed, more akin to other types of professional training. One can imagine much opposition in these universities since business was largely considered a trade at that time. The private commercial schools continued to prosper in this period. In 1876, there were 137 schools enrolling 25,000 students, and by 1890, they had grown to enroll almost 100,000 students (Haynes & Jackson, 1935).

The Struggle for Professionalization of Management: 1900–1928

In 1911, Frederick Taylor published *The Principles of Scientific Management* as the culmination of years of work and study into a new approach to management he began about 1900. Taylor is widely regarded as the father of American management thought and was the first to apply scientific principles to the practice of management. While many others had written about management before him, it was Taylor who first put forth a scientific theory and approach to management and the need to share it with managers and leaders in organizations.

In 1913, the National Association of Corporate Schools was formed. As the role of training broadened, the organization changed its name in 1920 to the National Association of Corporate Training. In 1922, that organization merged with the Industrial Relations Association of America (formerly the National Association of Employment Managers) to form the National Personnel Association. Very shortly after that in 1923, this group changed its name to the American Management Association (AMA). In 1924, the AMA absorbed the National Association of Sales Managers.

The AMA has continued to be a leader in the field of MLD and provided much of the early push to the field. Its principle mission was "to advance the understanding, principles, policies and practices of modern management and administration" ("Fifty Years of Management Education," p. 5). It was Mary Parker Follet who played a major influence in the early stages of the organization. In 1925, she voiced the need "to apply scientific methods to those problems of management which involve human relations ("AMA Management Highlights," p. 36). In 1926, the organization formed the Institute of Management "to promote scientific methods in management and to provide a forum for interchange of information" (Black, 1979, p. 38).

Higher education in business also experienced tremendous growth during this period. In 1900, there were only 4 business schools. By 1913, there were 25 new business schools on college campuses, 37 more by 1918, and by 1925 a total of 182 business schools thanks largely to the influx of veterans after the end of the war who needed training for jobs (Bossard & Dewhurst, 1931, p. 252). In 1916, the American Assembly of Collegiate Schools in Business was formed; by 1930, it had forty-two member schools. Its mission was to provide accreditation for schools and to set some standards for curricula.

Late in this era, management theory began to take a turn away from Taylor and scientific management. In 1927, Elton Mayo became involved in a recently completed series of experiments at Western Electric's Hawthorne plant begun in 1924. Sponsored by the National Research Council of the National Academy of Science, the experiments were originally designed to determine the relationship of illumination and individual productivity. While productivity went up dramatically, it was not as a result of the lighting. It was Mayo who suggested the now famous Hawthorne effect of paying attention to workers as a likely explanation. The outcome of these experiments was a call for the development of a new set of managerial skills: human behavior and interpersonal skills. Technical skills would not be enough (Wren, 1979, p. 313).

The Depression Era: 1929–1939

The unfortunate result of much of the enormous growth in business during the early part of the twentieth century was the Great Depression of 1929. There a few items of note occurred during this period. The first university-based executive or management development program was started at MIT's Sloan School in 1931 with the help and initiative of A. P. Sloan, chairman of General Motors Corporation. This program was designed for a group of selected executives with eight to ten years of experience who were released from their work for a year to attend. It was the forerunner of what would become a very important trend later.

The Management Development Boom: 1940–1953

This era was a critical one for the development of MLD. It is during this period that business thinking changed to accept management and leadership development as a necessary part of doing business. When World War II started in 1939, corporations needed managers quickly, so they turned to MLD activities to fill that need. After the war, the successes with management training made many companies realize that management and leadership development activities should be continued.

A significant new venture for university schools of business were the nondegree management and executive development programs. These programs were largely residential and required the manager or executive to leave the workplace for an extended period of time to return to school. In 1943, Harvard and Stanford were asked by the U.S. War Office to form the War Production Retraining Course. This was a fifteen-week course to retrain businessmen to manage the war production effort. By 1950, four such programs existed: MIT, Harvard, the University of Chicago, and Pittsburgh.

Another postwar phenomenon was the company-based MLD program. The Industrial Conference Board reported in 1935 that only 3.1 percent of over 2,400 companies surveyed had such programs, rising to only 5.2 percent of over 3,400 in 1946. By 1952, the American Management Association found that 30 percent of the companies it surveyed had MLD programs. While their sample was smaller and their definition a bit different, the growth trend is clear in this period and continued into the mid-1950s.

The Academy of Management began formal operations in 1941 after five years of discussions and meetings about the need for such a group (Wren, 1979, p. 380). In 1944, the American Society of Training Directors was organized. This organization would become the American Society of Training and Development and was a latecomer to the MLD business. Later it adopted management and leadership development as a key part of its mission.

The Management Reform Movement: 1953–1970

As MLD became a necessary part of the management profession, people in education and business began to take a close look at the quality of management education and the body of management knowledge that existed. They were not happy with what they found. Despite their growth, business schools in the 1950s were very similar to those in the 1920s.

One of the Ford Foundation initiatives was a comprehensive study of business education that included recommendations for the future growth of management education. Started in 1955, the study was conducted by Robert A. Gordon and James E. Howell. Published in 1959, the final report is now one of the landmark works in the field of management education and development. The recommendations of this study, and the Ford Foundation's other efforts, have shaped the field of MLD ever since. The report was critical of the vocationalism and specialization prevalent in business schools of the time, in essence calling for the transformation of business schools from vocational to professional schools.

Along with the reform in business schools came a period of strong growth for all aspects of MLD. Company-based MLD programs experienced significant growth. A 1955 AMA study found that 54 percent of the 460 companies it surveyed had some systematic plan, program, or method to facilitate the development of people in or for management responsibilities (*Current Practice in the Development of Management Personnel*, p. 3). A 1958 survey showed that of 492 top companies, 90.5 percent engaged in managerial development activities, with 84.8 percent of them conducting educational activity that required regular participation by management (Clark & Sloan, 1958, p. 14).

The Modern Management Era: 1970–2000

The early part of the modem era was really an extension of the reform movement. It was a time of consolidating gains made and continuing the progress started in the late 1950s and early 1960s. It was a time of change, although not the revolutionary change as in the previous era. Business continued to change dramatically and become even more complicated. The explosion in information technologies that started in the 1960s continued into the 1970s and reshaped the way managers approached their jobs. It simplified managers' jobs by giving them new tools with which to manage but also complicated them, because it involved adapting to new technologies. The pace of technological change continues to challenge the very underpinnings of business and industry and the ability of managers to keep pace. Markets have become more complex and are now global in scope. The economic, governmental, and social environments of business have also grown more complex. The rise of the service economy and Internet commerce has reshaped much of our thinking and the workforce has grown increasingly diverse.

Beyond general expansion, this era saw the development and growth of the non-university, non-company based MLD organization. Porter and McKibbon (1988) point out that these firms fall into several categories. First are the firms whose primary business is offering MLD programs such as Wilson Learning, The Forum Corp., and the nonprofit Center for Creative Leadership. A second category would be firms whose primary business is something other than training but who provide programs as a piece of their business such as Arthur D. Little, Inc., and the major accounting-consulting firms. Nonprofit organizations offering management programs have also expanded. Notable examples include the Brookings Advanced Study Program and the Aspen Institute, a program for executives in the humanities whose growth was assisted by the interest of the Bell system in its programs. Finally, a vast array of individual consultants offer programs as well.

The concept of continuing education and learning for managers is now firmly entrenched in corporate America, although the methods, quantity, and sources vary greatly. One study of one thousand medium and large companies showed that 90 percent of them used some type of formal MLD program (Johnson et al., 1988, p. 17). With the growth have come the critics. Two popular books that question the quality and integrity of both business schools and management consultants engaged in MLD are *Gravey Training: Inside the Business of Business Schools* (Crainer & Dearlove, 1999) and *The Witch Doctors: Making Sense of the Management Gurus* (Micklethwait & Wooldridge, 1996). The titles of these books challenge MLD in the twenty-first century to be theoretically sound and to demonstrate positive results.

EMERGENCE OF THE HRD RESEARCH COMMUNITY

The HRD profession was a very large field of practice with no university academic home until the late 1900s. Practitioners with university degrees came from many disciplines. Most were from education, business, psychology, and communication. For years universities acknowledged HRD as a career option for graduates without presenting a defined curriculum or disciplinary base.

Early University Programs

George Washington University

Len Nadler, considered by many to have coined the term human resource development in 1969, and his academic home base of George Washington University (GWU) deserve special status in the history of the HRD discipline. GWU has a large and dynamic HRD graduate program in which Nadler's influence continues beyond his retirement. Specific program features of the HRD consulting role and a focus on international HRD have had a long tradition at GWU.

Bowling Green State University

In the early 1970s, Bowling Green State University (BGSU) in Ohio supported separate programs in training and development and organization development. BGSU's organization development graduate program was headed by Glenn Varney, and its concentration in training and development was headed by Richard A. Swanson. Many innovative developments came out of BGSU for a number of years in spite of the fact that both were only master's-level programs.

Academy of Human Resource Development

The history of the Academy of Human Resource Development (AHRD) is relatively short and colorful. The academy was founded on May 7, 1993, during a passionate chartering conference. Numerous interesting events took place before and after the historical birthing of AHRD. The chartering conference produced about seventy-five scholar-members in 1993. There were over eight hundred scholar-members in 2000.

In reporting the AHRD's history, the first thing to acknowledge is that HRD has been a large field of practice dominated by practical techniques and reactive thinking. As an academic field, HRD is very young. Thus, the role of university-sponsored research and scholarship in the profession is only now taking hold. Over the last twenty years of the century, a cadre of HRD scholars has seized opportunities to advance the status of research and scholarship in the profession. They have struggled to have research lead the profession's practice. They edited special-issues journals from related disciplines on the topics of HRD, training, and organization development. They joined the research committees of American Society for Training and Development (ASTD) and other practitioner societies, contributed to HRD monographs, started HRD research columns in nonresearch journals, and in 1990 gave birth to the first HRD research journal, the *Human Resource Development Quarterly,* under the leadership of Richard A. Swanson, founding editor.

The unwieldy Professor's Network of ASTD (most members were vendors, not professors) and the independent and elitist University Council for Research on HRD (fourteen doctoral degree–granting institutions) provided birthing nests for the AHRD. Wayne Pace (Brigham Young University) was the amazing force and founding president of AHRD. Karen E. Watkins (University of Texas) represented the Professor's Network, Richard A. Swanson (University of Minnesota) represented the University Council for Research on HRD, and both became founding officers of the academy as they moved away from their former organizations.

The vision of the academy is to lead the HRD profession through research. The stated mission is to be the premier global organization focused on the systematic study of HRD theories, processes, and practices, the dissemination of the scholarly findings, and the application of those findings. Furthermore, the AHRD is meant to be a true community of scholars that cares deeply about advancing the scholarly underpinnings of the profession and about supporting one another in that journey.

The altruistic goal of wanting to advance the profession through research and scholarship eased the realignment of these two earlier groups into a new and independent Academy of Human Resource Development. The short history of the academy is a litany of positive events and a cobweb of partnerships. Many are highlighted in the concluding "HRD History Time Line."

HRD HISTORY TIME LINE

The following time line is a list of ideas, people, and developments of particular interest to scholars of human resource development:

500 B.C.–500 A.D.: The Influence of the Greeks and Romans
Greek disdain for menial work
Socrates: The Socratic method of inquiry
Plato's Republic: Bringing together the domains of politics, education, and philosophy
Aristotle: The father of scientific thought
The Romans: A pragmatic view

300–1300 A.D.: The Middle Ages
Augustine: The fusion of the classics and Christianity
Monastic schools
St. Thomas Aquinas
Merchant and craft guilds
Apprenticeships

1400–1700 A.D.: The Renaissance
Engineering and technical training in the Middle Ages
Secular education for boys and girls (Martin Luther)
Sensory learning (John Locke)
Experience, the best teacher (Jean-Jacques Rousseau)
Manual training (Johan Pestalozzi)

Transition from the Nineteenth to the Twentieth Centuries
Apprenticeship training
Industrial era
The decline of the apprenticeship in the United States
Technical training and corporation schools
First Chautauqua Assembly held on Lake Chautauqua, New York
Public education and technical training
The role of government in technical training

Twentieth Century
1911	Frederick Taylor publishes *The Principles of Scientific Management.*
1912	Society for the Promotion of Industrial Education (later to become the American Vocational Association) is established.
1913	National Association of Corporate Schools (later to become the American Management Association) is founded.
1914–18	World War I
1914	Charles Allen develops and implements the four-step job instruction training (JIT) method as part of the war effort.
1926	American Association for Adult Education organized.
1933	Elton Mayo publishes the Hawthorne Studies.
1937	Dale Carnegie publishes *How to Win Friends and Influence People.*

1937	Founding of the National Association of Industrial Teacher Educators.
1941–45	World War II
1943	Abraham Maslow publishes *A Theory of Human Motivation*.
1944	Founding of the American Society of Training Directors (later to become the American Society for Training and Development)
1945	Channing Dooley publishes *Training-within-Industry Report:1940–1945* (this massive World War II effort is the watershed in the birthing of the contemporary human resource development profession).
1946	Kurt Lewin launches the Research Center for Group Dynamics at Massachusetts Institute of Technology.
1947	Founding of the National Training Laboratories.
1947	Renis Likert pioneers the concept of survey-guided development.
1949	Eric Trist advances the idea of sociotechnical systems.
1954	Peter F. Drucker publishes *The Practice of Management*.
1956	K. E. Boulding publishes *General Systems Theory: The Skeleton of a Science*.
1958	B. F. Skinner builds the first teaching machine.
1958	Norm Crowder invents branching programmed instruction.
1959	Frederick Hertzberg et al. publish *The Motivation to Work*.
1959	Donald Kirkpatrick publishes magazine articles on the four-level evaluation model.
1961	Cyril O. Houle publishes *The Inquiring Mind*.
1962	Founding of the National Society for Programmed Instruction (later to become the National Society for Performance and Improvement and then the International Society for Performance Improvement).
1962	Robert Mager publishes *Preparing Instructional Objectives*.
1964	Gary S. Becker publishes *Human Capital: A Theoretical and Empirical Analysis, with Special Reference to Education*.
1965	Robert M. Gagne publishes *The Conditions of Learning*.
1968	Founding of the Organization Development Institute.
1960	Douglas McGregor publishes *The Human Side of the Enterprise*.
1964	*Training in Industry and Business* magazine begins publication (later called *Training*).
1965	Robert Craig (editor) publishes the first edition of the *Training and Development Handbook*.
1969	Leonard Nadler advocates the term *human resource development*.
1970	Malcolm Knowles publishes *The Modern Practice of Adult Education: From Pedagogy to Andragogy*.
1970	Leonard and Zeace Nadler publish *Developing Human Resources*.
1972	Cyril O. Hoyle publishes *The Design of Education*.
1972	International Federation of Training and Development Organizations (IFTDO) is founded in Geneva, Switzerland.
1973	U.S. military officially adopts the instructional systems development (ISD) model.
1973	Ontario Society for Training and Development publishes *Core Competencies for Training and Development*.
1974	Avice M. Saint publishes *Learning at Work: Human Resources and Organizational Development*.
1978	Patrick Pinto and James Walker publish *A Study of Professional Training and Development Roles and Competencies*.

1978	Thomas Gilbert publishes *Human Competence: Engineering Worthy Performance.*
1983	Patricia McLagan and Richard McCullough publish *Models for Excellence: The Conclusions and Recommendations of the ASTD Training and Development Competency Study.*
1983	*Organization Developments* journal begins publication.
1983	Founding of the Training and Development Research Center at the University of Minnesota (later named the Human Resource Development Research Center).
1987	Founding of the University Council for Research on Human Resource Development (later merged with the members of Professor's Network of ASTD to form the Academy of Human Resource Development in 1993).
1989	*Performance Improvement Quarterly* research journal begins publication. William Coscarelli is the founding editor. Sponsored by the National Society for Performance and Instruction (later called the International Society for Performance Improvement).
1990	*Human Resource Development Quarterly* research journal begins publication. Richard A. Swanson is the founding editor (sponsored by the American Society for Training and Development and cosponsored since 1997 with the Academy of Human Resource Development).
1990	Peter M. Senge publishes *The Fifth Discipline: The Art and Practice of the Learning Organization.*
1990	Geary Rummler and Alan Brache publish *Improving Performance: How to Manage the White Space on the Organizational Chart.*
1992	Chris Argyris publishes *On Organizational Learning.*
1993	Founding of the Academy of Human Resource Development (AHRD), an international academy of HRD scholars. Wayne Pace is the founding president.
1994	Karen E. Watkins becomes president of AHRD.
1995	Founding of the University Forum for Human Resource Development (based in the U.K. and later expanded to Europe).
1996	Richard A. Swanson becomes president of AHRD.
1997	*International Journal of Training and Development* journal begins publication. Paul Lewis is the founding editor (published by Blackwell).
1997	*Human Resource Development Research Handbook:* Linking Research and Practice is published by AHRD and ASTD.
1998	Elwood F. Holton III becomes president of AHRD.
1998	*Human Resource Development International* research journal begins publication. Monica Lee is the founding editor (sponsored by the AHRD and the University Forum for HRD, and published by Routledge).
1999	*Advances in Developing Human Resources* scholarly topical quarterly begins publication. Richard A. Swanson is the founding editor (sponsored by the AHRD and published by Berrett-Koehler and then Sage).

Twenty-first Century

2000	Gary N. McLean becomes president of AHRD.
2000	Channing R. Dooley (World War II Training within Industry Project) is first inductee and Malcolm S. Knowles (adult learning, andragogy) the second inductee in the HRD Scholar Hall of Fame (sponsored by AHRD).

2001	Inducted into the HRD Scholar Hall of Fame:

      • Lillian Gilbreth (human aspect of management)

      • Kurt Lewin (change theory)

      • B. F. Skinner (teaching machines)

      • Donald S. Super (career development theory)

      • Robert M. Gagne (conditions of learning)

      • Gary S. Becker (human capital theory)

      • Leonard Nadler (foundations of HRD)

2002   *Human Resource Development Review* begins publication as the theory quarterly of HRD. Elwood F. Holton III is the founding editor (sponsored by the AHRD and published by Sage).

REFLECTION QUESTIONS

1. Identify at least three discrete times in history, report on how human beings are viewed during that time, and note the HRD implications.

2. Identify three HRD related historical times or events of interest to you, and explain why they are of interest and what else you would like to know.

3. Why is the World War II Training within Industry project seen as so important to HRD?

4. What unique role does the Academy of Human Resource Development play in the HRD profession, and what are some of its accomplishments?

5. Identify two recurring themes in the history of HRD. Name them and describe them.

Theory and Philosophy in Human Resource Development

This section provides the critical theoretical and philosophical foundations of HRD. Both of these perspectives have generally been missing among HRD professionals and are believed to be essential for understanding and advancing the field.

CHAPTERS

The Role of Theory and Philosophy in HRD

In response to popular opinion to the contrary, Kurt Lewin, the famous early organization development innovator and scholar, presented his famous quote: "There is nothing so practical as good theory." It bears repeating. His description of practicality is in contrast to commonly held thoughts of theory being "half-baked ideas" disconnected from the "real world." A good theory is thorough and has been tested both intellectually and in practice. Lewin helps us from misusing the word *theory.*

Sound theory helps direct the professional energies to models and techniques that are effective and efficient. Sound theory also helps the profession confront celebrity professionals and infomercial-type consultants that riddle the profession. For example, to the unsubstantiated promises of accelerated learning, Torraco (1992) warned buyers to beware that it doesn't deliver on its promises. For the unfulfilled promise and premises of Kirkpatrick's (1998) flawed four-level evaluation model, Holton (1996b) warned the profession that after thirty-eight years, it still does not meet any of the criteria required of sound theories or models.

IMPORTANCE OF THEORY

The HRD profession continues to develop its core theories and to understand that theory building is a scholarly process, not soap box oratory. Following are a few organizing thoughts about theory. These ideas are important to highlight because some in HRD believe that it is not essential to the profession to have a theory or to clearly specify its underlying theory (McLean, 1998). An interpretation of this minimal view of theory is that the profession needs to have an ethical intent and to situationally draw upon as many theories as required in pursuit of its work. That is not the premise of this book.

Importance of Theory Building

Theory is particularly important to a discipline that is emerging and growing (Chalofsky, 1990). Sound theory is not pontificating or forcefully marketing the latest fad. Rather, theory in an applied field such as HRD is required to be both scholarly and successful in practice and can be the basis of advances in practice. Rhetoric that negates theory, or the promotion of the idea that theory is disconnected from practice, is an artifact of nontheoretical thinking.

Definition of Theory

The following two definitions of theory from HRD scholars capture the essence of theory and the theory challenge facing our profession:

- "A theory simply explains what a phenomenon is and how it works" (Torraco, 1997, p. 115). Torraco's definition poses the following questions: What is HRD, and how does it work?

- "Theory building is the process or recurring cycle by which coherent descriptions, explanations, and representations of observed or experienced phenomena are generated, verified, and refined"(Lynham, 2000b). Lynham's definition poses the following question: What commitments must individuals, the HRD profession, and its infrastructure make to establish and sustain theory-building research in the HRD profession?

Theory-Building Research

Theory-building research can be thought of as a never-ending journey for any discipline. Yet, it is reasonable to assume that there are points in the maturation of a field of study that cause it to press theory-building research to the forefront. We contend (1) that the demand for HRD theory is increasing, (2) that our present available theory, while substantial, must be further developed, and (3) that what we do is too important to wallow in atheoretical explanations.

RECOGNIZING THE THEORY-BUILDING JOURNEY AS SCHOLARSHIP

When a scholar takes a serious look at the theory building research journey, it is quite intricate and rigorous. An overview of this journey is contained in a recent article titled "Theory Building in the Human Resource Development Profession" (Lynham, 2000b); it is recommended reading for all those interested in HRD theory building. In addition, there are numerous benchmark theory-practice publications. "Workplace Learning: Debating the Five Critical Questions of Theory and Practice," edited by Rowden (1996), and *Systems Theory Applied to Human Resource Development,* edited by Gradous (1989), have provided excellent contributions to the theory in HRD. Gradous's classic monograph uses system theory as a springboard for thinking about the theory of HRD with arguments for and against a unifying theory in HRD. The perspectives in this monograph range from a call for focusing on system outputs—that is, being results driven versus activity driven (Dahl, 1989)—to the consideration of field and intervention theory, the theory of work design, critical theory, and human capital theory (Watkins, 1989). The idea of multiple theories that pay attention to people, organizational viability, along with a systematic and systemic understanding of the context emerged in this monograph. These far-ranging ideas are present in most theoretical debates about HRD.

Serious theory-building methodologies are challenging (Reynolds, 1971; Dubin, 1978; Cohen, 1991). Even the comparatively simple theory building tools and methods require significant effort for the theory builder (e.g. Patterson, 1983; Strauss and Corbin, 1998). The HRD profession needs to encourage and respect a full continuum of theory-building engagement. Examples are varied.

Seemingly elementary investigations into definitions and identification of the range of thought within HRD are important theory-building stepping stones. Specific examples include the following:

- "Commonly Held Theories of Human Resource Development" (Weinberger, 1998). Weinberger charts the history and the evolving definition of human resource development. Up to this point, this basic information has been scattered throughout the literature.

- "Operational Definitions of Expertise and Competence" (Herling, 2000). HRD methodically analyzes the literature on knowledge, competence, and expertise—core concepts in HRD. Even so, the HRD profession has not had clear scholarly literature defining human competence and expertise until Herling's work.

- "Organization Development: An Analysis of the Definitions and Dependent Variables" (Egan, 2000). Similar to Weinberger, Egan traces the definition of organization development over time with the added identification of declared outcomes.

- On the philosophical side, an example of theory research is "An Investigation into Core Beliefs Underlying the Profession of Human Resource Development" (Ruona, 1999). This study investigates the thought and value systems that permeate the discipline of HRD. Within her extensive findings, Ruona has determined that *learning* and *performance* are the two dominant philosophical views among HRD leaders.

- "Philosophical Foundations of HRD Practice" (Ruona & Roth, 2000) exposes core values in the field, while the "Theoretical Assumptions Underlying the Performance Paradigm of Human Resource Development" (Holton, in press-a) pushes to articulate the underlying assumptions related to the performance and learning paradigms and their common connection to learning.

It is important to recognize that each of these studies advances understanding of the HRD phenomenon.

Examples of straightforward theory-building efforts on the part of HRD scholars include the following. Each one of these cited pieces (and others) deserves forums with opportunity for reflection in an effort to advance the profession.

- "Systems Theory Applied to Human Resource Development" (Jacobs, 1989) presents system theory as a unifying theory for HRD.

- "Foundations of Performance Improvement and Implications for Practice (Swanson, 1999) discusses the underlying theory of HRD when performance improvement is viewed as the desired outcome.

- "A Theory of Intellectual Capital" (Harris, 2000) emphasizes the dynamic impact intellectual capital can have on an organization.

- "A Theory of Knowledge Management" (Torraco, 2000) helps us think theoretically about the supportive systems required of the phenomenon of knowledge management.

- "The Development and Validation of a Model of Responsible Leadership for Performance" (Lynham, 2000a) looks at leadership in context of purpose rather than the limited lens of leaders' traits and behaviors.

REQUIREMENTS OF A SOUND THEORY

Critics of HRD have chided the large number of HRD practitioners and commercial HRD products as being atheoretical (Swanson, 1998c; Holton, 1996). *Atheoretical* means there is no thorough scholarly or scientific basis for the ideas and products being promoted. Organizations seeking quick or magical solutions are vulnerable to the exaggerated promises of suppliers. Patterson (1983) has provided the following criteria for assessing the theory that undergirds sound practice: (1) importance, (2) preciseness and clarity, (3) parsimony and simplicity, (4) comprehensiveness, (5) operationality, (6) empirical validity or verifiability, (7) fruitfulness, and (8) practicality.

Reflective practitioners and scholars want to know about the completeness and integrity of ideas they adopt. Certainly, there are always new ideas, and those ideas generally deserve to be tried and tested. An ethical problem arises when unjustified claims are made in an attempt to market these ideas before they are fully developed and assessed.

PHILOSOPHY AND THEORY UNDERLYING HRD

There is tension in the academic world about the distinction between disciplines and fields of study. Some of the tension is rooted in history and tradition, some with singularity of focus in some fields, and some has to do with knowledge apart from practice. The debates around academic "turf" contain a number if issues. First, HRD is an old realm of practice and a relatively young academic field of study. While HRD is maturing, the stage of maturation varies within nations and between nations.

Most academic fields of study are applied (e.g., medicine, engineering, education, business, and communication) and draw upon multiple theories in articulating their disciplinary base. HRD is not alone. It is common for applied disciplines to create specializations that in time come to overshadow their hosts and to break away as independent disciplines. For example, university departments of adult education and vocational education have historically supported HRD in the United States. In the 1990s, many HRD programs became larger than their adult education and vocational education academic university hosts. Another point of confusion is that most disciplines are rooted in a set of theories, and some of those theories are shared by other disciplines.

A major question is "What theories make up the HRD discipline?" If psychological theory were determined to be one of them and HRD programs are hosted in colleges of the arts, engineering, business, and education—all would draw upon some aspect of psychological theory. What slice of psychological theory and for what purpose are what ultimately help distinguish the discipline. In that HRD has specific purposes, those purposes direct the profession to the relevant general theories and specific theories, while others might be ignored. Thoughtfully identifying core component theories from psychology and other theoretical domains for articulating the HRD discipline is essential for advancing its academic status. Furthermore, the blending of the core theories provides the true distinguishing theoretical base of HRD.

Take two theories often identified as foundational to HRD: system and anthropological theories. System theory is not as value laden as anthropology. Anthropologists are generally committed to not disturbing or changing the culture they study. In contrast, system theory almost always is thinking about understanding the system and the potential of improving it. Thus, it can be paradoxical to have HRD people espouse anthropological views with the intent to change the culture. This is a simple illustration of the missing logic that can occur when theory building is bypassed. Given the nature and purpose of HRD, easy arguments can be made that system theory is core to HRD and anthropology is secondary. Anthropology will likely provide situational methods and tools to be called upon as needed while never being central to the theory and practice of HRD.

A second example of missing logic within HRD is seen when HRD professionals claim a whole systems view (of the world, the organization, and the people in it) without having the rigorous system theory and tools to match those claims. Putting people into a guided group process and relying only on those interaction skills is adequate for whole system understanding. Such a view would limit "the" skill of the HRD professional to group interaction facilitation.

Theory has an enormous challenge and opportunity in the growing HRD profession. The concurrent questions are questions of philosophy: What is there? (ontology); How do you know? (epistemology), and Why should I? (ethics). The following essay by Dr. Karen Watkins (1989), a noted HRD scholar, provides alternative philosophical metaphors for thinking about HRD theory and practice.

PHILOSOPHICAL METAPHORS FOR HRD THEORY AND PRACTICE
Contributed by Karen E. Watkins

Theories from different disciplines attempt to explain the universe, using the tools and perspectives of that discipline. An interdisciplinary applied field like HRD can thus be expected to make use of many different theories. For example, general system theory is a robust and useful diagnostic theory, which befits a particular philosophical metaphor.

Just as different disciplines and different system levels may call for different theories, so may alternative *philosophies* for the role of human resource development call for different theories. Five such philosophical metaphors will be considered and are depicted in Figure 4.1: the human resource developer as organizational problem solver, organizational change agent/interventionist or helper, organizational

Person + Environment = Life Space

Figure 4.1   The Psychological Life Span

designer, organizational empowerer/meaning maker, and developer of human capital.

Organizational Problem Solver

For many years, the dominant image of the trainer has been one of a person who designs instructional programs to respond to organizationally defined problems. Training has been largely behavior oriented, in keeping with the emphasis on skills training. System theory is a useful tool for designing programs to respond to clearly defined problems. It enables people to attend to the whole and to classify and define the parts of a system. Depending on how broadly they define the system, they can think about the problem in increasingly broad terms. From the level of the individual to the "whole wide world environment," systems are made up of the same parts: contest, inputs, processes, outputs, and feedback loops. These parts not only help clarify the elements of a system but also have definable characteristics that can be tinkered with to produce alternative outputs. By increasing the number of inputs, by improving the processes that produce the outputs, or by drawing resources more effectively from the environment, or context, we can alter the cost and effectiveness of our outputs. Because system theory has been so useful for helping trainers think about the nature of the problems they are trying to solve, the theory has been widely favored. But there are problems with relying on it.

System theory is a useful diagnostic theory, but it does not help us decide which parts are working and which are not. It is not normative, so there is no hint about what might be a more ideal solution to the present situation. Moreover, system theory focuses more on problem solving than on problem finding, yet the complex, turbulent environments in which organizations find themselves today demand much greater emphasis on the problem identification phase of the problem-solving process.

System theory has grown out of the recognition that to solve the problems of the world, we need models that are more holistic than analytic, as were those in favor previously. Greenman (1978) suggests that efficient system models help people and organizations maintain purposeful, goal-directed behavior. He points out that there are inherent dilemmas in the use of systems models, such as the dilemma of oversimplifying complex environments or the dilemma of idealism versus realism. To accompany the classic systems model, Greenman developed a decision-making cycle that moves through three phases: *policy making, preplanning evaluation,* and *action implementation,* which therefore incorporates problem solving. Senge (1987) has noted that decision making is where most problems occur. Decision making is the product of a mental model, and if a manager's mental model is inadequate, he or she will make poor decisions.

Senge hypothesizes that managerial learning processes will be more effective if they are the result of a systemic and a dynamic perspective or worldview. He concludes that the task of HRD professions is to map, challenge, and improve existing mental models. The systems approach, when conceptualized broadly, may be a useful model for addressing short-term perspectives, truncated problem-solving processes, or limited worldviews.

Because system theory does not include even an implicit normative model, it is often coupled with other theories of organizational change or effectiveness to enable decision makers to move from diagnosing problems in a system to prescribing action. Systems thinking is often at a fairly macro or abstract level, and some other model or theory is needed to identify operational constructs that can be enacted in organizations. The following metaphors are often used in concert with system theory.

Organizational Change Agent/Interventionist or Helper

Many would argue that the most compelling metaphor for HRD is that of organizational change agent or helper (see Mink & Watkins, 1983). In this conception, human resource developers help people and organizations change. To do this, they need a theory of how human beings and groups are led to act as they do and what interventions might influence them to act differently. To start at the beginning, we must start with Kurt Lewin, the father of organizational change agentry.

Lewin's field theory is a comprehensive depiction of human behavior. First there was Sigmund Freud, who gave us a theory to help us understand the importance of individual history, and then there was Lewin, who helped us understand the group, especially as a means of understanding people (Argyris, 1952). These two remain the most influential thinkers in psychology. Lewin developed field theory out of the field concept in physics—the study of electromagnetic fields—which eventually led to Albert Einstein's theory of relativity. The first psychologists to use field theory were the Gestalt psychologists, who believed that the way an object is perceived is determined by the context in which it is embedded and that the relationship between the parts of that perceptual field is more important than the characteristics of those separate parts (Hall & Lindzey, 1970). Lewin, who was associated with these early Gestalt psychologists while at the University of Berlin, developed field theory as a way to represent psychological reality. He had three major premises:

- Behavior is a function of the field that exists at the time the behavior occurs. This has often been expressed as the equation $B = f(P,E)$, or behavior (B) is a function (f) of the interaction between a person (P) and his or her psychological environment (*E*).

- Analysis begins with the situation as a whole (the gestalt) from which we may differentiate parts.
- The concrete person in a concrete situation can be represented mathematically (Hall & Lindzey, 1970).

To amplify the first premise, Lewin termed the environment, as the person perceives and organizes it, the psychological field, or the *life space*. He suggested that the life space was made up of the person and his or her environment. He believed these parts were dynamically interrelated and held in equilibrium, with changes in any part affecting the whole just as in an electromagnetic field. Field theorists believe that a field not only surrounds the individual, but it also combines or overlaps with that of others to make up the *social field* (Argyris, 1952). Thus, by studying the organization in the individual, we can know the organization. A related idea in field theory is that past events only influence behavior in the present in terms of present conditions. For example, growing up with an alcoholic does not affect one's present behavior, but the mental "tapes" and embedded shame-based behavior one carries over from the past may.

Lewin sought to understand the psychological field with enough rigor that it could be represented mathematically. He even developed a new mathematic to help him represent psychological reality. Using topology, he could mathematically depict the connectedness of regions in the life space. Such concepts as Karl Weick's (1976) loose and tight coupling and the idea of having no permeable boundaries for the self illustrate ways we have conceptualized the degree of connectedness between regions. Although that degree of connectedness is more psychological than spatial, it is nevertheless clear and observable and hence may be represented mathematically. Organizational researchers, for example, sometimes measure the degree of loose or tight coupling in decision making by the number of decisions that organizational members say must go to the top of the organization.

Lewin developed "hodology," or a mathematic of path, to express psychological distance and direction. Lewin's concern was for powerful, scientific discourse, and the language of mathematics was considered the most powerful. He chose the mathematics of spatial relationships because he wanted to explain that it is the person in his or her life space. He depicted the person as a circle within a larger circle, much like the boy in a bubble. Thus, people have boundaries that differentiate them from each other and from their environment. Yet they also are included in a larger area or context, which also defines who they are. Bordering the entire life space is a *foreign hull,* which Lewin described as made up of all the data to which a person is not now attending but which is nevertheless part of his or her environment (Hall & Lindzey, 1970).

By varying the thickness of the circle around *P,* we can indicate a person's accessibility or inaccessibility. Lewin divided the life space into regions based on relevant psychological facts at any given moment. Those that are relevant to the person are *needs;* those that are relevant to the environment are *valences.* Needs are a system in a state of tension, or psychological energy, directed toward the boundaries of the system (Argyris, 1952). Needs are directed toward *goals*—regions in the life space that are attractive to the person or, in other words, have a positive valence. Here the electroganetic analogy seems clear. Lewin said there may be *barriers* in the life space that create resistance to goal attainment, and these barriers may be social, physical, or psychological. The clarity with which a person perceives the field in terms of structure, the amount of differentiation, and the relationships between regions is the *cognitive structure.* The regions of the personality are organized in definite relationships to each other; this arrangement is called the *psychological structure.*

Force in the psychological field is the tendency toward movement in people or groups. *It is the cause of change.* It is a vector with direction and magnitude or size. Every force in one direction has it opposite, so the direction of movement will depend on the strength of a given force. A force field is a constellation of forces. Human resource developers commonly use force field analysis to analyze conflict situations, to problem-solve, or to identify change strategies. It consists of analyzing the forces promoting and inhibiting change and determining the strength of each of those forces, followed by developing strategies to reduce the strength of the restraining forces and testing those strategies in action.

Lewin's theory can also be viewed in terms of adult development. Adults, he said, have more regions in their personality and are thus more differentiated than children. The boundaries between regions of the adult are less permeable, making adults more rigid but also less affected in one region by frustrations in another. In contrast, the child who wants an apple and can't have it will find that his frustration spreads to his play, his ability to concentrate, and so on. Long periods of frustration may produce dedifferentiation in adults. For example, when workers are underutilized, their behavior deteriorates in all areas of their lives.

The *social field* is made up of the group life space and may contain many subgroups or regions. The group has its own unique properties, both structural (the degrees of differentiation, stratification, and unity, as well as the type of organization or social hierarchy) and dynamic (group goals, ideal goals, style of living, and psychological and social climate) (Argyris, 1952).

Most people are part of many groups. Often these groups create *overlapping situations* for people. Chris Argyris (1952) used the example of a foreman who is both part of the worker groups and part of the management group. The degree of *consonance,* or similarity in values, norms, and goals between the groups will increase or decrease the amount of overlap, the valence or desirability of that overlap, and the nature of the barriers between the groups (Argyris, 1952). A clearer understanding of the nature of groups, intergroup conflicts, and the psychological reality internalized by individuals as members of groups grew out of Lewin's work.

Finally, people vary in terms of the relative accessibility of various regions in their life spaces. This concept is defined as their *space of free movement.* A person may view a region negatively or may have a barrier imposed around a region. In either case, movement toward personal goals will be impeded. For example, adults who have difficulty playing have limited their space of free movement. Also, in the case of a foreman in a newly unionized company, the union will circumscribe the foreman's ability to hire, fire, and work directly with the workers. Psychologically, the foreman's space of free movement also will be circumscribed.

Perhaps the most significant aspect of field theory is that it does not purport to be or to explain objective reality but rather to explain a person's psychological reality, which is not what is but what that person perceives reality to be. But Lewin did not develop his theory only to explain human behavior at an abstract level. Like most human resource developers, he was interested in observing these abstract concepts at work at the practical level. He believed that one had to have a theory that was broad enough to encompass the multifaceted nature of human action and that the way to test that theory was through a process called *action research.*

Action research can be thought of as a series of successive approximations. Interventions are developed while looking at the whole (at the individual level, at the life space, at the organizational level, and at the social field). Interventions are made and their effects studied. They are followed by new interventions, which are developed upon reflection of the previous effects on the whole. Lewin depicted the process of movement from a present state to a desired state through action and reflection as a process of unfreezing, changing, and refreezing.

Lewin's concepts will not lead to simple prescriptions or step-by-step instructions for human resource developers wondering what to do on Monday, but they do bring into sharper focus the architectural structure of human and organizational relationships in a way that permits a rich analysis of organizational life.

The work of Chris Argyris, who was one of Lewin's last students, furthers our understanding of how to use field theory in organizational change efforts. He defines intervention as entering "into an ongoing system of relationship, to come between or among persons, groups, or objects for the purpose of helping them" (1970, p. 15). In field theory terms, to intervene is to interrupt the forces in the life space in such a way as to disrupt the quasi-stationary equilibrium.

Argyris emphasized that the system exists independently of the intervenor and that despite the interdependencies that develop between the client system and the intervenor, the intervenor should focus on how to maintain or increase the autonomy of the client system, how to differentiate even more clearly the boundaries between the client system and the intervenor, and how to conceptualize and define the client system's health, independent of the intervenor. *The client must be the system as a whole regardless of where one initially begins to work,* he said. Interventions must, over time, provide all members with opportunities to enhance their competence and effectiveness (Argyris, 1970). Perhaps because of the ethical implications of tinkering with a person's or an organization's life space, the intervenor's primary tasks are to seek valid information, to provide for free and informed choice, and to encourage the client's internal commitment to the choices made in the interventions.

As HRD practitioners, our theories of practice usually contain intervention theories—theories of action aimed at increasing our effectiveness (Argyris & Schon, 1982). Because these theories are largely tacit, we need to reflect critically on what we actually do in order to examine and test our assumptions about what causes us to be effective. Argyris developed a normative theory of intervention. Having observed repeated patterns in people's theories of practice, he identified the pattern most commonly found in people's actual practice as a control orientation. In contrast to this pattern is a learning-oriented intervention theory that encapsulates Argyris's prescription for effective intervention.

Viewed from the perspective of field theory, Argyris can be seen to have defined the intervenor–client relationship in a way that will minimize the potential conflict in an overlapping situation (or field) in order to decrease the conflict that might be produced by attempts to control others and in order to permit learning to occur. His primary tasks for intervenors are designed to minimize the production of perceptual barriers in the form of defensiveness, negative attributions about the intervenors' motives, and other self-protective responses that could limit the intervenor's space of free movement and subsequent learning. By emphasizing the need for shared meaning between client and intervenor about goals and the personal causal responsibility of the client for actions and choices, Argyris hopes to increase the consonance between the two overlapping situations.

Action science (Argyris, Putnam, & Smith, 1985) has been defined as "an inquiry into how human beings design and implement action in relation to one another." It has three key features:

- empirically disconfirmable propositions that are organized into a theory;
- knowledge that human beings can implement in an action context;
- alternatives to the status quo that both illuminate what exists and inform fundamental change, in light of values freely chosen by social actors (p. 4).

These three propositions have traveled far from Lewin's three key tenets. Like Lewin, Argyris believes that human action is the result of subjective human perception that occurs within a behavioral world or a life space. Both agree that this knowledge of the perceptual world could inform and reform action. Lewin believes that for adults, education is most often reeducation, a process of unfreezing that begins with a disconfirmation of one's present beliefs or perception of reality, which leads to anxiety or guilt and finally to a search for psychological safety. The critical theory that people change as a result of an internal critique in which they perceive that their own action is in conflict with their own values has refined Argyris's concept of reeducation.

Argyris describes reeducation as a process of disconfirmation based on internal critique, which leads to a sense of personal causal responsibility (as in "I produced this mismatch—this action that conflicts with my values"), which can then lead to psychological success or congruence between one's internal critique and the external feedback one receives. Argyris notes that people and organizations develop elaborate defensive routines to deny that these mismatches occur and to save face. Only by interrupting those defensive routines will people and organizations experience psychological success.

In both Lewin's and Argyris's work, the emphasis is on a way of understanding people, especially in their social context. They offer not a technical prescription for action for change agents but rather a rich conceptual framework for action in any change situation.

Organizational Designer

A third metaphor for HRD is that of organizational designer. Organizational design is the process of first diagnosing and then selecting the structure and formal system of communication, authority, and responsibility to achieve organizational goals. Organizational designers attend to environmental flux, strategic choices, and the uncertainty or certainty of task or technology (Hellriegel, Slocum, & Woodman, 1986). People who work from this conception of metaphor see a clear connection between the structure of work and work organizations and the development of the organization's human resources. A foundational theory for students of organization design is Herb Simon's administrative decision-making theory.

Simon (1965) theorizes that individuals have a bounded rationality that leads to satisficing in decision making. Given the quantity of information we deal with, we need to find boundaries within which to make rational decisions. We may use heuristics or rules of thumb, which, experience suggests, usually lead to acceptable solutions; but heuristics may limit the search for solutions, especially in large, complex problem spaces (note the Lewinian image). In contrast, algorithms are more rigorous, systematic procedures. One goal of management science is to discover more algorithms by which managers may make more consistently effective decisions.

To meet this goal, we need to have a concept of the elements that make up decision-making activity. The response of managers to stimuli is a program, the basic element of Simon's theory. A program has basic parts:

- Stimuli—the information that evokes a program
- Inputs—both facts and values
- Content—a series of execution steps
- Outputs

There are programmed and unprogrammed activities: A programmed activity is prompted by a single clear stimulus. An unprogrammed activity is evoked when there is no tried-and-true method for handling the stimulus, either because it is a new situation, its nature is elusive and complex, or because it is so important that it deserves a customized response. Unprogrammed activity has three stages of individual activity, each stage of which is so rich that the stage itself has theories. The stages are as follows:

- Intelligence activity—searching the environment for conditions calling for a decision
- Design activity—inventing, developing, and analyzing course of action
- Choice activity—selecting a course of action from those available

For intelligence activity, theorists have explored the differences in problem framing between novices and experts. Schon (1983) has found that experts frame problems through a kind of artistry that defies routinization, whereas novices follow more of a technical, by-the-numbers process. Jaques (1985) suggests that individuals vary in cognitive complexity or work capacity. *Work capacity* is the longest time period one can plan a project or work without the need of feedback. This variable, Jaques said, is a given in individuals, like their height, and it varies enormously. Most people have a work capacity between three months and one year. A few scientists, politicians, and leaders have work capacities that exceed their lifetimes; they are designing new worlds. People with limited work capacities cannot fall back far enough to view a problem with a wide-angle lens, nor can they conceive of long-term solutions or parallel implications. Thus, they are limited in the scope of work that they can design.

Design activity has also been studied extensively. We see design as having both a conceptual and an aesthetic quality, whether we conceive of it

- in the dictionary sense, as in conceiving an idea or a form, planning and shaping a structure, using tools and materials creatively, and making something useful;
- in the broader context used by Simon, as in converting actual to preferred situations;
- or in accordance with C. West Churchman's (1971) notion that design is occurring whenever we consciously attempt to change ourselves and our environment to improve the quality of our lives (p. vii).

Churchman (1971) states that design is "thinking behavior which conceptually selects among a set of alternatives in order to figure out which alternative leads to the desired goals or set of goals" (p. 5). Schon (1983, 1987) understands design to be a process of problem framing or problem setting, in which the artistry of expert practitioners is a "reflective conversation with a situation," which may lead to a reframing of the situation and thence to an architectural plan or a therapeutic intervention. Pfeiffer and Jones (1973) describe the design process in training as dependent on four considerations:

- The parameters of the situation (time, place, resources, staff, etc.)
- The skill needed to design
- The components to be designed

- Outcome criteria, which are defined in terms of client needs

Those considerations will be influenced greatly by the conceptual skill (thinking behavior) and the design expertise (artistry) of the designer. Design is artistic, because in these nonroutine, unprogrammed activities, we must create a new artifact, plan, or training program.

Most of what human resource developers do is unprogrammed activity. Organizational design has emerged as a distinct field within the study of organizations. Galbraith (1974) notes that "the ability of the organization to successfully utilize coordination by goal setting, hierarchy, and rules depends on the combination of the frequency of exceptions and the capacity of the hierarchy to handle them" (p. 29).

Organizational design was thus the creation of responses to uncertainty, which he said could be done by either

- reducing the need for information processing through creating slack resources or self-contained tasks or
- increasing the organization's capacity to process information through investment in vertical information systems or through the creation of lateral relationships.

Lorsch (1971) focuses on the design dimensions of differentiation and integration. In each of these theoretical models, organizational design is triggered through a process of assessing the gap between where the organization is now and where it needs to be, based on a normative model of organizational effectiveness.

Design theory has emerged from the literature of art, architecture, computer science, decision making, and education. Houle, in *The Design of Education* (1972), finds that design is a two-part process consisting of first examining the situation in which the learning activity occurs and then applying a framework to that situation. The framework can be system theory, field theory, or some other theory; although designers who operate only out of a credo or belief system, such as Malcolm Knowles's andragogy, will find that their frameworks are not broad enough to guide a program design process. Thus, the systems approach is a useful theoretical tool to guide the design stage, but other theories may be more useful for Simon's other two stages of unprogrammed activity.

Organizations increase productivity by increasing the level of routinization. Thus, a major task for human resource developers is to help managers design routine responses for nonroutine, unprogrammed activities. There are many ways to do this, from designing a learning program for training machine operators to use a new machine, to designing strategic systems for monitoring unstable or unpredictable processes. General system theory is an analytical process model, not a content model. To develop models for diagnosis and prescriptions for action, organizational design theorists add to system theory other normative content theories, such as a theory of an open, healthy person or a theory of organizational effectiveness.

Organizational Empowerer/Meaning Maker

Theorists who embrace this metaphor seek to transform people and organizations in order to foster long-term health and effectiveness. They view the organization and its people as repressed and disenfranchised. As adherents of the philosophy that meanings are in people, they would agree with Smirich (1983) that "organizations are socially constructed systems of shared meaning" (p. 221). In modern terms, they follow the prescripts of critical theory. Critical theories are aimed at producing enlightenment in those who hold them and are inherently emancipatory in that they help people free themselves from self-imposed coercion.

Critical theorists contrast their type of knowledge, which is "reflective," with that of normal science, which is "objectifying." They argue that because knowledge is never objective, the search for objectivity in normal science tends to objectify people and natural phenomena. Critical theory emancipates by offering a critique of "what is" from the perspective of "what might be." It seeks to stimulate self-reflection so that people may freely choose to transform their world. Geuss (1981) has defined emancipation as a movement, or transformation, from an initial state to a final state. The initial state is one of false consciousness, error, and unfree existence, in which

- this false consciousness is interconnected with the oppression,
- the false consciousness is self-designed, and the oppression is self-imposed,
- the power in the above lies in the fact that people do not realize their oppression is self-imposed.

The final stage is one in which people are free of false consciousness (enlightened) and free of self-imposed constraints (emancipated).

People move from one state to another by engaging in a process of self-reflection, or critical reflectivity, in which they

- dissolve the illusion of objectivity,
- become aware of their own origin, and
- bring to consciousness the unconscious determinants of their action (Geuss, 1981).

As a result of this reflection, a perspective transformation will occur (Mezirow, 1981), and the person will generate new knowledge, which may be generalized into a critical theory. This reflective thinking has also been referred to as an *internal critique of a person's epistemic beliefs* (second-order beliefs about which beliefs are acceptable) in which the person's values are seen to contradict his or her ideal of a good life.

The critical theory so generated will consist of three parts:

- A demonstration that change is possible
- A depiction of the practical necessity of the change, as the present situation has produced frustration and suffering and is only thus because peo-

ple hold a particular world view that, upon critical reflection, is no longer acceptable

- An assertion that the movement or transformation can only come about if people accept the critical theory as their "self consciousness" (Geuss, 1981, p. 76)

The best-known critical theories are psychoanalysis for individuals and Marxism for social systems. Action science comes closest to operationalizing the idea of a critical theory for organizations.

The strategies used to transform perspectives in action science include determining the potential unintended or unjust consequences of action strategies; ensuring that participants feel personal causal responsibility for their actions; and offering an alternative for action in the form of learning-oriented behavior rather than coercive or control-oriented behavior.

Developer of Human Capital

The fifth and final metaphor of the human resource developer is that of the developer of human capital. A derivative of economics, human capital theory refers to "the productive capabilities of human beings that are acquired at some cost and that command a price in the labor market because they are useful in producing goods and services (Parnes, 1986, p. 1). Flamholtz (1985) emphasizes that it is the "expected realizable value" of a person, given opportunities for training, expected turnover, age to retirement, promotability, and so on, that has ultimate value in a human resource accounting system. Value is typically perceived as the relationship between costs and benefits (or the return on investment). Gordon (in LaBelle, 1988) outlines the economic assumptions that underlie human capital theory: "Product and labor markets are competitive, firms attempt to maximize profits, workers seek to maximize earnings, and the labor force has both knowledge and mobility to take advantage of the best opportunities available" (p. 206).

Salaries are seen in supply-and-demand terms. A worker's skills and abilities are a form of capital because they influence the worker's productivity for the organization as well as the worker's opportunities for higher wages, greater economic security, and increased employment prospects. Education, or training, is seen in the human capital model as a major tool to influence workers' acquisition of the needed knowledge and skills.

Dierkes and Coppock (1975) suggest that human needs are met in organizations as the result of a chain of interventions that have allowed a problem to bubble up from a state of recognition by subgroups in society, to legislation, to organizational enforcement of new human resource standards. An example is the human need for equal pay for equal work. A more proactive approach—one that attends to the organization's long-term human resource needs—is human resource accounting.

To illustrate how difficult it is to justify training without the concept of human resource accounting, Dierkes and Coppock compared how we now account for management's spending $100,000 on a new piece of equipment and how we account for spending the same amount on employee training or on efforts to improve the quality of the work environment. When purchasing equipment, the manager anticipates amortizing the costs over the expected life of the equipment and being able to document benefits by listing the equipment as an asset over a number of years. When purchasing human resource development, the manager anticipates incurring costs for the current year, with no amoritization over the useful life of the skills gained.

Human resource accounting systems have been developed to attempt to overcome this short-range distortion in measuring organizational economic effectiveness. Initially, the focus was on developing accounting procedures to determine investments in human capabilities. Human resource information systems attempted to inventory human resources, determine outlay and replacement costs, and determine the economic value of the human resources employed in the organization. Succession plans and lists of high-potential employees are recent outgrowths of organizational attempts to develop inventories of their human resource assets. These approaches led to a definition of the economic value of human resources as "the present discounted value of their [individuals'] future contributions less the costs of acquiring, maintaining, and utilizing these resources in the organization" (Pyle, in Dierkes & Coppock, 1975, p. 313).

The first extension of the application of human resource accounting systems was to health and safety measures, because, if people are assets, anything that diminishes those assets will diminish the organization's expected realizable value. The costs of investments in employee health, rehabilitation, safety measures, and safety training can be compared with the costs of days lost because of accidents and illnesses. It is a short step from there to examining the economic impact of the psychological work environment. The research and literature on job satisfaction, matching jobs and people, climate, leadership, motivation, etc., illustrate the high degree of interest in this approach. However, research linking these tertiary effects to productivity typically involves assumptions of correlation when, for example, both climate and productivity change in value without careful concomitant control of any intervening social, historical, demographic, or political variables. Such research is difficult to conduct. Rensis Likert and David Bowers (1973) made perhaps the most comprehensive attempt to capture such relationships. In analyzing the result of a large number of studies, they found a .67 correlation between organizational climate and subordinates' satisfaction and a .42 correlation between subordinates' satisfaction and total productive efficiency. Given the large number of studies they used, these are fairly strong relationships, which suggest that climate influences satisfaction and leads to at least modest gains in productivity.

Human capital theory provides a strong, bottom-line-oriented justification for HRD. It breaks down the barriers that now exist between organizational development approaches that attempt to influence climate and quality of work life, employee assistance, and other employee health and safety areas, and the more conventional training and development arena of HRD. Each area makes its contribution to the organization's long-term effectiveness. The human capital, or human resource accounting approach, is perhaps most valuable for this long-term emphasis.

Changing demographics and higher labor participation by women and minorities along with recent technological changes are creating an enormous need for long-range thinking. "It becomes increasingly clear that economic security in the post-industrial economy depends less on expertise and more on *flexpertise*— the ability to continually adapt individual knowledge and skill. . . . Virtually the entire adult population needs retraining and new learning to be economically productive. . . . The emergence of a knowledge-based economy requires a new synthesis of the functions of training, education, and other forms of communication and learning under the single umbrella of the learning enterprise" (Perelman, 1984, pp. xvi–xvii).

Carnavale (1984) has offered a similar analysis of the role of training and development in developing human capital. According to Carnavale, workplace learning and formal education account for more growth in economic output than employee health, capital, the composition of the workforce, population size, or resource adaptation. Workplace learning, he states, accounts for 85 percent of the variance in lifetime earnings. The relationship between learning and training and economic returns for both people and organizations enjoys a distinguished, currently prominent place among the theoretical underpinnings for HRD.

Critics of human capital theory point to the limits of capitalism and to economic explanations of what people gain from investments in learning. In the first instance, they discuss the role of training as a means of social control, using as examples

- training as a means of despoiling, or "cooling out," the aspirations of many people so they will accept low-level jobs and

- organizational training programs to socialize newcomers into conforming to the organization's norms and values.

Moreover, the inherent class structure and objectification of workers in bureaucratic organizations may produce lower productivity despite training efforts (LaBelle, 1988).

People gain considerably more from training than simply an enhanced economic value. Intrinsic satisfaction, enhanced life skills, the increased capacity to function effectively as parents, as citizens are alternative benefits derived from training. In fact, people often regard training as a fringe benefit—a view human resource developers deplore, as it often leaves training budgets seeming as expendable as other fringe benefits. Yet this perspective may also correctly capture a more holistic, value-added approach to understanding the benefits of training.

Summary

The underlying root philosophies and theories of HRD are rich and varied. Figure 4.2 offers a brief comparison as presented in this chapter. Increasing understanding among practitioners of their potential to enrich and improve practice often requires translations, such as Peter Senge's translation of system theory to management practice, and Chris Argyris's translation of field theory to HRD practice. When human resource developers come to embrace many different theoretical foundations, practice will be enlarged and will rise to the level demanded by the present complex, nonroutine, ambiguous business environment. Not one, but many metaphors, can be used to guide our understanding of the field of our practice.

CONCLUSION

Theory, research, development, and practice together compose a vital cycle that allows ideas to be progressively refined as they evolve from concepts to practices and from practices to concepts. The theory-research-development-practice cycle (Figure 4.2) illustrates the systematic application of inquiry methods working to advance the knowledge used by both HRD researchers and practitioners.

There are those who caution us in constructing the relationships among theory, research, development, and practice. In offering the notion of a scientific *paradigm*, Kuhn (1970) compelled philosophers and researchers to rethink the assumptions underlying the scientific method and paved the way for alternative,

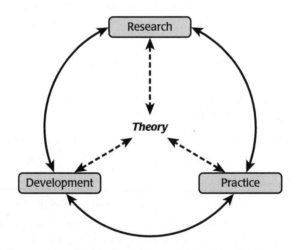

Figure 4.2   Theory-Research-Development-Practice Cycle (*Source:* Swanson, 1997, p. 14.)

postpositivistic approaches to research in the behavioral sciences. Ethnography and naturalistic inquiry allow theory to emerge from data derived from practice and experience; theory does not necessarily precede research as theory can be generated through it. The model of theory, research, development, and practice for HRD embraces these cautions (see Figure 4.2).

The cyclical model brings HRD theory, research, development, and practice together in the same forum. The union of these domains is itself an important purpose of the model. Two other purposes also exist. First, each of the four domains makes a necessary contribution to HRD. There is no presumption about the importance to the profession of contributions from research, practice, punctuated development efforts, and theory itself. The model demonstrates the need for all domains to inform each other in order to enrich the profession as a whole. Second, exchange among the domains is multidirectional. Any of the domains can serve as an appropriate starting point for proceeding through the cycle. Improvements in the profession can occur whether one begins with theory, research, development, or practice. Thus, each of the cycle's domains both *informs* and *is informed by* each of the other domains.

In summary, HRD philosophy and theory results in powerful and practical *explanations, principles,* and *models* for professionals to carry out their work in organizations. The problem facing almost every organization, and those who work in them, is in meeting the constant demand for high performance. In that organizations are human-made entities, they require human expertise to perform, grow, and adapt. These demands include everything from assuring sustainable financial growth of the organization to satisfying the next customer standing in the front row. Without a holistic mental model of human resource development within an organizational system and improvement context working through people, the practitioner is left with the task of dissecting and interpreting each and every HRD situation they face. Or worse yet, they simply charge ahead in a trial-and-error mode.

REFLECTION QUESTIONS

1. Why would someone argue that good theory is practical?
2. What is theory? Give a definition and an explanation.
3. Of the HRD theory references cited, which one interests you the most? Why?
4. Which of the five philosophical metaphors for HRD theory makes the most sense to you? Explain why?
5. Which of the five philosophical metaphors for HRD theory makes the most sense to a high-tech business organization? Explain why.

The Theory of Human Resource Development

CHAPTER OUTLINE

This chapter is based on four papers that articulate a theoretical foundation of human resource development. All four papers were originally presented at an Academy of Human Resource Development theory symposium in 1998 by Holton (1998), Ruona (1998), Swanson (1998a), and Torraco (1998). The first section is "The Discipline of Human Resource Development" by Richard A. Swanson. The purpose of this section is to frame the discipline of HRD by identifying its model, boundaries, definition, context, foundational theories (psychological theory, economic theory, and system theory), and propositions arising from the theory. Each of these three underlying theories is discussed in depth.

In terms of psychological theory, Elwood F. Holton's section is titled the "Psychology and the Discipline of HRD—Contributions and Limitations." He notes that psychology has long provided a core theoretical base for HRD. Contemporary HRD extends beyond psychology to embrace multiple theoretical bases. This second section examines psychology's theoretical contributions to the discipline of HRD. It is argued that psychological theories are both powerful and limited as a foundation for HRD. Specific psychological theories and their conceptual relationships with economics and system theory are discussed.

The third section, "Economics—Human Capital Theory and Human Resource Development," was written by Richard J. Torraco. He argues that the development of a theory base to support the rapidly growing field of HRD is the most important issue facing HRD scholars today. The pressures on HRD to meet the needs of a diverse workforce in a rapidly changing work environment demand the inclusion of economics as a foundational theory of the HRD. He further argues for human capital theory as the economic theory relevant to HRD.

The final section by Wendy E. A Ruona, "System Theory as a Foundation for HRD," investigates the contribution of system theory to HRD. The treatise offers a framework to organize themes emerging from the literature on how system theory supports HRD. Finally, some current challenges and how system theory relates to economics and psychology are discussed.

THE DISCIPLINE OF HUMAN RESOURCE DEVELOPMENT
Contributed by Richard A. Swanson

"A theory simply explains what a phenomenon is and how it works" (Torraco, 1997, p. 115). The purpose of this section is to propose one theory of HRD believed to be supported by both research and practice.

Assumptions, Context, Definition, and Model of HRD

The bias of HRD has been the belief that organization, work process, group, and individual performance are mediated through human expertise and effort. In contrast to this belief, the performance scorecards available to organizational decision makers generally ignore the human element. The most evident example is the short-term financial view of company performance as judged by daily stock market data.

The journey of understanding performance improvement for those having the "human resource perspective" has not been easy. The range of performance perspectives in organizations forces the HRD profession to face the realities of how others strategically view HRD and how HRD views itself (Torraco & Swanson, 1995; Swanson, 1995a, 1995b). It appears as though HRD has taken a detour during the past fifty years. The clear vision and practice during World War II was lost in the 1950s and began returning in the 1980s.

The massive Training within Industry (TWI) project that culminated with the ending of World War II is seen as the origin of contemporary HRD (Dooley, 1945; Ruona & Swanson, 1998a; Swanson & Torraco, 1994; Swanson, 2001). The performance language was simpler then—"Is it a production problem?" they would ask. If yes, they would use performance improvement tools that were masquerading under the name of "training." Besides operating under a training title that they quickly outgrew, the TWI project delivered on organization, process, and individual performance outputs using simple and powerful tools they called *job instruction, job relations,* and *job methods.*

In the 1950s, a psychology-only perspective took over the personnel and training professions. As far back as 1950, Peter Drucker warned that while this thinking freed managers from the viciously bad ideas about working with people, it never provided substantive alternatives (1964, p. 278). He went on to chide the profession for an inadequate focus on the work and for inadequate awareness of the economic dimensions of work (pp. 278–279).

The reality is that most decision makers in organizations pursue performance and improvement, with or without professional HRD interventions. This simple fact confronts the HRD profession with the need to think about performance with and without the human resource perspective. The willingness to let go *temporarily* of the human bias in favor of performance improvement at all levels is the key to elevating HRD to its fullest potential. Without this fundamental mental shift, HRD will awkwardly keep trying to claim system performance (organization) through subsystem thinking (individuals). I have enough confidence that the best HRD theory and practice will invariably validate the contribution of human expertise and the unleashing of it as integral to performance at multiple levels.

The basic decision to begin with the host system of HRD as the primary avenue to performance alters the models, thinking, and tools of an HRD effort. Without this shift beyond the individual, the human resource development lens remains clouded, the HRD model is fragmented, and the underlying theory remains unclear.

Performance as the Ultimate Outcome Variable of HRD

To perform is "to fulfill an obligation or requirement; accomplish something as promised or expected" (*American Heritage College Dictionary*, 1993, p. 1015). Performance is not system design, capability, motivation, competence, or expertise. These, or other similar performance taxonomies, can best be thought of as *performance variables* (or *performance drivers*), but not performance. Performance may be aligned within missions, goals, and strategies—but not always. *Performance is the valued productive output of a system in the form of goods or services.* The actual fulfillment of the goods and/or services requirement is thought of in terms of *units of performance.* Once these goods and/or services units of performance are identified, they are typically measured in terms of production quantity, time, and quality features (Swanson & Holton, 1999; Swanson, 2001).

Chasing after individual or organization change without first specifying a valid unit of performance is foolhardy and a waste of time. This is because change can take place while "real" performance decreases! One example is to pursue employee satisfaction with the assumption that production will increase. Numerous studies have demonstrated that employee satisfaction can increase while actual production decreases or remains the same. The recent reengineering fad is another example of the pursuit of change with the majority of instances ending up in losses in performance instead of gains (Micklethwait & Wooldridge, 1996). There are those in the profession speaking directly to the topic of performance in an attempt to clarify the relationships among performance *drivers* (Holton, 1998) and/or performance *variables* (Swanson, 1994, 1996a).

System theory informs us that (1) there are systems and subsystems, and (2) all systems are open systems. The realization that there are tiers of subsystems and larger host systems and that systems are open entities constantly changing is humbling. These realizations help prevent professionals from thinking and acting simply and mechanically. HRD practitioners and scholars should not lose sight of the constantly evolving state of overall systems.

The larger frame in which HRD functions includes organizations and the milieu in which they function. Organizations are the host systems for most HRD activity. Some of these systems are profit-making organizations that produce goods and/or services for consumers. Some are nonprofit organizations that produce goods and/or services for consumers. Some are publicly owned, some are shareholder owned and publicly traded, and some are owned by individuals or a group of individuals. All these organizations function in an ever present political, cultural, and economic milieu. Each has its own mission/strategy, structure, technology, and human resource mix. Additionally, each has core processes related to producing the goods and services it produces.

Definition and Model of Human Resource Development
The expectation is that HRD efforts will logically culminate with important performance improvements for its host organization. Thus, the operational definition of HRD is as follows:

> Human resource development (HRD) is a process of developing and unleashing human expertise through organization development (OD) and personnel training and development (T&D) for the purpose of improving performance.

- The domains of performance include organizations, work processes, and groups, and individuals.
- OD is the process of systematically implementing organizational change for the purpose of improving performance.
- T&D is the process of systematically developing expertise in individuals for the purpose of improving performance.

Additionally, HRD itself can be viewed and pursued as an improvement process functioning within the host organization. This is graphically portrayed in Figure 5.1. This model of HRD illustrates HRD as a five-phase process working in concert with other core organizational processes, all functioning in the organizational context and the larger environmental context. The boundaries of HRD relate to the system hosting HRD. In most instances, this is an organization such as a business, industry, government, or nonprofit agency. In some instances, the host organization for HRD could be a geopolitical region or a nation.

While performance will likely always demand multiple interpretations, performance and, more important, performance improvement are not simply abstract notions about desirable ways to reach a better state. In every organization, the concrete determinants of performance are reflected in people, their ideas, and the material resources through which their ideas reach the marketplace. Performance cannot be described or improved without specifying its determinants, accounting for the sophisticated processes through which performance is expressed (e.g., human behavior, work process innovation, stock market performance), and making some judgment about whether performance has, in fact, improved. Performance improvement can only be manifest through outputs, and

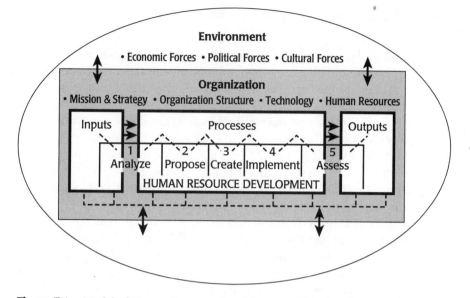

Figure 5.1   Model of Human Resource Development within the Organization and Environment

change in outputs can only be assessed through some form of measurement. Thus, performance is a concept that can be systematically operationalized in any organization when we set out to demonstrate whether or not it has improved.

Theory versus Model

Models of HRD have been developed and disseminated through books, seminars, and consulting projects. Many of these models are based on extensive practical experience with development and improvement (Nadler, Gerstein, & Shaw, 1992; Rummler & Brache, 1995; Schwartz, 1991; Swanson, 1994; Weisbord, 1987). Other models have been embraced as ways to solve problems by simply calling them multidimensional and demanding multidimensional thinking.

Armed with a flow chart and a description of its components, HRD professionals using their personal models can find that while they may be powerful enough to effect change, they are most likely too superficial to *explain* the complex dynamics of HRD and its connection to results. In short, a model derived from logic is no substitute for sound theory. Such models can guide improvement efforts through hypothesized relationships without having those relationships ever tested. You can have a model and no theory, you can have a theory with no model, and you can have a theory accompanied by a supporting model. A model by itself is not theory.

Theoretical and Disciplinary Foundations of HRD

HRD as a discipline is broader than any single theory. Reflecting the reality that most successful strategies for system and subsystem improvement require multi-faceted interventions, HRD draws from multiple theories and integrates them in a unique manner for the purposes of HRD. This section develops a core theoretical foundation for HRD that draws upon contributions from several respected theoretical domains. The purpose is to understand the model of human resource development within the organization and environment (Figure 5.1).

While "a theory simply explains what a phenomenon is and how it works" (Torraco, 1997, p. 115), "a discipline is a body of knowledge with its own orga-nizing concepts, codified knowledge, epistemological approach, undergirding the-ories, particular methodologies, and technical jargon" (Passmore, 1997, p. 201). The belief that HRD is a discipline that draws upon many theories is widely held. This overly generous idea has served as fools' gold to the profession. In the at-tempt to be inclusive of so many theories—staking its claim so broadly—HRD has come up with no theory. However, many believe that efforts in developing core HRD theory are essential to the maturation of the profession.

Having well-defined core HRD theories in no way limits the utility of hun-dreds of available theories that could inform HRD research or the development of specific practitioner tools and methods.

Theory Components of HRD

Presently there is no universal view or agreement on the theory or multiple the-ories that support HRD as a discipline. Furthermore, no theory alternatives are being visibly proposed in the literature or debated by the profession. On one hand, some have called for system theory to serve as a unifying theory for HRD to access all useful theories as required (Gradous, 1989; Jacobs, 1989; McLagan, 1989); on the other hand, many have proposed sets of principles in the forms of comparative lists of added value, products, processes, and expertise (e.g., Gilley & Maycunich, 2000).

The alternative to having a sound theoretical and disciplinary base for the HRD profession is the present state of rudderless random activity aggressively sponsored by atheoretical professional associations and greedy consultants (Micklethwait & Wooldridge, 1996; Swanson, 1997). This present state celebrates short-term results without having deep understanding of the ability to replicate the results or the utility of those results. For this reason, a discrete and logical set of theories as the foundation of HRD is proposed as a means of understanding the model of human resource development within the organization and environ-ment. The discipline of HRD and the model of HRD are believed to be supported and explained through the three core theory domains of psychological theory, economic theory, and system theory (Passmore, 1997; Swanson, 1995a, 1995b). Economic theory is recognized as a primary driver and survival metric of organi-zations; system theory recognizes purpose, pieces, and relationships that can maximize or strangle systems and subsystems; and psychological theory acknowledges human beings as brokers of productivity and renewal along with the cultural and behavioral nuances. Each of these three theories is unique, complementary, and robust. Together they make up the core theory underlying the discipline of HRD.

The theories have been visually presented as comprising a three-legged stool, with the three legs providing great stability for HRD as a discipline and field of practice that is required to function in the midst of uneven and changing conditions (see Figure 5.2). In recent years, particularly with the demands of the global economy and an unbridled free-market condition, the stool has been positioned on an ethical rug—a filter, if you will—between its three theories and the context in which HRD functions. Thus, the three theories are at the core of the HRD discipline, and ethics plays an important moderating role. Furthermore, the ethical concerns are believed to be best expressed through recognition and adherence to the following core beliefs:

1. Organizations are human-made entities that rely on human expertise in order to establish and achieve their goals.

2. Human expertise developed and maximized through HRD processes for the mutual long- and/or short-term benefits of the sponsoring organization and the individuals involved.

3. HRD professionals are advocates of individual/group, work process, and organizational integrity.

The *whole* theory of HRD is proposed to be the integration of psychological, economic, and system theories within an ethical frame. This integrative state is

Figure 5.2   The Theoretical Foundations of Human Resource Development

central to securing HRD as a discipline, not in just knowing the elements. The journey to this integrative state results in the organizing concepts, codified knowledge, underpinning theories, particular methodologies, and the unique technical jargon of HRD. The *whole* of any integrated HRD theory will be larger than the sum of the parts and unique to HRD. On its own, psychological theory, economic theory, or system theory is inadequate for understanding HRD and producing reliable results. Thus, the overarching proposition or HRD is as follows:

> *The theory integration proposition:* HRD must integrate its core psychological, economic, and systems theories into a holistic HRD theory and model for practice.

For example, business process reengineering, according to Hammer and Champy (1994), focused on cost reductions through low-level system analysis. Had they considered the larger frame system and sustainable economic performance and not ignored the psychological domain, the intervention and its total effects would have been very different. The premise is that the three theories constitute the core theory framework for the discipline of HRD. As such, they must be understood not only individually but, more important, in their wholeness and integration. The implications of economic, system, and psychological theories in guiding the overarching approach to HRD practice follows.

Economic Theory Component of HRD

Any minimization of economic theory in HRD is untenable. The widely used book on organization development, *Organization Development and Change* (Cummings & Worley, 1993), does not have the words *economic, financial,* or *cost–benefit analysis* in its index. The organization development literature addresses the psychological theory leg of the theory stool and a portion of the system theory leg, but it regularly ignores the economic leg. As a result, what is called organization development is reduced to individual development or team development in hopes of achieving improvement in organizational performance. While there is still much to be learned, a substantial amount of information about the economics of short-term interventions (Swanson, 2001) and broader-based investments is available (Becker, Huselid, & Ulrich, 2001; Fitz-enz, 2000; Lyau & Pucel, 1995).

How could responsible HRD not include direct analysis, action, and measurement of economic outcomes? Over time, organizations must generate more income than they spend in order to exist. Unless expenditures on HRD contribute to the viability and profitability of an organization, those expenditures will almost certainly be reduced or eliminated. Three specific economic theory perspectives are believed to be most appropriate to the discipline of HRD: (1) scarce resource theory, (2) sustainable resource theory, and (3) human capital theory.

Scarce Resource Theory

Scarce resource theory informs us that there are limitations to everything. The limitations in money, raw materials, time, and so on, require us to make choices as to how capital will be utilized in order to gain the greatest return. Decision makers choose among options based on their forecasted return on investment. This is a simple and powerful notion that forces decision makers to separate the most valuable and worthy initiatives from the many things that they would like to do if there were no resource limitations (Swanson & Gradous, 1986).

Sustainable Resource Theory

Sustainable resource theory is much like scarce resource theory except for one major point: the concern for the long-term versus short-term agenda. Thurow (1993) informs us that "in the future, sustainable advantage will depend on new process technologies and less on new product technology. New industries of the future depend . . . on brain power. Man-made competitive advantages replaces the comparative advantage of Mother Nature (natural-resources endowment) or history (capital endowments)" (p. 16).

Human Capital Theory

Becker's (1993) classic book, *Human Capital: A Theoretical and Empirical Analysis with Special Reference to Education* (1993), illustrates this domain. Becker implores the reader, "I am going to talk about a different kind of capital. Schooling, a computer training course, expenditures on medical care, and lectures on the virtues of punctuality and honesty are capital too, in the true sense that they improve health, raise earnings, or add to a person's appreciation of literature over a lifetime. Consequently, it is fully in keeping with the capital concept as traditionally defined to say that expenditures on education, training, and medical care, etc., are investments in capital" (pp. 15–16). These are not simply costs but investments with valuable returns that can be calculated.

The Economic Theory Propositions for HRD

The economic principles for HRD revolve around managing scarce resources and the production of wealth. Most people who talk about performance can mentally convert units of performance into monetary units. HRD itself has costs and benefits that need to be understood and are not always favorable. As they are better understood in terms of theory and practice, the HRD discipline and profession will mature. The economic propositions for HRD appear elementary yet must be addressed through sound economic theory and practice:

> *Scarce resource theory:* HRD must justify its own use of scarce resources.

> *Sustainable resource theory:* HRD must add value to creating sustainable long-term economic performance.

> *Human capital theory:* HRD must add short- and long-term value from investments in the development of knowledge and expertise in individuals and groups of individuals.

In conclusion, economist Alfred Marshall (1949) argues that the most valuable of all capital is that invested in human beings. Since HRD takes place in organizations that are economic entities, HRD must call upon economic theory at its core. In addition, management theories and methods should be properly viewed as useful derivatives of economic theory (see Drucker, 1964).

Psychological Theory Component of HRD Theory

The psychological theory from which HRD can draw is immense. It includes theories of learning, human motivation, information processing, group dynamics, and psychology-based theories of how we make decisions and behave in organizations. Yet it has been poorly interpreted by the profession. Most practitioners grab onto a small and relatively irrelevant slice of psychological theory and act upon it in exaggerated ways. Examples include the fascination with whole-brain theory and personality types. Passmore (1997) informs us, "Psychology is the science of behavior and mental processes of humans and other animals. Beyond that, we have something that resembles a teenager's closet" (p. 210).

While psychological theory may have something for everybody, HRD has yet to capitalize fully on its psychology leverage to improve performance. Interestingly, the widely used book on training, *Training in Organizations: Needs Assessment, Development and Evaluation* (Goldstein, 1993), is almost exclusively focused on the behaviorist school of psychology and does not deal in any meaningful way with Gestalt psychology or cognitive (purposive-behaviorism) psychology. At best, the HRD literature addresses the psychological theory leg of the theory stool in an unpredictable manner. Add to this the fact that HRD interventions are rarely systematically connected to the economic agenda via a systematic analysis of the organization and its goals (Swanson, 1994), and it is no wonder that HRD interventions based only on psychological theory are often dismissed as irrelevant by organization leaders.

Fascination appears be the watchword of the psychological leg as questions from psychology are typically narrow and/or disconnected from the core purpose of the organization, the work process, and often even the individual. For example, the continued intrigue of such topics as transfer of training from the psychology perspective mostly focuses on the individual and individual perceptions. The response to this limited perspective in HRD is best expanded through the addition of systems and economic theory, not by psychological theory alone (Holton, 1996c).

How could responsible HRD not integrate and use the vast body of knowledge from psychological theory? With such vast and divergent psychological theory available, it is more appropriate to focus on core understandings related to behavior and learning rather than fringe psychology theories and techniques. Three specific psychological theory perspectives are proposed here to be most appropriate to the discipline of HRD: (1) Gestalt psychology, (2) behavioral psychology, and (3) cognitive (purposive-behaviorism) psychology.

Gestalt Psychology

Gestalt is the German term for configuration or organization. Gestalt psychologists inform us that we do not see isolated stimuli but stimuli gathered together in meaningful configurations. We see people, chairs, cars, trees, and flowers—not lines and patches of color. Gestaltists believe that people add something to experience that is not contained in the sensory data and that we experience the world in meaningful wholes (Hergenhahn & Olson, 1993). Thus, learning involves moving from one whole to another. Words associated with Gestalt psychology include introspection, meaning, closure, insight, life space, field theory, humanism, phenomenology, and relational theory. The holistic view of individuals and their own need for holistic understanding is in sharp contrast to a mechanistic and elemental view of human beings.

Behavioral Psychology

Behavioral psychology is concerned with what can be seen, and therefore behavior is what is studied. Behavioral psychologists inform us that individuals respond the only way they can given their capacity, experience, and present forces working on them. No more introspection, no more talk of instinctive behavior, and no more attempts to study the vague notions of human conscious or unconscious mind. Words associated with behaviorism include *readiness, law effect, exercise, recency, frequency, stimulus, response, reinforcement, punishment, programmed learning,* and *drives.*

Cognitive Psychology

Tolman's (1932) term of *purposive-behaviorism* has been selected as the exemplar of this third important perspective from psychology. Purposive-behaviorism attempts to explain goal-directed behavior and the idea that human beings organize their lives around purposes. Purposive-behaviorism (and other cognitive psychologies) attempts to integrate theory from Gestalt and behavioral psychology.

"For Purposive Behaviorism, behavior, as we have seen, is purposeful, cognitive, and molar, i.e., 'Gestalted.' Purposive Behaviorism is molar, not a molecular" (Tolman, 1932, p. 419). Words associated with cognitive psychology, including purposive-behaviorism, include *drive discriminations, field-cognition modes, cognitive map, learning by analogy, learned helplessness, structuring, information processing, short- and long-term memory,* and *artificial intelligence.*

The Psychological Theory Propositions for HRD

The psychology principles for practice revolve around the mental processes of humans and the determinants of human behavior. Among scholars and practitioners of psychology, the schisms and gimmicks reported under the psychology banner abound with little integration. As the three psychology subtheories here are interpreted in terms of the theory and practice relevant to HRD, the discipline and profession will mature. While the psychological propositions appear to be elementary, they are regularly ignored in practice:

Gestalt psychology: HRD must clarify the goals of individual contributors, work process owners, and/or organization leaders.

Behavioral psychology: HRD must develop the knowledge and expertise of individual contributors, work process owners, and organization leaders.

Cognitive psychology (purposive behaviorism): HRD must harmonize the goals and behaviors among individual contributors, work process owners, and organization leaders.

In conclusion, since HRD takes place in organizations that are psychologically framed by those who invented them, operate in them, and renew them, HRD must call on psychology as being core (see Argyris, 1993; Bereiter & Scardamalia, 1993; Dubin, 1976). In addition, learning theories such as constructivism and situated cognition should be properly viewed as useful derivatives of psychological theory. Performance cannot be improved if people choose not to perform, put forth little effort, or do not persist in their efforts (Bereiter & Scardamalia, 1993). Moreover, systematically designed learning experiences and workplace systems provide a durable foundation for performance improvement. Thus, theories of learning, human motivation, information processing, and other psychologically based theories provide a core theoretical foundation for the discipline of HRD.

System Theory Component of HRD

System theory, a small body of knowledge compared to economics and psychology, contains a harvest of low-hanging fruit for HRD. From a system theory perspective, a wide range of systemic disconnects is adversely affecting performance. They include (1) not being able to clearly specify the required outcomes of the host organization and (2) not having a systematically defined HRD process (see Rummler & Brache, 1995).

System theory is a relatively young discipline made up of "a collection of general concepts, principles, tools, problems and methods associated with systems of any kind" (Passmore, 1997, pp. 206–207). Gradous's (1989) classic monograph set the stage for serious consideration of system theory by the HRD profession. Jacobs's (1989) chapter, "Systems Theory Applied to Human Resource Development," called for the profession to adopt an individual contributor view of system theory as the unifying theory. Seeing this as limited, McLagan (1989) proposed the larger organization and societal views in her chapter titled "Systems Model 2000: Matching Systems Theory to Future HRD Issues." Her challenge was for HRD to think about, and work within, a more expansive and tiered world of systems.

Three specific system theory perspectives are proposed here to be appropriate to HRD: (1) general system theory, (2) chaos theory, and (3) futures theory.

General System Theory

At the core, general system theory (GST) forces us to talk intelligently about inputs, processes, outputs, and feedback. Furthermore, GST informs us of the reality of open systems (vs. closed systems), that systems engineering focuses on the less dynamic aspects of the organization, and of the limitations of a single personality theory in predicting human behavior (Bertalanffy, 1962).

Boulding's (1956a) classic article on general system theory describes the paradox of a theory so general as to mean nothing and the seeming inability of a single theory from a single field of study to ever reach a satisfactory level of theory generality. He goes on to talk about the power of a "spectrum of theories"—a "system of systems" that would perform the function of a "gestalt" in theory building. "General systems theory may at times be an embarrassment in pointing out how far we still have to go" (Boulding, 1956a, p. 10).

Chaos Theory

"Where chaos begins, classical science stops. . . . Chaos is a science of process rather than a state, of becoming rather than of being" (Gleick, 1987, pp. 3–5). Chaos theory confronts Newtonian logic head-on by offering a revised motto away from determinism to something much softer: "Given an approximate knowledge of a system's initial conditions and an understanding of natural law, one can calculate the approximate behavior of the system" (Gleick, 1987, p. 15). Chaos theory purposefully acknowledges and studies phenomena that are unsystematic, that do not appear to follow the rules.

Futures Theory

Futures theory is "not necessarily interested in predicting the future, it is about the liberation of people's insights" (Schwartz, 1991, p. 9). Thus, futures theory, in the context of planning for future in uncertain conditions, in no way resembles the reductionist view of most strategic planning efforts that end up with a single strategy. The language and tools of *alternative futures* and *scenario building* are intended to create a true picture of the facts, the potential flux in those facts, and the decision-making agility required of the future. Futures theory is critical for sustainable performance in that it prepares one to recognize and cope with an evolving future state.

System Theory Propositions for HRD

The system theory principles for practice are organic. The system elements, their arrangements, the interdependencies—the complex nature of the phenomenon under study—must be faced. The system theory principles for practice require serious thinking, sound theory-building research, and the utilization of new tools for sound practice. A full pursuit of the following simple propositions in HRD would reshape the HRD purpose and the tools utilized in practice:

> *General system theory:* HRD must understand how it and other subsystems connect and disconnect from the host organization.
>
> *Chaos theory:* HRD must help its host organization retain its purpose and effectiveness given the chaos it faces.
>
> *Futures theory:* HRD must help its host organization shape alternative futures.

In conclusion, since HRD takes place in organizations that are themselves systems and subsystems functioning within an environmental system that is ever-changing, system theory is at its core (see Buckley, 1968; Gradous, 1989). In addition, engineering technology theories and methods should be viewed as useful derivatives of system theory, even though they have a longer scholarly history (see FitzGerald & FitzGerald, 1973; Davenport, 1993).

Ethics in HRD

As noted earlier, ethics is viewed as the supporting theory for HRD, but not a core theory. It serves as the filter among the three core theories of economics, psychology, and systems within the performance improvement context.

From the ethical beliefs perspective, some argue about the exploitive nature of organizations and would criticize HRD as an unthinking arm of management (Korten, 1995), challenging the profession to act as the agent of democracy and equity (Dirkx, 1996). Others argue that exploitation is a much more expansive concept (e.g., employees can exploit their employers) and that it must be addressed as such (Swanson, Horton, & Kelly, 1986). The ethical issue is not with performance. It is the distribution of the gains realized from performance. The ethical distribution among contributors and stakeholders is the bogeyman behind most of the emotional performance discussions in HRD. It should be dealt with directly and apart from the pursuit of performance.

Summary

The purpose of this section was to frame the discipline and theory of human resource development by identifying its definition, model, component theories, and the propositions raised by the theory.

Research in the realm of theory requires that theories be developed through rigorous theory-building research methods (Dubin, 1969; Hearn, 1958; Torraco, 1997; Lynham, 2000b) and that the journey is continuous. If theory just happened as a result of practice, the development of HRD theory bucket would be overflowing. Instead, the massive field of HRD practice is still experiencing a "theory application deficit disorder" (Swanson, 1997). Fulfilling HRD's performance improvement mission through building the HRD discipline around the proposed theories is fundamental to the maturation of the profession. The following three sections of this chapter provide extended and alternative views of the contributions of psychological, economic, and system theories to HRD.

PSYCHOLOGY AND THE DISCIPLINE OF HRD—CONTRIBUTIONS AND LIMITATIONS
Contributed by Elwood F. Holton III

Psychology has been identified as one of the core theories of human resource development (Passmore, 1997; Swanson, 1994). There can be little question that the discipline of psychology has made, and continues to make, major contributions to the discipline of HRD. Indeed, references from industrial psychology, educational psychology, cognitive psychology, and developmental psychology are common in our research. It is psychology that keeps HRD's focus on the individual.

However, there are those who practice HRD as if it were little more than applied psychology. This approach results in overemphasis on the individual to the exclusion of other vital components of our discipline. The thesis of this section is that there can also be little question that psychology is inadequate *by itself* to define the discipline of HRD. The purpose of this section is to systematically identify some key issues surrounding psychology's contribution to defining the discipline of HRD.

Psychology and HRD

Understanding Psychology as a Discipline

To understand psychology as a field, one must first differentiate between what are alternately called *foundational* or *framework theories* (Wellman & Gellman, 1992) and systems of psychology (Lundin, 1991) versus specific theories. "Framework theories outline the ontology and the basic causal devises for their specific theories, thereby defining a coherent form of reasoning about a particular set of phenomena" (Wellman & Gellman, 1992, p. 342). A *system* has been defined as "a framework or scaffolding which permits the scientist to arrange his data in an orderly meaningful way" (Lundin, 1991, p. 2). In psychology, these systems are also known as *movements* or *schools*.

System or framework theories then inspire specific theories that propose specific formal propositions. For example, behaviorism is a framework theory or system because is defines a particular set of assumptions about human behavior. Within that system are a variety of theorists (e.g., Watson, Skinner) who vary in their specific propositions about behaviorism but nonetheless agree as to the underlying epistemology. Our interest here is not in specific theories but rather the underlying framework theories or systems from psychology that are in turn foundational theories for the discipline of HRD. Continuing the previous example, we will not discuss which theory of behaviorism is appropriate but rather whether behaviorism is a foundational theory for HRD.

No universal agreement prevails among psychology scholars as to which theories are specific versus foundational theories, and some theorists are "bridge" theorists in that they attempt to integrate multiple systems. Furthermore, many noted psychologists can be classified in multiple categories (e.g., is Bandura a behaviorist or a cognitivist?). Thus, it is difficult to find one "best" classification. For this discussion, Lundin's (1991) and Brennan's (1994) classifications of twentieth-century psychology systems have been integrated to generate the following list of candidates to be included as foundational theories for HRD: functionalism, behaviorism, Gestalt (classic and field theory), psychoanalysis, "third force" (humanistic and existential), cognitive, and emerging systems (social psychology and developmental psychology).

Interestingly, some psychologists have called for the creation of a "metadiscipline" of theoretical psychology to recapture the theoretical roots of psychology (Slife & Williams, 1997). They use some of the same language that scholars in HRD do to bemoan movement away from theory "toward models, techniques, and microtheories in the more modern sense" (Slife & Williams, 1997, p. 118). Due in large part to the emergence of applied or functional psychology in the early 1900s (Watson & Evans, 1991), psychology has moved away from the creation of broad theories such as behaviorism and cognitivism, to the scientific testing of theories and models.

Psychological Theories for HRD

Within psychology, Swanson (1998a) proposes three foundational psychological theories: Gestalt, behavioral, and cognitive psychology. Figure 5.3 summarizes these three foundational theories and selected contributions to the discipline of HRD.

Relationship to Other Core Theories of HRD

Swanson (1998a) also proposes that the other two foundation theories of HRD are economics and system theory. Yet unresolved is the relationship between psychology and the other two core domains. While there may be many microlevel linkages, at the macrolevel possible relationships are as follows:

- *Behaviorism* provides the link between psychology of the individual and economic theory. One of behaviorism's strengths is its emphasis on exter-

Figure 5.3 Foundational Psychological Theories and Their Contribution to HRD

Foundation Theory	*Representative Theorists*	*Contributions to HRD*
Gestalt	Wertheimer, Kofka, Kohler, Lewin	• Focus on the whole person • Holistic view of organizations and individuals
Behaviorism	Watson, Pavlov, Thorndike	• How external environments affect human behavior • Reward and motivation systems • Goal setting
Cognitive	Piaget, Bruner, Tolman	• How humans process information • Foundation for instructional design • How humans make meaning of their experiences

nal reinforcers of human behavior. Human behavior within organizations is deeply affected by organizational performance goals as represented by individual performance criteria and associated rewards. This performance system is largely economic, as described by Torraco (1998). Behaviorism provides the theoretical linkage between the external performance system and individual behavior.

- *Gestalt* psychology is primarily concerned with the integration of the parts of the self into the whole person. Conceptually, this is the same contribution that system theory makes to understanding organizations—the focus on the whole and the interaction of the parts, rather than reducing it to just its parts. In addition to helping the HRD profession focus on the whole person, the emphasis on holism also logically leads to a holistic view of the person embedded in the organizational system.

- *Cognitivism* is primarily focused on the self. Cognitive psychology explains how individuals make meaning of what they experience. It emphasizes that individuals are not simply influenced by external factors but make decisions about those influences and their meaning. In the constellation of psychological theories relevant to HRD, it is cognitive psychology that exclusively focuses on the internal processes of individuals. It helps explain how people learn and how they make sense of the organizational system.

Emerging Foundational Theories of Psychology

There is little question that, of the well-established foundation theories in psychology, these three are the appropriate ones. Others, such as functionalism and psychoanalytic theory, simply do not fit. That said, two other emerging psychological theories point out possible weaknesses in this scheme and offer possible theoretical solutions.

Individual Growth Perspective

None of these three theories fully recognizes the potential that humans have to expand and develop capabilities well beyond those immediately apparent. Gestalt psychology comes closest but still is focused primarily on how people perceive, think, and learn in the here and now (Hunt, 1993). It still leaves unexplained the human processes that underlie the motivation to grow and develop. It is this potential for growth and expansion of human capabilities that undergirds human capital theory in economics.

Humanistic psychology is still a somewhat loosely formed movement that views humans as self-actualizing, self-directing beings. It is one of the roots for much of adult learning theory (Knowles, Holton, & Swanson, 1998). Two of its most recognizable names are Carl Rogers and Abraham Maslow. While still not as theoretically "tight" as behaviorism or cognitivism, it nonetheless makes contributions in explaining individuals' motivation and potential. A core presumption of some HRD models is that employees have intrinsic motivation to grow. While some growth can be explained from the behavioristic notion that people grow to seek organizational rewards, a strictly behaviorist view of this phenomenon is much too limited. The three psychological theories proposed earlier (Gestalt, behaviorism, and cognitive) may fall short in supporting HRD's position that humans are capable of reaching far higher potential, justifying long-term investment to build expertise.

Social System of Organizations

A second area of concern is whether these three psychological theories, along with system theory and economic theory, provide adequate theory to account for individuals within the social system of organizations. Organization development specialists are particularly focused on elements of the social system such as organizational culture, power and politics, group dynamics, intergroup communication, and how these social systems change (Cummings & Worley, 1997). The question is whether the core theories proposed provide an adequate foundation to understand the individual within the organizational social system.

It is these very concerns that have led to the emergence of social psychology, which studies interactions between people and groups. It, too, is seen by some as an eclectic discipline lacking any unifying theory (Hunt, 1993), while others are more generous in describing it as still emerging in its theoretical base (Brennan, 1994). In some respects, social psychology is much like HRD, building on other theories while creating a new theory of its own. Wiggins, Wiggins, and Vander Zanden (1994) define *social psychology* as "the study of behavior, thoughts, and feelings of an individual or interacting individuals and their relationships with larger social units" (p. 17). According to them, social psychology consists of four theoretical streams, the first two from psychology and the second two from sociology:

- *Behavioral perspective*—social learning and social exchange theory
- *Cognitive perspective*—field theory, attribution theory, and social learning of attitudes
- *Structural perspective*—role theory, expectation states theory, and postmodernism
- *Interactionist perspective*—symbolic interaction theory, identity theory, and ethnomethodology

Frankly, I offer it more as a "placeholder" than with certainty that it is a foundational theory. What social psychology emphasizes, and which seems lacking in this HRD discipline model, is some theory base that defines the social system of an organization. There are deep roots in some aspects of HRD that have relationships with social psychology. For example, social psychologist Kurt Lewin's force field theory is a core model for organizational change and development. Social psychology also focuses on humans in groups, which is clearly a major issue in HRD. If social psychology is not the correct foundational theory, then we must identify a component that provides a base for HRD's work in the social systems of organizations.

In summary, Kuhn (1970) cautions us that the emergence of new theory is rarely an orderly or quick process. While both humanistic and social psychology lack the conceptual clarity of cognitivism, behaviorism, and Gestalt psychology, they emerged to fill the need to explain human phenomena that the others did not adequately explain. The question for HRD to debate is whether these same holes are important considerations for HRD theory. If so, then these two emerging areas of psychology—or some other theory—should be carefully considered.

Limits of Psychology

Issue 1: Domains of Performance

Two predominant performance frameworks are the Rummler and Brache (1995) model and Swanson's (1994) expanded framework. Because Swanson's framework uses five performance variables, it is a more powerful lens for this analysis. Swanson suggests that there are three levels of performance and five performance variables. By definition, psychology's primary focus is on the individual. Psychologists do consider organizational context, but as environmental influences on the individual, not as a core area of focus.

Historically, HRD was also defined at the individual level (Ruona & Swanson, 1997). It is increasingly considering multiple levels (individual, group, work process, and organizational) as core areas of focus. The implications of this for HRD as a discipline are significant. If the discipline of HRD is a multilevel discipline, then we can draw heavily upon psychology as a foundation discipline but also must realize it is inadequate by itself.

The psychological lens, while powerful, leads to incorrect or inadequate conceptions of HRD when used alone. For example, Barrie and Pace (1997) state:

> The question of whether the field of human resource development is in the business of improving *performance* or of enhancing learning in organizations has not been sufficiently explored. Succinctly put, advocates argue that the field should focus on creating *behavioral* changes or on fostering a cognitive perspective in organization members. (p. 335; emphasis added)

The authors equate the performance perspective with the behavioral perspective in psychology, which is incorrect. Performance theory is concerned with the outputs and outcomes of humans in organizations and the extent to which cognitive strategies improve them. From an applied psychology definition of HRD, theirs is the logical conclusion. From a broader theoretical base, their argument is incorrect.

Issue 2: Building Capacity for Performance

Holton (1999) presents an expanded framework for conceptualizing performance domains in HRD that offers another lens within which to consider psychology's contribution to HRD. One important addition is the integration of Kaplan and

Norton (1996) to two categories of performance measures: outcomes and drivers. Unfortunately, they do not offer concise definitions of either. For our purposes, *outcomes* are measures of effectiveness or efficiency relative to core outputs of the system, subsystem, process, or individual. The most typical are financial indicators (profit, return on investment [ROI], etc.) and productivity measures (units of goods or services produced) and are often generic across companies. According to Kaplan and Norton, these measures tend to be lag indicators in that they reflect what has occurred or has been accomplished in relation to core outcomes.

Drivers measure elements of performance that are expected to sustain or increase system, subsystem, process, or individual ability and capacity to be more effective or efficient in the future. Thus, they are leading indicators of future outcomes and tend to be unique for particular business units. Together with outcome measures, they describe the hypothesized cause-and-effect relationships in the organization's strategy (Kaplan & Norton, 1996). Thus, drivers should predict future outcomes. For example, for a particular company, ROI might be the appropriate outcome measure that might be driven by customer loyalty and on-time delivery, which in turn might be driven by employee learning so internal processes are optimized. Conceptually, performance drivers could be added as a third axis to Swanson's performance levels and performance variables.

This lens further defines the limits of psychology's contribution to HRD:

- At the individual level, psychology pays only limited attention to building future capacity for individual performance.
- At other levels, performance drivers are not an area of focus for psychology.

Some areas of psychology are preoccupied with current performance and outcomes, while HRD has a more balanced view of building capacity for future performance in addition to present performance (see Figure 5.4).

Summary

As part of a series of papers on the core theories of HRD, this treatise was primarily designed to initiate an ongoing dialogue to continue defining the discipline of HRD. HRD has, and always will have, psychology as one of its core theories. It is psychology that reminds us that our discipline is one concerned with humans in organizations. It is important that we recognize its contributions, as well as its limitations as a lens through which to view HRD.

ECONOMICS–HUMAN CAPITAL THEORY AND HUMAN RESOURCE DEVELOPMENT
Contributed by Richard J. Torraco

This section addresses the most important issue facing HRD scholars today: developing a theoretical foundation to provide the intellectual basis for the further

Figure 5.4 Performance Domains and Metrics

Domains of Performance	Typical Metrics for Measuring Performance Domains	
	PERFORMANCE OUTCOMES	PERFORMANCE DRIVERS
Mission	Economic returns External metrics Market share Profitability Mortality rate Poverty level	Societal benefits Innovation Knowledge capital Management/leadership Strategy Social responsibility
Process	Customers Quality Cost Time Product features Market share (in product category)	Customer (needs satisfaction) Quality Innovation

Critical performance subsystem (team, department, etc.)	Team effectiveness
	Structural subunits
	  performance
	Productivity (resource
	  efficiency)
	Internal metrics
	Work outputs
		Innovation
		Team/group climate
		Management/leadership
		Ethical performance

Individual	Productivity Work output	Knowledge, expertise Learning Renewal and growth Human relations Ethical performance Turnover Absenteeism

development of the HRD field. The increasing demands on HRD practice, and the need for research to guide practice, have already far outstripped HRD's emerging theory base. HRD is among the youngest disciplines in the social sciences. If HRD is to grow beyond its present stage—now barely into the "adolescence" of its life—it needs its own unique theory base. An important need exists for further theory development in HRD.

Beyond directing the attention of HRD scholars to theory building, the main premise of this section is that economics be included as a central element of HRD's theoretical foundation. To this end, this treatise discusses economics in general and human capital theories and their importance to HRD's core theory base. An exposition of the central values and principles in organizations supported by economics is provided. Finally, as a prelude to further theory development in HRD, the nature of theory building is briefly explored.

The Challenge to HRD Posed by Theory

Interrelationships among the behavioral sciences such as education, psychology, sociology, and organization behavior necessitate a certain cross-fertilization of theory across these fields. One would expect the theories of related fields that all address human behavior in social contexts, as these fields do, to share common theoretical elements. Theories of learning, motivation, group dynamics, and social/organizational structures are common to these fields. In addition to the elements of theory that are shared among fields, each discipline generates theory unique to its own domains of research and practice. Psychologists and economists, although both representing social sciences, view the world through their own unique disciplinary lenses. The psychologist is more interested in factors related to individual behavior, whereas the economist is concerned with the allocation of resources at higher levels of aggregation. Consequently, each discipline relies on distinct bodies of knowledge supported by theory, some of which is unique to that discipline.

A theory robust enough to support both the present knowledge base and the need for further developments in both research and professional practice requires a rich, conceptual system synthesized from multiple, relevant theories. Some of these theoretical components are existing theories; others must be developed for this purpose. Some are unique to the field, while other theoretical components are shared across fields. Theory development in HRD is in its infancy. The challenge for HRD scholars is that so much theorizing remains to be done to synthesize new HRD theory that effectively and continuously supports our ever-changing field of professional practice.

The purpose here is to stimulate discussion among HRD scholars about the importance of theory to HRD's future development and the rightful components of such a core theory base. Arguments for including economics as a core element of HRD's theoretical foundation are also made.

What Is Economics?

Economics addresses the allocation of resources among a variety of human wants. It represents human wants and the scarcity of resources as essential and perennial elements in the study of any human activity. Like other social sciences, economics deals with human behavior that cannot be controlled as can, for example, the physical mechanisms used by an engineer. Economics uses society as its laboratory and cannot engage in the kind of experimentation favored by the physicist or chemist. As with the social sciences in general, economics is not an exact science, and predictions of economic developments are subject to error. According to Lewis (1977), however, economics is the social science "with the most sophisticated body of theory—that is, the one with the greatest predictability accuracy of all the social sciences" (p. 43). For comprehensive treatments of economics, please see Samuelson (1980), Milgrom and John (1992), and Shughart, Chappell, and Cottle (1994).

What Is Human Capital Theory?

Human capital theory is considered the branch of economics most applicable to HRD. While Theodore Schultz's (1961) address to the American Economic Association was the first presentation of research on the return-on-investment in human capital, Gary S. Becker is generally credited as the leading developer of human capital theory. Classical economic theory considers labor as a commodity that can be bought and sold. Because of the negative connotations associated with the exploitation of labor by capital, it is understandable that human capital theory is still suspect in some circles. However, unlike the meaning traditionally associated with the term *labor, human capital* refers to the knowledge, expertise, and skill one accumulates through education and training.

Emphasizing the social and economic importance of human capital theory, Becker (1993) quotes the economist Alfred Marshall's dictum that "the most valuable of all capital is that invested in human beings" (p. 27). Becker distinguishes firm-specific human capital from general-purpose human capital. Examples of firm-specific human capital include expertise obtained through education and training in management information systems, accounting procedures, or other expertise specific to a particular firm. General-purpose human capital is knowledge gained through education and training in areas of value to a variety of firms such as generic skills in sales and marketing, or expertise in human resource management. Regardless of the application, Becker considers education and training to be the most important investments in human capital. Figure 5.5 presents the key relationships in human capital theory and the assumptions underlying these relationships.

Key relationships and assumptions of human capital theory are represented in Figure 5.5 by the numbered brackets 1, 2, and 3.

- *Relationship 1* represents the concept of production functions as applied to education and training. The key assumption underlying this relationship is that investments in education and training result in increased learning. Relationship 1 includes the human capital variables assessed using cost-effectiveness analysis.

- *Relationship 2* represents the human capital relationship between learning and increased productivity. The key assumption underlying this relationship is that increased learning does, in fact, result in increased productivity.

- *Relationship 3* represents the human capital relationship between increased productivity and increased wages and business earnings. The key assumption underlying this relationship is that greater productivity does,

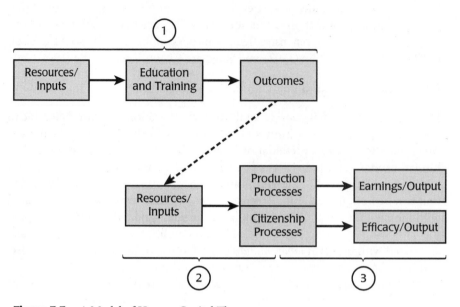

Figure 5.5 A Model of Human Capital Theory

in fact, result in higher wages for individuals and earnings for businesses. An equally important human capital relationship represented by relationship 3 is that between the citizenship processes affected by education (e.g., community involvement, voting) and enhanced social efficacy.

- *The entire human capital continuum* represented in Figure 5.5 (i.e., all the bracketed relationships as a single continuum) is assessed using return-on-investment analysis or cost–benefit analysis.

Several key concepts from economics and human capital theory are apparent in the practices and context of HRD. In this following section, these concepts are briefly reviewed and applied to HRD. This exposition reveals many of the core values and principles espoused by economics.

Macroeconomic Theory

Macroeconomic theory addresses the aggregate performance of an entire economy or economic system (e.g., the European economy or world economy). Macroeconomics is concerned with fiscal and monetary policy and the interaction of major determinants of economic developments such as wages, prices, employment levels, interest rates, capital investments, the distribution of income, and other factors. It is contrasted with microeconomics, which focuses on the individual consumer, family, or firm and the determinants of each of these factors (i.e., wages, interest rates) in particular.

Human capital theory has both macroeconomic and microeconomic implications for HRD in important areas. Workforce development on a regional or national level is what economists might call "human capital deepening" on a macroeconomic scale. The increased value of human capital derived from workforce development is likely to influence productivity, wages, prices, and other factors at an aggregate level of the economy. Conversely, the decisions made by HRD professionals in organizations are microeconomic in scope—that is, they influence the economic performance of individual firms, groups, or members.

Supply and Demand

The supply of, and demand for, education and training affects the competitive position of organizations such that HRD's role becomes central to the organization's long-term viability. Classical economics posits that, on average, scarce resources are more valuable than plentiful resources. Although developed independent of economic theory, Wright, McMahan, and McWilliams's (1994) resource-based view of the firm is based on the concept of supply and demand. They suggest that human resources, and HRD in particular, substantially increase the competitive position of the firm because they enhance the value of the firm's human resources in ways that are (1) rare, (2) inimitable, (3) valuable, and (4) nonsubstitutable. Indeed, it is difficult or impossible to compete with firms whose greatest assets are embedded in their people (Barney, 1991).

Elasticity of Demand

This concept is an elaboration of the popular economic concept of supply and demand. *Elasticity of demand* indicates the degree of responsiveness of the quantity of a product or service demanded by consumers to changes in the market price of the product or service. Elastic demand exists when a price reduction leads to a substantial increase in demand for the product or service (and an increase in total revenue despite the price cut). Inelastic demand exists when a price reduction leads to a decrease in total revenue despite the price cut. Elastic demand is said to exist for some leisure- and recreation-related goods (e.g., airfares, vacation cruises, resort rates). Inelastic demand is said to exist for gasoline prices, railroad service, and certain necessities (e.g., foods, medicine) for which acceptable substitutes are unavailable.

The elasticity of demand for HRD can be viewed in a number of contexts. For example, how elastic is the demand for education/training when its cost increases relative to the cost of alternative activities in the workplace (e.g., attend training vs. remain on the job)? Will attendance or support for an HRD intervention increase, despite its increased cost, if the intervention is perceived as crucial to organizational growth or survival (e.g., an organization development or performance improvement effort)? To what degree does the availability of substitutes for HRD (e.g., outsourcing, other non-HRD interventions) influence the elasticity of demand for HRD?

Opportunity Costs

Opportunity costs are the value of opportunities foregone due to participation in a given project or intervention. By electing a particular course of action among alternatives, one necessary foregoes the opportunities offered by the alternatives. Human capital theory involves opportunity costs at several levels of HRD practice. At the individual level, participation in HRD, especially during normal working hours, incurs the opportunity costs associated with lost productivity on the job. This opportunity cost has traditionally been a major source of management reluctance to support certain types of HRD. Similar opportunity costs are involved at the group or department level when work activities are foregone to participate in HRD. At the organization level, the value of opportunity costs is necessarily higher, just as is the value of increased human capital, when applied across the organization. Opportunity costs are the flip (and sometimes unnoticed) side of the benefits of HRD.

Agency Theory

Agency theory derives from a branch of organization theory concerned with reconciling the behavior of self-interested individuals with conflicting goals within a larger organizational context where collaboration among individuals is sought. Levinthal's (1988) agency theory proposes that principals (i.e., owners) monitor performance of agents (i.e., employees) and use incentives such that employees work to achieve the principal's goals in spite of their own self-interests. Given discretion in the direction and degree of investments in human capital, agency theory suggests that principals are far more likely to promote firm-specific human capital over general-purpose human capital, which increases the ease with which employees can move to other firms.

Production Functions

Production functions are the technical or physical relationships between the inputs and outputs in a value-added process. With respect to education and training investments in human capital, we wish to know the precise inputs (resources) that enter the production process (e.g., education, training), the precise relationship between factors within the production process, and the outputs (benefits) that result from these production processes in education (Lewis, 1977). The production function for education is represented as relationship 1 in Figure 5.5. Production functions in HRD are represented by the training options of in-house development versus vendor training, traditional versus technology-based training programs, the level of involvement and role of supervisors and managers in HRD programs, and other alternatives that are available for accomplishing HRD outcomes.

Screening Theory of Education

The screening theory of education suggests that, as opposed to affecting the productivity increases espoused by human capital theory, education serves a screening function in which individuals are ranked by ability, achievement levels, and grading. Any productivity gains apparent from education are, therefore, a function of the traits of those being educated, not a product of the education process. Some evidence exists in support of the screening theory of education (Stiglitz, 1975). The implications of this theory extend to HRD in that HRD might also be seen as a screening activity and thus perceived as providing little or no developmental value. HRD might be viewed as a screening process for promotion, transfer, or other personnel action.

In addition to these key human capital concepts, several economic realities facing the organizations served by HRD should influence the development of a theory base robust enough to support and extend HRD research and practice:

- The most frequently used measures in organizations, of any sort, are financial measures.

- HRD professionals are reluctant to express their work in financial terms, even though their organizations are financially driven.

- Efficiency is a universal value, not limited to economics. Efficiency is simply a ratio of the optimal level of accomplishments relative to the effort and resources required to achieve them.

Theory Development for HRD

Dubin (1978) provides a comprehensive methodology for theory building that is particularly relevant for applied fields such as HRD. This methodology is frequently used as a template for building theories in the behavioral sciences. More so than other theory-building strategies, Dubin's eight-phase methodology for theory building lays out an explicit road map for the theorist to follow. The eight phases are (1) *units* (i.e., concepts) of the theory, (2) *laws of interaction* (among the concepts), (3) *boundaries of the theory* (the boundaries within which the theory is expected to apply), (4) *system states* of the theory (conditions under which the theory is operative), (5) *propositions* of the theory (logical deductions about the theory in operation), (6) *empirical indicators* (empirical measures used to make the propositions testable), (7) *hypotheses* (statements about the predicted values and relationships among the units), and (8) *research* (the empirical test of the predicted values and relationships). The first five phases of the methodology represent the theory-building component of Dubin's model; the last three phases represent the process of taking the theory into real-world contexts to conduct empirical research. Although theorists must consider the entire scope of Dubin's model, theory building and empirical research are often separated, and each of these is conducted as a distinct research effort.

Summary

The values and principles supported by economics and human capital theory discussed here are part of the basic fabric of the organizations in which HRD professional carry out their work. Ideology aside, the reality in our culture is that economic choices are among the most important decisions made in the workplace.

Given the centrality of economics, the question for HRD theory is not "Is economics an element of HRD theory?" but rather "How important is economics as an element of HRD theory?"

SYSTEM THEORY AS A FOUNDATION FOR HRD
Contributed by Wendy E. A. Ruona

It is widely acknowledged that HRD is a discipline rooted in multiple theories. While it is true that HRD utilizes many theories, all of these theories are not foundational or core to HRD. A foundation is the basis on which a thing stands and is composed of those elements that are essential to its survival. For a profession such as HRD, a foundation must be theoretically sound and its professionals must be well versed in what comprises that core. Indeed, Warfield (1995) regards the specification of foundations as central to the progress of a discipline when he states, "Science is a body of knowledge consisting of three variously integrated components: foundations, theory, and methodology. Foundations inform theory and the theory informs the methodology" (p. 81).

System theory has been proposed here as one of three theories that constitute HRD. This proposition is unlikely to be met with much opposition as many professionals and scholars have acknowledged that it is an essential component of HRD work. While many are committed to system theory implicitly, if not explicitly, the incorporation of it into our foundational base, theories, and methodologies has yet to fully take hold. The goal of this section is to investigate the contribution of system theory to HRD.

What Is System Theory?

System theory is simply a theory concerned with systems, wholes, and organizations. Beyond this elementary description, there is not one correct way to define it. Even Bertalannfy (1968), who is widely acknowledged as the father of general system theory, does not offer one clear definition but rather focuses on describing its scope and meaning.

Scope
Describing this burgeoning theory is increasingly difficult as various facets of the approach develop. Multiple fields claim to be descendants of system theory. Although all these related fields are distinctively different, they align in their concern with system. Four of these fields in particular are dominating current discussion in system theory.

General System Theory   General system theory is known for focusing multiple disciplines on wholes, parts, the organization and connectedness of the various parts, and the relationships of systems to their environment.

Cybernetics   *Cybernetics* is the science of information, communication, feedback, and control both within a system as well as between a system and its environment. Its focus is more on how systems function, rather than the *structure* issues emphasized in general system theory. The result of much of its core work has been defining heterogeneous interacting components such as mutuality, complementarily, evolvability, constructively, and reflexivity (Joslyn, 1992).

Chaos   *Chaos theory* is the "qualitative study of unstable aperiodic behavior in deterministic non-linear dynamically systems" (Kellert, 1993, p. 2). This theory revolutionized science through its discovery that complex and unpredictable results were actually not random but rather could be expected in systems that are sensitive to their initial conditions. Behavior that had been assumed to be random in systems of every type was actually found to be bounded and operating within recognizable patterns. Now it is widely recognized that forces in a system endlessly rearrange themselves in different yet similar patterns. The resulting hidden qualitative pattern is coined chaotic, fractal, or strange. Chaos theory seeks to understand this ordered randomness and enables scientists to discover and study chaotic behavior.

Complex Adaptive Systems   This subfield has emerged most recently out of chaos theory. It inquires into a more holistic view of the behavior of complex systems. Recent research has revealed that chaos is only one of four possible states into which behavior of complex systems may be classified (Phelan, 1995). The theory of complex adaptive systems proposes that complex systems emerge and maintain on the edge of chaos—the narrow domain between frozen constancy and chaotic turbulence (Heylighten, 1996). It proposes that systems function in an area of complexity between chaos and order. Furthermore, systems in this state conduct self-organizing and learning processes, which include structural change through self-renewal (replication, copy, and reproduction), nonlinear flows of information and resources, and "far-from-equilibrium conditions that create a dynamic stability where paradox abounds" (Dooley, 1996, p. 20).

Meaning

The meaning of system theory may do more to define it than the descriptions offered here. A synthesis of literature illuminates that system theory is a few distinct things. It is (1) an ontology—a philosophy of nature and systems, (2) an epistemology—a way to view or understand the world, and (3) a unifying theory.

An Ontology: The Nature of the World and Systems   System theory began with a reorientation of the philosophy of nature. It is, at its most fundamental level, a belief about the world—a belief that the world is made up of set(s) of interacting components and that those sets of interacting components have properties, when viewed as a whole, that do not exist within any of the smaller units (Heylighten &

Joslyn, 1992). System theory reveals a multitiered world comprised of subsystems within systems within environment—all of which are regulated through a set of relationships. Second, system theory provides a storehouse of information about the nature of systems. New discoveries about systems' structures and processes offer increasing detail crucial to understanding the basic workings of the world.

An Epistemology: A Way to View the World   System theory is also a fundamentally different way of viewing reality. It is now thought to be a complement, rather than a substitute to more specialized ways of seeing the world. It is all-embracing, incorporating reductionist perspectives as simply one aspect of a general conceptualization. A premise of system theory is that systems ultimately are mental constructs. System theory, or systems thinking, fosters a way of understanding the world in a more holistic way, demanding that the pieces of the world are not viewed separately. Rather, it provides a way to see and know the world—realizing the connections and the dynamics that make the whole something more than the sum of its parts.

Although system theory contributes the two distinct meanings described earlier, Laszlo and Laszlo (1997) capture the somewhat indescribable meaning of system theory when they state:

> Systems sciences defy classification as constituting either an epistemology or ontology. Rather, they are reminiscent of the Greek notion of gnosilogy concerned with holistic and integrative exploration of phenomena and events. There are aspects of the systems approach that are ontological and aspects that are epistemological, and aspects that are at once both and should not be circumscribed to either. (p. 8)

A Unifying Theory   A primary goal of system theory was to revive the unity of science (Bertalanffy, 1968). System theory argues that no matter how complex or diverse the world, it is possible to find different types of organization in it and that this organization can be described by principles that are independent from the specific domain being investigated. The uncovering of these general laws will provide a way to analyze and solve problems in any domain pertaining to any type of system. System theory serves as a unifying theory in that it provides a "framework of structure on which to hang the flesh and blood of particular disciplines and particular subject matters in an orderly and coherent corpus of knowledge" (Boulding, 1956, p. 10). Acting as a metatheory per se, it capitalizes on parallelisms in multiple disciplines and organizes concepts, objects, and relationships in such a way as to overcome the limitations of any one theory.

Why System Theory?

After this brief review of the scope and meaning of system theory, the question must be raised as to whether HRD has any choice but to embrace system theory fully. If we agree that we serve those in organizations, even organizations themselves, we must adopt the science of systems.

Organizations are systems. A *system* is defined here as a collection of elements in which the performance of the whole is affected by every one of the parts and the way that any part affects the whole depends on what at least one other part is doing. Although there remains some critique of using the "organization as organism" metaphor, organizations can be viewed as living systems of discernible wholes with lives of their own that they manifest through their processes, structures, and subsystems (Jaros & Dostal, 1995). The biggest difference between organizations and other living systems is that they are multiminded, a fact that HRD has never disputed.

System theory provides a common conception of organizations—an organizer or conceptual frame through which HRD can ensure holistic understanding of its subject. It also provides analysis methodologies capable of including multiple variables. For these important two reasons, it is viewed as the only meaningful way to comprehend the organization as a system.

The Support Provided to HRD by System Theory

It is not possible to provide a comprehensive review of the multiple ways in which system theory contributes valuable knowledge to HRD. However, some general themes can be drawn from the literature and grouped into conceptual categories. A cross-section of the systems leg of the three-legged stool proposed by Swanson (1998) visually depicts these three categories—three ways that system theory supports HRD (Figure 5.6). It provides (1) information—knowledge

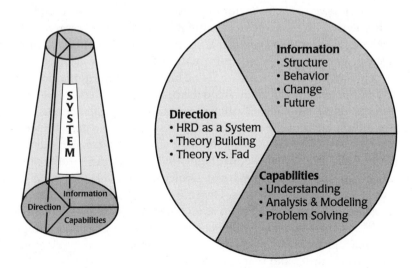

Figure 5.6 A Cross-section of the Systems Leg: Contributions of System Theory

or data about systems, (2) capabilities—the potential to act, and (3) direction—guidance for a fields' activities and development.

Information Provided by System Theory
A primary goal of system theory is to uncover information about systems. During the last forty years, a large amount of knowledge has been compiled that can help HRD professionals understand the basic structure and essences of system parts and wholes. Four distinct themes, or areas, of information began to emerge from the literature review conducted by this author. A description of each area as well as a cursory discussion of the implications resulting from that knowledge are provided in the following sections.

Structure of Systems   System theory has sought to understand the basic structure of systems—the way that their parts are arranged, the interrelation of parts to other parts and of wholes to the environment, and the purposes of the system design. Although some systems scientists propose that the structure of a system is hardly separable from its functioning or behavior, others study structure specifically and agree that there are specific elements that provide necessary infrastructure (e.g., boundaries, feedback structures, and mechanisms that serve specific purposes). Prigogine and Stengers (1984), for example, discovered that systems in disequilibrium produce new structures spontaneously from the disorder. Field theory, commonly discussed related to organizational development, emerged in the 1970s as an explanation of the empty space in systems that affect the structure. Finally, the issue of levels in complex systems has begun to attract scholarly attention.

Behavior of Systems   The behavior of a system must be understood before it can be influenced. System theorists conduct considerable research into the processes and behaviors of a system. It is not possible here to offer a comprehensive inventory of the plethora of information in this area. A brief account, though, demonstrates how extensive it is and how much key information is available for HRD to tap to better understand the behavior of systems.

Katz and Kahn (1966) identify nine common characteristics of open systems that help inform HRD of the basic character of systems. To date, seventeen laws of complexity have been discovered and can be classified in a matrix particularly relevant to behavior outcomes (Warfield, 1995). McLagan (1989) discusses processes unique to self-creating systems. Dooley (1996) offers theoretical propositions of complex adaptive systems. The entire field of cybernetics exists for the primary goal of understanding information processing and how nonlinear feedback guides systems behavior. Finally, chaos and emerging fields of complexity inform us that apparent random behavior of a system actually reveals an underlying pattern and order and that complex systems are deterministic (i.e., they have something that is determining their behavior).

Change Processes   System theory acknowledges that change is part of the very fabric of systems. A systems subfield, population ecology, focuses almost entirely on the potential evolution of the system and posits that actual equilibrium in a system is equal to death, underscoring how systems must evolve, grow, and change to survive. It has taught us to view change as the activation of a system's inherent potential for transformation. The field of ontogeny supports this evolutionary perspective in developing ways to study the history of structural change in a unity without loss of organization in that unity (Dooley, 1995).

System theory is also increasingly probing for a deeper understanding of the nature and processes of change in systems. Findings inform us that systems sensitive to initial conditions are fairly unpredictable in that minor changes can cause huge fluctuations through amplification or, conversely, that some changes in systems can have no apparent effect at all. We also know from the theory that (1) systems behavior gets worse before it grows better, (2) systems tend toward equilibrium (thus, to expect resistance to incremental change), and (3) changes in the essential nature of a system take place when a control parameter passes a critical threshold or bifurcation point (Dooley, 1996). From the field of chaos and complexity, we are growing to understand that a system is creative not when all of its components pull in same direction but when they generate tension by pulling in contradictory directions (Stacey, 1992). System theory renders the complex dynamics of change more comprehensible through the uncovering of general principles about the nature of change.

The Future in Systems   Many distinguished systems scientists have also been very active in the study of the future. System theory contributed a rather revolutionary element to futures theory in that it surfaced the reality that the future is *emergent*—it is created by and emerges from self-organization and the interaction of its members (Stacey, 1992).

What does this mean? Emergent systems are adaptable, evolvable, boundless, and resilient and *not* optimal, controllable, or predictable. The literature emerging out of chaos, in particular, informs us that the future is unpredictable due to a system's sensitivity to initial conditions as well as specific characteristics being discovered about emergent systems. Attempting to perform traditional strategic planning given this information is a rather futile exercise. In a systems approach, rather, the focus of inquiry is on the general character of a system's long-term behavior. There is ongoing pressure to develop improved ways of understanding the qualitative patterns that emerge, how to increase the ability of a system to cope with its emerging future, and how to use evolution as a tool.

Capabilities Offered by System Theory

System theory offers a specific contribution that, beyond simply the information described so far, affects how things are seen or done. It is in this way that system theory provides HRD with *capabilities*—the potential to act.

Understanding of Wholes and Complexity   Some might find it strange that this theme has been categorized as a capability. However, it is placed here to sufficiently recognize the perspective contributed by the ontology and epistemology discussed earlier. Information provided by system theory is simply raw data without professionals to use it to act in ways that are unique in what can often be a mechanistic, reductionist environment. This perspective enables HRD professionals to see wholes. It enables us, if we accept and utilize systems as a foundational theory, to set critical standards for our profession that demand the unfolding of the whole to seek understanding. The conceptual importance of the "whole" cannot be minimized in HRD, and it has great implications. It acknowledges that systems have a life of their own separate from their parts, focuses on the interactions between the parts rather than the variables themselves, concedes that cause and effect are distant in time and space, and emphasizes that the nature of a system is a continuing perception and deception—a continual reviewing of the world.

System theory also offers a unique capability rooted in its perspective on the complexity that organizations face. This includes understanding the environment and its impact on systems as well as the complexities within systems. These types of understandings better position systems professionals to deal with the unpredictability inherent in systems and, in fact, to recognize the need for nonlinear feedback and structural instability as a source of innovation and growth. Furthermore, current chaos literature reveals that chaos methods are being discussed as tools to simplify decisions made in conditions of complexity. Guastello (1995) asserts that the tool kit of nonlinear dynamic system theory consists of attractor and repellor forces, stabilities and instabilities, bifurcation and self-organization, fractal geometry, the distinction between evolutionary and revolutionary change, and catastrophes and discontinuous change. Although that may be somewhat overstated, it does redirect the potential of HRD to act and forces the development of a new capabilities.

Methodologies for Analysis and Modeling   System theory offers much in the way of describing, analyzing, and creating models of systems. These methods facilitate the analysis and modeling of complex interpersonal, intergroup, and human–nature interactions without reducing the subject matter to the level of individual agents. The key is to utilize methods that allow the abstraction of certain details of structure and component, while concentrating on the dynamics that define the characteristic functions, properties, and relationships—this simplification is coined *reduction to dynamics* (Laszlo & Laszlo, 1997). Many analysis and modeling approaches grounded in the systems approach may be reviewed in the literature. Generally they entail identification of multiple elements around and in a system and a refocusing on the whole, integrating what was learned in an understanding of the overall phenomena.

Problem-Solving Approaches   System theory offers two things in terms of approaching problem solving in applied sciences such as HRD. First, systems theorists actually start from the problem, not some preconceived notion of a model or a solution. Once the manifestation of the problem has been identified and described, they proceed inward to the subsystems and outward to the environment (Laszlo & Laszlo, 1997). Second, system theory is the antithesis of the "one tool fits all" mentality. Rather, the theory accepts complexity, freeing problem solvers from causality and linearity and fostering the identification of patterns and tools that apply to different entities. Furthermore, system theory encourages drawing on multiple disciplines without being unduly restricted from points of view within those disciplines (McLagan, 1989).

Direction Provided by System Theory

Finally, it is suggested that system theory can serve as a guiding force that offers direction for a discipline's activities and future. Interpretations grounded in system theory can help build the case for the structure and behavior of HRD.

HRD as a System   There continues to be much discussion about the purpose, function, and definition of HRD (Ruona & Swanson, 1998a). Further work on how HRD will conceive of itself is imperative to ensure a robust future for the field. While multiple proposals have been made to conceive of HRD as a system, there continues to be no firm agreement or discussion of the implications of such a conception (Willis, 1997). System theory provides guidance for identifying the field's contexts and boundaries; actual versus desired goals, inputs, processes, and outputs; modes of operation; constraints; various systems states; and roles.

Theory Building in HRD   System theory can enhance the development of theory in HRD in a few ways. First, it serves as a unifier with other disciplines and sciences in the spirit of its founder. Bertalanffy (1968) called for the unity of science through an interdisciplinary theory that sought to integrate findings into "an isomorphy of laws in different fields" (p. 48). This isomorphy needs to be built at two levels. On a microlevel, it can assist in the organization of HRD's "various practical experiences into some formal, theoretical structure that will be useful in advancing our practice and that in turn will provide a basis for further theory building" (Jacobs, 1989, p. 27). On a macrolevel, system theory provides a foundation on which to acknowledge how interdisciplinary it really is and contribute to the isomorphy integrating those disciplines.

Second, system theory provides relief from mechanistic approaches and a rationale for rejecting principles based on the closed-system mentality (Kast & Rosenzwig, 1972). The theory requires a new heuristic other than reducing things to their components—that is, focusing on wholes, dynamics, and general theory constructs.

Finally, system theory provides great insight into the process of theory building. It offers guidance about the limits of theoretical generalization. Although a motivation undergirding the theory is the unity of science and discovery of general systems principles and laws, it should be noted that systems scientists take great pains to avoid the trap of creating theory that explains "everything" but actually explains nothing. The goal of system theory is to build theory that explains a lot and has tentacles linking it to other general theories whose purposes are to describe a particular class of phenomena (Guastello, 1995).

Theory versus "Fad"   System theory provides knowledge of the nature and behavior of systems. In this knowledge is once again found a capability—the capability to fight against the propagation of fads. Most of these types of solutions are only partial, focusing on parts that gurus can easily see, rather than a holistic view. They typically lack an overall understanding of complexity and how a system copes with the implications. System theory is not a panacea or an easy "six-step" kind of thing. It is difficult. However, it provides a foundation that facilitates a thorough understanding of complex situations and systems. This is the strongest way to increase the likelihood of appropriate action. Professionals embracing system theory as a foundation of HRD are best positioned to influence other practitioners to change their perception of the development and the unleashing of expertise in systems. This is the very nature of scientific revolution (Kuhn, 1970).

Current Limitations of System Theory as a Foundation for HRD

Even in the limited space of these pages, it would be incomplete not to acknowledge that system theory has its limitations. Some of the current limitations are noted in Figure 5.7 in terms of how they impact theory and practice. These issues provide ample challenges to HRD professionals. Most of the issues can be overcome through research, development, and increased dialogue between theoreticians and practitioners as well as those who prescribe to system theory and those that do not.

Relation to Other Proposed Theoretical Foundations

Swanson (1998) proposes that three theoretical foundations comprise the foundation of HRD. Implicit in this proposal, at least for this author, is that it is the *integration* of these three theories that will equip HRD to contend with the challenges it is called upon to address. In this sense, the whole of the integrated theory stemming from these foundations will be larger than the sum of the parts and will be unique to HRD (Ruona & Swanson, 1997, 1998a). The disciplines complement one another nicely. There appears to be nothing inherently in conflict between the theories. There are only minor issues that arise and may need to be addressed as HRD begins to integrate the theories.

Economic Theory

Economics is quite aligned with system theory in acknowledging that the ultimate purpose of systems is survival. The two theories agree that systems are teleological—

Figure 5.7   Current Limitations of System Theory as a Foundation for HRD

Theoretical Limitations	*Practical Limitations*
• Is complex and "big" • Provides more information about dynamics between the parts than it does about the parts themselves • Biological model may ignore social-psychological nature of social systems (Katz & Kahn, 1966) • Can be misinterpreted as not offering a definite body of knowledge since not one mainstream approach • Lacking in reliable methods of "total" conception of the whole • Requires subjectivity • Normative implications of system theory not clarified (Dash, 1995) • Requires more empirical data on systems applications and concepts relative to theoretical formulations • Risk of losing scientific depth in favor of breadth • Places great demands on the field in terms of theory building • Requires knowledge and skill that are not readily available in academia	• Can be viewed as constraint to practitioners because time-consuming and costly • Raises the risk of becoming obsessed with system and forgetting individual (Bierema, 1997) • Responsibilities of the systems practitioners have yet to be clearly articulated and developed. • Necessitates interventions that may lie outside the mandate of the "client" (Dash, 1995) • Coercive structures in organizations have to be confronted as they undermine the pluralist spirit of systems approach (Dash, 1995)

working toward a desired end result. However, current-day teleology has expanded its notions to differentiate between purposes and goals. It acknowledges that a system may have many goals that must be considered. System theorists are cautioned to not blur goals with the idea of functioning. A second disconnect that may arise is an organization's limited view of economics that may discourage truly systemic ideas that do not show their benefits until the long run.

Psychological Theory

System theory and psychological theory align in the belief that the organization is composed of multiminded individuals engaging in patterned activities (Jaros & Dostal, 1995). However, system theory goes further to acknowledge that the organization is exists separate from the sum of its parts—a proposition not embraced by psychologists who remain individually focused. The implications of this disconnect will need to be more fully processed.

Summary

This discussion has attempted to investigate the contribution of system theory to HRD. It offers a unique synthesis of the literature in describing its scope and meaning as well as a framework to organize its multiple contributions to HRD theory and practice.

CONCLUSION

The twenty-first century will most surely see a burst of HRD theory-building research. It will be spurred on by the maturing of the academic side of the HRD profession and the high expectations organizations have for the HRD contribution. The new HRD theory and review journal, *Human Resource Development Review,* under the leadership of Elwood F. Holton III, editor, and Richard J. Torraco, associate editor, will provide a dramatic boost to HRD theory research and theory visibility.

REFLECTION QUESTIONS

1. Explain how models and theories differ. Also, discuss whether it is possible to have one without the other.
2. What is the argument for multiple theories supporting the discipline of HRD?
3. From the section on "The Discipline of Human Resource Development," what do you see as the connection between the definition of HRD and the model of HRD?
4. What do you think the main contribution of psychological theory is to HRD? Why?
5. What do you think the primary contribution of economic theory is to HRD? Why?
6. What do you think the main contribution of system theory is to HRD? Why?

Perspectives of Human Resource Development

This section explicates the learning and performance paradigms of HRD and associated models within each. An attempt is made to clarify the learning–performance perspectives and their logical connection.

Paradigms of HRD

CHAPTER OUTLINE

Like most professional disciplines, HRD includes multiple paradigms of practice and research. A *paradigm* is defined as a "coherent tradition of scientific research" (Kuhn, 1996, p. 10). Thus, paradigms represent fundamentally different views of human resource development, including its goals and aims, values, and guidelines for practice. It is important to understand each one as they may lead to different approaches to solving HRD problems and to different research questions and methodologies. It is also important that each person develop a personal belief system about which paradigm or blend of paradigms will guide his or her practice. This chapter will review the different paradigms, discuss the learning-versus-performance debate, and examine core philosophical and theoretical assumptions of each paradigm.

OVERVIEW OF HRD PARADIGMS

For our purposes, we divide HRD into two paradigms as shown in Figure 6.1: (1) learning paradigm and (2) performance paradigm. These two paradigms will be discussed in this chapter because they are the most clearly defined and dominate most HRD thinking and practice today. A third paradigm, the meaning of work, is an emerging perspective that is relatively ill formed at this point. It seems to have arisen from a backlash against the workplace created as a result of downsizings, layoffs, and other corporate actions that have left workers feeling disenfranchised. One important HRD role is helping people create a sense of meaning in their work. It has also been called the spirituality at work approach. It will be discussed in the last chapter as it is still very much an emerging perspective.

The first paradigm, the learning paradigm, has been the predominant paradigm in U.S. HRD practice. As shown in Figure 6.1, this perspective has three different streams. The first, *individual learning* (column 1a), focuses primarily on individual learning as an outcome and the individual learner as the target of interventions. Two characteristic approaches within this paradigm are adult learning (Knowles et al., 1998) and traditional instructional design (Gagne, 1965; Gagne, Briggs, & Wager, 1992; Gagne & Medsker, 1996).

Most HRD practice has now advanced to at least the second or third streams, *performance-based learning* or *whole systems learning*. The key change when moving from individual learning to these two streams is that the outcome focus changes to performance, though it is still performance improvement as a result of learning. The primary intervention continues to be learning, but interventions are also focused on building organizational systems to maximize the likelihood that learning will improve performance. *Performance-based learning* (column 1b) is focused on individual performance resulting from learning. Performance-based instruction (Brethower & Smalley, 1998) and transfer of learning (Baldwin & Ford, 1988; Ford & Weissbein, 1997; Holton, Bates, & Ruona, 2000) are two examples of this paradigm. *Whole systems learning* (column 1c) focuses on enhancing team and organizational performance through learning in addition to individual performance. It does so by building systems that enhance learning at the individual, team, and organizational levels. Most representative of this perspective is learning organization theory (Dibella & Nevis, 1998; Marquardt, 1995; Watkins & Marsick, 1993).

The second paradigm, the *performance paradigm,* is quite familiar to those who have embraced performance improvement or human performance technology (HPT) (Brethower, 1995). From these perspectives, the outcome focus is on

Figure 6.1 Comparison of the Learning and Performance Paradigms

	1 Learning Paradigm			2 Performance Paradigm	
	(A) INDIVIDUAL LEARNING	(B) PERFORMANCE-BASED LEARNING	(C) WHOLE SYSTEMS LEARNING	(A) INDIVIDUAL PERFORMANCE IMPROVEMENT	(B) WHOLE SYSTEMS PERFORMANCE IMPROVEMENT
Outcome focus	Enhancing individual learning	Enhancing individual performance through learning	Enhancing multiple levels of performance through learning	Enhancing individual performance	Enhancing multiple levels of performance
Intervention focus	• Individual learning	• Individual learning • Organizational systems to support individual learning	• Individual, team, and organizational learning • Organizational systems to support multiple levels of learning	• Nonlearning individual performance system interventions • Learning if appropriate	• Nonlearning multiple-level performance system interventions • Multiple-level learning if appropriate
Representative research streams	• Adult learning • Instructional design	• Performance-based instruction • Transfer of learning	• Learning organization	• Human performance technology	• Performance improvement

total performance, but the intervention focus is on nonlearning as well as learning interventions. It is the incorporation of nonlearning components of performance and associated interventions that distinguishes this group from the learning systems perspective.

Within the performance systems perspective are also two approaches. The *individual performance improvement* approach (column 2a) focuses mostly on individual level performance systems. Human performance technology (Gilbert, 1978; Stolovich & Keeps, 1992) is representative of this approach. *Whole systems performance improvement* is the broadest perspective, encompassing learning and nonlearning interventions occurring at multiple levels in the organization. What is generically called *performance improvement* (Holton, 1999; Rummler & Brache, 1995) or *performance consulting* (Robinson & Robinson, 1995) is representative of this approach.

DEBATES ABOUT LEARNING AND PERFORMANCE

Since 1995, an intense debate in the U.S. research literature has revolved around the learning versus performance paradigms of HRD (Watkins & Marsick, 1995; Swanson, 1995a, 1995b). This has occurred in spite of the fact that U.S. human resource development practice has been found to be increasingly focused on performance outcomes and developing systems to support high performance (Bassi & Van Buren, 1999).

In this debate, the performance paradigm of HRD has come under increasing criticism, some of which reflects misconceptions about the basic tenets of performance-based HRD. For example, Barrie and Pace (1998) argue for a more educational approach to HRD manifested through an organizational learning approach. They are also particularly critical of the performance paradigm as it is focused on the individual:

> Performance consists of the demonstration of specific behaviors designed to accomplish specific tasks and produce specific outcomes (Swanson & Gradous, 1986). Improvements in performance are usually achieved through behavioral control and conditioning. Indeed, performance may be changed or improved through methods that allow for very little if any willingness and voluntariness on the part of the performers. In fact, behavioral performance may be enhanced decidedly by processes that allow for minimal or no rational improvement on the part of performers in the change process. Their willingness of consciousness as rational agents is neither encouraged nor required. Such persons function in a change process purely as "means" and not "ends." (Holding, 1981, p. 50)

Recently, their criticisms became even harsher (Barrie & Pace, 1999): "It is the performance perspective that denies a person's fundamental and inherent agency and self-determination, not the learning perspective. All of the negative effects of training come from a performance perspective" (p. 295).

Bierema (1997) calls for a return to a focus on individual development and appears to equate the performance perspective to the mechanistic model of work. She says, "The machine mentality in the workplace, coupled with obsessive focus on performance, has created a crisis in individual development" (p. 23). She goes on to say that "valuing development only if it contributes to productivity is a viewpoint that has perpetuated the mechanistic model of the past three hundred years" (p. 24). Provo (1999) also equates the performance paradigm with behaviorism.

Dirkx (1997) offers a somewhat similar view when he says that "HRD continues to be influenced by an ideology of scientific management and reflects a view of education where the power and control over what is learned, how, and why is located in the leadership, corporate structure, and HRD staff" (p. 42). He goes on to say that the traditional view in which learning is intended to contribute to bottom-line performance leads "practitioners to focus on designing and implementing programs that transmit to passive workers the knowledge and skills needed to improve the company's overall performance and, ultimately, society's economic competitiveness. In this market-driven view of education, learning itself is defined in particular ways, largely by the perceived needs of the sponsoring corporation and the work individuals are required to perform" (p. 43).

What is striking about these comments and others offered by critics of the performance paradigm of HRD is that they all contain rather gross errors and misunderstandings. In reality, there is less of a gap between the performance and learning paradigms than is represented by learning paradigm advocates. Simply, when properly and clearly framed, the performance paradigm is not what the learning paradigm advocates present it to be. While there can be no denying that some tension will always exist between the learning systems and work systems in an organization (Van der Krogt, 1998), there is actually more common ground than has been portrayed by performance critics.

Our purpose in this chapter is *not* to argue for a unifying definition or perspective of HRD. Rather, we present a framework for understanding paradigms of HRD to highlight both the common ground and the differences between the perspectives. As Kuchinke (1998) has articulated, it is probably not possible or even desirable to resolve paradigmatic debates, but the sharp dualism that has characterized this debate is also not appropriate or necessary.

PHILOSOPHICAL VIEWS OF LEARNING AND PERFORMANCE

Underlying this debate is a tension around whether performance is inherently "bad" and learning "good." From a philosophical perspective, this is a discussion about the ontology of learning and performance because it focuses on making the fundamental assumptions about the nature of these phenomena explicit and clearly articulated (Gioia & Pitre, 1990; Ruona, 1999). In this section, we define the multiple perspectives of performance and learning that can be identified within the learning versus performance debate and argue that neither performance or learning can be considered inherently "good" or "bad" and that human resource development can embrace both as humanistic (Holton, 2000).

Three Views of Performance

Performance has largely been a practice-based phenomenon with little philosophical consideration. Three basic views pervade the thinking about the performance paradigm: performance as (1) a natural outcome of human activity, (2) necessary for economic activity, and (3) an instrument of oppression.

Performance as a Natural Outcome of Human Activity

In this view, performance is accepted as a natural part of human existence. Human beings are seen as engaging in wide varieties of purposeful activities with performance as a natural and valued outcome. Furthermore, the accomplishment of certain outcomes in these purposeful activities is regarded as a basic human need. That is, the belief is that few people are content not to perform.

Many of these activities occur in work settings where we traditionally think of performance; however, they may also take place in leisure settings. For example, a person may play softball for leisure but be quite interested in winning games. Or, a person might be heavily involved with church activities such as membership drives or outreach programs and exert great effort to make them successful. In both of these examples, performance is a desired aspect of their freely chosen behavior.

In this view, for HRD to embrace performance is also to embrace enhancing human existence. It is this perspective that many, although not all, performance-based HRD professionals advocate. This view of performance-based HRD views advancing performance and enhancing human potential as perfectly complementary (Holton, 2000).

Performance as Necessary for Economic Activity

This perspective is a more utilitarian view that considers performance to be an instrumental activity that enhances individuals and society because it supports economic gains. More value-neutral than the first perspective, this view sees performance as neither inherently good nor bad but rather as a means to other ends. It is largely a work-based view of performance. Performance is seen as necessary for individuals to earn livelihoods, be productive members of society, and build a good society. In this recursive process, performance at the individual level leads to enhanced work and careers, and performance at the organizational level leads to stronger economic entities capable of providing good jobs to individuals.

Some models and concepts of performance improvement can be associated with this perspective as they attempt to enhance the utility of learning by linking learning to individual and organizational performance outcomes. While this objective is worthy by itself, it is critiqued for lacking the intrinsic "goodness" of the first ontological perspective. As the performance paradigm has matured, it has broadened to embrace the first perspective.

Performance as an Instrument of Organizational Oppression

From this perspective, performance is seen as a means of control and dehumanization. Through focusing on performance, organizations are seen as coercing and demanding behaviors from individuals in return for compensation. Performance is viewed as threatening to humans and potentially abusive. As such, it is largely a necessary evil that denies human potential.

It is this perspective that seems to be represented in critics of performance-based HRD. For example, Barrie and Pace (1998) say that "it is the performance perspective that denies a person's fundamental and inherent agency and self-determination" (p. 295). Others (Bierema, 1997; Peterson & Provo, 1999) refer to the mechanistic or machine model of work when referring to the performance perspective.

The underlying presumption of this perspective is that performance is antithetical to human potential. It seems to be most closely aligned with critical theorists who wish HRD to challenge organizational power structures that seek to control performance outcomes.

Three Views of Learning

Much philosophical work has focused on learning and adult education since ancient times (Gutek, 1998; Elias & Merriam, 1995; Lindeman, 1926; Bryson 1936; Hewitt & Mather, 1937). For purposes of this discussion, we group the views of learning into three analogous ontological views of learning as (1) a humanistic endeavor, (2) value-neutral transfer of information, and (3) a tool for societal oppression.

Learning as a Humanistic Endeavor

The primary purpose of learning in this perspective is to enhance human potential. Most closely aligned with humanistic psychology and existentialist philosophy, humans are seen as growing, developing beings. Learning is viewed as a key element in helping individuals become more self-actualized and as inherently good for the person. Most HRD scholars view learning from this perspective. They believe deeply in the power of learning to enhance human potential. It is important to note that most within performance-based HRD also see learning in this way (Holton, in press-a).

Learning as a Value-Neutral Transmission of Information

Learning in this view has instrumental value in that it transfers information that individuals need and desire. Closely aligned with Dewey's (1938) pragmatic philosophy, learning is seen as a means to solve problems of everyday living. Instructional designers and many organizational trainers approach learning from this perspective as their primary task is to transfer information effectively. A large part of training practice in the United States is grounded in this perspective that sees learning as largely value-neutral and instrumental.

Learning as a Tool for Societal Oppression

Largely overlooked by most HRD scholars in the United States is the fact that learning can also be a tool for oppression, particularly outside organizational settings. For example, communists use learning to control people, cults use learning to brainwash people, religion has used learning to restrict worldviews of people, and education has used learning to restrict history by eliminating black and female perspectives of history. Freire (1970) and Mezirow (1991) are examples of scholars who have warned about the potentially oppressive nature of learning. Thus, learning can also be a tool for oppression and control.

Comparing Philosophical Foundations

The first conclusion is that neither learning nor performance are inherently good or bad. Both can be instruments of oppression or means to elevate human potential. We maintain that human resource development can elevate human potential and enhance the human experience by focusing on *both* performance and learning.

It is disturbing that debates in the literature have reflected diverse ontological assumptions about performance without explicitly owning and acknowledging them. Specifically, critics of "the" performance-based HRD have categorized all emerging views of performance into the third perspective, an instrument of organizational oppression. As a result, learning has been incorrectly portrayed as inherently "good" and performance as inherently "bad." It is equally possible for performance to be "good" and learning to be "bad" in a given situation. Any notion that either performance or learning has these inherent qualities should be abandoned in future debates.

Performance-based HRD should adopt the perspective that *both* learning and performance are inherently good for the individual because both are natural parts of human existence. It is hard to imagine a life without learning or without performance. The challenge for the human resource development profession is to ensure that neither one becomes a tool for oppression but rather elevates human potential.

LEARNING PARADIGM OF HRD

The learning paradigm is familiar territory to most HRD professionals. In this section the learning paradigm will be defined and its core assumptions explicated.

Definition of the Learning Paradigm

Watkins (1995) offers a useful definition of the learning paradigm of HRD: "HRD is the field of study and practice responsible for the fostering of a long-term work-related learning capacity at the individual, group, and organizational level of organizations" (p. 2). Furthermore, she says that HRD "works to enhance individual's capacity to learn, to help groups overcome barriers to learning, and to help organizations create a culture which promotes conscious learning" (p. 2).

Core Theoretical Assumptions of the Learning Paradigm

The core assumptions of the learning paradigm have not been clearly articulated by any one individual. Ruona (2000, 1998) provides particularly good insights in her study of the core beliefs of ten scholarly leaders in HRD. Barrie and Pace (1998), Watkins and Marsick (1995), Bierema (1997), and Dirkx (1997) have offered particularly strong arguments in favor of what we are calling the learning paradigm. Drawing on these sources (and others), the following nine core assumptions have emerged.

Assumption 1: Individual education, growth, learning and development are inherently good for the individual. At the heart of the learning paradigm is the notion that learning, development, and growth is inherently good for each individual. This assumption is drawn from humanistic psychology, which stresses self-actualization of the individual. This assumption is also central to all of human resource development practice and is unchallenged by any paradigm of HRD.

Assumption 2: People should be valued for their intrinsic worth as people, not just as resources to achieve an outcome. Learning advocates object to characterizing people as "resources" to be utilized to achieve a goal, particularly in an organization. For HRD to value people only with regard to their contribution to performance outcomes is offensive because it invalidates them as human beings. Furthermore, it leads to workplaces that devalue people and that can quickly become abusive to employees. From this perspective, HRD should value people for their inherent worth, not seek to use them to accomplish a goal. Thus, learning and development should be a means to enhance people and their humanness, not to accomplish performance goals.

Assumption 3: The primary purpose of HRD is development of the individual. From this paradigm, the needs of the individual should be more important than the needs of the organization, or equally important at a minimum. Those learning advocates who are concerned about power structures in society would argue that the learning and development needs of the individual should take precedence over the needs of the organization (Bierema, 2000; Dirkx, 1997). Others might take a more moderate view that the needs of the individual need to be balanced against the needs of the organization. Regardless, the primary goal of HRD from this perspective is to help individuals develop to their fullest potential.

Assumption 4: The primary outcome of HRD is learning and development. In this paradigm, learning is considered to be the primary outcome of human resource development. While performance is acknowledged, the core outcome variable is learning. As stated in the overview, there are variations within this paradigm such that some focus mostly on individual learning while others take a whole systems approach (individual, team, and organizational). Regardless, the end result is some form of learning and development.

Assumption 5: Organizations are best advanced by having fully developed individuals. Performance outcomes that benefit the individual and the organization are presumed to occur if the individual is developed to full potential. That is, the specific performance behaviors desired by the organization are best achieved by focusing on the individual's development. Performance, then, flows naturally from development instead of having performance drive development. As Bierema (1996) states, "A holistic approach to the development of individuals in the context of a learning organization produces well-informed, knowledgeable, critical-thinking adults who have a sense of fulfillment and inherently make decisions that cause an organization to prosper" (p. 22). Indeed, learning and development are presumed to be able to nourish the individual to higher levels of performance than can be achieved by a focus on well-defined performance outcomes.

Assumption 6: Individuals should control their own learning process. This assumption is deeply rooted in the democratic as well as humanistic principles of adult learning. Individuals are presumed to have the inherent capacity and motivation to direct their own learning in a way that is most beneficial to them. Because of this, HRD is presumed not to need to specify performance outcomes because learners are able to determine their own course to high performance and will actively seek to do so. Deeply rooted in the inherent belief of the goodness of people and the concept of self-organizing systems, this assumption frees HRD from focusing on performance outcomes by striving to create nourishing learning situations.

Assumption 7: Development of the individual should be holistic. For people in organizations to achieve their fullest potential, they must be developed holistically, not just with specific skills or competencies for specific tasks (Barrie & Pace, 1998). HRD, from this paradigm, should focus on all aspects of individual development.

> Holistic development integrates personal and professional life in career planning, development, and assessment. Holistic development is not necessarily linked to the present or future job tasks, but the overall growth of the individual with the recognition that this growth will have an effect on the organizational system. (Bierema, 1996, p. 25)

Assumption 8: The organization must provide people a means to achieve their fullest human potential through meaningful work. This assumption extends Assumption 3 to say that organizations have a duty and responsibility to help individuals develop to their full potential. Furthermore, one of the primary vehicles for this is human resource development.

Assumption 9: An emphasis on performance or organizational benefits creates a mechanistic view of people that prevents them from reaching their full potential. This assumption is particularly important because it creates the largest gap with the performance paradigm. Learning advocates tend to think that emphasizing performance outcomes in HRD, and targeting HRD interventions to improve performance, results in an overly mechanistic approach to HRD and organizational life. As a result, people in organizations are limited and many fail to reach their full potential. Rather than unleashing the fill power of human potential, learning advocates argue that performance-based HRD creates a machinelike approach to development. Such an approach fails to tap into the capabilities people have to accomplish great things, leaving them more alienated from the organization and ultimately hurting the organization.

PERFORMANCE PARADIGM OF HRD

The performance paradigm of HRD has seen renewed interest in the 1990s. As shown in Chapter 3, it actually has very deep roots in training practices throughout history. It has come to the forefront of HRD debates because changes in the global economy have put renewed pressure on HRD for accountability.

Definition of the Performance Paradigm

Holton (in press-a) points out that the performance paradigm of HRD has not been formally defined in the literature, although there are definitions of HRD that are performance based (Weinberger, 1998). He offers several useful definitions. First, *performance* is defined as

accomplishing units of mission-related outcomes or outputs.

He defines a *performance system* as

any system organized to accomplish a mission or purpose.

It is important to note that the term *performance system* is used instead of *organization*. Performance systems are simply purposeful systems that have a specified mission. All organizations are performance systems, but some performance systems are not an organization. For example, a community could become a performance system if it adopts a mission.

Then, the performance paradigm of HRD is defined as follows:

The performance paradigm of HRD holds that the purpose of HRD is to advance the mission of the performance system that sponsors the HRD efforts by improving the capabilities of individuals working in the system and improving the systems in which they perform their work.

Core Theoretical Assumptions of the Performance Paradigm

In this section, eleven core assumptions are presented (Holton, in press-a). It is important to remember that the performance paradigm has evolved over the last decade with only limited work to explicitly define it (Swanson, 1999; Holton,

1999). Thus, these core assumptions represent a snapshot of the performance paradigm at this point. Clearly literature from ten years ago might appear to represent different perspectives because the performance paradigm was just emerging. Indeed, in their zeal to get performance added to the HRD framework, early performance advocates focused mostly on performance variables and may have unintentionally appeared to exclude learning and human potential.

Assumption 1: Performance systems must perform to survive and prosper, and individuals who work within them must perform if they wish to advance their careers and maintain employment or membership. The performance paradigm views performance as a fact of life in performance systems (e.g., organizations) that is not optional. For example, if organizations do not perform, they decline and eventually disappear. Performance is not defined only as profit, but rather by whatever means the organization uses to define its core outcomes (e.g., citizen services for a government organization). Every performance system has core outcomes and constituents or customers who expect them to be achieved. Even nonprofit and government organizations face restructuring or extinction if they do not achieve their core outcomes.

By extension, then, if individual employees do not perform in a manner that supports the system's long-term interests, they are unlikely to be seen as productive members of the system. Thus, in an organization persons may not advance and may ultimately lose their jobs. This is not to suggest that employees must blindly follow the organization's mandates. In the short term they are expected to challenge the organization when necessary, but over the long term every employee must make contributions to core outcomes. Thus, the greatest service HRD can provide to the individual and to the performance system is to help improve performance by enhancing individual expertise and building effective performance systems.

Assumption 2: The ultimate purpose of HRD is to improve performance of the system in which it is embedded and which provides the resources to support it. The purpose of HRD is to improve performance of the system in which it is embedded (or within which it is working in the case of consultants) and that provides the resources to support it (Swanson & Arnold, 1997). All interventions and activities undertaken by HRD must ultimately enhance that system's mission-related performance by improving performance at the mission, social subsystem, process, and individual levels (Holton, 1999). Aside from general ethical responsibilities (Dean, 1993), HRD's primary accountability is to the system within which it resides.

The system's mission and the goals derived from it specify the expected outcomes of that system. Every purposefully organized system operates with a mission, either explicitly or implicitly, and the role of the mission is to reflect the system's relationship with its external environment. If the system has a purpose, then it also has desired outputs, so performance theory is applicable. Performance occurs in everything from churches (e.g., number of members, money raised, individuals helped), to government (e.g., health care in a community, drivers' licenses issued, crime rates), to nonprofits (e.g., research funded, members), and, of course, to profit-making organizations. Under this broad definition, performance is not seen as inherently harmful or nonhumanistic but rather as an important fact of life in systems organized for purposeful activity.

The particular system's definition of its performance relationship with the external environment is fully captured by the mission and goals of the organization. In that sense, this model differs from that of Kaufman and his associates (see Kaufman, Watkins, Triner, & Smith, 1998; Kaufman, 1997), who have argued that societal benefits should be included as a level of performance. This difference should not be interpreted to mean that societal benefits are unimportant. Rather, the relationship between the performance system and society is most appropriately captured by the mission of that system.

Assumption 3: The primary outcome of HRD is not just learning but also performance. The argument over learning versus performance has positioned the two as equal and competing outcomes. In reality, this is an inappropriate theoretical argument. Performance and learning really represent two different levels of outcomes that are complementary, not competing. Multilevel theory building has become increasingly popular as a means to integrate competing perspectives (Klein, Tosi, & Cannella, 1999). In management, this divide has been characterized as the "micro" domain where the focus is on the individual and the "macro" domain where the focus is on the organization. Multilevel theory integrates the two by acknowledging the influence of the organization on the individual, and vice versa:

> Multilevel theories illuminate the context surrounding individual-level processes, clarifying precisely when and where such processes are likely to occur within organization. Similarly, multilevel theories identify the individual-level characteristics, behaviors, attitudes and perceptions that underlie and shape organization-level characteristics and outcomes. (Klein et al., p. 243)

From the multilevel perspective, then, neither level is more or less important. Furthermore, individual learning would be seen as an integral part of achieving organizational and individual goals.

Assumption 4: Human potential in organizations must be nurtured, respected, and developed. Performance advocates believe in the power of learning and the power of people in organizations to accomplish great things. It is important to distinguish between the performance paradigm of HRD and simple performance management. The latter does not necessarily honor human potential in organizations as performance-oriented HRD does. Performance-oriented HRD advocates remain HRD and human advocates at the core. Performance advocates do not believe that emphasizing performance outcomes invalidates their belief in and respect for human potential.

The performance paradigm of HRD recognizes that it is the unleashing of human potential that creates great organizations. While performance advocates emphasize outcomes, they do not demand that outcomes be achieved through control of human potential. Performance advocates fully embrace notions of empowerment and human development because they will also lead to better performance when properly executed (Huselid, 1995; Lam & White, 1998). Furthermore, they see no instances where denying the power of human potential in organizations would lead to better performance. Thus, they see it as completely consistent to emphasize both human potential and performance.

Assumption 5: HRD must enhance current performance and build capacity for future performance effectiveness in order to create sustainable high performance. Kaplan and Norton (1996) suggest two categories of performance measures: outcomes and drivers. Unfortunately, they do not offer concise definitions of either. For our purposes, outcomes are measures of effectiveness or efficiency relative to core outputs of the system, subsystem, process or individual. The most typical are financial indicators (profit, ROI, etc.) and productivity measures (units of goods or services produced) and are often generic across similar performance systems. According to Kaplan and Norton, these measures tend to be lag indicators in that they reflect what has occurred or has been accomplished in relation to core outcomes.

Drivers measure elements of performance that are expected to sustain or increase system, subsystem, process, or individual ability and capacity to be more effective or efficient in the future. Thus, they are leading indicators of future outcomes and tend to be unique for particular performance systems. Together with outcome measures, they describe the hypothesized cause and effect relationships in the organization's strategy (Kaplan & Norton, 1996).

From this perspective, performance improvement experts who focus solely on actual outcomes, such as profit or units of work produced, are flawed in that they are likely to create short-term improvement but neglect aspects of the organization that will drive future performance outcomes. Experts who focus solely on performance drivers such as learning or growth are equally flawed in that they fail to consider the actual outcomes. Only when outcomes and drivers are jointly considered will long-term, sustained performance improvements occur. Neither is more or less important, but work in an integrated fashion to enhance mission, process, subsystem, and individual performance. Performance-based HRD advocates do not support such "performance at all costs" strategies. Long-term sustainable high performance, which is the goal that performance-oriented HRD advocates, requires a careful balance between outcomes and drivers. High short-term performance that cannot be sustained is not really high performance.

Assumption 6: HRD professionals have an ethical and moral obligation to ensure that attaining organizational performance goals is not abusive to individual employees. Performance advocates agree that the drive for organizational performance can become abusive and unethical. In no way should performance-oriented HRD support organizational practices that exceed the boundaries of ethical and moral treatment of employees. Clearly, there is ample room for disagreement as to the specifics of what is ethical and moral, but the basic philosophical position is that performance improvement efforts must be ethical. This is not viewed as hard to accomplish because of the assumption (described shortly) that effective performance is good for individuals and organizations.

Assumption 7: Training/learning activities cannot be separated from other parts of the performance system and are best bundled with other performance improvement interventions. The broadest approach, and the one advocated by performance-based HRD, is the whole systems performance improvement approach. This approach focuses on improving performance outcomes at multiple levels with nonlearning and learning interventions. In most organizations there is no profession or discipline charged with responsibility for assessing, improving and monitoring performance as a whole system. This void is directly responsible for the proliferation of "quick fixes" and faddish improvement programs, most of which focus on only a single element or a subset of performance variables. Because HRD is grounded in system theory and the whole systems perspective of organizations, it is the logical discipline to take responsibility for whole system performance improvements in organizations.

Assumption 8: Effective performance and performance systems are rewarding to the individual and to the organization. Performance clearly benefits the organization. However, lost in the literature is the recognition that effective performance benefits the individual equally. In many instances, performance is presented as almost antithetical to individual benefits, implying one must choose between them. In fact, a variety of research tells us that people like to perform effectively:

- The goal-setting literature indicates that individuals build self-esteem by accomplishing challenging goals (Katzell & Thompson, 1990).
- Hackman and Oldham's (1980) job characteristics model and the research supporting it have shown that experienced meaningfulness of work and responsibility for work outcomes are two critical psychological states that individuals seek.
- Self-efficacy is built when individuals experience success at task performance that is referred to as *enactive mastery* (Wood & Bandura, 1989).
- The relationship between job satisfaction and performance has been shown to be a reciprocal relationship, with performance enhancing job satisfaction and vice versa (Katzell, Thompson, & Guzzo, 1992; Spector, 1997).
- Success at work is seen as important to an individual's basic adult identity because it helps them see themselves as productive, competent human beings (Whitbourne, 1986). Conversely, failure or frustration threatens an individual's self-concept of competence.

- Work allows the individual to implement his or her self-concept and fulfill their unique goals and interests. Work and life satisfaction depend on the extent to which individuals finds outlets for their needs and abilities (Super, Savickas, & Super, 1996).

- Success at work fulfills an individual's innate drive for what has been called *self-actualization* (Maslow, 1970) or the need for achievement (McClelland, 1965).

- Self-determination theory and research suggest that humans have three innate needs that are essential to optimal functioning and well-being: the needs for competence, relatedness, and autonomy (Ryan & Deci, 2000). Thus, effective performance will contribute to an individual's sense of well-being by enhancing feelings of competence.

- Certain individuals have high levels of a dispositional trait called *conscientiousness* that is a valid predictor of job performance (Barrick & Mount, 1991). For these individuals failure to perform would be very frustrating.

- Performance also helps individuals achieve instrumental goals. It may lead to more career advancement and career opportunities in organizations as well as valued intrinsic and extrinsic rewards as a result of performance

This list is not offered as being a comprehensive presentation of ways that performance benefits individuals. Rather, it is representative enough to conclude safely that performance benefits individuals in a myriad of ways. People do not want to fail to perform in their jobs. Therefore, to the extent that HRD helps them be more successful in their jobs, performance-oriented HRD is just as valuable to the individual as the organization. Effective performance can make a significant contribution to individuals as well as their organizations.

Assumption 9: Whole systems performance improvement seeks to enhance the value of learning in an organization. Performance-based HRD actually seeks to increase the value of the individual employee and individual learning in the system, not diminish it. It fully agrees that enhancing the expertise of individual employees is fundamentally important. However, performance-based HRD suggests that individually oriented HRD violates the fundamental principles of system theory (Bertalanffy, 1968), which tell us that no one element of the system can be viewed separately from other elements. Intervening in only one element of the system without creating congruence in other parts of the system will not lead to systemic change. Furthermore, intervening in the whole system to improve outcomes or drivers alone is also flawed. For example, a company that downsizes drastically may increase profits (outcomes) in the short run, but it will leave itself without any intellectual capital (driver) for future growth. Human performance technologists (Stolovich & Keeps, 1992) and needs assessors (Moore & Dutton, 1978) have understood the need to view the individual domain within the larger organizational system in order to make individual domain performance improvement efforts more effective. Whole systems performance improvement goes a step further to analyze and improve performance of the whole system through a balanced emphasis on outcomes and drivers in the four performance domains.

Assumption 10: HRD must partner with functional departments to achieve performance goals. One common lament from HRD practitioners is that the performance approach forces them to deal with organizational variables over which they have no control (e.g., rewards, job design, etc.). Performance-oriented HRD acknowledges this and stresses that HRD must become a partner with functional units in the organization to achieve performance improvement, even through learning. Opponents often suggest that HRD should focus on learning because they can influence learning. Yet, classroom learning is the only variable in the performance system over which HRD professionals have the primary influence. Learning organization advocates stress the fact that much of the really valuable learning that takes place in organizations occurs in the workplace, not the classroom (Watkins & Marsick, 1993). Performance-oriented HRD advocates suggest that if HRD is not willing to be a performance partner, then it is doomed to play only small roles in organizations with minimal impact and with great risk for downsizing and outsourcing.

Assumption 11: The transfer of learning into job performance is of primary importance. Because the dependent variable in performance-oriented HRD is not just learning but individual and organizational performance, considerable emphasis is placed on the transfer of learning to job performance. As Holton et al. (2000) point out, researchers are still working to operationalize the organizational dimensions important to enhancing transfer. Nonetheless, there is widespread recognition that the transfer process is not something that occurs by chance or is assured by achieving learning outcomes but rather that it is the result of a complex system of influences (Baldwin & Ford, 1988; Broad, 2000; Ford & Weissbein, 1997; Holton & Baldwin, 2000). Learning is a necessary, but not sufficient, condition for improving job performance through increased expertise (Bates, Holton, & Seyler, 2000; Rouillier & Goldstein, 1993; Tracey, Tannenbaum, & Kavanaugh, 1995). Expertise has emerged as a construct integrating the performance component of HRD with learning (Swanson & Holton, 1999). Defined as "human behaviors, having effective results and optimal efficiency, acquired through study and experience within a specialized domain" (p. 26), expertise focuses HRD on core outcomes from learning.

Performance advocates are known for emphasizing measurement of HRD outcomes to see whether outcomes are achieved. Measuring performance is a common activity in organizations, so it is logical that performance-oriented HRD would also stress measurement. This emphasis stems from two key observations. First, it seems that important performance outcomes in organizations are almost always measured in some manner. Thus, if HRD is to improve performance, then it must measure its outcomes. Second, components of organizational systems that are viewed as contributing to the organization's strategic mission are usually able to demonstrate their contribution through some measurement. Thus, if HRD is to be a strategic partner, it must measure results.

Myths about the Performance Paradigm

It should be apparent that a variety of the criticisms leveled at the performance about the performance paradigm are actually myths.

Performance is behavioristic. The performance paradigm is not the same as behaviorism. The performance paradigm is most concerned that performance *outcomes* occur, but in no way should it be interpreted to restrict the *strategies and interventions* employed to behavioristic ones. Barrie and Pace's (1998) contention that "improvements in performance are usually achieved through behavioral control and conditioning" is simply wrong. Similarly, Bierema's (1997) view that the performance approach is "mechanistic" and Dirkx's (1997) view that it leads organizations to "transmit to passive workers the knowledge and skills needed" are also wrong. The performance paradigm advocates none of these things, nor must it lead organizations in that direction. This myth probably arose because of the early work in performance technology that indeed grew out of behaviorism (Gilbert, 1978). It may persist for two reasons: (1) the performance paradigm places considerable emphasis on building effective systems, in addition to individual development, and (2) performance-based HRD sanctions interventions that change the system in which the individual works but do not involve the individual.

It is perfectly possible for a performance-oriented person to take a humanistic approach to HRD, as long as that approach will lead to performance outcomes. For example, interventions that attempt to spark more creativity and innovation in an organization can rarely be done using a behavioristic strategy. Or, a more spiritual approach to adding meaning to employees' lives may be quite appropriate, if it leads to performance outcomes. Furthermore, the performance paradigm would not restrict learning solely to the objectivist paradigm (Mezirow, 1996) but would also embrace critical and transformational learning if needed to improve performance. In fact, many organizational change interventions to improve performance encourage employees to think more critically about their work and the organization. The performance paradigm can and does adopt any type of HRD strategy, as long as outcomes occur that further the mission of the system.

Performance is deterministic. Another mistaken belief is that the performance paradigm demands that outcomes of HRD interventions be predetermined before the interventions. If that were true, then the only interventions that would be acceptable would be those for which outcomes could be determined in advance, thereby leaving out strategies such as the learning organization. In fact, the performance paradigm advocates no such thing. Performance advocates are just as comfortable as learning advocates with less certain outcomes, provided that outcomes do occur at some point. For example, in a learning organization, an organization does not need to know exactly *where* the performance improvement will occur. However, performance advocates would say that they should expect to see that performance improvements do occur at some point and be able to assess outcomes when they do occur.

Performance ignores individual learning and growth. The performance paradigm honors and promotes individual learning and growth just as much as a learning paradigm does. The key difference is that the performance paradigm expects that learning and growth will benefit the performance system in which it is embedded. That is, learning and growth for the sole benefit of the individual and which will never benefit the organization is not acceptable for *organization-sponsored HRD*. Note that many performance HRD advocates would honor learning and growth of the individual as a core outcome for other circumstances, but not for organization-sponsored HRD.

Performance is abusive to employees. There is little doubt that a performance approach *can* be abusive to employees, particularly when organizations use cost cutting through downsizing as a substitute for sound performance improvement. However, this is a problem of implementation, not one that is inherent in the theoretical framework. Research (e.g., Huselid, 1995; Lau & May, 1998) clearly shows that creating an environment that is supportive and respectful of employees is not only the morally right thing to do, but also results in improved performance. When properly implemented, performance-based HRD is not abusive to employees.

Performance is focused on the short term. Once again, this is a problem of implementation, not theory. It is true that many organizations place too much emphasis on short-term results. However, most organizations have learned that focusing on short-term performance and not building capacity for long-term success simply does not work. There is nothing inherent in performance theory that says it must be short-term. Many long-term interventions have been abused by companies and inappropriately conducted with a short-term perspective (e.g., TQM). Performance-oriented HRD is no different—some will do it right, and others will not.

RECONCILING THE TWO PARADIGMS

In recent years, more energy has gone into reconciling the two paradigms and finding common ground. It is fair to say that there is much greater understanding between groups representing both views. Substantial overlap exists between the two paradigms. In particular:

- A strong belief in learning and development as avenues to individual growth
- A belief that organizations can be improved through learning and development activities

- A commitment to people and human potential
- A deep desire to see people grow as individuals
- A passion for learning

It is this common ground that keeps people within the two paradigms in the field of human resource development. They represent a strong uniting bond that clearly defines the field and separates it from other disciplines.

At the same time, unresolved issues persist between the two paradigms. The differences seem to be deeply held values and philosophical assumptions (Ruona, 1999). Because of that, they are very difficult to resolve, as there are few "right" answers when the differences are defined at the value level. Let's review some key differences.

The issue of organizational control over the learning process and outcomes is a difficult one for those who believe that only the individual should control his or her learning process (Bierema, 2000). It may be the one issue about which no agreement is possible because it is a philosophical issue that triggers passionate feelings. The performance paradigm accepts the premise that the organization and the individual should share control of the individual's learning if the organization is the sponsor of the intervention. However, performance advocates would argue that ignoring performance in favor of individual control might ultimately be bad for the individual if the organization is not able to survive or prosper. The individual employee presumably needs the benefits of employment (e.g., economic, psychological, instrumental) that will exist only if the organization thrives. Thus, sharing control in order to advance organization performance is viewed as appropriate and beneficial to both parties. Learning advocates would argue that learning is inherently an individual and personal experience that should never be controlled. That is, to control a person's learning is to control the person, which is objectionable.

The other argument for shared control is an economic one. Simply, if the performance system or organization is paying for the HRD efforts, it has a right to derive benefits from it and share control over it. This is one area of criticism that performance advocates truly struggle to understand. It is difficult to understand how organizations can be expected to pay for HRD efforts yet have those efforts focus primarily on what is good for the individual. To performance advocates, this sounds perfectly appropriate for schools and universities in a democratic society, but not for organization-sponsored HRD. In fact, most would wholeheartedly support the individually oriented philosophy for learning activities outside of organizations. Yet, most performance advocates also understand there are deeply held fears about institutional control over individual learning. Nonetheless, they view the situation as different once HRD crosses the organizational boundary and employers fund HRD efforts.

Many of the learning paradigm tenets are best understood by remembering that their roots are in adult education. Adult education is a broader and different field of practice than human resource development, although some would debate this. Adult education is grounded in the idea that education should be used to maintain a democratic society, which is best accomplished by building individuals' power through education and knowledge. When viewing adult learning in a broader societal context, this makes perfect sense. Where the differences arise is when learning is moved inside the boundaries and sponsorship of a purposeful system like an organization. Then performance advocates believe a different set of assumptions is warranted. Learning advocates, on the other hand, believe that a very similar set of assumptions still applies.

We acknowledge that our bias is toward the performance paradigm. Perhaps the best way of thinking about the importance of the performance paradigm is to ask this question: Could HRD sponsored by a performance system survive if it did *not* result in improved performance for the system? Most would agree that the answer is no. Second, will it thrive if it does not contribute in a *substantial* way to the mission of the organization? Again, most would answer no. Like all components of any system or organization, HRD must enhance the organization's effectiveness. The challenge is to consider how performance is incorporated in HRD theory and practice, not whether it will be.

The performance paradigm is the most likely approach to lead to a strategic role for HRD in organizations. HRD will only be perceived as having strategic value to the organization if it has the capability to connect the unique value of employee expertise with the strategic goals of the organization (Torraco & Swanson, 1995). Performance advocates see little chance that HRD will gain power and influence in organizations by ignoring the core performance outcomes that organizations wish to achieve. By being *both* human and performance advocates, HRD stands to gain the most influence in the organizational system. If HRD focuses only on learning or individuals, then it is likely to end up marginalized as a staff support group.

CONCLUSION

While it would be naive to think that the performance and learning paradigms would ever converge, it is important to realize that there may be much more common ground than has been stated by learning advocates. Further scholarly research and debate are needed to articulate the similarities as well as the differences more clearly. This chapter is a step in that direction as we have attempted to define core assumptions of each paradigm in order to discuss differences and common ground more accurately. In the end we believe HRD is probably best served by the integration of the two paradigms.

REFLECTION QUESTIONS

1. Which paradigm do you feel most comfortable with and would you adopt as your own personal belief system?

2. Do you see the learning and performance paradigms as competing paradigms or as mutually reinforcing?

3. How can HRD operate from a performance paradigm and ensure that human development is honored and supported?

4. How can HRD operate from a learning paradigm and play a core strategic role in organizations?

5. How would an employee, an employee's manager, and a corporate CEO view this issue?

6 If knowledge and expertise are now considered a competitive advantage for many organizations, how would knowledge management fit into these paradigms?

Perspectives on Learning in HRD

Learning has always been at the heart of HRD, and it continues to be a core part of all paradigms of HRD. Whatever the debates about paradigms of HRD, nobody has ever suggested that HRD not embrace learning as an organizing construct for the field. In this chapter we take a closer look at some representative theories and research on learning in HRD. First, five metatheories of learning are discussed. Then, representative middle-range learning theories at the individual and organizational level are reviewed. The purpose of this chapter is to provide not a comprehensive review but rather key foundational perspectives.

METATHEORIES OF LEARNING

In chapter 5, two metatheories of learning, behaviorism and cognitivism, were introduced as being core parts of our theory of HRD. Figure 7.1 provides a summary of metatheories of learning for HRD, which include humanism, social learning, and constructivism as well as behaviorism and cognitivism. These five are metatheories because they apply to learning in all settings, for all age groups, and for all types of learning events. In this section, each metatheory is described along with its primary contribution to HRD. Each has been the subject of extensive thinking, writing and research.

Figure 7.1 clearly shows that each approach represents a fundamentally different view of learning. Each would define learning differently, prescribe different roles for the teacher, and seek different outcomes from learning. Each has made a substantial contribution to learning in human resource development, and will continue to inform practice. This section provides only a brief summary of each. Readers interested in a more thorough presentation are encouraged to consult Ormond (1999), Hergenhahn and Olson (1997), or Merriam and Cafferella (1999).

It is important to realize that very few HRD professionals or HRD interventions utilize only one of these metatheories. Most are quite eclectic, using a combination of approaches that fit the particular situation. Thus, these five approaches should not be read as either-or choices but rather as five different approaches to be drawn upon as appropriate to your particular needs. They are presented here in their more pure form to enhance your understanding of each. However, in practice they are usually adapted and blended to accomplish specific objectives. Your challenge is to understand them so as to make sound judgments about which to utilize in a given situation. It is important not to reject any single theory as each one has its strengths and weaknesses.

Behaviorism

Behaviorists are primarily concerned with changes in behavior as a result of learning. Behaviorism has a long and rich history, having been originally developed by John Watson, who introduced the term in 1913 and developed it in the early twentieth century (Ormond, 1999). Six prominent learning theorists are mostly commonly included in this school: Ivan Pavlov, Edward L. Thorndike, John B. Watson, Edwin R. Guthrie, Clark L. Hull, and B. F. Skinner. Pavlov and Skinner are the best-known contributors, with Pavlov having developed the classical conditioning model and Skinner the operant conditioning model. While each of these six men had different views of behaviorism, Ormond (1999) identifies seven core assumptions that they share:

1. Principles of learning apply equally to different behaviors and to different species of animals.
2. Learning processes can be studied most objectively when the focus of study is on stimulus and response.

Figure 7.1 Five Orientations to Learning

Aspect	Behaviorist	Cognitivist	Humanist	Social Learning	Constructivist
Learning theorists	Thorndike, Pavlov, Watson, Guthrie, Hull, Tolman, Skinner	Koffka, Kohler, Lewin, Piaget, Ausubel, Bruner, Gagne	Maslow, Rogers	Bandura, Rotter	Candy, Dewey, Lave, Piaget, Rogoff, von Glaserfeld, Vygotsky
View of the learning process	Change in behavior	Internal mental process (including insight, information processing, memory, perception)	A personal act to fulfill potential	Interaction with and observation of others in a social context	Construction of meaning from experience
Locus of learning	Stimuli in the environment	Internal cognitive structuring	Affective and cognitive needs	Interaction of person, behavior and environment	Internal construction of reality by individual
Purpose of education	Produce behavioral change in desired direction	Develop capacity and skills to learn better	Become self-actualized, autonomous	Model new roles and behavior	Construct knowledge
Teacher's role	Arranges environment to elicit desired response	Structures content of learning activity	Facilitates development of whole person	Models and guides new roles and behavior	Facilitates and negotiates meaning with learner
Manifestation in adult learning	• Behavioral objectives • Competency-based education • Skill development • Skill development and training	• Cognitive development • Intelligence, learning, and memory as function of age • Learning how to learn	• Andragogy • Self-directed learning	• Socialization • Social roles • Mentoring • Locus of control	• Experiential learning • Self-directed learning • Perspective transformation • Reflective practice

Source: Merriam and Caffarella (1999, p. 264). Used with permission.

3. Internal cognitive processes are largely excluded from scientific study.
4. Learning involves a behavior change.
5. Organisms are born as blank slates.
6. Learning is largely the result of environmental events.
7. The most useful theories tend to be parsimonious ones.

As discussed earlier, behaviorists put primary emphasis on how the external environment influences a person's behavior and learning. Rewards and incentives play a key role in building motivation to learn. In classic behaviorism, the role of the learning facilitator is to structure the environment to elicit the desired response from the learner.

Behaviorism has played a central role in human resource development. Its key contributions include the following:

- *Focus on behavior.* The focus on behavior is important because performance change does not occur without changing behavior. Although behavior change alone without internal cognitive changes is usually not desirable, neither is cognitive change alone. Thus, behaviorism has led to popular practices such as behavioral objectives and competency-based education.

- *Focus on the environment.* Behaviorism reminds us of the central role the external environment plays in shaping human learning and performance. An individual in an organization is subjected to a number of factors (e.g., rewards and incentives, supports, etc.) that will influence their performance. As discussed in chapter 5, behaviorism thus provides the link between psychology and economics in HRD.

- *Foundation for transfer of learning.* Behaviorism also provides part of the foundation for transfer of learning research. Transfer of learning is concerned with how the environment impacts the use of learning on the job. Transfer research (e.g., Rouiller & Goldstein, 1993) shows that the environment is at least as important, if not more important, than learning in predicting use of learning on the job.

- *Foundation for skill development training.* As indicated in Figure 7.1, behaviorism has provided much of the foundation for skill or competency oriented training and development. Behavioral objectives are another contribution from behaviorists.

Behaviorism has also been heavily criticized, primarily by adult educators who prefer a more humanistic and constructivist perspective. The chief criticism is that behaviorism views the learner as being passive and dependent. In addition, behaviorism does not account for the role of personal insight and meaning in learning. These are legitimate criticisms and explain why behaviorism is rarely the only learning theory employed. On the other hand, there are training interventions that are appropriately taught in a behavioral approach. For example, teaching police officers how to respond when attacked is an appropriate use of behavioral methods because officers have to respond instinctively.

Behavioristic interventions are also objectionable to some HRD professionals because they find it offensive at a value level. This is particularly true of those who favor an adult learning perspective that abhors external control over a person's learning process. We believe that there are legitimate uses of behaviorism, but only when the situation warrants this type of learning. We question the objections in training such as the police example or in situations where certification of skills externally mandated is essential for safety. For example, airplane pilots, chemical plant operators, and nuclear plant operators all must pass rigorous certification programs that are behavioristic but that few of us would want changed.

Cognitivism

Cognitivism arose as a direct response to the limits of behaviorism, particularly the "thoughtless" approach to human learning. The early roots can be traced back to the 1920s and 1930s through the work of Edward Tolman, the Gestalt psychologists of Germany, Jean Piaget, and Lev Vygotsky (Ormond 1999). However, contemporary cognitivism did not begin to appear until the 1950s and 1960s. Ormond (1999) identifies seven core assumptions of contemporary cognitivism:

1. Some learning processes may be unique to human beings.
2. Cognitive processes are the focus of study.
3. Objective, systematic observations of people's behavior should be the focus of scientific inquiry; however, inferences about unobservable mental processes can often be drawn from such behavior.
4. Individuals are actively involved in the learning process.
5. Learning involves the formation of mental associations that are not necessarily reflected in overt behavior changes.
6. Knowledge is organized.
7. Learning is a process of relating new information to previously learned information.

Cognitivists are primarily concerned with insight and understanding. They see people not as passive and shaped by their environment but as capable of actively shaping the environment. Furthermore, they focus on the internal process of acquiring, understanding, and retaining learning. Because of that, they suggest that the focus of the learning facilitator should be on structuring the content and the learning activity so learners can acquire information optimally.

Gestalt theory, mentioned in chapter 5, is one type of cognitivist theory. Some very well-known names within HRD fit under this umbrella, including Kurt Lewin (organization development), Jean Piaget (cognitive development), Jerome Bruner (discovery learning), and Robert Gagne (instructional design). Contemporary cognitivism can be thought of as having three perspectives: information-processing theory, constructivism, and contextual views (situated cognition).

Cognitivism has made significant contributions to HRD and adult learning. Some key ones include the following:

- *Information processing.* Central to cognitivism is the concept of the human mind as an information processor. Figure 7.2 shows a basic schematic view of the human information processing system. Notice that there are three key components: sensory memory, short-term memory, and long-term memory. Cognitivists are particularly concerned with the processes shown by arrows in this schematic. These arrows represent the mental processes of moving information from sensory memory to short-term memory, and from short-term memory to long-term memory, and retrieving information from long-term memory.

- *Metacognition.* Along with these basic information-processing components, cognitivism also focuses on how individuals control their cognitive processes, which is called metacognition. This concept is more commonly known in HRD and adult learning as "learning how to learn."

- *Cognitive development.* Another important contribution has been the focus on how cognition develops over the life span. It is now generally accepted that cognitive development continues throughout adulthood. Chapter 13 will discuss adult cognitive development in more detail.

Cognitivism has not received the same degree of criticism that behaviorism has. For the most part, cognitivism has made important contributions and is

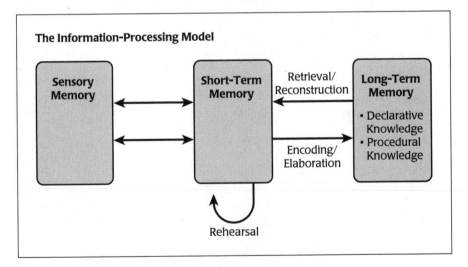

The Information-Processing Model

Sensory Memory ⟷ Short-Term Memory ⟷ Retrieval/Reconstruction ← Long-Term Memory
- Declarative Knowledge
- Procedural Knowledge

Encoding/Elaboration

Rehearsal

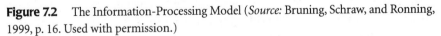

Figure 7.2 The Information-Processing Model (*Source:* Bruning, Schraw, and Ronning, 1999, p. 16. Used with permission.)

widely utilized in HRD. At the same time, it is viewed in some circles as incomplete because it views the human mind as too mechanical.

Humanism

Humanism did not emerge as a learning metatheory but rather as a general approach to psychology. The work of Abraham Maslow (1968, 1970) and Carl Rogers (1961) provides the core of humanistic psychology. Buhler (1971), a leading humanistic psychologist (Lundin, 1991) suggests that the core assumptions of humanism are as follows:

1. The person as a *whole* is the main subject of humanistic psychology.
2. Humanistic psychology is concerned with the knowledge of a person's entire life history.
3. Human existence and intention are also of great importance.
4. Life goals are of equal importance.
5. Human creativity has a primary place.
6. Humanistic psychology is frequently applied to psychotherapy.

Rogers (1980) put forth his principles of significant learning by saying that such learning must have the following characteristics:

- *Personal involvement:* The affective and cognitive aspects must come from within.
- *Self-initiated:* A sense of discovery must come from within.
- *Pervasive:* The learning makes a difference in the behavior, the attitudes, and perhaps even the personality of the learner.
- *Evaluated by the learner:* The learner can best determine whether the learning experience is meeting a need.
- *Essence is meaning:* When experiential learning takes place, its meaning to the learner becomes incorporated into the total experience.

Humanism adds yet another dimension to learning and has dominated much of adult learning. It is most concerned with development by the whole person and places a great deal of emphasis on the affective component of the learning process largely overlooked by other learning theories. The learning facilitator has to take into account the whole person and his or her life situation in planning the learning experience. Humanists view individuals as seeking self-actualization through learning and of being capable of controlling their own learning process. Adult learning theories, particularly andragogy, best represent it in HRD. In addition, self-directed learning and much of career development are grounded in humanism. (Andragogy will be discussed in much more detail in the next section.)

In many respects, humanism is absolutely central to the field of human resource development. If humans are not viewed as motivated to develop and improve, then some of the core premises of HRD disappears. At the same time, humanism is also a primary source of debate within the field because the performance paradigm is viewed by some as violating the humanistic tenants of the field. As we have stated, we do not believe they are contradictory. However, if a person believes completely in the humanistic view of learning, then allowing for behavioral components in the learning process is uncomfortable. We prefer to see them coexist.

Social Learning

Social learning focuses on how people learn by interacting with and observing other people. This type of learning focuses on the social context in which learning occurs. Some people view social learning as a special type of behaviorism because it reflects how individuals learn from people in their environment. Others view it as a separate metatheory because the learner is also actively making meaning of the interactions.

A foundational contribution of social learning is that people can learn vicariously by imitating others. Thus, central to social learning processes is that people learn from role models. This was in direct contradiction to behaviorists who said that learners had to perform themselves and be reinforced for learning to occur. Thus, the facilitator must model new behaviors and guide learners in learning from others. Albert Bandura is probably the best-known name in this area. It was his works in the 1960s and extending through the 1980s that fully developed social learning theory.

Ormond (1999) lists four core assumptions of social learning theory:

1. People can learn by observing the behaviors of others and the outcomes of those behaviors.
2. Learning can occur without a change in behavior.
3. The consequences of behavior play a role in learning.
4. Cognition plays a role in learning.

Social learning also occupies a central place in HRD. One contribution is in classroom learning in which social learning focuses on the role of the facilitator as a model for behaviors to be learned. Facilitators often underestimate their influence as a role model and forget to utilize role modeling as part of their instructional plan.

Social learning may make its biggest contribution through nonclassroom learning. One area is in new employee development, in which socialization processes account for the largest portion of new employee development (Holton, 1996c; Holton & Russell, 1999). *Socialization* is the process by which organizations pass on the culture of the organization to new employees and teach them how to be effective in the organization. It is an informal process that occurs through social interactions between new employees and organizational members. Another key area is mentoring, which is a primary means of on-the-job development in many organizations. It is often used to develop new managers. This is clearly a social learning process as mentors teach and coach protégés. Yet another key area is on-the-job training whereby newcomers learn their jobs from job incumbents, in part by direct instruction but also by observing the incumbent and using the incumbent as a role model.

There are few critics of social learning as it mostly contributes to learning theory in HRD without inciting any sharp arguments. Social learning is widely accepted as an effective and important learning process. When properly applied, it enhances learning and contributes learning that often cannot occur in the classroom.

Constructivism

While controversial, especially in its more radical versions, constructivism is emerging as a useful perspective for some adult learning situations (Wiswell & Ward, 1987). Constructivism stresses that all knowledge is context bound and that individuals make personal meaning of their learning experiences. Thus, learning cannot be separated from the context in which it is used. It also emphasizes the cumulative nature of learning. That is, new information must be related to other existing information in order for learners to retain and utilize it. For adults, experience might be conceptualized as creating a giant funnel of previous knowledge, whereby new information that enters the top of the funnel cascades downward and eventually falls out unless it "sticks" to some element of prior knowledge. The facilitator's role is to help learners make meaning of new information.

Many learning theorists, including Ormond (1999), do not view constructivism as a separate metatheory but rather as a special type of cognitivism. Adult learning theorists (e.g., Merriam & Cafferella, 1999) are more inclined to differentiate it from cognitivism because of its importance for adult learning.

The contributions of constructivism to HRD are still emerging. The emphasis on how adults make meaning of new information by relating it to previous experience largely support the andragogical view of learning (Knowles et al., 1998). In fact, the parallels between moderate views of contructivism and andragogy are rather striking. Both stress ownership of the learning process by learners, experiential learning, and problem-solving approaches to learning. However, andragogy and the more extreme views of constructivism are not compatible. Constructivism plays an important role in understanding informal and incidental learning, self-directed learning, and perspective transformation.

Summary

Most learning theories in HRD can be embedded in one or a blend of these five metatheories of learning. Each metatheory makes unique contributions and adds power to learning practice in HRD. Readers are advised to understand and master each so that they can be employed in appropriate situations. We reiterate that no one approach is best, but in any given situation one or a combination of approaches is likely to be most powerful.

MIDDLE-RANGE LEARNING MODELS AT THE INDIVIDUAL LEVEL

This section reviews four middle-range models of learning. First, andragogy is discussed as a core adult learning model that has played a central role in adult learning within HRD. Also, the andragogy in practice model (Knowles et al., 1998; Holton, Swanson, & Naquin, 2001) is presented as a more comprehensive elaboration of andragogy. Next, Kolb's experiential learning model is considered, followed by informal and incidental learning. Last, transformational learning is discussed.

Andragogy: The Adult Learning Perspective

In the late 1960s when Knowles introduced andragogy in the United States, the idea was groundbreaking and sparked much subsequent research and controversy. Since the earliest days, adult educators have debated what andragogy really is (Henschke, 1998). Spurred in part by the need for a defining theory within the field of adult education, andragogy has been extensively analyzed and critiqued. It has been alternately described as a set of guidelines (Merriam, 1993), a philosophy (Pratt, 1993), and a set of assumptions (Brookfield, 1986). Davenport and Davenport (1985) note that andragogy has been called a theory of adult learning/education, a method or technique of adult education, and a set of assumptions about adult learners. The disparity of these positions is indicative of the perplexing nature of andragogy. But, regardless of what it is called, "it is an honest attempt to focus on the learner. In this sense, it does provide an alternative to the methodology-centered instructional design perspective" (Feur & Gerber, 1988).

Despite years of critique, debate, and challenge, the core principles of adult learning advanced by andragogy have endured (Davenport & Davenport, 1985; Hartree, 1984; Pratt, 1988), and few adult learning scholars would disagree with the observation that Knowles's ideas sparked a revolution in adult education and training (Feur & Gerber, 1988). Brookfield (1986), positing a similar view, asserts that andragogy is the "single most popular idea in the education and training of adults" (p. 91). Adult educators and HRD professionals, particularly beginning ones, find them invaluable in shaping the learning process to be more effective with adults.

The Core Andragogical Model

Popularized by Knowles (1968), the original andragogical model presents core principles of adult learning and important assumptions about adult learners. These core principles of adult learning are believed to enable those designing and conducting adult learning to design more effective learning processes for adults. The model is a transactional model (Brookfield, 1986) in that it speaks to the characteristics of the learning transaction. As such, it is applicable to any adult learning transaction, from community education to human resource development in organizations.

Depending on which citation is consulted, various authors present andragogy in different ways. Accordingly, it has often been difficult to ascertain both the number and content of the core principles of andragogy. This difficulty stems from the fact that the number of andragogical principles has grown from four to six over the years as Knowles refined his thinking (Knowles, 1989). The addition of assumptions and the discrepancy in the number cited in the literature has led to some confusion (see Holton et al., 2001, for a complete review of the history of the andragogical assumptions). The current six core assumptions or principles of andragogy (Knowles et al., 1998) are as follows:

1. Adults need to know why they need to learn something before learning it.

2. The self-concept of adults is heavily dependent on a move toward self-direction.

3. Prior experiences of the learner provide a rich resource for learning

4. Adults typically become ready to learn when they experience a need to cope with a life situation or perform a task.

5. Adults' orientation to learning is life centered, and they see education as a process of developing increased competency levels to achieve their full potential.

6. The motivation for adult learners is internal rather than external.

These core principles provide a sound foundation for planning adult learning experiences. Absent any other information, they offer an effective approach to adult learning.

The second part of the andragogical model is what Knowles (1995, 1984) called the *andragogical process design* for creating adult learning experiences. Originally, he presented this as seven steps (Knowles 1984, 1990). Recently, he added a new first step, preparing learners for the program, which brought the total to eight steps (Knowles, 1995):

1. Preparing learners for the program

2. Establishing a climate conducive to learning

3. Involving learners in mutual planning

4. Involving participants in diagnosing their learning needs

5. Involving learners in forming their learning objectives

6. Involving learners in designing learning plans

7. Helping learners carry out their learning plans

8. Involving learners in evaluating their learning outcomes

Figure 7.3 shows the andragogical process elements and andragogical approaches as presented and updated by Knowles (1992, 1995).

Integrated System or Flexible Assumptions?

In early works, Knowles presented andragogy as an integrated set of assumptions. However, following years of experimentation, it now seems that the power of andragogy lies in its potential for more flexible application. As others have noted (Brookfield, 1986; Feuer & Geber, 1988; Pratt, 1998), over the years the assumptions became viewed by some practitioners as somewhat of a recipe implying that all adult educators should facilitate the same in all situations. Clear evidence indicates that Knowles intended for them to be viewed as flexible assumptions to be altered depending on the situation. Knowles (1984) reiterated this point in the conclusion to his casebook examining thirty-six applications of andragogy. He noted that he had spent two decades experimenting with andragogy and had reached certain conclusions, including these:

Figure 7.3   Process Elements of Andragogy

Element	*Andragogical Approach*
Preparing learners	Provide information Prepare for participation Help develop realistic expectations Begin thinking about content
Climate	Relaxed, trusting Mutually respectful Informal, warm Collaborative, supportive
Planning	Mutually by learners and facilitator
Diagnosis of needs	By mutual assessment
Setting of objectives	By mutual negotiation
Designing learning plans	Learning contracts Learning projects Sequenced by readiness
Learning activities	Inquiry projects Independent study Experiential techniques
Evaluation	Learner-collected evidence validated by peers, facilitators, and experts Criterion referenced

Source: Developed from Knowles and Knowles (1992, 1995).

1. The andragogical model is a system of elements that can be adopted or adapted in whole or in part. It is not an ideology that must be applied totally and without modification. In fact, an essential feature of andragogy is flexibility.

2. The appropriate starting point and strategies for applying the andragogical model depend on the situation. (p. 418)

More recently, Knowles (1989) states in his autobiography, "So I accept (and glory in) the criticism that I am a philosophical eclectic or situationalist who applies his philosophical beliefs differentially to different situations. I see myself as being free from any single ideological dogma, and so I don't fit neatly into any of the categories philosophers often want to box people in" (p. 112). He further says that "what this means in practice is that we educators now have the responsibility to check out which assumptions are realistic in a given situation" (Knowles, 1990, p. 64).

It seems clear that Knowles always knew, and then confirmed through use, that andragogy could be utilized in many different ways and would have to be adapted to fit individual situations. Unfortunately, he never offered a systematic framework of factors that should be considered when determining which assumptions are realistic in order to adapt andragogy to the situation. As a result, the andragogical assumptions about adults have been criticized for appearing to claim to fit all situations or persons (Davenport, 1987; Davenport & Davenport, 1985; Day & Baskett, 1982; Elias, 1979; Hartree, 1984; Tennant, 1986). While a more careful read of Knowles's work shows that he did not believe this, andragogy is nonetheless open to this criticism because it fails to account for the differences explicitly.

Several researchers have offered alternative contingency models in an effort to account for the variations in adult learning situations. For example, Pratt (1988) proposes a useful model of how the adult's life situation affects not only their readiness to learn but also their readiness for andragogical-type learning experiences. He recognizes that most learning experiences are highly situational and that a learner may exhibit very different behaviors in different learning situations. For example, it is entirely likely that a learner may be highly confident and self-directed in one realm of learning but very dependent and unsure in another. Pratt operationalizes this by identifying two core dimensions within which adults vary in each learning situation: direction and support.

Cross's (1981) Characteristics of Adult Learners (CAL) model also embodies a range of individual characteristics as well as some situational characteristics. Pratt (1998) discusses five different perspectives on teaching based on an international study of 253 teachers of adults. Grow (1991) also offers a contingency framework for self-directed learning.

The Andragogy in Practice Model
Andragogy in practice, the framework depicted in Figure 7.4, is an enhanced conceptual framework to apply andragogy more systematically across multiple

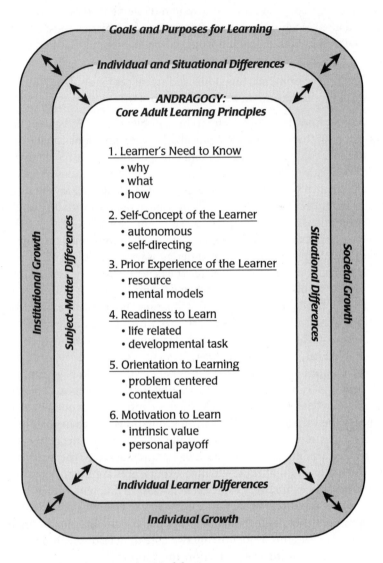

Figure 7.4 Andragogy in Practice Model

domains of adult learning practice (Holton et al., 2001; Knowles et al., 1998). The three dimensions of andragogy in practice, shown as rings in the figure, are (1) goals and purposes for learning, (2) individual and situational differences, and (3) andragogy: core adult learning principles.

In contrast to the traditional model of andragogy, this approach conceptually integrates the additional influences with the core adult learning principles. The three rings of the model interact, allowing the model to offer a three-dimensional process for adult learning situations. The result is a model that recognizes the lack of homogeneity among learners and learning situations and illustrates that the learning transaction is a multifaceted activity. This approach is entirely consistent with most of the program development literature in adult education that in some manner incorporates contextual analysis as a step in developing programs (e.g., Houle, 1972; Knox, 1986; Boone, 1985).

Goals and Purposes for Learning   Goals and purposes for learning, the outer ring of the model, are portrayed as developmental outcomes. The goals and purposes of adult learning serve to shape and mold the learning experience. In this model, goals for adult learning events may fit into three general categories: *individual, institutional,* or *societal.* Knowles (1970, 1980) used these three categories to describe the missions of adult education, though he did not directly link them to the andragogical assumptions. Beder (1989) employed a similar approach to describe the purposes of adult education as facilitating change in society and supporting and maintaining good social order (societal), promoting productivity (institutional), and enhancing personal growth (individual).

Merriam and Brockett (1997) discuss seven content-purpose typologies (Bryson, 1936; Grattan, 1955; Liveright, 1968; Darkenwald & Merriam, 1982; Apps, 1985; Rachal, 1988; Beder, 1989), using Bryson's (1936) five-part typology (liberal, occupational, relational, remedial, and political), noting that the purposes for adult learning have changed little since then. Bryson's (1936) typology would also fit into Knowles's three-part typology with liberal, relational, and remedial fitting into the individual category; occupational fitting into the institutional category; and political fitting into the societal category. Thus, Knowles's three-category typology can be seen as also encompassing all of the categories found in other major typologies of purposes for adult learning.

Individual growth. The traditional view among most scholars and practitioners of adult learning is to think exclusively of individual growth. Representative researchers in this group might include some mentioned earlier such as Mezirow (1991) and Brookfield (1987, 1984). Others advocate an individual development approach to workplace adult learning programs (Bierema, 1997; Dirkx, 1997). At first glance, andragogy would appear to fit best with individual development goals because of its focus on the individual learner.

Institutional growth. Adult learning is equally powerful in developing better institutions, as well as individuals. Human resource development, for example, embraces organizational performance as one of its core goals (Brethower & Smalley, 1998; Swanson & Arnold, 1996), which andragogy does not explicitly embrace, either. From this view of human resource development, the ultimate goal of learning activities is to improve the institution sponsoring the learning activity. Thus, control of the goals and purposes is shared between the organization and the individual. The adult learning transaction in an HRD setting still fits nicely within the andragogical framework, although the different goals require adjustments to be made in how the andragogical assumptions are applied.

Societal growth. Societal goals and purposes that can be associated with the learning experience are illustrated through Paulo Freire's work (1970). This Brazilian educator sees the goals and purposes of adult education as societal transformation, contending that education is a consciousness-raising process. He says that the aim of education is to help participants put knowledge into practice and that the outcome of education is societal transformation. Freire is clearly concerned with creating a better world and the development and liberation of people. As such, the goals and purposes within this learning context are oriented to societal as well as individual improvement.

Individual and Situational Differences   Individual and situational differences, the middle ring of the andragogy in practice model, are portrayed as variables. We continue to learn more about the differences that impact adult learning and which act as filters that shape the practice of andragogy. These variables are grouped into the categories of *individual learner differences, subject-matter differences,* and *situational differences.*

Subject-matter differences. Different subject matter may require different learning strategies. For example, individuals may be less likely to learn complex technical subject matter in a self-directed manner. Or, as Knowles stated in the earlier quote, introducing unfamiliar content to a learner will require a different teaching/learning strategy. Simply, not all subject matter can be taught or learned in the same way.

Situational differences. The situational effects category captures any unique factors that could arise in a particular learning situation and incorporates several sets of influences. At the microlevel, different local situations may dictate different teaching/learning strategies. For example, learners in remote locations may be forced to be more self-directed, or perhaps less so. At a broader level, this group of factors connects andragogy with the sociocultural influences now accepted as a core part of each learning situation. This is one area of past criticism that seems particularly appropriate.

Jarvis (1987) sees all adult learning as occurring within a social context through life experiences. In his model, the social context may include social influences prior to the learning event that affect the learning experience, as well as the social milieu within which the actual learning occurs. Thus, situational influences before the learning event could include anything from cultural influences to learning history. Similarly, situational influences during learning can be seen as including the full range of social, cultural, and situation-specific factors that may alter the learning transaction.

Individual differences. The last decade has witnessed a surge of interest in linking the adult education literature with psychology to advance our understanding of how individual differences affect adult learning. Analyzing psychological theories from an adult learning perspective, Tennant (1997) argues for psychology as a foundation discipline of adult education. Interestingly, a group of educational psychologists have recently argued for building a bridge between educational psychology and adult learning, calling for creation of a new subfield of adult educational psychology (Smith & Pourchot, 1998).

This may be the area in which our understanding of adult learning has advanced the most since Knowles first introduced andragogy. A number of researchers have expounded on a host of individual differences affecting the learning process (e.g., Dirkx & Prenger, 1997; Kidd, 1978; Merriam & Cafferella, 1999). This increased emphasis on linking adult learning and psychological research is indicative of an increasing focus on how individual differences affect adult learning. From this perspective, there is no reason to expect all adults to behave the same, but rather our understanding of individual differences should help shape and tailor the andragogical approach to fit the uniqueness of the learners.

Jonassen and Grabowski (1993) present a typology of individual differences that impact on learning incorporating three broad categories of individual differences: *cognitive* (including cognitive abilities, controls, and styles), *personality,* and *prior knowledge.* Figure 7.5 shows their list of individual differences that may impact on learning.

Another area of individual differences in which our understanding is expanding rapidly is adult development. Adult development will be discussed more thoroughly in chapter 13.

An understanding of individual differences helps make andragogy more effective in practice. Effective adult learning professionals use their understanding of individual differences to devise adult learning experiences in several ways. First, they tailor the manner in which they apply the core principles to fit adult learners' cognitive abilities and learning style preferences. Second, they use them to know which of the core principles are most salient to a specific group of learners. For example, if learners do not have strong cognitive controls, they may not initially emphasize self-directed learning. Third, they employ them to expand the goals of learning experiences. For example, one goal might be to expand learners' cognitive controls and styles to enhance future learning ability. This flexible approach explains why andragogy is applied in so many different ways (Knowles, 1984).

Applying the Andragogy in Practice Framework

The andragogy in practice framework is an expanded conceptualization of andragogy that incorporates domains of factors that will influence the application of core andragogical principles. We suggest a three-part process for analyzing adult learners:

1. The core principles of andragogy provide a sound foundation for planning adult learning experiences. Without any other information, they reflect the sound approach to effective adult learning.

2. Analysis should be conducted to understand (a) the particular adult learners and their individual characteristics, (b) the characteristics of the

Cognitive
1. General Mental Abilities
   • Hierarchical abilities (fluid, crystallized, and spatial)

2. Primary Mental Abilities
   • Products
   • Operations
   • Content

3. Cognitive Controls
   • Field dependence/independence
   • Field articulation
   • Cognitive tempo
   • Focal attention
   • Category width
   • Cognitive complexity/simplicity
   • Strong versus weak automatization

4. Cognitive Styles: Information Gathering
   • Visual/haptic
   • Visualizer/verbalizer
   • Leveling/sharpening

5. Cognitive Styles: Information Organizing
   • Serialist/holist
   • Conceptual style

6. Learning Styles
   • Hill's cognitive style mapping
   • Kolb's learning styles
   • Dunn and Dunn learning styles
   • Grasha-Reichman learning styles
   • Gregorc learning styles

Personality
7. Personality: Attentional and Engagement Styles
   • Anxiety
   • Tolerance for unrealistic expectations
   • Ambiguity tolerance
   • Frustration tolerance

8. Personality: Expectancy and Incentive Styles
   • Locus of control
   • Introversion/extraversion
   • Achievement motivation
   • Risk taking versus cautiousness

Prior Knowledge
9. Prior knowledge
   • Prior knowledge and achievement
   • Structural knowledge

Figure 7.5 Individual Learner Differences (*Source:* Jonassen and Grabowski, 1993.)

subject matter, and (c) the characteristics of the particular situation in which adult learning is being used. Adjustments necessary to the core principles should be anticipated.

3. The goals and purposes for which the adult learning is conducted provide a frame that puts shape to the learning experience. They should be clearly identified and possible effects on adult learning explicated.

This framework should be used in advance to conduct what we call *andragogical learner analysis*. As part of needs assessment for program development, andragogical learner analysis is used to determine the extent to which andragogical principles fit a particular situation (see Holton et al., 2001, for more details on applying the model).

Experiential Learning Model

Kolb (1984) has been a leader in advancing the practice of experiential learning. He defines learning as "the process whereby knowledge is created through transformation of experience" (p. 38). For Kolb, learning is not so much the acquisition or transmission of content as the interaction between content and experience, whereby each transforms the other. The educator's job, he says, is not only to transmit or implant new ideas but also to modify old ones that may get in the way of new ones.

Kolb bases his model of experiential learning on Lewin's problem-solving model of action research, which is widely used in organization development (Cummings & Worley, 2001). He argues that it is very similar to Dewey's and Piaget's as well. Kolb suggests that there are four steps in the experiential learning cycle (see Figure 7.6):

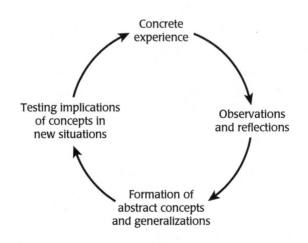

Figure 7.6   Kolb's Experiential Learning Model

1. *Concrete experience*—being fully involved in here-and-now experiences

2. *Observations and reflection*—reflecting on and observing their experiences from many perspectives

3. *Formation of abstract concepts and generalization*—creating concepts that integrate their observations into logically sound theories

4. *Testing implications of new concepts in new situations*—using these theories to make decisions and solve problems

Kolb goes on to suggest that these four modes combine to create four distinct learning styles.

Kolb's model has made a major contribution to the experiential learning literature by providing (1) a theoretical basis for experiential learning research and (2) a practical model for experiential learning practice. The four steps in his model are an invaluable framework for designing learning experiences for adults. At a macrolevel, programs and classes can be structured to include all four components, as well as, at a microlevel, units or lessons. Shown here are examples of learning strategies that may be useful in each step:

Kolb's Stage	Example Learning/Teaching Strategy
Concrete experience	Simulations, case studies, field trips, real experiences, demonstrations
Observe and reflect	Discussion, small groups, buzz groups, designated observers
Abstract conceptualization	Sharing content
Active experimentation	Laboratory experiences, on-the-job experiences, internships, practice sessions

Research on Kolb's model has focused mostly on learning styles he proposes. Unfortunately, research has done little to validate his theory, due in large part to methodological concerns about his instrument (Cornwell & Manfredo, 1994; Freedman & Stumpf, 1980; Kolb, 1981; Stumpf & Freedman, 1981).

Human resource development practitioners, while always valuing experience, are increasingly emphasizing experiential learning as a means to improve performance. Action reflection learning is one technique developed to focus on the learner's experiences and integrate experience into the learning process. Transfer of learning researchers are also focusing on experiential learning as a means to enhance transfer of learning into performance (Holton, Bates, Seyler, & Carvalho, 1997; Bates, Holton, & Seyler, 2000) and to increase motivation to learn (Seyler, Holton, & Bates, 1997). Structured on-the-job training (Jacobs & Jones, 1995) has emerged as a core method to capitalize more systematically on the value of experiential learning in organizations and as a tool to more effectively develop new employees through the use of experienced coworkers (Holton, 1996c). Experiential learning approaches have the dual benefit of appealing to the adult learner's experience base, as well as increasing the likelihood of performance change after training.

Informal and Incidental Learning

While many people think first of formal training in HRD, much of the learning that occurs in organizations happens outside formal training or learning events. Informal and incidental learning has deep roots in the work of Lindeman (1926) and Dewey's (1938) notion of learning from experience, although it was Knowles (1950) who introduced the term *informal learning* (Cseh, Watkins, & Marsick, 1999).

Watkins and Marsick (1992; Marsick & Watkins, 1990, 1997) and their associates have been responsible for much of the recent work on informal and incidental learning. They define the constructs in this way:

> *Formal learning* is typically institutionally-sponsored, classroom-based, and highly structured. *Informal learning*, a category which includes incidental learning, may occur in institutions, but is not typically classroom-based or highly structured, and control of learning rests primarily in the hands of the learner. *Incidental learning* is defined as a byproduct of some other activity, such as task accomplishment, interpersonal interaction, sensing the organizational culture, trial-and-error experimentation, or even formal learning. Informal learning can be deliberately encouraged by an organization or it can take place despite an environment not highly conductive to learning. Incidental learning, on the other hand, almost always takes place although people are not always conscious of it. (Marsick & Watkins, 1990, p. 12; emphasis added)

Thus, informal learning can be either intentional or incidental. Examples of informal learning include self-directed learning, mentoring, coaching, networking, learning from mistakes, trial and error, and so forth. Incidental learning can also lead to embedded assumptions, beliefs and attributions that can later become barriers to other learning. Argyris (1982) and Schon (1987) refer to *double-loop learning* (or *reflection in action*) as the learning process required to challenge the implicit or tacit knowledge that arises from incidental learning. Tacit knowledge is increasingly being recognized as an important source of knowledge for experts and innovation (Glynn, 1996).

Watkins and Marsick (1992; Cseh et al., 1999) have developed a model of informal and incidental learning, the most recent version of which is shown in Figure 7.7. This model clearly shows how the learning is embedded within the individual's daily work and is highly contextual. Furthermore, it indicates that learning occurs as a result of some trigger (internal or external) and an experience. This is in sharp contrast to the planned learning approach of formal learning events.

The question of whether informal or incidental learning can and should be facilitated is unsettled. On the one hand, it seems that there are efforts HRD organizations should use to facilitate the process. For example, Raelin (2000) suggests

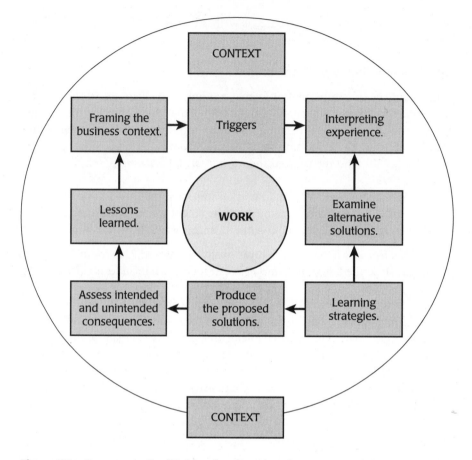

Figure 7.7 Reconceptualized Informal and Incidental Learning Model (1999) (*Source:* Cseh et al., 1999, p. 354. Used with permission.)

using action learning, communities of practice, action science, and learning teams in management development to encourage informal work-based learning. Piskurich (1993) takes a similar approach to self-directed learning, while Jacobs and Jones (1995) and Rothwell and Kasanas (1994) advocate a structured approach to on-the-job training. On the other hand, there is also a danger in attempting to overfacilitate informal and incidental learning to the point that it really becomes formal learning.

Transformational Learning

Transformational learning has gained increasing attention in HRD. The fundamental premise is that people, just like organizations, may engage in incremental learning or in deeper learning that requires them to challenge fundamental assumptions and meaning schema they have about the world. This concept has appeared in a variety of forms in the literature.

Rummerlhart and Norman (1978) propose three different modes of learning in relation to mental schema: *accreation, tuning,* and *restructuring.* Accretion and tuning involve no change or only incremental changes to a person's schemata. Restructuring entails the creation of new schema and is the hardest learning for most adults.

Argyris (1982) labels learning as either "single-" or "double-loop" learning. *Single-loop learning* is learning that fits prior experiences and existing values, which enables the learner to respond in an automatic way. *Double-loop learning* is learning that does not fit the learner's prior experiences or schema; generally it requires learners to change their mental schema in a fundamental way. Similarly, Schon (1987) talks about "knowing in action" and "reflection in action." *Knowing in action* is the somewhat automatic responses based on our existing mental schema that enable us to perform efficiently in daily actions. *Reflection in action* is the process of reflecting while performing to discover when existing schema are no longer appropriate, and changing those schema when appropriate.

Mezirow (1991) and Brookfield (1986, 1987) are leading advocates for transformational learning in the adult learning literature. Mezirow (1991) calls this *perspective transformation,* which he defines as "the process of becoming critically aware of how and why our assumptions have come to constrain the way we perceive, understand, and feel about our world; changing these structures of habitual expectation to make possible a more inclusive, discriminating, and integrative perspective; and finally, making choices or otherwise acting upon these new understandings" (p. 167).

The concept of deep transformational change is found throughout the HRD literature. It is easy to see that transformational change at the organization level (discussed in chapter 13) is not likely to happen unless transformational change occurs at the individual level through some process of critically challenging and changing internal cognitive structures. Furthermore, without engaging in deep learning through a double-loop or perspective transformation process, individuals will remain trapped in their existing mental models or schemata. It is only through critical reflection that emancipatory learning occurs and enables people to change their lives at a deep level. Thus, transformational change processes are vitally important to HRD.

MIDDLE-RANGE LEARNING MODELS AT THE ORGANIZATIONAL LEVEL

While individual learning has long dominated HRD practice, in the 1980s and particularly the 1990s, increased attention turned to learning at the organizational level. The literature refers to two related but different concepts: organizational learning and the learning organizations. A *learning organization* is a prescribed set of strategies that can be enacted to enable organizational learning. It is important to recognize that *organizational learning* is different and that the terms are not interchangeable.

Organizational learning is learning occurring at the system level rather than at the individual level (Dixon, 1992). It does not exclude the learning that occurs at the individual level, but it is greater than the sum of the learning at the individual level (Fiol & Lyles, 1985; Kim, 1993; Lundberg, 1989). Organizational learning is more specifically defined as "the intentional use of learning processes at the individual, group and system level to continuously transform the organization in a direction that is increasingly satisfying to its stakeholders" (Dixon, 1994). It is learning keenly perceived at the system level and it arises from processes surrounding the sharing of insights, knowledge, and mental models (Stata, 1989).

According to Kim (1993), the key element differentiating individual and organizational learning revolves around mental models. When individuals make their mental models explicit and organizational members develop and take on shared mental models, organizational learning is enabled. Learning becomes organizational learning when these cognitive outcomes, the new and shared mental models, are "embedded in members' minds, and in ... artifacts ... in the organizational environment" (Argyris & Schon, 1996). Organizational learning is embedded in the culture, organizational systems, and work procedures and processes.

The Learning Organization Strategy

The learning organization has been a focus of attention in the organizational literature in recent years. Interest in this organizational development (OD) intervention has been spurred by the constantly changing work and business environments, which have been prompted by technological advances, increased levels of competition, and globalization of industries. Senge and other researchers have described the characteristics of the learning organization and made suggestions for organizational implementation (Kline & Saunders, 1993; Marquardt, 1996; Pedler, Bourgoyne, & Boydell, 1991; Senge, 1990; Watkins & Marsick, 1993).

The dimensions commonly described in the literature as being associated with a learning organization are not new concepts, but their coordination into a system focused on organizational learning is. However, there is no single definition of what the learning organization is. Senge (1990) defines a *learning organization* as "a place where people are continually discovering how they create their reality" (p. 13). Watkins and Marsick (1993) define it as "one that learns continuously and transforms itself" (p. 8). A comprehensive definition of a learning organization is offered by Marquardt (1996): "an organization which learns powerfully and collectively and is continually transforming itself to better collect, manage, and use knowledge for corporate success. It empowers people within and outside the company to learn as they work. Technology is utilized to optimize both learning and productivity" (p. 19).

There appears to be some common recognition and agreement about the core characteristics of a learning organization. Researchers suggest that individuals and teams work toward the attainment of linked and shared goals, communication is open, information is available and shared, systems thinking is the norm, leaders are champions of learning, management practices support learning, learning is encouraged and rewarded, and new ideas are welcome (Marquardt, 1996; Senge, 1990; Watkins & Marsick, 1993). The learning outcomes found in a learning organization are expected to include experiential learning, team learning, second-loop learning, and shared meaning (Argyris, 1977; Argyris & Schon, 1978; Dodgson, 1993; Senge, 1990). As a result of this learning, organizations are believed to be capable of new ways of thinking.

Senge's Foundation Theory

Peter Senge (1990) is credited with popularizing the learning organization, even though considerable work was done on it in the 1980s. In laying out the foundation for his model of the learning organization, Senge (1992, 1993) speaks about the three levels of work required of organizations. The first level focused on the development, production, and marketing of products and services. This organizational task is dependent on the second level of work: the designing and development of the systems and processes for production. The third task undertaken by organizations centers around thinking and interacting. Senge (1993) claims that the first two levels of organizational work are affected by the quality of this third level. That is, the quality of the organizational thinking and interacting affects the organizational systems and processes, and the production and delivery of products and services. This belief places organizational thinking in a pivotal position affecting the ability of an organization to accomplish goals and perform effectively.

It is the third level of organizational work that Senge addresses with his concept of learning organizations. In defining a learning organization, he states, "We can build learning organizations, where people continually expand their capacity to create the results they truly desire, where new and expansive patterns of thinking are nurtured, where collective aspiration is set free, and where people are continually learning how to learn together" (1990, p. 3).

Senge (1990) suggests that organizations need to develop five core disciplines or capabilities to accomplish the following defined goals of a learning organization:

- Personal mastery
- Mental models
- Shared vision
- Team learning
- Systems thinking

Systems thinking, the fifth discipline, acts to integrate the other four disciplines. It is described as the ability to take a systems perspective of organizational reality. Senge (1990) discusses strategies that organizations can implement to develop and encourage the five core disciplines of a learning organization. The recommended strategies involve the following organizational variables: climate, leadership, management, human resource practices, organization mission, job attitudes, organizational culture, and organizational structure.

Watkins and Marsick's Perspective

Watkins and Marsick (1993) suggest that learning is a constant process and results in changes in knowledge, beliefs, and behaviors. They also believe that, in a learning organization, the learning process is a social one and takes place at the individual, group, and organizational levels. They propose six imperatives that form the basis for the organizational strategies recommended to promote learning:

1. Create continuous learning opportunities.
2. Promote inquiry and dialogue.
3. Encourage collaboration and team learning.
4. Establish systems to capture and share learning.
5. Empower people toward a collective vision.
6. Connect the organization to its environment.

Figure 7.8 shows the interrelationship of these six imperatives across the individual, team, and organizational levels.

These six imperatives are similar to the disciplines suggested by Senge (1990, 1994). Marquardt (1996) similarly focuses on a learning system composed of five linked and interrelated subsystems related to learning: the organization, people, knowledge, technology, and learning. Most theories of a learning organization appear to focus on the values of continuous learning, knowledge creation and sharing, systemic thinking, a culture of learning, flexibility and experimentation, and finally a people-centered view (Gephart, Marsick, Van Buren, & Spiro, 1996).

Learning Organization and Performance Outcomes

Much of the learning organization literature is conceptual and descriptive. While there are numerous descriptive accounts and suggestions about why the process works, we have few concrete descriptions about *how* it works to achieve performance improvement. Learning organizations perceive learning as the means to long-term performance improvement (Guns, 1996). However, there is little data supporting the claim that performance improvement is directly related to adoption of the learning organization's suggested behaviors or policies. One exception is recent evidence that firm performance is associated with those strategies (Ellinger, Ellinger, Yang, & Howton, 2000) and that learning organization strategies are related to perceived innovation (Holton & Kaiser, 2000).

LEARNING ORGANIZATION ACTION IMPERATIVES

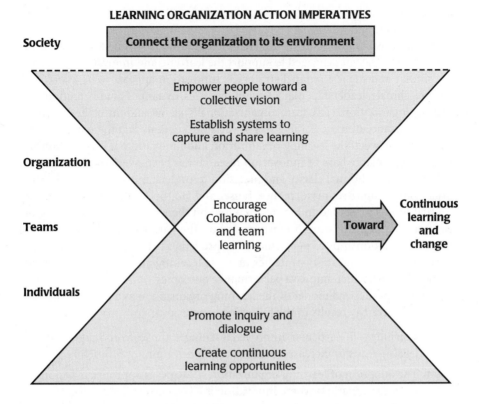

Figure 7.8 Watkins and Marsick's Learning Organization Action Imperatives (*Source:* Watkins and Marsick, 1993, p. 10. Used with permission.)

Kaiser and Holton (1999) suggest that innovation provides the critical link between learning organization strategies and performance. Just as the learning organization has been described as an organizational response to the dramatically changing work environment, so has innovation been described as finding its genesis in "shocks that may be either internal or external to an organization" (Van de Ven & Rogers, 1988, p. 644). Innovation is conceived as an organizational response to environmental change by Damanpour and Evan (1984) and by Brown and Duguid (1991). Put simply, innovation is a new idea (Galbraith, 1982; Van de Ven, 1986) that may be created by or adopted by the organization. The expected result is improvement in the achievement of goals and organizational performance (Damanpour, 1991; Damanpour & Evan, 1984).

The learning organization and the innovating organization are both dependent on the acquisition of information, the interpretation of information, the creation of meaning, and the creation of organizational knowledge. The stated end goal of both the learning system and the innovating system is improved organizational performance. The similarities between the two literatures are striking: the linking pin in both is knowledge; the goal in both is performance improvement.

A comparison of both literatures (Kaiser & Holton, 1999) suggests that the organizational strategies engaged to support the learning and innovating endeavors are similar and suggest parallel strategies. Innovation appears to be affected by culture, climate, leadership, management practices, dynamics of information processing, organizational structure, organizational systems, and the environment.

The existence of these parallel sets of variables suggests that there may be a relationship between the learning organization and innovation. If this relationship is true, then a large base of innovation research has been overlooked that would help provide additional clarity and precision to understanding how the learning organization improves performance. Kaiser and Holton (1999) propose the conceptual model presented in Figure 7.9 based on their review of the learning organization and innovation literatures and on the parallel sets of variables and theorized relationships to performance improvement. This model hypothesizes that learning organization strategies increase learning and innovation (performance drivers), which improve performance outcomes.

This hypothesized model of the learning organization as a performance improvement strategy results in the following conclusions:

- Learning—in particular, improved learning at the team and organizational levels—leads to increased organization innovation.

- The adoption of learning organization strategies is appropriate for organizations in markets where innovation is a key performance driver.

- Innovation is expected to result in improved performance outcomes, leading to competitive advantage for the organization.

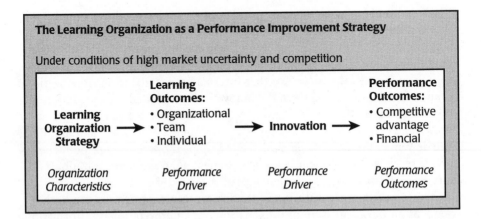

Figure 7.9 Learning Organization Performance Model (*Source:* Kaiser and Holton, 1999.)

CONCLUSION

The good news for HRD is that learning has never been as highly regarded in organizations as it is today. HRD is entrusted with developing the expertise in organizations to enable them to be competitive and effective in a challenging global economy. HRD must continue to research and define effective learning processes. While much is known about learning, much remains to be discovered about learning in the workplace.

REFLECTION QUESTIONS

1. If learning is a defining construct for the HRD discipline, how can learning be made more powerful in organizations?
2. Think about all the models or methods of learning that you know are advocated in HRD. Where do they fit into the metatheories of learning?
3. How can the andragogy in practice model be applied to enhance the application of adult learning in HRD?
4. Do you believe that organizations can learn? Or, are organizations merely the sum of individual learning?

Perspectives on Performance in HRD

CHAPTER OUTLINE

Disciplinary Perspectives on Performance
Individual-Level Performance Models
    Campbell's Taxonomy of Individual Performance
    Gilbert's Performance Engineering Model
Multilevel Performance Models
    Rummler and Brache's Performance Model
    Swanson's Performance Diagnosis Matrix
    Organization Development Performance Model
    Holton's Integrated Taxonomy of Performance Domains
Conclusion
Reflection Questions

This chapter examines core theories of performance that inform the performance perspective of HRD. Unlike learning theory, performance theory is a much more recent phenomenon. Whereas learning philosophy and theory can be traced back to Socrates and Plato, performance theory is very much a modern creation. Thus, readers should expect to find it much less developed and more diverse than learning theory.

One of the hallmarks of performance theories is that they all attempt to capture the complexity of organizational systems more completely while still presenting a set of constructs parsimonious enough to be usable. Organizational systems are complex enough that it is easy to develop a model that is so complex as to be unwieldy. Thus, each performance theory takes a particular perspective so as to define a more limited range of useful performance constructs while maintaining their integrity with system theory. Imagine picking up a crystal and turning it in the light—each perspective yields a slightly different view. Such is the case with performance theory as each theory is an attempt to capture adequate complexity but still be useful.

DISCIPLINARY PERSPECTIVES ON PERFORMANCE

HRD is not the only discipline that is interested in performance and performance improvement. To clarify perspectives of performance, a search was conducted for representative performance models in disciplines closely associated with HRD. The results, shown in Figure 8.1, are meant to be representative, not comprehensive.

Figure 8.1   Perspectives on Domain of Performance

Perspective	*Author*	*Domains of Performance/Analysis*
Performance improvement	Rummler and Brache (1995, 1990)	Organization Process Individual
HRD	Swanson (1994)	*Levels* Organization Process Individual *Measures of Outputs in Terms of:* Quantity Time Quality features
Human performance technology	Gilbert (1996)	Philosophical Cultural Policy (institutional) Strategic (role or job performance) Tactics (tasks) Logistics
Human performance technology	Kaufmann, Rojas, and Mayer (1993)	*Organizational Elements* *Model Results* Mega—outcomes impacting society and community Macro—outputs deliverable to society Micro—intermediate products delivered to internal clients *Means* Processes—means to produce the products Resources—inputs to the system (human, capital, materials, etc.)
		(Continued)

Figure 8.1 Continued

Perspective	Author	Domains of Performance/Analysis
Human performance technology	Tosti and Jackson (1987) as discussed in Silber (1992)	*Organizational Alignment Model* Organization People Work
Human performance technology	Langdon (1995)	Business unit Work groups Processes Individuals
Human performance technology	Silber (1992)	All organizations in society All organizations in system Whole organization One unit of organization
HRD Needs assessment	McGehee and Thayer (1961) Moore and Dutton (1978) Sleezer (1991)	Organizational Work/task Individual
HRD Needs assessment	Ostroff and Ford (1989)	*Levels* Organizational Subunit Individual *Content* Organizational Task Person
Psychology	Campbell (1990)	*Individual level* Job-specific task proficiency Nonspecific task proficiency Written and oral communication Demonstrating effort Maintaining personal discipline Facilitating peer and team performance Supervision Management/administration
Organization development	Cummings and Worley (1993)	Organizational Group Individual

(Continued)

Perspective	Author	Domains of Performance/Analysis
Organization development	Rashford and Coghlan (1994)	Organizational Interdepartmental group Face-to-face team Individual
Strategic management	Kaplan and Norton (1996)	Financial Customer Internal business process Learning and growth (employee based)
Strategic management	Porter (1980)	Society Industry Company
Strategic management	Hitt, Ireland, and Hoskisson (1997)	Corporate level Competitive dynamics Business level
Industrial engineering	Sink, Tuttle, and Devries (1984)	Nation Industry Firm Division Plant Function Department Work group Individual
Quality	Juran (1992)	Customer needs Product features Processes
Reengineering	Hammer and Champy (1993)	Process
Social responsibility	D. L. Swanson (1995a, 1995b)	Societal impacts Organizational ethical performance Individual ethical performance
HRM—performance management	Schneir (1995)	Company Work process Unit Team Individual

(Continued)

Figure 8.1 Continued

Perspective	Author	Domains of Performance/Analysis
HRM—general	Lewin and Mitchell (1995)	Firm Plant Individual
Economics—human capital	Becker[1] (1993)	Society/economy Firm Individual
Economics—macroeconomics	Case and Fair (1996)	Society/economy
Economics—microeconomics	Case and Fair (1996)	Markets Firm Individual
Intellectual capital	Edvinsson and Malone (1997)	Financial Customer Process Renewal and development Human focus
Strategic performance improvement	Hronec (1993)	*Quantum Performance* *Matrix Levels* Organization Process People *Measures* Cost Quality Time
Sociology—general	Kammeyer, Ritzer, and Yetman (1997)	Society Cultures Organizations Groups Individuals
Sociology—industrial	Hodson and Sullivan (1995)	Workplaces (firm) Occupation Industry Labor force Worker
Sociology—industrial	Ford (1988)	Macro (society, social systems, culture) Mezzo (organizations and associations) Micro (social groups, roles, and norms/rules)

[1]Derived from analysis of levels discussed in the book.

These models illustrate the diversity of performance perspectives and point to key considerations in performance theory:

- *Performance is a multidisciplinary phenomenon.* It should be apparent from Figure 8.1 that many different disciplines study performance. This search revealed performance models in a wide range of disciplines, including psychology, human resource management, ethics, quality, sociology, economics, strategic management, and industrial engineering. This wide range of disciplines is consistent with performance improvement competency models that indicate that a performance improvement professional must be proficient in skills drawn from multiple disciplines (Stolovich, Keeps, & Rodrigue, 1995).

- *Performance models have a disciplinary bias.* Each discipline has defined performance to fit its unique needs. For example, psychology, which focuses on individuals, has defined performance through the *individual* lens (Campbell, 1990). The quality movement, which focuses on improving organizational processes, sees performance through a *process* lens (Juran, 1992). Strategic management, which focuses on positioning the organization competitively, views performance through the *organization* and *industry* lens (Porter, 1980). While nothing is inherently wrong with a disciplinary bias, it does indicate a need for caution when viewing performance models from other disciplines.

- *There is no such thing as a single view of performance.* Each discipline or perspective has defined performance in a way that fits its purpose. The search for a single model of performance may be a futile search, or at least likely to result in a model so complex as to be unusable. Each discipline has had to limit its performance models to focus on aspects of performance appropriate for that discipline. The lesson is that HRD must define performance in a manner that fits its unique role in performance improvement and that acknowledges the legitimate role of other disciplines. It is not essential that HRD's model define every possible view of performance. As professionals responsible for improving performance in predominantly work-related social systems (Dean, 1997), HRD needs to define performance domains that fit that purpose.

- *Types (levels) of performance and indicators of performance are confused in some models.* One persistent source of confusion in the literature is between levels of performance and indicators or metrics of performance. For example, several models include "customer" as a level of performance (Edvinsson & Malone, 1997; Juran, 1992; Kaplan & Norton, 1996). Clearly customer satisfaction is important, but it is an indicator of process and organizational performance, not a level of performance. Similarly, several models define some aspect of employee behavior such as learning (Edvinsson & Malone, 1997; Kaplan & Norton, 1996), demonstrating effort (Campbell, 1990), or individual ethics (D. L. Swanson, 1995) as a level of performance. All are really indicators of individual performance but are defined as levels due to disciplinary biases.

Sleezer, Hough, and Gradous (1998) point out that performance is usually not measured directly. What is measured are attributes of performance and their indicators. Performance indicators and metrics are vitally important but must not be confused with performance itself. And, as Sleezer et al. point out, multiple levels of measurement may be involved. For example, customer satisfaction may be an indicator of process performance, but it is also measured in multiple ways. That is, we do not measure all possible dimensions of satisfaction directly but could use a metric such as repeat visits to a store as an indicator of satisfaction.

- *Subsystems in the models vary widely.* Part of the disciplinary bias is reflected in the subsystems included in the models. Organization development (Cummings & Worley, 1993) defines groups as its primary subsystem because OD focuses on interpersonal dimensions of an organization. Needs assessment (McGehee & Thayer, 1961; Sleezer, 1991) defines work or task as its primary subsystem because of it focuses on analyzing work-related learning needs. Others (Rummler & Brache, 1995; Swanson, 1994) include process as their subsystem, reflecting current emphasis on process improvement. In the case of human capital or strategic management, the organization becomes the subsystem, with society as the larger system. There seems to be little uniformity in terminology.

INDIVIDUAL-LEVEL PERFORMANCE MODELS

Because HRD has its roots in individual learning, it was logical that individual-level performance models would be the first to develop. These models are now known collectively as *human performance technology* (Stolovich & Keeps, 1999) models. The common characteristic of these models is that they attempt to define individual performance and key factors that impact upon individual performance. Two representative models are John Campbell's taxonomy of individual performance and Thomas Gilbert's human performance engineering model.

Campbell's Taxonomy of Individual Performance

Campbell's (1990) model of individual performance is considered one of the preeminent performance models in industrial psychology. Campbell developed it because he noted that psychologists had paid little attention to the dependent variable (performance), focusing most of their energy on the independent variables. As he said, "the literature pertaining to the structure and content of performance is a virtual desert. We essentially have no theories of performance" (1990, p. 704).

Campbell's theory has three key parts: performance *components,* performance *determinants,* and *predictors* of performance determinants. First, he suggests that the predictors of performance fall into three groups (see Figure 8.2). Predictors of declarative and procedural knowledge include ability, personality,

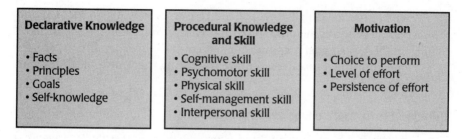

Figure 8.2 Campbell's Job Performance Components (*Source:* Campbell, 1990.)

interests, education, training, experience, and the interaction of these components. Predictors of motivation vary depending on which theory of motivation one uses.

Campbell (1990) then proposed eight components that are hypothesized to collectively be sufficient to describe performance in all jobs in the *Dictionary of Occupational Titles.* They are as follows:

1. *Job-specific task proficiency*—the degree to which an individual can perform the core substantive or technical tasks central to his or her job

2. *Non-job-specific task proficiency*—the degree to which an individual can perform the tasks or execute behaviors that are not specific to his or her particular job

3. *Written and oral communication*—the proficiency with which an individual can write or speak, independent of the correctness of the subject matter

4. *Demonstrating effort*—the consistency of an individual's effort day by day, the degree to which he or she will expend extra effort when required, and the willingness to work under adverse conditions

5. *Maintaining personal discipline*—the degree to which negative behaviors are avoided (e.g., abusing alcohol, breaking laws and rules, etc.)

6. *Facilitating peer and team performance*—the degree to which the individual supports his or her peers, helps them with job problems, and helps train them. It also encompasses how well an individual is committed to the goals of the groups and tries to facilitate group functioning by being a good model, keeping the group goal directed, and reinforcing participation by group members.

7. *Supervision*—proficiency in the supervisory component includes all the behaviors directed at influencing the performance of supervisees through face-to-face interpersonal interaction and influence

8. *Management/administration*—includes the major elements in management that are independent of direct supervision. It includes the performance behaviors directed at articulating goals for the unit or

enterprise, organizing people and resources to work on them, monitoring progress, helping solve problems or overcome crises that stand in the way of goal accomplishment, controlling expenditures, obtaining additional resources, and representing the unit in dealings with other units.

Gilbert's Performance Engineering Model

Tom Gilbert's 1978 book *Human Performance: Engineering Worthy Performance* is regarded as one of the classics in human performance technology. While the more recent multilevel performance models discussed in the next section are more comprehensive, Gilbert's work remains as an important benchmark in individual-level performance improvement. This section provides an overview of his model and its contributions.

Gilbert presents his work in a series of theorems which he called "Leisurely Theorems." His first theorem states:

> Human competence is a function of worthy performance (W), which is a function of the ratio of valuable accomplishments (A) to costly behavior (B).

Mathematically, this is stated as

$$W = \frac{A}{B}$$

According to Gilbert, this theorem tells us that having large amounts of work, knowledge, and outcomes without accomplishment is not worthy performance. Performance, he points out, is not the same as activity but rather is a function of the worth of the accomplishment for a given unit of effort (similar to return on investment). Thus, systems that reward people for effort, not worthy accomplishments, encourage incompetence according to Gilbert. Similarly, rewarding accomplishment without examining the relative worth of those accomplishment squander people's energies.

Measuring performance alone does not give us a measure of competence, according to Gilbert. To measure competence, Gilbert (1978) proposes his second theorem:

> Typical performance is inversely proportional to the potential for improving performance (the PIP), which is the ratio of exemplary performance to typical performance. The ratio, to be meaningful, must be stated for an identifiable accomplishment, because there is no "general quality of competence. (p. 30)

Mathematically, this is stated as

$$PIP = \frac{W_{ex}}{W_t}$$

The PIP tells us how much competence we have and how much potential we have for improving it. For example, simply knowing that a person can produce ten widgets a day tells us little about competence. If the best performance possible is ten widgets, then this person is an exemplary performer. On the other hand, if the best performance is twenty widgets, then this person is only at 50 percent of exemplary performance and has a high potential for improving performance.

The third theorem deals directly with the engineering human behaviors to create the accomplishments. It states:

> For any given accomplishment, a deficiency in performance always has at its immediate cause a deficiency in a behavior repertory (P), or in the environment that supports the repertory (E), or in both. But its ultimate cause will be found in a deficiency of the management system (M).

Gilbert (1978, p. 88) then provides what may be the most well-known part of this model, the behavior engineering model (see Figure 8.3).

Figure 8.3 Gilbert's Behavior Engineering Model			
	S^D *Instrumentation*	R *Instrumentation*	S_T *Motivation*
E *Environmental supports*	Data 1. Relevant and frequent feedback about the adequacy of performance 2. Descriptions of what is expected of performance 3. Clear and relevant guides to adequate performance	Instruments 1. Tools and materials of work designed scientifically to match human factors	Incentives 1. Adequate financial incentives made contingent upon performance 2. Nonmonetary incentives made available 3. Career development opportunities
P *Person's repertory of behavior*	Knowledge 1. Scientifically designed training that matches the requirements of exemplary performance 2. Placement	Capacity 1. Flexible scheduling of performance to match peak capacity 2. Prosthesis 3. Physical shaping 4. Adaptation 5. Selection	Motives 1. Assessment of people's motives to work 2. Recruitment of people to match the realities of the situation

Source: Gilbert (1978).

Gilbert's notion of human performance is clearly grounded in behavioral psychology. The strength of his framework is that he emphasizes both the individual and the individual's environment, unlike Campbell's model that focuses solely on the individual. While modern conceptualizations of performance encompass more than just behaviorist notions of human behavior, Gilbert's emphasis on the environmental influences on behavior are fundamental to performance improvement. In addition, his emphasis on the worth of behavior as a measure of wise investments in competence remains fundamental to performance-based HRD.

One serious drawback to Gilbert's emphasis on behaviorism is that it has helped give performance-based HRD a bad name. As seen in chapter 6, many of the criticisms leveled at performance-based HRD suggest that it is mechanistic or dehumanizing. This stems in part from early works like Gilbert's that were strictly behavioristic. As was pointed out, this is no longer the case, but it has been a tough label to shed.

MULTILEVEL PERFORMANCE MODELS

Scholars of organizational performance have long been frustrated with piecemeal approaches to performance improvement. System theory tells us that interventions that focus on only a subset of organizational performance variables are usually doomed to failure unless they are embedded in the context of whole-system performance improvement. Thus, efforts to improve performance using an individual-level model such as Campbell's are missing key elements of the organizational context. Fundamentally, this is the reason that the performance-based HRD perspective has developed and become popular. Training or skill development is often futile unless it is embedded in a systems approach to organizational performance improvement.

When viewed from a systems perspective, organizations are extremely complex social systems. In fact, they become so complex that the average person has trouble comprehending them, let alone improving them. Thus, various scholars have attempted to reduce the complexity of organizational systems to a more manageable form by creating taxonomic models of key performance variables. These models usually embrace multiple levels of performance and multiple dimensions of performance within those levels. This chapter looks at four multilevel models: Rummler and Brache's (1995) performance model, Swanson's (1994) performance diagnosis matrix, an OD performance model from Cummings and Worley (2001), and Holton's (1999) integrated taxonomy of performance system domains.

Rummler and Brache's Performance Model

Rummler and Brache (1995) provide an integrated framework for achieving competitive advantage by learning how to manage organizations, processes, and individuals effectively. Beginning with a holistic view of the organization, they set forth a rational, clear, yet simple view of the organizational skeleton, process levels, and interdependencies. Their model hypothesizes that organizational failure is due not to lack of desire or effort, but lack of understanding of the variables that influence organizational, process, and individual performance. Rummler and Brache call these variables "performance levers" (p. 2). With a complete understanding and holistic management of these variables, high performance should result.

To guide the management of organizations as systems, Rummler and Brache present the nine-cell matrix described here and in Figure 8.4. They define three levels of performance:

- *Organizational level*—emphasizes the organization's relationship with its market and the basic skeleton of the major functions that comprise the organization
- *Process*—the work flow, how the work really gets done
- *Job/performer*—the individuals doing various jobs

Within each of these three levels are three performance variables:

- *Goals*—specific standards that reflect customers' expectations for product and service quality, quantity, timeliness, and cost
- *Design*—the structure needs to include the necessary components, configured in a way that enables the goals to be efficiently met
- *Management*—management practices that ensure goals are current and being achieved

Organizational Level

According to Rummler and Brache (1995), "if executives [leaders] do not manage at the organization level, the best they can expect is modest performance improvement. At worst, efforts at other levels will be counterproductive" (p. 33).

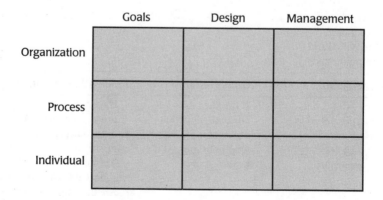

Figure 8.4 Rummler and Brache's Performance Model (*Source:* Rummler and Brache, 1995.)

This "level emphasizes the organization's relationship with its market and the basic 'skeleton' of the major functions that comprise the organization" (p. 15). They further suggest that organization-level performance addresses the set of core questions shown in Figure 8.5.

Process Level

According to Rummler and Brache (1995), an organization is only as good as its processes. Organizational processes describe the actual work of an organization and are responsible for producing goods and services (i.e., outputs) for customers. For the process level, the analyst must go "beyond the cross functional

---

Figure 8.5   Questions at Each Level of the Rummler and Brache Model

Organization Goals	*Organization Design*	*Organization Management*
• Has the organization's strategy/direction been articulated and communicated? • Does the strategy make sense, in terms of the external threats and opportunities and the internal strengths and weaknesses? • Given this strategy, have the required outputs of the organization and the level of performance expected from each output been determined and communicated?	• Are all the relevant functions in place? • Are all functions necessary? • Is the current flow of inputs and outputs between functions appropriate? • Does the formal organization structure support the strategy and enhance the efficiency of the system?	• Have appropriate function goals been set? • Is relevant performance measured? • Are resources appropriately allocated? • Are the interfaces between functions steps being managed?
Process Goals	*Process Design*	*Process Management*
• Are goals for key processes linked to customer and organization requirements?	• Is this the most efficient/effective process for accomplishing process goals?	• Have appropriate process subgoals been set? • Is process performance managed? • Are sufficient resources allocated to each process? • Are the interfaces between process steps being managed?

Job/Performer Goals	Job Design	Job/Performer Management
• Are job outputs and standards linked to process requirements (which are in turn linked to customer and organization requirements)?	• Are process requirements reflected in the appropriate jobs? • Are job steps in a logical sequence? • Have supportive policies and procedures been developed? • Is the job environment ergonomically sound?	• Do the performers understand the job goals (outputs they are expected to produce and the standards they are expected to meet)? • Do the performers have sufficient resources, clear signals and priorities, and a logical job design? • Are the performers rewarded for achieving the job goals? • Do the performers know if they are meeting the job goals? • Do the performers have the necessary skills and knowledge to achieve the job goals? • If the performers were in an environment in which the five questions listed above were answered yes, would they have the physical, mental, and emotional capacity to achieve the job goals?

boundaries that make up the organization chart, we see the work flow—how the work gets done." "At the process level, one must ensure that processes are installed to meet customer needs, that those processes work effectively and efficiently, and that the process goals and measures are driven by the customers' and the organizations' requirement" (p. 17). The Rummler and Brache model describes the cells of the process level to include process goals, process design, and process management.

Rummler and Brache (1995) make these arguments for the importance of focusing on processes in performance systems:

- Process is the least understood and least managed domain of performance
- A process can be seen as a value chain, with each step adding value to the preceding steps

- An organization is only as effective as its processes.
- Enhancing organizational and individual effectiveness will only improve performance as much as the processes allow.
- Strong people cannot compensate for a weak process (p. 45).

Individual Level

Finally, Rummler and Brache (1995) identify three performance variables at the job/performer level: job/performer goals, design, and management, and developed the core questions shown in Figure 8.5. "At the individual level it is recognized that processes . . . are performed and managed by individuals doing various jobs" (p. 17). These performance levels determine effectiveness at the individual job/performer level and contribute to the efficiency of the process and organizational levels.

Swanson's Performance Diagnosis Matrix

Swanson (1994) has extended Rummler and Brache's (1995) model by expanding the number of performance variables included in the model. Initially advanced as part of his performance analysis system, the core performance model also stands alone as one definition of an organizational performance system. Similar to Rummler and Brache's model, Swanson's has two key components: performance levels and performance variables.

Performance Levels

Three levels are identified that are the same as the Rummler and Brache model and consistently referred to throughout the performance diagnosis phases:

- Organization
- Process
- Individual

These three levels have been carefully presented by FitzGerald and FitzGerald (1973). System theory helps us understand the three levels. For example, the cause of a company sending a customer a contract bid containing an inaccurate budget and an incomplete list of services may lie in any or all three levels. Even so, the decision maker may be falsely convinced early on that the cause is lodged at a single level. For example:

- "There is so much bureaucracy around here that it is a miracle anything even gets done!" or
- "The financial computer program has a glitch in it!" or
- "Our financial analysts are incompetent!"

Performance Variable

The second component is five performance variables that occur at each of the three performance levels:

Figure 8.6   Swanson's Performance Diagnosis Matrix

	Performance Levels		
Performance Variables	**ORGANIZATIONAL LEVEL**	**PROCESS LEVEL**	**INDIVIDUAL LEVEL**
Mission/goal	Does the organization mission/goal fit the reality of the economic, political, and cultural forces?	Do the process goals enable the organization to meet organization and individual missions/goals?	Are the professional and personal mission/goals of individuals congruent with the organization's:
System design	Does the organization system provide structure and policies supporting the desired performance?	Are processes designed in such a way to work as a system?	Does the individual face obstacles that impede their job performance?
Capacity	Does the organization have the leadership, capital, and infrastructure to achieve its mission/goals?	Does the process have the capacity to perform (quantity, quality, and timeliness)?	Does the individual have the mental, physical, and emotional capacity to perform?
Motivation	Do the policies, culture, and reward systems support the desired performance?	Does the process provide the information and human factors required to maintain it?	Does the individual want to perform no matter what?
Expertise	Does the organization establish and maintain selection and training policies and resources?	Does the process of developing expertise meet the changing demands of changing processes?	Does the individual have the knowledge, skills, and experience to perform?

Source: Swanson (1994).

- Mission/goals
- System design
- Capacity
- Motivation
- Expertise

These performance variables, matrixed with the levels of performance— organization, process, and/or individual—provide a powerful perspective in diagnosing performance. For example, a work process may have an inherent goal built into it that is in conflict with the mission and/or goal of the organization or a person working in the process. The questions presented in the performance variable matrix help the diagnostician sort out the performance overlaps and disconnects (see Figure 8.6).

Like all multilevel models, Swanson emphasizes that bad systems almost always overwhelm good people. This idea was most evident in the World War II performance improvement efforts (Dooley, 1945). How else to explain the failure of high-aptitude workers? When the work system ties the hands of competent persons behind their backs and then punishes them for doing their best, they either quit and leave or quit and stay! Likewise, when a well-designed work process is coupled with organizational policies and procedures that hire employees lacking the capacity to perform the work, no reasonable amount of training will get the employees up to required performance standards.

Organization Development Performance Model

Another representative multilevel performance model comes from organization development. Figure 8.7 shows the Cummings and Worley (2001) organizational diagnosis model. This model is typical of performance models found in the OD field.

There are several clear differences between the OD model and the Rummler and Brache or Swanson models. The biggest difference is in the levels defined. Instead of including a process performance level, most OD models include a group or team performance level. The other two levels are usually the same—organization and individual. The group level reflects a clear difference in values and perspective by OD professionals who place a great deal of emphasis on groups and interpersonal dynamics in organizations. The OD model underemphasizes process performance, while the Rummler–Brache and Swanson models appear to underemphasize groups and teams.

The other clear difference is in the performance variables included in the model, which are called *design components* in this model. Sixteen variables are included across the three levels, roughly equivalent to the other models. The variables at the organization level are similar, encompassing strategy (goals), design, systems, and management. Notice, however, that one key variable explicitly included is organization culture, another variable of key interest to OD but not as explicit in other models. At the group and individual levels, the variables included represent

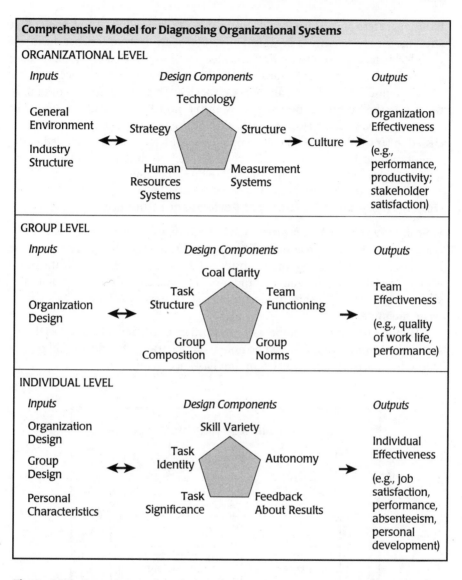

Figure 8.7   Cummings and Worley's Organization Development Performance Model
(*Source:* Cummings and Worley, 2001.)

traditional areas of concern for OD professionals. They emphasize elements that affect the social dynamics in organizations and that are likely to enhance quality of work life. In fact, this model explicitly includes quality of work life, job satisfaction, and personal development as outcome variables along with performance.

This model provides yet another perspective on performance in organizations. Like the Rummler–Brache and Swanson models, it is firmly grounded in system theory. While a close examination of the three multilevel models discussed so far would reveal that all components of each model are included in the other two models, the structure of each model reflects different emphasis on the different components by the authors and their subdisciplines.

Holton's Integrated Taxonomy of Performance Domains

Holton (1999) presents an integrated taxonomy of performance system domains in an attempt to reconcile differences between the OD domains and the Rummler–Brache and Swanson models (see Figure 8.8). In addition, he wanted to change the language of the model to make it more universal and to address criticisms of other models that performance was viewed as a short-term phenomenon.

Holton proposes four domains of performance: mission, process, social subsystem, and individual. It should be noted that he originally called *social subsystem* "critical performance subsystem" but has since changed it.

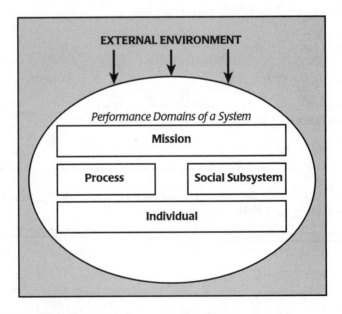

Figure 8.8 Holton's Integrated Taxonomy of Performance Domains (*Source:* Holton, 1999.)

Mission Domain

The system's mission, and the goals derived from it, specifies the expected outcomes of that system. Every purposefully organized system operates with a mission, either explicitly or implicitly, and the role of the mission is to reflect the system's relationship with its *external* environment. For a business organization, the mission may reflect its relationship with its industry, society, and competitors. For a nonprofit organization, its mission may reflect its relationship with the community and society. It is not necessary to specify in the taxonomy what the possible levels of impact outside the system are, because the mission will reflect that system's understanding of its responsibilities to the external environment.

It is important to note that the concept of "performance system" was used instead of "organization." A mission may be defined for any system organized to accomplish some purpose. If the system has a purpose, then it also has desired outputs, so performance theory is applicable. In many instances, the mission domain will be the same as the organization domain, particularly in for-profit firms. However, for a trade association, the mission domain may focus on an entire industry, or an entire profession for a professional association. For example, the Academy of Human Resource Development's mission is the advancement of the HRD profession through research. In other situations, the mission may include community outcomes, or societal outcomes.

The particular system's definition of its performance relationship with the external environment is fully captured by the mission and goals of the organization. In that sense, his model differs from that of Kaufman and his associates (see Kaufman et al., 1998; Kaufman, 1987), who have argued that societal benefits should be included as a level of performance. This difference should not be interpreted to mean that societal benefits are unimportant. Rather, Holton believes that the mission of that system most appropriately captures the relationship between the performance system and society. The degree to which the performance system targets societal outcomes will be incorporated in its mission. The actual level of societal performance targeted will vary greatly, depending on the performance system.

For business organizations, the mission-level metrics are likely to be dominated by traditional business outcome measures, including economic outcomes (more on metrics later). However, the mission domain for a government organization may be dominated by metrics assessing societal benefits. The notion that the performance perspective only embraces economic returns as the system's mission (Bierema, 1997; Dirkx, 1997) is fundamentally flawed. Performance metrics are defined by and depend on the mission of the organization.

Process Domain

The process domain in his model was identical to Rummler and Brache's and Swanson's. Holton notes that one of the positive outcomes of the quality and reengineering movements is the realization that managing and designing effective processes is an essential part of performance improvement. A number of performance experts have clearly articulated the need for including the process domain of performance (Hammer & Champy, 1993; Hronec, 1993; Juran, 1992; Kaplan & Norton, 1996; Rummler & Brache, 1995; Swanson, 1994). Readers desiring a deeper understanding of the importance of process to performance improvement should consult these sources.

Social Subsystem

This taxonomy includes a domain for social subsystems, defined as an *internal* social entity (group, team, department, etc.) for which performance goals have been set that are derived from, and contribute to, the mission of the overall system. Thus, the core difference between this domain and the mission domain is that the mission domain defines performance outcomes relative to the external environment, while this domain defines internal performance subsystems that do not always directly connect with the external environment. Social subsystem is a more general construct than "group" or "team" although it encompasses both of these terms.

One of the weaknesses of prominent integrated performance models (Rummler & Brache, 1995; Swanson, 1994) is that they do not appear to embrace social subsystems within an organization. That is, by appearing to ignore teams, divisions, departments, functions, and so forth, the integrated performance models appear to neglect organizational realities. In addition, they appear to neglect the interpersonal domain of teams and groups that is so central to many organizations today (McIntyre & Salas, 1995). In the case of structural subunits, it is easier to see how the "organization" domain can be redefined to be "department" or "division" than for team performance that has unique components.

The social subsystem is an important point of analysis. For example, the following questions may have to be answered:

- What are the social subsystems that are critical to accomplishing the system's mission?
- What are the explicit social subsystems? The implicit ones?
- Are the explicit and implicit subsystems congruent?
- Are the social subsystems appropriate for the mission of the system?
- Are the relationships between social subsystems optimal?
- Do organizational factors help or hinder subsystem performance?
- Are appropriate metrics in place?

Individual Domain

This domain is also identical to the Rummler–Brache and Swanson models.

Drivers and Outcomes in Each Performance Domain

Kaplan and Norton (1996) suggest two categories of performance measures: outcomes and drivers. Unfortunately, they do not offer concise definitions of either.

For our purposes, *outcomes* are measures of effectiveness or efficiency relative to core outputs of the system, subsystem, process, or individual. The most typical are financial indicators (profit, ROI, etc.) and productivity measures (units of goods or services produced), and they are often generic across similar performance systems. According to Kaplan and Norton, these measures tend to be lag indicators in that they reflect what has occurred or has been accomplished in relation to core outcomes.

Drivers measure elements of performance that are expected to sustain or increase system, subsystem, process, or individual ability and capacity to be more effective or efficient in the future. Thus, they are leading indicators of future outcomes and tend to be unique for particular performance systems. Together with outcome measures, they describe the hypothesized cause-and-effect relationships in the organization's strategy (Kaplan & Norton, 1996). Thus, drivers should predict future outcomes. For example, for a particular company return on investment might be the appropriate outcome measure, which might be driven by customer loyalty and on-time delivery, which in turn might be driven by employee learning so internal processes are optimized. In a state government department of revenue, an outcome measure might be the percentage of tax returns processed correctly within two weeks of receipt. A performance driver for that outcome might be number of quality improvement initiatives successfully implemented.

Kaplan and Norton (1996) go on to say:

> Outcome measures without performance drivers do not communicate how the outcomes are to be achieved. . . . Conversely, performance drivers without outcome measures may enable the business unit to achieve short-term operational improvements, but will fail to reveal whether the operational improvements have been translated into expanded business with existing and new customers, and, eventually, to enhanced financial performance. A good balanced scorecard should have an appropriate mix of outcomes (lagging indicators) and performance drivers (leading indicators) of the business unit's strategy. (pp. 31–32)

From this perspective, performance improvement models that focus solely on actual outcomes, such as profit or units of work produced, are flawed in that they are likely to create short-term improvement but neglect aspects of the organization that will drive future performance outcomes. Models that focus solely on performance drivers such as learning or growth are equally flawed in that they fail to consider the actual outcomes. Only when outcomes and drivers are jointly considered will long-term sustained performance improvement occur.

The correct perspective is illustrated in Figure 8.9. This figure shows that performance drivers and performance outcomes should be linked within each performance domain. Neither is more or less important but work in an integrated fashion to enhance mission, process, subsystem, and individual performance.

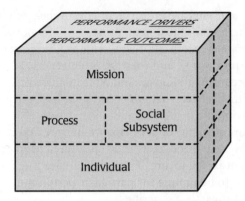

Figure 8.9   Integrated View of Performance Domains, Outcomes, and Drivers

CONCLUSION

The integration of performance models into HRD has introduced an entirely new perspective to HRD thinking, research, and practice. Their primary contribution is that they all remind us that the individual is embedded in a performance system that has a major effect on the individual's performance. Even if one believes that the primary purpose of HRD is to enhance individual development, the individual is embedded in an organizational system so HRD professionals must understand the system and its effects on the individual. A broader view suggests that enhancing human performance means working on the system as well as developing individuals. The broadest application of these models suggests that HRD professionals should work to improve all aspects of the performance system.

REFLECTION QUESTIONS

1. Which performance model do you think best represents performance constructs of concern to HRD? Explain why.
2. What are the implications of multilevel, multiattribute performance models for HRD practice?
3. Do performance models enhance or diminish the value of learning in organizations?
4. Performance models are often seen as useful to management, but not a tool to benefit employees. What is your position on this?
5. How can HRD lead change in each of the performance variables?
6. What is the future of performance-oriented HRD?

P A R T　　F O U R

Developing Human Expertise through Personnel Training and Development

This section captures the essence of the personnel training and development component of HRD as well as the nature of human expertise. Illustrations of personnel training and development practice that exist in host organizations are presented along with variations in core thinking, processes, interventions, and tools.

CHAPTERS

Overview of Personnel Training and Development

Personnel training and development (T&D) constitutes the largest realm of HRD activity. *Training and development* is defined as a process of systematically developing work-related knowledge and expertise in people for the purpose of improving performance. Within personnel training and development, more effort is focused on *training* than on *development*. Also, *training* is more likely focused on new employees and those entering new job roles in contrast to long-term *development*. To be clear, the *development* portion of training and development is seen as "the planned growth and expansion of knowledge and expertise of people beyond the present job requirements" (Swanson, 1996b, p. 6). In the majority of instances, *development* opportunities are provided to people who are high potential contributors to the organization. In all cases, people at all levels in all organizations need to know how to do their work (expertise) and generally need help with their learning. Davis and Davis (1998) provide an explanation that helps frame this chapter:

> Training is the process through which skills are developed, information is provided, and attributes are nurtured, in order to help individuals who work in organizations to become more effective and efficient in their work. Training helps the organization to fulfill its purposes and goals, while contributing to the overall development of workers. Training is necessary to help workers qualify for a job, do the job, or advance, but it is also essential for enhancing and transforming the job, so that the job actually adds value to the enterprise. Training facilitates learning, but learning is not only a formal activity designed and encouraged by specially prepared trainers to generate specific performance improvements. Learning is also a more universal activity, designed to increase capability and capacity and is facilitated formally and informally by many types of people at different levels of the organization. Training should always hold forth the promise of maximizing learning. (p. 44)

VIEWS OF T&D

Fortunately, no single view of T&D exists. There is so much variety in the nature of organizations, the people that work in them, the conditions surrounding the need for human expertise, and the process of learning that one lens would be inadequate. Alternative views are useful. Two useful models include the taxonomy for performance (Swanson, 1996) and the informal and incidental learning model (Marsick & Watkins, 1997).

Taxonomy of Performance

One way of gaining perspective of the expertise required of organizations to function is through the taxonomy of performance (Swanson, 1996; see Figure 9.1). The taxonomy first illustrates the two large challenges that every organization

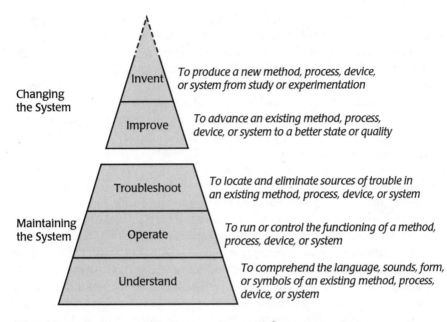

Figure 9.1 Taxonomy of Performance *(Source:* Swanson, 1994, p. 57.)

faces: *maintaining the system* and *changing the system.* Keeping any system up and running is hard work. Workplace systems erode in many ways. For example: equipment wears out, customers demand more than the work processes can produce, and expert workers leave their employment for a variety of reasons.

Even though a work system is mature and reasonably predictable, conditions can change and things can go wrong. A variety of forces cause systems to erode. Thus, managers and workers have the continuing pressure of "maintaining" their work systems. When there is inadequate expertise, training can be applied. Furthermore, the "Maintaining the System" subcategories of understanding, operation, and troubleshooting of work systems allow for clearer specification of the performance required and what it takes to achieve it. You could not expect a person experiencing training that only deals with "understanding" the work system to be able to go into the workplace with the expertise required to "operate" and "troubleshoot" in that setting. A fundamental error in HRD practice would be to provide training to employees at one level and expect them to demonstrate expertise at a higher level. It is generally assumed that people who have designed and worked in a system are subject-matter experts on that system. Thus, these people are key resources to T&D professionals wanting to analyze what a person needs to know and be able to do to maintain the system. In addition, support information about the existing system is usually available that can also be used in putting together sound training.

In contrast to the challenge of "maintaining systems," the challenge of "changing systems" is posed by the taxonomy of performance. Changing the system can be either *improving* it or *inventing* a whole new system. Changing the system strikes another chord. What a person needs to know and be able to do in order to change a system is to engage in activity that is primarily outside the maintaining realm. A person needs to be involved in problem identification and problem-solving methods apart from the system operation methods. For example, human factors design, process redesign, and statistical process control are specific strategies for *improving the system* that must be learned in order to apply them to an existing work system. A person can be an expert in this *improvement* work without being an expert in the system he or she wishes to improve. This individual typically partners with people having system-specific expertise. In other situations, organizations train people who are experts of existing systems on methods for *improving the system* with the expectation that they can apply those invention methods to change the very system in which they work. Thus, they are expecting the same people to be able to *maintain* and *improve* systems.

The *invention* level of "changing the system" has little regard for the existing system. Totally new ways of thinking and doing work are entertained. One measure of success is that the existing system goes away as a result of being replaced by the new system and that the new challenge is to maintain the new system. This cycle of renewal is fed by HRD interventions and ends up requiring new HRD interventions. It is part of the dynamic of the HRD profession that both these demands of maintaining the system and changing the system go on—go on simultaneously in organizations and go on simultaneously in individual contributors.

Experts on changing the system (see Deming, 1986; Rummler & Brache, 1995) provide us fair warning about the domains of maintaining the system and changing the system in organizations. An organization that is in crisis will first need to focus itself on the core issue of *maintaining the system* before it goes about *improving the system*. While improving the system may be more appealing, it would be analogous to rearranging the chairs on the deck of the *Titanic*. More than once we have started with an OD "changing the system" project only to discover that there was a frantic need to develop core expertise so as to get the system back to where it was (maintain)—to the point that *changes to the system* could then be entertained.

It is important to note the role the learning and performance paradigms (discussed in chapters 7 and 8) play in meeting the challenges posed by the taxonomy of performance. With learning viewed as a driver of performance, it is easy to make a short-term connection between learning and performance when there are system maintenance issues. In comparison, it is not as easy to make the long-term learning-to-performance connection when T&D is involved in system change issues. Just the time frame involved in changing a work system makes it more difficult to fly the performance banner and suggests that intermediate evidence of learning and new behaviors as legitimate goals in themselves.

The traditional lines that have been drawn between those people in a system responsible for maintaining it and those responsible for changing it have been blurred. Some of the traditional thoughts about short-term versus long-term investments in T&D have also been blurred.

Informal and Incidental Learning

While we knew it all along, only recently did T&D professionals acknowledge the unstructured learning journey. Most T&D professionals had been only thinking about their structured training view of the world and not acknowledging the unstructured or trial and error role learning in the organization. The classic rival to structured T&D has been unstructured T&D, which has not been viewed favorably. Swanson and Sawzin (1976) carefully define each, noting that the difference was whether or not there was a plan for learning coming from the organization. Planning is at the heart of the argument. The conscious acknowledgment of informal and incidental workplace learning has matured in recent years. This realization is based on the fact that the majority of what people actually learn related to their work performance is not planned in the way T&D professionals have traditionally talked about work-related learning.

Marsick and Watkins (1997) have provided an "informal and incidental learning model" to understand this phenomenon (see Figure 9.2). Their model is based on a core premise that the behavior of individuals is a function of their interaction with their environment (Lewin, 1951). One could argue that the moment an organization begins thinking about, planning, and taking actions to

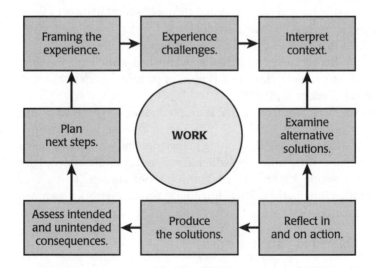

Figure 9.2 Marsick and Watkins's Informal and Incidental Learning Model (*Source:* Marsick and Watkins, 1997, p. 299. Used with permission.)

encourage informal and incidental learning, the process is no longer informal or incidental. Such an argument would be shortchanging the confidence in the capability and integrity of workers as learners that the informal and incidental learning view brings to the debate. What they argue for is the power of the context—the organization and the work—both to ignite the learning process and to serve as the primary learning aid. It provides the challenge to learn, to define problems, to solve problems, and to reflect.

It is no wonder that organizational leaders are interested in ideas that embrace *action learning* that results in learning *and* possible solutions to real contextual problems and *team problem solving* that results in solutions to contextual problems *and* learning and possible learning on the part of team members. Both action learning and team problem solving rely on the power of work and context in their structured T&D experiences, while the work and the context are at the very core of informal and incidental workplace learning.

KEY T&D TERMS

Key personnel training and development concepts and terms provide a basis of understanding the profession. The following definitions are categorized as basic terms, forms of T&D, and subject matter.

Basic Terms Related to T&D

Knowledge—the intellective mental components acquired and retained through study and experience

Expertise—the human state, acquired through a combination of knowledge and experience, that enables individuals to consistently achieve performance outcomes that meet or exceed the performance requirements

Learning—the process of acquiring new knowledge and expertise in people

Informal learning—learning that is predominantly experiential and noninstitutional (Cseh et al., 1998)

Incidental learning—learning that is unintentional, a byproduct of another activity (Cseh et al., 1998).

Training—the process of developing knowledge and expertise in people

Development—the planned growth and expansion of the knowledge and expertise of people beyond the present job requirements. This is accomplished through systematic training, learning experiences, work assignments, and assessment efforts.

Terms Related to T&D Strategies

Structured training and development—the systematic development of workplace knowledge and expertise. Within organizations, structured training and development is the effective and efficient development of expertise in personnel through carefully selected knowledge, practice, and/or experiences that result in criterion behavior.

Unstructured training and development—the unplanned and undocumented process of developing expertise

On-the-job training and development—training that takes place at the job site while the employee is simultaneously expected to produce. It can be either structured (planned) or unstructured (unplanned).

Customized training and development—structured training produced to address organization-specific training needs

Off-the-shelf training and development—structured training produced to address general or generic training needs

Training and development program—a stand-alone learning experience designed to develop specific expertise

Training and development program title—a title derived from a job title, job task, work concept, work system, work process, or hardware

Terms Associated with Major Subject Matter of T&D

Technical skills training and development—focuses on content that is system- or tool-specific and can be either information or hardware oriented. It is generally thought of as people-thing or people-procedure, or people–process focused.

Management and leadership training and development—addresses the challenges of both maintaining the work system and changing the work system. Manager and supervisor tasks primarily focus in getting the work done—maintaining the system—with a lesser concern with improving and changing the system. In comparison, leadership tasks are more focused on concerns about the future state of the system while not losing sight of the present.

Motivational training and development—focuses on content that is attitudinal in nature in the forms of values and beliefs. It is generally pursued through intense structured experiences such as emotional presentations role model presenters to placing people into unfamiliar settings such as wilderness or survival situations that are actually quite safe.

Career development—an extended view of the learning and expertise development journey. A simple explanation would be to plan and construct a pattern of training and learning experiences purposefully with an eye toward more holistic development around one's career. A significant shift took place in the 1980s in U.S. firms: firms that once groomed people to move up in a system that was fairly stable sponsored career development programs. Once the realization hit that firms were changing at such a fast rate, the locus of control for career development moved from the firm to the individual. Thus, when a person is asked today, "Who is in charge of your career development?" the answer is most likely "I am." The void that presently exists is that neither companies nor schools are adequately preparing to manage their own career development.

Three common ways to categorize T&D are generic (content), task/role/job (people), and process/technology (business). Examples of generic T&D categories include: technical and skills T&D, management T&D, and motivational T&D. Examples of *job/role/task* T&D categories are executive development, management training, sales training, technical training, safety training, and new employee and benefits training.

Sample T&D Program Titles

- Gas line inspector (job); gas line inspection (role or task)
- Plant supervision (role)
- Sales manager (job)
- Coaching (task)

Examples of *process/technology* T&D categories include hardware systems, software systems, information systems, and sociotechnical systems.

Sample T&D Program Titles

- Market analysis (information system/process)
- Plastic pipe extrusion (process/hardware)
- Total quality management (sociotechnical/process)
- Microsoft Word—basic training (process)
- Heart pacemaker basics (technology/hardware)

THE GENERAL T&D PROCESS

We have defined HRD as essentially a problem-defining and problem-solving method. For those who react negatively to the notion of problems, we suggest they use the positive word of their choice (e.g. *opportunity, improvement,* etc). We also characterize T&D as a five-phase process. We use variations in the wording for the HRD, T&D, and OD processes to capture the common thread and varying elements. Here are all three variations:

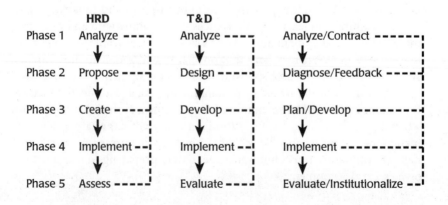

	HRD	**T&D**	**OD**
Phase 1	Analyze	Analyze	Analyze/Contract
Phase 2	Propose	Design	Diagnose/Feedback
Phase 3	Create	Develop	Plan/Develop
Phase 4	Implement	Implement	Implement
Phase 5	Assess	Evaluate	Evaluate/Institutionalize

T&D professionals with HRD almost universally talk about their work in terms of the ADDIE process (analyze, design, develop, implement, and evaluate). The origins of the ADDIE process are rooted in the instructional systems development (ISD) model developed by the U.S. military in 1969 (United States, 1969; Campbell, 1984). The Training for Performance System (TPS) is one of a number of training systems that calls upon the ADDIE process.

INSTRUCTIONAL SYSTEMS DEVELOPMENT (ISD)

The instructional system development (ISD) model of procedures was developed by the U.S. military for the purpose of going about training in a systematic and effective manner in the context of an enormous military training enterprise. Furthermore, it was meant to provide a common language and process that transcended the various branches of the military service.

The ISD model is illustrated in Figure 9.3. The first level of the graphic shows the five phases of the training process in its original form as analysis, design, develop, implement, and control. The *control* phase was later changed to *evaluation* in most adaptations of the original work. The second tier of the graphic specifies the numerous steps within the phases.

In that the original ISD was designed for the military, it is best suited to the following conditions:

- Large numbers of learners must be trained.
- A long lifetime is expected for the program.
- Standard training requirements must be maintained.
- High mastery levels are required because of criticality, such as safety or high cost of errors.
- Economic value is placed on learner's time.
- Training is valued in the organizational culture (Gagne & Medsker, 1996).

The original IDS model started with the assumption in the analysis phase that training was required. Thus, the beginning point of the analysis phase was to analyze the job, and the ending points were to assess trainee behaviors and to revise programs as needed. The sheer size of the military and the degree of standardization in personnel and equipment helped shape the original ISD model with features incompatible with most business and industry training requirements.

TRAINING FOR PERFORMANCE SYSTEM (TPS)

The training for performance system (TPS) is a process for developing human expertise for the purpose of improving organization, process, and individual performance. The TPS was originally developed in 1978 by Richard A. Swanson

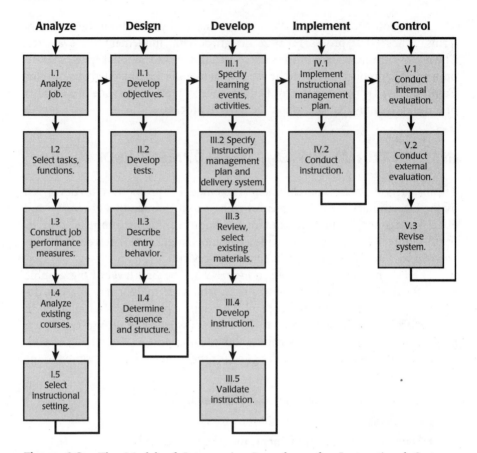

Figure 9.3 The Model of Interservice Procedures for Instructional Systems Development (ISD)

for a major United States manufacturing firm. The firm wanted a comprehensive training process that would embrace all training at all levels (corporate, division, and plant; management, technical, and motivational), thus allowing for a common systematic approach and common language for personnel training throughout the company. The system was originally called the "training technology system." The name was changed to reflect better the true purpose of the training system and eliminate the misinterpretations that were given to the word *technology* (Swanson, 1980).

When the TPS was developed in the late 1970s, the sponsoring firm raised several issues about the existing state of the training profession. First, there was a concern about the inadequacy of the dominant ISD model to connect with core business performance requirements at the analysis phase. Second, the firm pointed out the inadequacy of the tools and processes being used in management training and development in getting at the substance of knowledge work. Third, it was similarly concerned about the inadequacy of the tools and processes being used in technical T&D in getting to the heart of systems/process work. Finally, there was a concern about the inadequacy of the dominant ISD model to connect with core business performance outcomes at the evaluation phase.

The TPS embraces the titles of the traditional five phases of training presented in most models (Swanson, 1996): analyze, design, develop, implement, and evaluate. This five-phase model, as already mentioned, is generally referred to as the *ADDIE model*. In addition, the critical overarching task of "leading the training and development process" is added to the ADDIE process.

TPS Model

The TPS model is illustrated in two forms in Figures 9.4 and 9.5. Figure 9.4 shows the five phases of the training process being integrated and supported through leadership. Figure 9.5 specifies the major steps within the phases and the leadership component.

It is important to note that the systematic process of the TPS has integrity and can be maintained even in the simplest of situations (severe time and budget constraints) or can be violated in the most luxurious situations (generous time and budget allocations). Professional expertise—training process knowledge and experience—is what is necessary to maintain training integrity.

Phases of the TPS and Leading the Process

The TPS is a process for developing human expertise for the purpose of improving organization, process, and individual performance. Let's take a closer look now at its five phases and the overarching concern for leading the process.

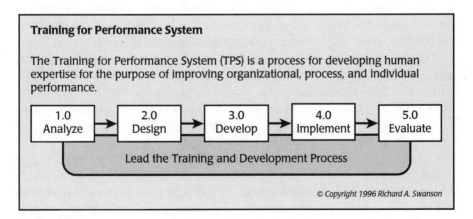

Training for Performance System

The Training for Performance System (TPS) is a process for developing human expertise for the purpose of improving organizational, process, and individual performance.

| 1.0 Analyze | 2.0 Design | 3.0 Develop | 4.0 Implement | 5.0 Evaluate |

Lead the Training and Development Process

© Copyright 1996 Richard A. Swanson

Figure 9.4 Training for Performance System

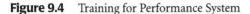

Steps within the Process Phases of the Training for Performance System				
1.0 Analyze	**2.0 Design**	**3.0 Develop**	**4.0 Implement**	**5.0 Evaluate**
1.1 Diagnose Performance and Propose Intervention	2.1 Design Training Program	3.1 Develop Training Materials	4.1 Manage Training Program	5.1 Evaluate Training Effectiveness
1.2 Document Expertise	2.2 Design and Plan Lessons	3.2 Pilot-test Training Program	4.2 Deliver Training	5.2 Report Training Effectiveness

Lead the Training and Development Process:
• Champion T&D Mission/Goals • Manage the Process • Improve the Process

© Copyright 1996 Richard A. Swanson

Figure 9.5   Steps within the Process Phases of the Training for Performance System

Phase 1: Analyze

Diagnose the performance requirements of the organization that can be improved through training and document the expertise required to perform in the workplace. The integrity of the TPS is in its connection to important performance goals and in answering one or more of the following questions positively after the program: (1) Did the organization perform better? (2) Did the work process perform better? (3) Did the individuals (group) perform better?

The front-end organizational diagnosis is essential in clarifying the goal and in determining the performance variables that work together to achieve the goal. It requires the analyst to step back from T&D and to think more holistically about performance. This diagnosis culminates with a performance improvement proposal with the likely need of human expertise being a part of the improvement effort. The overall process is portrayed in Figure 9.6.

Given the need for human expertise, the documentation of what a person needs to know and be able to do (expertise) is the second part of the analysis phase. The TPS addresses job and task analysis with special tools for documenting procedural, system, and knowledge work. Task analysis invariably requires close careful study and generally spending time with a subject-matter expert in their work setting. The process is portrayed in Figure 9.7.

Phase 2: Design

Create and/or acquire general and specific strategies for people to develop workplace expertise. T&D design is at the program and lesson/session levels. At the program

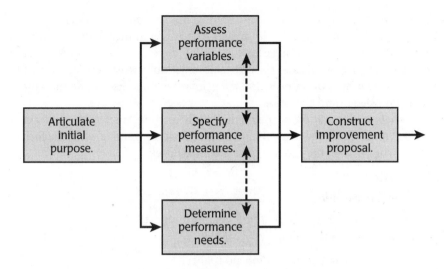

Figure 9.6   Diagnosing Performance (Swanson, 1994, p. 45)

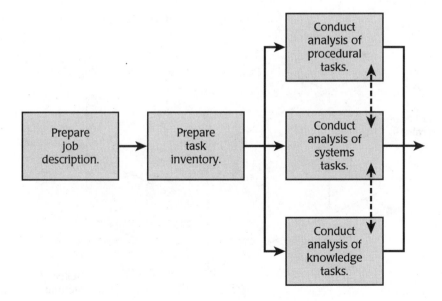

Figure 9.7   Documenting Expertise (Swanson, 1994, p. 102)

design level, the overall design strategy must be economically, systemically, and psychologically sound. Critical information that will influence the program design is gathered. The "Training Strategy Model" depicted in Figure 9.8 allows the program designer to consider the critical interaction between the stability of the content, the number of trainees, and the primary method used to develop the required knowledge and expertise.

Here is an illustration of the media-led through instructor-led continuum. All T&D methods would likely use media; the dividing point is when the locus of delivery control is in the instructor or the media itself.

Media Led

- Interactive video
- Computer-based training/performance support
- Programmed instruction (video/audio/paper)
- Programmed instruction/job aid (paper)

Instructor Led

- Off-site classroom
- On-site classroom
- Structured on-the-job training
- Learning team

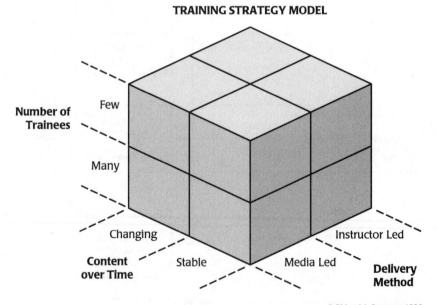

TRAINING STRATEGY MODEL

© Richard A. Swanson, 1996

Figure 9.8   Training Strategy Model

T&D Design Templates   The Whole-Part-Whole Learning Model (Swanson & Law, 1993) serves as the basis for T&D design templates. Basic psychological need for the "whole" (as explained by Gestalt psychology) and the "parts" (as explained by behavioral psychology) are utilized to structure whole-part-whole (W-P-W) learning templates. The W-P-W model can be applied at the program and individual lesson/session levels.

General Whole-Part-Whole Model

Whole-Part
1.   Whole
2.   Part
3.   Whole

A. Whole-Part-Whole Technical T&D Design Template
Whole-Part
1.   Operation/equipment/system overview
2.   Startup
3.   Operation
4.   Shutdown
5.   Defects/faults
6.   Troubleshooting
7.   Solo performance

B. Whole-Part-Whole Management T&D Design Template
Whole-Part
1.   Objectives/purpose of training
2.   Illustration of good/bad performance
3.   Conceptual model
4.   Elements of the model
5.   Techniques
6.   Practice/role playing
7.   Managerial implications discussion

C. Whole-Part-Whole Motivational T&D Design Template
Whole-Part
1.   Acceptance of group/individuals
2.   Problem/opportunity
3.   Fear/greed illustrations (with role models)
4.   The solution
5.   Solicit commitment to solution
6.   Vision success

Lessons/Session Plan Design   The lesson/session plan is the final and official document in the design phase. It carries the burden of bringing together the original performance requirement, the documentation of expertise, and the resulting training objectives into the "artful" articulation of content and method.

The lesson/session plan is not a private document. It is the property of the sponsoring organization, and it should be detailed to the point that another knowledgeable trainer could take the lesson/session plan and the supporting materials and teach essentially the same content via the same method in the same period of time.

Phase 3: Develop

Develop and/or acquire participant and instructor training materials needed to execute the training design. There is an almost unlimited range of instructor- and media-based T&D materials and media options available to the T&D profession. The development of training materials is a paradox. While the range of creative options is enormous, most training programs actually utilize very limited materials as portrayed in level 1 of the following five-level portrayal:

Level 1

- No planned instructor materials
- No planned participant materials

Level 2

- Overhead transparencies or slides
- Paper copies of the transparencies or slides for the participants

Level 3

- Overhead transparencies or slides
- Trainees print materials in the form of a structured trainee notebook (including paper copies of the transparencies or slides for the participants)

Level 4

- Overhead transparencies or slides
- Trainees print materials in the form of a structured trainee notebook (paper copies of the transparencies or slides for the participants included).
- Workplace objects and artifacts from the tasks to be learned
- Dynamic or interactive support materials such as video, interactive video, in-basket case, and simulation

Level 5

- Materials are designed to the level that they can mediate the development of knowledge and expertise *without* the need of a trainer.

There are practical reasons for producing materials at level 2. It is easy to visualize a situation in which only one to two trainees are participating and the content is unstable. In such an instance, structured on-the-job training would likely be the best method with inexpensive level 2 training materials (see Sisson, 2001). In a similar vein, practical considerations are the primary basis for choosing any of the levels.

Once materials are developed, the critical issue emerges of testing T&D programs prior to program implementation. Organizations can approach pilot-testing of training programs in five ways:

1. Conduct a full pilot test of the program with a representative sample of participants.

2. Conduct a full pilot test of the program with a group of available participants.

3. Utilize the first offering of the program as the pilot test, being sure to inform the participants of this fact and gain their support in providing improvement information.

4. Conduct a "walk-through" of the entire program with a selected group of professional colleagues and potential recipients.

5. Presenter of the program conducts a dry run by him- or herself.

Most organizations rely on 5, 4, *and* 3 to meet the pilot test requirements. For programs with limited offerings, options 4 and 5 are used.

Phase 4: Implement

Manage individual training programs and their delivery to participants. The issues around managing and delivering T&D to participants suggest that the strategies for both have been thought through and planned into program materials.

Managing individual T&D programs should not be confused with leading or managing a T&D department. The focus here is on managing individual programs that will most likely be offered on numerous occasions by a variety of presenters. Managing T&D programs should be thought of as those activities (things, conditions, and decisions) necessary to implement a particular training program. They can also be thought of as generally taking place before, during, or after the training event with time specifications recorded in weeks (or days) for the "before" and "after" time periods and hours (or minutes) on the lesson plans for the "during" period of the training event.

Either a simple paper- or computer-based project management system is what is typically used. It first requires specification of the activity, activity details, initial and completion dates, and the responsible party for each. These data can be matrixed into a management chart or placed in a simple computer database for assignments and follow-ups.

Delivery of T&D to participants is pressure point in the T&D process. Presenters want to succeed, and participants want high-quality interaction. Critics of T&D bemoan the fact that this often causes presenters to digress to gimmicks and entertainment instead of facing and managing delivery problems. One study identified the following twelve most common delivery problems of beginning trainers and the general tactics used by expert trainers in addressing those problems (Swanson & Falkman, 1997):

Delivery Problems		Expert Solutions
1. Fear		A. Be well prepared.
		B. Use ice breakers.
		C. Acknowledge fear.
2. Credibility		A. Do not apologize.
		B. Have an attitude of an expert.
		C. Share personal background.
3. Personal experiences		A. Report personal experiences.
		B. Report experiences of others.
		C. Use analogies, movies, famous people.
4. Difficult learners		A. Confront problem behavior.
		B. Circumvent dominating behavior.
		C. Use small groups for timid behavior.
5. Participation		A. Ask open-ended questions.
		B. Plan small-group activities.
		C. Invite participation.
6. Timing		A. Plan well.
		B. Practice, practice, practice.
7. Adjustment of instruction		A. Know group needs.
		B. Request feedback.
		C. Redesign during breaks.
8. Questions	*Answering:*	A. Anticipate questions.
		B. Paraphrase learners' questions.
		C. "I don't know" is OK.
	Asking:	A. Ask concise questions.
		B. Defer to participants.
9. Feedback		A. Solicit informal feedback.
		B. Do summative evaluations.
10. Media, materials, facilities	*Media:*	A. Know equipment.
		B. Have backups.
		C. Enlist assistance.
	Material:	A. Be prepared.
	Facilities:	A. Visit facility beforehand.
		B. Arrive early.
11. Openings and closings	*Openings:*	A. Develop an "Openings" file.
		B. Memorize.
		C. Relax trainees.
		D. Clarify expectations.
	Closings:	A. Summarize concisely.
		B. Thank participants.

12. Dependence
    on notes

A. Notes are necessary.
B. Use cards.
C. Use visuals.
D. Practice.

Phase 5: Evaluate

Determine and report training and development effectiveness in terms of performance, learning, and perceptions. The TPS draws upon a results assessment system (Swanson & Holton, 1999) that is conceptually connected to the first phase—analysis. In effect, it is first and foremost a checkup on those three goal-focused questions from the analysis phase: (1) Does the organization perform better? (2) Does the work process perform better? (3) Do the individuals (group) perform better? With learning being an important performance variable, assessing learning in terms of knowledge and expertise is seen as an essential intermediate goal. To a lesser extent, the perception of T&D participants and program stakeholders is viewed as important.

Based on an analysis of actual T&D practices, there have traditionally been three domains of expected outcomes: performance (individual to organizational), learning (knowledge to expertise), and perception (participant and stakeholder). To focus on a single realm changes the purpose, strategy, and techniques of an intervention. If an intervention is expected to result in highly satisfied participant-learners (perceptions), T&D professionals will engage in very different activities than if the expected outcome was to increase organizational performance. With organizational performance as the desired outcome, T&D professionals will spend time with managers, decision makers, and subject-matter experts close to the performance setting throughout the T&D process. If the outcome is satisfied participant-learners, T&D people will likely spend time asking potential participants what kind of T&D experience they like, will focus on "fun-filled" group processes, and will have facilities with pleasing amenities.

It is not always rational to think that every T&D program will promise and assess performance, learning, and perception outcomes. Furthermore, it is irrational to think that a singular focus on one domain (performance, learning, or perception) will result in gains in the other. For example:

- A demanding T&D program could leave participants less than thrilled with their experience.

- Participants may gain new knowledge and expertise that cannot be used in their work setting.

- Participants can thoroughly enjoy a T&D program and actually learn little or nothing.

Being clear about the expected outcomes from T&D is essential for good practice. As Mager (1997) notes, "If you do not know where you are going, you will likely end up some place else."

Leading the Training and Development

Lead and maintain the integrity of the personnel training and development process.
The leadership task is the most important task within the T&D effort. The training process requires strong individuals to champion the mission, goals, process, and specific efforts of training in context of the organization. To do this, the champion must clearly articulate to all parties the outputs of training and their connection to the organization, the process by which the work is done, and the roles and responsibilities of the training stakeholders.

Outputs of Training   The output of the TPS is human expertise for the purpose of improving performance. Such a decision radically affects the training process and the training stakeholders. The TPS acknowledges that training by itself can develop expertise and that workplace performance is beyond the training experience. Thus:

- To obtain workplace performance almost always requires line manager actions as well as training.
- Managers must be fully responsible partners in performance improvement interventions that rely on training.

Other common, *and less effective,* outputs of training have been

- clock hours of training or the number of people trained;
- meeting compliance requirements from external or internal source of authority;
- management and/or participant satisfaction apart from measures of knowledge, expertise, and performance;
- knowledge gains that are marginally connected to performance requirements; and
- expertise gains that are marginally connected to performance requirements.

Process of Training   Training leaders must have expertise in a defined training process. The TPS is one such process. Training leaders must advocate for the training process while relying on findings from research and experience.

Training Stakeholders   Expertise among the stakeholders is required to carry out the defined training process. Leaders select or develop the professional training expertise required by the defined training process. Roles and responsibilities of those working in the process—the stakeholders—must also be defined and managed (see the next section).

T&D ROLES AND RESPONSIBILITIES

T&D leaders manage and improve the training process. Having a defined process, such as the TPS, is a first critical step. Having people with adequate expertise to function in their assigned training process roles is another critical component. Even with these conditions in place, the training process will not necessarily work or work smoothly, let alone be improved.

It is therefore important to identify the specific stakeholder roles in the training process, their responsibilities, and the process quality standards. The TPS phases and steps constitute the process. The roles, responsibilities, and process quality standard decisions could vary with specific organizations, but generally they would include the following:

Roles

- Upper management
- Line manager
- Training manager
- Program leader
- Program evaluator
- Training specialist
- Subject-matter expert
- Support staff
- External consultant
- External provider

Responsibilities

- Leads program
- Manages program
- Produces outputs per program, phase, and/or step
- Determines whether phase-/step-level outputs meet quality standard
- Provides information about program, phase, and/or step
- Gets information about program, phase, and/or step

T&D Process Quality Standards Categories (applied to each TPS phase or step outputs)

- Quality features
- Timeliness
- Quantity

Best decisions as to the specifics on how the three sets of data interact should be made, recorded, and communicated as a means of further defining the training process for the purpose of ensuring the highest quality of training. These training roles, responsibilities, and quality standards decisions would approximate (or actually become) training policy. Once they are stabilized and adhered to, improvements to the training process can be based on solid data and experience.

COMPARISON OF SELECTED T&D MODELS

Numerous training systems have been reported in the literature. Six are identified here for the purpose of illustration and comparison. For each main feature, strengths and weaknesses are noted.

Four-Step Training Method

C. R. Dooley, 1945

Main Features

- Starts with the assumption that training must address a production problem
- T&D phases: Getting ready to instruct (four phases) and how to instruct (four phases)

Strengths

- Simple model designed to engage all experts in the workplace as trainers
- Support and participation from top management required
- Well grounded in economic, system, and psychological "logic"

Weakness

- Core method narrowly focused on trainer–trainee interactions

Instructional System Development (ISD)

U.S. Military, 1969

Main Features

- Starts with assumption that the training need has already been established
- T&D phases: analyze, design, develop, implement, and evaluate

Strengths

- Well grounded in psychological theory and system theory; no economic theory
- Has an integrated set of "tools"

Weaknesses

- System and tools that are too complex
- Best suited to technical training

Training in Organizations

Irwin L. Goldstein, 1974 (2001)

Main Features

- Starts with assumption that training may not be the basis of improving employee performance
- T&D phases: needs assessment, training and development, evaluation, and training goal

Strength

- Well grounded in psychological theory and some system theory; no economic theory

Weakness

- Does not have an integrated set of "tools"

Approaches to Training and Development

Dugan Laird, 1978 (1985)

Main Features

- Starts with the primary assumption that training is a basis for improving employee performance
- T&D phases: define standard, secure people, use inventory expertise, train on difference, test, and support

Strengths

- Grounded in psychological theory; some system theory
- Provides practical "tools"

Weakness

- Too "teacher" oriented

Training for Performance System (TPS)

Richard A. Swanson, 1978 (2000)

Main Features

- Starts with assumption that training may not be the basis of improving organization, work process, *and/or* employee performance.
- T&D phases: analyze, design, develop, implement, and evaluate

Strengths

- Well grounded in psychological, economic, and system theory
- Has an integrated set of practical "tools"

Weakness

- Analysis phase often viewed as too time-consuming

Training across Multiple Locations

Stephen Krempl and Wayne Pace, 2001

Main Features

- Starts with the T&D purpose of enhancing individual performance and organizational capacity
- T&D phases: analyze, design, develop, implement, and evaluate

Strengths

- Well grounded in system theory; some economic and psychological theory
- Integrated planning tools including information technology

Weakness

- Does not have any traditional trainer presentation and delivery "tools"

CONCLUSION

Personnel training and development is a process that has the potential of developing human expertise required to maintain and change organizations. As such, T&D may be strategically aligned to its host organization. It also has the potential of developing the expertise required to create new strategic directions for the host organization.

REFLECTION QUESTIONS

1. How would you define T&D and describe its relationship to HRD?
2. What is the role of informal and incidental learning in T&D?
3. What are the unique aspects of the training and development component of HRD?
4. What is the purpose of each of the five phases of T&D and the relationship between the phases?
5. How does T&D help with organizational challenges of managing the system and changing the system?

The Nature of Human Expertise

CHAPTER OUTLINE

The concept of human expertise lies at the core of human resource development. The definition of HRD posited by this book describes HRD as a process of developing and unleashing human expertise, with T&D on the developing side and OD on the unleashing side.

The success of an HRD-initiated and -managed intervention, regardless of the philosophy in which it may be based—learning or performance—is achieved through the development and utilization of an organization's human resources. The development of human resources requires an ability to understand human expertise. While human expertise is not fully understood, a basic grasp of the characteristics of expertise makes it possible to formulate an operational defini-tion of human expertise applicable to HRD. The following treatise on expertise and competence provides the understanding of the nature of human expertise that is required of HRD professionals.

OPERATIONAL DEFINITIONS OF EXPERTISE AND COMPETENCE
Contributed by Richard W. Herling

At the core of human resource development is the concept of human expertise. This discussion is a simple distillation of related ideas, not a meta-analysis of the literature but a synthesis of a concept of expertise. The intent of this section is twofold: first, to assist the reader in developing a basic conceptual understanding of expertise as it specifically applies to individual performance and, more gener-ally, to the context of HRD; and second, to apply this conceptual understanding of expertise to the formulation of an *operational definition* of human expertise applicable to the theory and practice of HRD.

In the process of developing an operational definition, and because of the tendency to interchange inadvertently the terms *expert* and *expertise,* several as-sumptions are necessary. The first presumes that expertise represents a journey, not a destination; that expertise characterizes the output of an active process from which experts periodically emerge. The second assumes that every person, while not each an expert, possesses some level of expertise. The final assumption is that, for the purposes of this section, human expertise is of primary interest and importance to HRD.

THE RATIONALE FOR AN OPERATIONAL DEFINITION OF EXPERTISE

After a decade of downsizing, right-sizing, restructuring, reorganizing, and reengineering (various perceived methods of attaining profitability), organiza-tions are beginning to realize that the operating expense most easily reduced, their workforce, is also the one resource that has the biggest impact on attaining and maintaining long-term profitability and growth. An organization's human resources are now being recognized as a significant competitive advantage and one of the hidden forces behind growth, profits, and lasting value (Pfeffer, 1994; Reichheld, 1996). As Torraco and Swanson (1995) note, "business success in-creasingly hinges on an organization's ability to use its employee's expertise as a factor in the shaping of its business strategy" (p. 11). It is the skills, knowledge, and experience of the organization's human resources—in short, its expertise—that have become the new secret weapon in the competitive marketplace.

Competence, as a Standard for HRD, Is No Longer Enough

Caring about their human competence base and how it is developed is beginning to make sense to organizations as they start to realize how their market value increasingly relies on the knowledge and skills of their employees (McLagan, 1997). A competent workforce is well within the grasp of any organization, but competence is not enough.

Competence suggests that an employee has an ability to do something satisfactory, not necessarily outstandingly or even well. The potential to use specific sets of knowledge and skills is what Jacobs (1997b) defines as *employee competence,* noting that "employee competence should be viewed within its proper performance context" (p. 281). Organizations are complex, adaptive, open systems guided by their own internal criteria and feedback and influenced by the economic, political, and cultural forces of their respective environments. In such systems change is inevitable, the proper performance context is constantly being redefined, and individuals who can work in complex organizations are becoming invaluable.

As represented by Swanson's (1994, p. 57) taxonomy of performance, the skills and knowledge required to maintain a system are significantly different from the expertise required to change the system. To remain competitive, organizations, and the individuals within those organizations, are required to be more flexible, to be able to adapt to the "constantly changing world of new strategies, memberships on multiple teams, customer requirements, and competitive maneuvers" (McLagan, 1997, p. 45). To gain competitive advantage, organizations are requiring that employees be top performers; thus, it is the development of workplace expertise, not competence, that is becoming vital to optimal organization performance, and HRD holds the key to "improving performance through the development and/or unleashing of human expertise" (University of Minnesota, HRD Faculty 1994).

An Operational Definition of Expertise Is Clearly Needed

In the context of individual performance and human resource development, expertise is defined as "the optimal level at which a person is able and/or expected to perform within a specialized realm of human activity" (Swanson, 1994, p. 94). As a descriptive definition of human expertise, this provides clarity and focus, and expertise is generally thought of as the possession of superior skills or knowledge in a particular area of study. Expertise is also generally recognized as implying proficiency, with an understanding that the individual gains expertise, and thus proficiency, only through experience and training.

Although the actual measurement of expertise has never been fully defined, the importance of quantifying expertise has long been recognized. The general level of expertise possessed by an individual is readily observable through his or her actions. This ease of recognition has promoted what can be interpreted as a misdirected attempt to quantify human expertise; the classification and reclassi-fication of individual levels of expertise. From the traditional terminology of the craft guilds of the Middle Ages to Jacobs's (1997b) recently proposed taxonomy of expertise for HRD, a myriad of terms, ranging from *novice* to *expert,* have been used to describe and define human expertise (Jacobs, 1997b; Hoffman, Shadbolt, Burton, & Klein, 1995; Bereiter & Scardamalia, 1993). Unfortunately, the classifi-cation of human expertise, without the ability to measure expertise quantita-tively, has limited utility.

Linking Expertise to Performance through Measurement

It is well accepted that the performance of an organization can be evaluated and addressed at three levels—organization, process, and individual job performer (Rummler & Brache, 1995; Swanson, 1994)—and that the primary tool for link-ing the three levels of performance together for taking improvement action is measurement. In fact, Rummler and Brache (1995) argue that "without measures we don't get the desired performance" (p. 135), that "measurement is the founda-tion for managing organizations as systems" (p. 134), and that it is only through measurement that performance can be monitored, managed, and improved. Swanson (1994), in a more direct manner, simply notes that "it is foolhardy to talk about development, change, and performance improvement without speci-fying the measure of performance" (p. 53).

Thus, logic dictates that the quantification and measurement of expertise is necessary for the enabling of an organization to improve its performance and the performance of its human resources, and the obvious dictates that current de-scriptive definitions of expertise do not meet this need. To be able to quantify ex-pertise, one must first be able to define operationally what expertise is.

THE THEORETICAL PERSPECTIVES OF EXPERTISE

In the past thirty years, entire books, complete chapters, and numerous papers have been written in response to the question "What is expertise?" (Chi, Glaser, & Farr, 1988; Slatter, 1990; Ericcson & Smith, 1991; Bereiter & Scardamalia, 1993; Swanson, 1994). The answers have been numerous, and the next section discusses the nature of expertise from several theoretical perspectives.

An Overview of the Cognitive Theories of Expertise

All focused research on experts and expertise began with the study of chess play-ers by deGoot and his published findings in 1965. As summarized by Kuchinke (1997), the theories in cognitive psychology and cognitive sciences on experts and expertise have now transitioned to a third generation of thinking.

First-generation research explored the individual's basic information-processing capabilities and resulted in "theories of problem-solving being stated in terms of the human information-processing system" and a search for general rules of thumb (Kuchinke, 1997).

Second-generation theories of expertise focused on complex problem solving and the characteristics of experts as the key to human expertise, as opposed to generic methods of conceptualizing solutions to unique situations. The outcome of this refocused research effort, as summarized by Glaser and Chi (1988) and included in Kuchinke's (1997) update of the current theories and literature, was the identification of several key characteristics of experts. These were descriptive characteristics associated with either how experts solve problems or how experts acquire, process, and retrieve information. As examples, experts, in their area of expertise, (1) know more, (2) use the information they have differently, (3) have better recall, (4) solve problems faster, (5) see problems at a deeper level, (6) analyze problems qualitatively, and (7) are more aware of their ability to make mistakes.

The third generation of research on expertise theory is still evolving. Based on a realization that there may be no single *expert way,* current theory and research work are examining expertise as an "ability to rapidly organize and process small bits of information into meaningful and creative solutions to specific problems" (Kuchinke, 1997).

An Overview of the Knowledge Engineering Theories of Expertise

Whereas cognitive psychologists and scientists attempt to discover how an expert thinks and what was required to be an expert, knowledge engineering (KE), another area of study highly interested in human expertise, takes a different approach.

The focus of knowledge engineers is in the replication of human expertise. Through the processes of trying to create artificial intelligence, knowledge engineering has paralleled the work done in the cognitive fields. In KE, the evolution of expertise theory has resulted in five major model classifications of human expertise: heuristic models, deep models, implicit models, competence models, and distributed models (Slatter, 1990).

Expertise, as loosely defined by the heuristic models, involves the acquisition of lots of information, including heuristic knowledge, about a specific domain. The heuristic knowledge is composed of the know-how or rules of thumb of a specific domain. In the heuristic models, expert problem solving entails the extraction and application of domain specific information and heuristic knowledge.

The KE *deep models* advance the general theory of expertise by suggesting that experts use a variety of *deep knowledge* structures (as opposed to the *shallow knowledge* structures emphasized by the heuristic models). The deep knowledge of a subject includes the "hierarchical relationships, causal models and specialist representation of domain objects . . . capturing the temporal, spatial, and/or analogical properties" of the domain (Slatter, 1990, p. 138). It is believed that these "deep mental models" created by the domain expert result in better problem solving and better explain expertise than the ones bounded by the limitations of the heuristic models.

The KE *implicit models* attempt to explain expertise by differentiating between implicit knowledge and explicit knowledge. In this context, *explicit knowledge* is defined as the combination of shallow and deep knowledge, while *implicit knowledge* is representative of the "nonarticulable experience-base knowledge that enables a skilled expert to solve a task in an effortless, seemingly intuitive fashion" (Slatter, 1990, p. 141).

Competence models make a distinction between domain knowledge (static knowledge) and task knowledge (action knowledge), with the implication being that expertise is a competence-level term denoting the potential for *doing something*. These models of expertise recognize that experts know a great deal about a specific domain and that they use this knowledge to solve problems effectively. The task knowledge, which is gained from the practice of domain specific behaviors, is compiled by the expert within his or her domain of knowledge in an ongoing search for better ways to do things, including problem solving.

The fifth class of KE expertise models, unlike the first four, is considered to be multiagent. *Distributed models* equate expert knowledge as a combination of domain knowledge, task knowledge, and cooperative knowledge (knowledge about how one communicates and interacts with others). The underlying assumption of distributed models is that, in a complex technological society, the expertise needed to solve a problem may be distributed among many individuals. Consequently, these models are more concerned with what an expert must know to solve problems cooperatively with others.

The Elements of Expertise

Based on the diversity represented in even this small sampling, an operational definition of expertise applicable to the needs of HRD seems unlikely. Even though a large body of knowledge has been, and continues to be, added to our understanding of the nature of expertise by the cognitive psychologists, cognitive scientists, and knowledge engineers, after thirty years of advancing research on this topic these groups, whose research has been focused on the domain and processes of expertise, have not agreed on what expertise is, let alone defined it in measurable terms suitable to the needs of HRD.

In fact, Kuchinke's (1997) review of the expertise theories and Slatter's (1990) summary explanation of the KE expertise models have shown, through a lack of consensus, that human expertise cannot be operationally defined by its processes. While the lack of a definition is disappointing, the combined summaries of the reviewers has brought to light several shared elements in the various theories of expertise:

- Expertise is a dynamic state.
- Expertise is domain-specific.

- The basic components of expertise are knowledge, experience, and problem solving.

Figure 10.1 is a representation of the relationship of these three foundational concepts of expertise.

Working from this perspective, the most important concept of human expertise is that it is a dynamic state. Expertise is seen by the theorists as an internal process of continuous learning by the individual; a constant acquisition of knowledge, reorganization of information, and progressive solving of problems. The importance of recognizing expertise as a dynamic state lies in the realization that a person never stops acquiring expertise. Bereiter and Scardamalia (1993) summarize the dynamic characteristic of expertise in their descriptive comparison of experts and nonexperts. The "career of the expert is one of progressively advancing on problems constituting a field of work, whereas the career of the non-expert is one of gradually constricting the field of work so that it more closely conforms to the routines the non-expert is prepared to execute" (p. 11).

The second shared element, that of expertise being domain specific, may have the most impact on the future creation of programs designed to develop expertise in individuals. How significant is this second foundational concept? Research indicates that "there is little evidence that a person highly skilled in one domain can transfer the skill to another" (Glaser & Chi, 1988, p. xvii). The demonstration of expertise in one domain is no guarantee of expertise in other areas, however, it may be that "certain task domains are more generalized then other areas, such as applied mathematics" (Glaser, 1985, p. 7). Cognitive psychologists have theorized that "there are some domains where nearly everyone becomes an expert, like reading English words" (Posner, 1988, p. xxxi). Nevertheless, the majority of research suggests that extensive, specialized knowledge is "required for excellence in most fields" (Gleespen, 1996, p. 502).

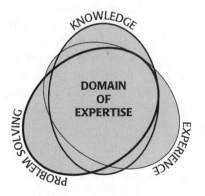

Figure 10.1   The Basic Components of Expertise

The third foundational concept highlighted by the earlier review of the expertise models and theories is that expertise is composed of a few basic components. While researchers do not always agree as to which component took precedence, all identify in some manner (1) knowledge, (2) experience, and (3) problem solving as being the distinguishing points of difference between experts and nonexperts. These three common elements can be viewed as the fundamental components of human expertise, and it is reasonable to expect that from this third foundational concept an operational definition of expertise can be developed—for example, "Human expertise is a combination of domain specific knowledge, experience, and problem-solving skills."

Each of these elements is measurable, but an operational definition, like a theory, must have utility, simplicity, and coherence (Gilbert, 1978, p. 3). As a possible operational definition, this core definition of expertise has simplicity, and in its conceptual application it appears to have utility. However, to validate the proposed definition, a closer examination of each of the three components is required.

The Component of Knowledge

Knowledge appeared in every reviewed theory and model of expertise, and in almost every case either it was descriptively different, or there were multiple types of knowledge specified. For example, the KE distributed model of expertise identified, as one of its requirements, three types of knowledge: domain knowledge, task knowledge, and cooperative knowledge.

Depending upon the theories or models being examined, the knowledge required for expertise could be implicit, explicit, shallow, deep, or heuristic. Bereiter and Scardamalia (1993), in their inquiry into the nature of expertise, note that "every kind of knowledge has a part in expertise" (p. 74). Their definition for every kind of knowledge includes what they classify as the obvious kinds of knowledge—procedural knowledge and formal knowledge—as well as what they refer to as the less obvious kinds—informal knowledge, impressionistic knowledge, and self-regulatory knowledge.

While there may be some disagreement among the theories and models regarding the specific type of knowledge required for expertise, theorists agree on two points. First, for the purposes of expertise, knowledge is, and has to be, domain-specific. Second, knowledge is an interactive component of expertise, one of the requirements for expertise, but not expertise in itself. As noted by Bereiter and Scardamalia (1993), nonexperts as well as experts have knowledge; "the difference is in how much they have, how well integrated it is, and how effectively it is geared to performance" (p. 74).

The Component of Experience

The second common component gleaned from the theories of expertise is that of experience. Just as it is recognized that all experts are knowledgeable, it is also understood that all experts are experienced. Based on their studies of master's-level chess players (Chase & Simon, 1973, cited in Posner, 1988), "Herbert Chase reasoned that to achieve a master level of expertise a player had to spend between 10,000 and 20,000 hours staring at chess positions" (p. xxxi). A number of years later, through the studied biographies of experts in many fields, it was generalized that ten thousand hours was the amount of time required to gain expert experience (cited in Bereiter & Scardamalia, 1993, p. 17). Thus, it has been hypothesized from the research, but not verified, that to become an expert one must have the equivalent of ten years of combined studies and related work experience.

Based on the experience component of expertise, the important question would seem to be not what is expertise but rather what can be done to speed up the process of acquiring expertise. Taking actions in this direction, however, would be premature for two reasons. First, the term *experience,* like *expertise,* has varied meanings currently lacking qualifying and quantifying boundaries. Second, when related to expertise, and specifically to the development of human expertise, experience (like knowledge) is an interactive component of expertise and is heavily dependent upon the type and quality, as well as the quantity, of the events experienced by the individual. As Bereiter and Scardamalia (1993) have observed in the performance of equally experienced schoolteachers, based on the training received and the number of years worked, experience "distinguishes old-timers from beginners, but does not distinguish experts from experienced non-experts" (p. 81).

The Component of Problem Solving

The key to expertise thus appears to lie in the third component, an individual's propensity to solve problems. The knowledge engineers, in attempting to replicate the process of applying expertise, have viewed problem solving as the core concept of expertise and, as with the concept of knowledge, have ended up describing and identifying a multitude of problem-solving processes.

Problem solving, as the term is currently used in cognitive psychology, constitutes some amount of searching and/or deliberation in order to find a way to achieve a goal, a concept that defines a problem as any nonroutine purposeful activity (Bereiter & Scardamalia, 1993).

The concept of problem solving as the primary component of expertise has also been heavily supported by the research of cognitive psychologists and scientists, as summarized by Glaser (1987) in his *Thoughts on Expertise* (cited in Chi, Glaser, & Farr, 1988). Bereiter and Scardamalia (1993) take the emphasis on this concept one step farther by describing problem solving as the dynamic element in the growth of expertise.

Wertheimer, an early Gestalt psychologist whose studies and research centered on insightful learning, focused on the abilities required by the individual to solve problems effectively. In his book *Productive Thinking,* Wertheimer (1945) places the emphasis on the type of solution used for solving a problem rather than on the problem itself. He identifies two types of solutions: Type A solutions, in which there is originality and insight, and Type B solutions, in which "old rules" are applied (Hill, 1971). Wertheimer believes that both types of solutions depended on the previous experience of the problem solver, noting that "the prime difference was in the originality used by the problem-solver to organize information," a characteristic unique to Type A solutions (Hill, 1971, p. 102). He also believes that true problem solving involved a "real understanding" of both the problem and the environment in which the problem was framed. Applying Wertheimer's theory of true problem solving to the concepts of human expertise, we can reason that understanding implies not merely a logical correctness but a perception of the problem as an integrated whole, which in turn leads to an insightful solution. An interesting concept but not readily measurable.

Wertheimer's concepts of real understanding and insightful solutions can also be seen at the core of Bereiter and Scardamalia's (1993) comparison of expert and nonexpert problem solving. Experts are progressive problem solvers, while "the problem-solving efforts of the non-expert is taken over by well learned routines . . . aimed at eliminating still more problems thus reducing the activity even further" (p. 81).

THE FORMULATION OF AN OPERATIONAL DEFINITION OF HUMAN EXPERTISE

From this examination of the foundational components of expertise, we can see that nonexperts can have vast amounts of knowledge, nonexperts can have many years of experience, and nonexperts can also solve problems. While basing an operational definition of expertise on the combined elements of knowledge, experience, and problem solving has simplicity and utility, it is also obvious that attempting to define expertise by its components fails to meet the desired criterion of coherence.

Unable to decipher from the theories and models of human expertise an operational definition of expertise founded on the expert's cognitive processes, and unable to base an operational definition on the identified components of expertise, we have as a final option to work from the earlier premise (that we know expertise when we see it) and attempt to base the definition on the characteristics of displayed behavior. This approach carries with it a degree of practicality as it is generally agreed that the presence of expertise is readily recognized in an individual's actions.

Experts are capable of doing things at a higher level; they have more knowledge, a greater skill level, and better solutions (VanLehn, 1989). The expert–novice research of different occupations (domains) has verified that this is true (Glaser & Chi, 1988; VanLehn, 1989; Ericcson & Smith, 1991). The fundamental basis of expert research has been driven by the recognized fact that there were observed differences in the displayed behavior of individuals engaged in the same activities. Thus, the concept of "demonstrated behavior" must be the foundational core of an operational definition of human expertise.

Behavior, as applied to the discussion of human expertise, implies an intended behavior, or action, on the part of the individual; and an action has a consequence—it terminates with a result. Results, and the actions which lead to them, are measurable. Gilbert (1978), acknowledged as a performance improvement pathfinder (Dean & Ripley, 1997), states that the result of behavior should be viewed in the context of value, "the consequence as a valuable accomplishment," a "valuable performance" (p. 17). He defines individual performance with the aid of a mathematical formula (Performance = Behavior > Consequence), equating individual performance to a transactional relationship involving both a behavior and its consequence (p. 16).

Performance, especially a valuable output, can be quantified by comparison of the value of the result to a predetermined standard. The measurement of performance can be applied to the individual, process, or organization (Rummler & Brache, 1995; Swanson, 1994) and assessed in terms of (1) time, (2) quality, (3) quantity, and ultimately, (4) cost. At the individual level, performance is thus representative of the effectiveness of the consequences of an individual's intended behavior, or actions, what some recognize as competence or "the capacity to think about performance and also to perform" (Barrie & Pace, 1997, p. 337).

Morf (1986) attempts to operationalize this relationship of individual performance to competence by stating that it "is a function of the interaction of the person and the work environment" (p. 113). He also reduces his definition of individual performance to a formula (Performance = Competence × Work Environment), claiming that his formula demonstrates a relationship between the three unobservable constructs, thereby "help[ing] to structure and explain the chaotic and confusing empirical world around us" (p. 111). The purpose of introducing this formula here is to show that there has been a recognized need for quantifying the relationship that exists between individual performance and demonstrated behavior, the representative factor of expertise.

Morf (1986) defines the variable *competence* as the product of "the worker's motivational dispositions and abilities that are relevant in the context of work" (p. 15). This is a key point in the present discussion because Morf is basing his performance theory/formula on the premise that "the aspect of the worker most frequently influenced by performance is ability levels," which he equates to the "new skills developed and new knowledge acquired in the very process of doing a job" (p. 14). In other words, the key element in Morf's formula for performance is expertise.

Gilbert (1978), in his book *Human Competence: Engineering Worthy Performance,* discusses the concept of human competence and individual performance in depth. However, unlike Morf, Gilbert sees competence not as a *component* of performance but as a *function* of "worthy performance" expressed as "the ratio of valuable accomplishments to costly behavior (Worthy Performance = Valuable

Accomplishment/Costly Behavior)" (p. 18). In Gilbert's mind, competent people are those individuals who can create valuable results without using excessively costly behavior. Gilbert uses the quantified term *competence* as the measure of efficient behavior, and his standard of competence is exemplary performance. He qualifies exemplary performance as the "historically best instance of performance" (p. 30), stating that "exemplary performers do things more easily than others do them" (p. 40).

The worthy performance of Gilbert's (1978) competent individual, the exemplary performer, can be shown to be a product of the work environment and the individual's repertory of behavior. Gilbert's explanation of a person's repertory of behavior highlights specialized responses, knowledge, and an understanding of a specific area (p. 75), and emphasizes the need to recognize that "knowledge deficiencies were the most important problems of behavior repertory" (p. 107). In short, Gilbert identifies experts (exemplary performers) and expertise (repertory of behavior) as the standard and the key element of competence, respectively.

Competence can thus be seen in its proper perspective, as a displayed characteristic of expertise, not as expertise itself but as very behavior-specific, definable, and measurable subsets within an individual's domain of expertise (Figure 10.2).

From this examination of the characteristics of individual performance and competence, as displayed behavior that is effective, efficient, and thus measurable, the remaining pieces of an operational definition of human expertise have been uncovered. As previously stated, we recognize expertise in others by their demonstrated actions. Expanding on this observation: We recognize experts as those individuals who do things better than anyone else. Experts, in their area of expertise, demonstrate their acquired expertise through outstanding performance, which means that experts can consistently do things more effectively and efficiently than nonexperts.

Human expertise can thus be operationally defined by these two desired characteristics of displayed behavior: *the consistent demonstrated actions of an individual that are both (1) efficient in their execution and (2) effective in their re-*

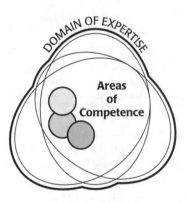

Figure 10.2 Competence of a Subset of Expertise

sults. In short, human expertise is the ability of the individual to do consistently the right thing in the right way.

However, before completely accepting this definition of human expertise, a question may be raised regarding the lack of, or the need for, a reference to *outstanding performance* and the associated expectation that it is readily observable within the domain of expertise as well as periodically seen in related domains. One cannot deny the importance of the level of expertise achieved by some individuals, but outstanding performance is a descriptive characteristic of the desired destination, not of the journey. Outstanding performance becomes a comparative characteristic of individuals, and the intent of this chapter is not to define, identify, or quantify the term of expert but to develop an operational definition of human expertise, and simply being able to quantifiably distinguish between minimal performance and optimal performance satisfies that intent.

THE IMPLICATIONS FOR HRD

As a general premise, HRD exists to serve the organization. Therefore, any answer to the posed question of implication of the proposed definition of human expertise will reflect the perspective from which one chooses to view HRD's role. The preeminent points of view see HRD as either a passive function within the organization, focused on the activities and outcomes of learning; or as an active function focused on improving organizational, process, and individual performance. While the activity of learning can contribute to performance, from the organization's perspective it is only those activities that clearly improve performance that will be seen as value added. Optimal performance has precedence over minimal performance, and in this context the ability to quantify expertise—efficient and effective behavior—can be seen as having significant implications to HRD.

One could attempt to argue that defining expertise adds no value because performance is reflective of only the lowest level of responsive behavior and that it is competence that promotes efficiency (Barrie & Pace, 1997). Consequently, this argument would conclude that it must be the competence provided to the organization by HRD through the development of core competencies, and not expertise, that is the desired outcome. Such an argument lacks merit, for while clearly linked and unquestionably similar in nature, expertise and competence are distinctly different. Figure 10.3 illustrates, by the relationship to expertise, the limitations of competence as the ultimate desired outcome.

Competence, or what can be depicted as core competencies, can be visualized as subsets of expertise. In other words, competence reflects very task-specific actions and is therefore found within an individual's domain of expertise, not encircling it. An addition, competence, with its primary goal being efficient action, can be seen as both narrowing in its nature and static, unlike expertise, which is dynamic and expanding. Competence is seen and described as an outcome (McLagan, 1997), a destination, while expertise is clearly a process (Bereiter & Scardamalia, 1993), a

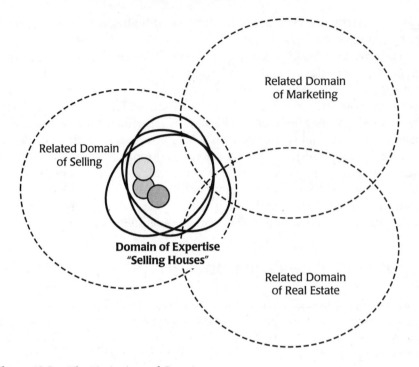

Figure 10.3   The Limitations of Competence

journey. Finally, competence is limited to a specific domain of knowledge or expertise, while the individual's area of expertise, though also recognized as domain-specific, is not limited to a single domain but often extends into several related domains. As shown by the example in Figure 10.3, the competencies are tasks specific to selling houses, but the specific domain of expertise—Selling Houses—overlaps the related but more general domains of Selling, Marketing, and Real Estate. As this example suggests, HRD must look past competence and focus on the development of expertise as a desired outcome in the process of improving performance.

This is not to say that the need or importance of learning, and the competencies that it supports, is diminished. It has always been generally understood that the acquisition of expertise required study, practice, and experience, although it has never been clear as to how much of each was needed. The result of this lack of understanding has often been a "more is better" approach to providing training. Equipped with an operational definition of human expertise, a definition that has simplicity, utility, and coherence, the HRD professional is positioned to gain a better understanding of the requirements for improving performance through the development of the organization's human resources.

The proposed operational definition of human expertise, reinforced with the analysis tools currently available to HRD, allows the actions of exemplary performers within an organization to be benchmarked in qualitative and quantitative terms. This in turn permits HRD the opportunity to focus on the development and implementation of training interventions designed to accelerate both the acquisition of specific knowledge and skills and the transfer of this expertise. However, even in this focused activity there is a potential danger should the goal of these activities be misconstrued by HRD to be the development of experts instead of expertise. As Rummler and Brache (1995) have emphasized, while failure to measure the right things results in no performance improvement, choosing to measure the wrong things (or measuring the right things for the wrong reasons) results in a loss of performance.

CONCLUSION

Human expertise is clearly a complex, multifaceted phenomenon, but by the means of an operational definition, expertise can be expressed in measurable terms. Human *expertise* can be defined as

> displayed behavior within a specialized domain and/or related domain in the form of consistently demonstrated actions of an individual that are both optimally efficient in their execution and effective in their results.

Human *competence,* a related construct and component of expertise, can also be expressed in measurable terms and defined as

> displayed behavior within a specialized domain in the form of consistently demonstrated actions of an individual that are both minimally efficient in their execution and effective in their results.

Through the use of an operational definition of human expertise and the recognition of domain specific (1) knowledge, (2) experience, and (3) problem solving as being the core elements of human expertise, the HRD profession gains conceptual access to one of the most powerful tools for improving performance: human expertise.

REFLECTION QUESTIONS

1. What exactly is expertise?
2. Cite a personal experience that illustrates the concept of expertise.
3. What is the difference among knowledge, competence, and expertise?
4. How would HRD/T&D differ if it committed to knowledge versus expertise?
5. How would HRD/T&D differ if it committed to competence versus expertise?
6. What issues arise from focusing on expertise as an outcome of T&D?

Personnel Training and Development Practices: From Individuals to Organizations

System-wide Knowledge and Expertise through T&D
Conclusion
Reflection Questions

Part Four has dealt with personnel training and development (T&D). Chapter 9 captured the essence of the T&D component of HRD, and chapter 10 delved deeper into the nature of human expertise. This third and final chapter in this part of the book provides illustrations of T&D practice as it exists in host organizations along with variations in core thinking guiding T&D practices, interventions, and tools.

VARIATIONS IN T&D PRACTICES

The practices in personnel T&D are extremely varied, because of a number of overarching variables. They include variability in mission of the host organization, purpose of the T&D function in the host organization, T&D professional expertise, content of the T&D program, and expected results from the T&D program. Commentary on each of these variables follows.

Mission and Culture of the Host Organization

Organizations vary greatly in terms of their missions and strategies, organizational structure, technology, and human resources. T&D in a high-tech financial firm that designs and manufactures heart pacemakers will look very different from T&D in a professional lawn care service.

Purpose of the T&D Function in the Host Organization

T&D that is based out of a general human resources function primarily focused on new employee training will be very different from T&D that is directly under a business unit such as sales or manufacturing.

T&D Professional Expertise

People hired into T&D positions because of their subject-matter expertise (e.g., a financial investment expert) are different from those hired because of their T&D process expertise.

Purpose of the T&D Program

T&D programs with the purpose of creating participant understanding or awareness will be very different from one with the purpose of producing expert performers upon completion of the program.

Content of the T&D Program

T&D programs having content related to values and beliefs will be very different from programs focused on technical procedures for using a particular tool or programs having to do with a particular planning method.

Expected Results from the T&D Program

T&D programs aimed at a high-profile performance problem will be looked at very differently from a program dealing with a nice-to-know topic such as general communication skills or new employee orientation.

CORE T&D PRACTICES

T&D has a number of fairly standard practices. Six standard practices are presented in the following sections.

T&D Revolves around the ADDIE Process

While the analyze, design, develop, implement, and evaluate phases are usually followed, T&D departments will supplement their expertise as needed. One example is using external consultants having high expertise and credibility for the analysis and evaluation phases on key projects. Another example is a T&D department holding on tightly to the analysis and evaluation phases and outsourcing the design, development, and implementation as a means of maintaining control while being flexible. Done this way, a relatively small T&D department focused on the analysis and evaluation phases can multiply its impact by being flexible in terms of staff allocation and obtaining staff expertise as required on a consulting or contract basis.

Use of Subject-Matter Experts

Some would argue that relying on subject-matter experts is overdone in that so many people are hired into T&D roles who have not had formal T&D or related professional preparation. People who are considered experts in a subject-matter domain and who have good people skills are regularly recruited into the T&D profession because of their subject-matter expertise. They are the best salesperson, the best manager, or the best computer repair person. The organization wants to "multiply" that expertise. The alternative strategy is to utilize subject-matter experts as members of the HRD team on a project-by-project basis. In this way they continue on with their work with a temporary T&D assignment or spend just a portion of their work time training people in their realm of expertise.

Professionally trained T&D practitioners operate from the perspective that they are experts in the T&D *process,* not just the subject matter of a given T&D program. They are experts in the T&D process and as such are skilled at identifying and using subject matter experts as assistants in the process. The argument can be made that the very best T&D professionals are experts in the T&D process and the subject domains in which they function.

Interesting and Effective Delivery

T&D has a tradition of wanting to conduct interesting and effective programs. The good reason is the commonsense goal of believing that T&D should be a positive experience, not a negative one. The idea of engaging learners with interesting activities has led to a perverted "fun-filled" training goal that plays into one of the false ideas that exist in T&D practice. It is not true, for example, that the more participants like a program, the more effective it is. Best practice would say you need to be effective first and worry about being interesting second. The research is clear about this. You can get very high satisfaction ratings from participants who have not learned and who have not changed when back on the job after the program (Alliger & Janak, 1989; Dixon, 1990).

Transfer of Learning to the Workplace

The goal of transfer is the full application of new knowledge and skills to improve individual and/or group performance in an organization or community. Important actions by a learning project manager and other stakeholders to support transfer of new knowledge and expertise are required for learning transfer.

When managing support for learning transfer becomes part of the organization's way of doing business, there are no universal "start" or "stop" points. Stakeholder support becomes integrated into an organization-wide strategy. HRD professionals need to share responsibilities and actions with the client and stakeholders as partners. Without visible involvement by managers, learners do not perceive the behavioral change as strategically important to their organization. The learning transfer process from the HRD professional perspective is as follows (Broad, 2000):

- Develop/maintain expertise in managing learning transfer.
- Identify performance requirements (including learning).
- Meet with client.
- Identify stakeholders.
- Meet with client and stakeholders.
- Analyze organizational context for transfer barriers and support.
- Develop learning design.
- Identify support for learners.
- Identify specific stakeholder transfer strategies.
- Implement learning project.
- Implement/manage transfer system.

Effective Use of Information Technology

The T&D component of HRD has had a long tradition of utilizing instructional and information technology in doing its work. This tradition was heightened with the teaching machines work of Crowder and Skinner in the 1950s. Over the years, many media have and continue to be used. Some include audio records and tapes, filmstrips, slides, opaque and transparency projections, movies, and videotapes. Contemporary T&D is presently using CD-ROMs and Web-based training.

CIGNA HealthCare's "Applying Underwriting Skills" CD-ROM computer-based instruction (CBI) program designed for salespeople with less than one year's experience in their company. The module contains basic- to intermediate-level underwriting information. As with many such technology-based training programs, this course was produced by CIGNA personnel in partnership with external consultants. It was systematically developed using the ADDIE process.

Extensive lesson design documentation was carried out, including the whole-part-whole template, flow charts, content, checkpoints, and formative tests. The extensive documentation of the design was generated by a team made up of CIGNA and external provider professionals.

The CBI materials were designed to the level that they mediate the development of participant knowledge and expertise without the need of a trainer. A well-organized "Applying Underwriting Skills Reports Binder" was distributed to personnel. It contained a table of contents, twenty cases, job aids, and the CBI disc. In that this program is self-instructional CBI, implementation was driven by the requirement to successfully "test out" the training modules.

The T&D design and development in this case were exemplary. It was conscious, purposeful, and orderly. The company project staff utilized external consultants in this work while maintaining full control over the project (e.g., design documentation was provided to project staff for review and approval). The case studies were "real" company cases and directly connected training to work performance requirements. This project utilized existing technological infrastructure (portable computers, company local area network [LAN], and general communication technology) to achieve its core goal of developing core workplace knowledge and expertise.

INDIVIDUAL-FOCUSED T&D PRACTICES

It is common to consider T&D in terms of individuals. Organizations that think in terms of individually focused T&D engage in some unique practices. The historical roots of T&D are in technical training, and it is easy to visualize the worker at a workstation surrounded by tools and materials doing his or her craft. Training in this mental image has to do with that person needing to know how to use a tool or operate a piece of equipment. The work system is well defined, and the worker needs to learn it. Thus, the focus is on the individual. The individual performer focus of T&D can be thought of in two ways: a single person requiring T&D or a number of single performers within a job classification requiring the same T&D. For example, a small community bank may need to train one teller every six months, while a major metropolitan bank may train fifty tellers each quarter.

Single-Person T&D

Two general strategies are employed for meeting single-person T&D requirements. One is to engage in on-the-job efforts that embrace the work site as a learning site and the utilization of a subject-matter expert as the instructor. Hands-on training captures the essence of on-the-job training while assuring a reasonable amount of structure, to avoid the pitfalls of it being a trial and error learning experience. Sisson's (2001) recent book opens with the following story:

> Tim Horton was having a tough time on his new job. He knew it, his boss knew it and so did everyone else. It wasn't as if he didn't try, but the computer system was complex, and there were a lot of tricks to learn. Tim spent a week in formal training and had done well. Once he got on the job, however, he couldn't keep up with the workload. Two of Tim's co-workers had tried to help. It didn't work. Tim seemed like he simply wasn't catching on.
>
> Tim's boss, Shauna Davis, was now getting pressure to replace Tim with someone who could get the job done. But Shauna was reluctant to bring in yet another new person while there was still a chance that Tim might improve. "Maybe it isn't Tim's fault. Maybe he isn't getting the right kind of help . . . after all, there is a difference between the classroom and the job," she thought.
>
> Shauna decided to have Tim work with a woman named Linda Hart. Linda was one of the very best people in their department. Linda was the semi-official department trainer and had been to a class about how to do hands-on training. But Linda was very busy. If she was going to help Tim, it would have to happen fast . . . three or four days at the most. They couldn't afford more than that.
>
> Tim met Linda in the break room. Linda spent a few minutes getting to know him better and asked about his training so far. Then they went out to Tim's area and Linda watched him work for a while. As she watched, Linda began to notice a couple of patterns. Tim was going through too many steps, and he was making a number of mistakes. He was making the job more complicated than it really was. Linda asked if she could show Tim a couple of better techniques. She went through each one step-by-step, clearly explaining what to do. One procedure at a time, she had Tim do the job. As Tim practiced, Linda watched carefully. She asked him to say what he was doing and why. When Tim got it right, she told him so. When he made a mistake, she showed him how to do it better and had him try again. She asked questions to make sure Tim really understood. This went on for the rest of the day. It was smooth, it was natural and it was effective.

The next morning Linda started by reviewing what they covered the day before. Then she had Tim go back to work while she watched. Linda was very careful to give Tim all the help and advice he needed. After a couple of hours, she started to leave Tim alone for a while and by noon, Linda wasn't even around. (pp. 1–2)

Multiple–Job Holder T&D

Martelli (1998) reports on a T&D case involving a Midwest steel company. In this instance there was a very expensive steel mill modernization investment. Given the new technology, there was "a need for a structured operator training program for ladle preheater operators" (p. 89). The case highlights the fact that the firm was so eager to get the new technology operating that they ignored training until they realized the fact that the new technology required a definitive body of knowledge and expertise for proper and safe operation. As the training was being produced, existing workers were unsuccessfully trying to learn on the job. Equipment damage and shutdown occurred during this period. Using systematic ADDIE training, a T&D program was produced and delivered. All the operators were trained, tested, and returned to the job. In a matter of months, the training resulted in 135 percent return on investment. The conclusion is that in this case training was both cost-effective and educationally effective. Martelli goes on to note that project managers in organizations need to be aware that their system changes impact on other organizational and human aspects and the T&D needs to be proactive in these change efforts.

GROUP-FOCUSED T&D PRACTICES

In recent years, there has been a realization that a "group of heads" is better than one. In addition, natural work teams that are already in place, or newly formed work groups poised to take on a new organizational challenge, are seen as logical focal points for T&D. This shift in perspective was primarily a result of Japanese views on group work, group problem solving, and group learning in the 1980s to 1990s.

Group-focused T&D practices have almost always utilized a real work-related problem facing the group and the learning that must occur to address the problem adequately. The pivot point between two perspectives on group T&D practices has to do with the relative importance of learning versus solving the problem:

- *Action learning* is committed to participant learning as the outcome—with the use of an actual problem that may or may not end up being solved.
- *Team problem* solving is committed to solving an actual problem—which may or may not end up with all the participants learning.

The difference is subtle yet important. It is subtle because in practice the two perspectives often end up looking alike and end up with the same result. They are different in the fact that what an organization is approving up front is a different potential outcome—learning versus a solved problem. More on these two perspectives follows.

Action Learning

Action learning is defined as "an approach to working with and developing people that uses work on an actual project or problem as a way to learn. Participants work in small groups to take action to solve their problem and to learn from that action. Often a learning coach works with the group in order to help the members learn how to balance their work with the learning from that work" (Yorks, O'Neil, & Marsick, 1999, p. 3). The preface of an action learning monograph edited by Yorks et al. (1999) provides a vivid example of action learning:

> In a multi-national food products company, an action learning team's recommendations for change result in savings of over $500,000 in a single division in their company. The company is awarded a Corporate Excellence award by a national human resource management association in the process.
>
> Struggling with breaking down strong business unit boundaries that had existed for years in the organization, a company creates a cross-functional action learning team to put together a plan for globally centralizing its materials management process. The very people in those business units who would be impacted by this centralization work together to come to a consensus on a plan that anticipated and addressed the issues driven by existing business unit boundaries created by the change.
>
> An organization in a highly regulated industry has to move rapidly into a competitive environment. There has been resistance to the kind of changes needed to address this challenge. After involvement in an action learning effort, individuals say things such as "Learning is ongoing, it never ends. I've learned how to learn. We've changed our outlook to 'we' and will go out to meet the competition."
>
> Stories such as these have fostered increasing interest in the use of action learning as an intervention that can produce individual, team, and organizational learning, and improve performance. (pp. v–vi)

Team Problem Solving

Team problem solving can take many forms. In almost all cases the team members learn one or more methods of problem solving and then apply the methods to a particular problem. In applying the method, the members must learn in order to solve the problem.

Scholtes (1988) identifies fourteen specific strategies for team problem solving. One well-known strategy is the plan-do-check-act (PDCA) approach developed by Walter Shewhart and popularized by W. Edwards Deming in the 1980s during the quality improvement movement in business and industry. Scholtes offers the following example of team problem solving:

An equipment maintenance department in a government agency realized that to cut the number of complaints they received, they'd have to find out what their customers wanted and start addressing those needs.

A group of mechanics and supervisors talked to representatives of each department they served to identify customer needs. They found two key concerns: First, the customers had different priorities than the maintenance department—despite severe cutbacks, the customers were still more concerned about safety than repair costs. Second, the customers felt that the repair process took too long.

The maintenance team then split into two groups. One found ways to resolve conflicting priorities by developing appropriate solutions. The second studied the repair process, localizing problems, looking for causes, and developing solutions.

Conflicts in priorities are now settled between a maintenance supervisor and a designated person in each department, The repair process has been streamlined with unnecessary steps cut out entirely. Other delays in repairs have been eliminated by revising purchasing policies of equipment is more standardized, and by keeping better records of failure so that they can stock the right spare parts. (pp. 35–36)

WORK PROCESS–FOCUSED T&D PRACTICES

In recent years, T&D has learned to think in terms of work processes, not just jobs. The job perspective uses the job as the basis for thinking about and carrying out T&D. When job roles were stable, T&D could be organized around jobs and job hierarchies such as machine attendant, machine operator, lead operator, technician, supervisor, manager, and executive. Given the instability of jobs and the increased focus on how the work gets done, work processes have become increasingly important.

Process-focused T&D can be thought of in two forms. One is related to understanding and studying processes, and the other is developing knowledge and expertise that is derived from work processes (vs. traditional job and task analysis).

Understanding and Studying Processes

A major producer of consumable goods was experiencing extreme problems in the quality of its product. An initial performance diagnosis made it clear that training was required as a result of the loss of expertise in the workplace. Worker turnover and changes in worker demographics were root causes of this loss.

The work involved a continuous production process and no analysis or documentation of the process existed. The T&D manager chose to teach a team of workers how to analyze their job and particularly to analyze systems tasks using systems task analysis (Figure 11.1) as the basis for creating a T&D program for existing and future workers.

The amazing thing that happened was that workers who were not experts in their own work were taught the tools required to analyze expertise. Then they

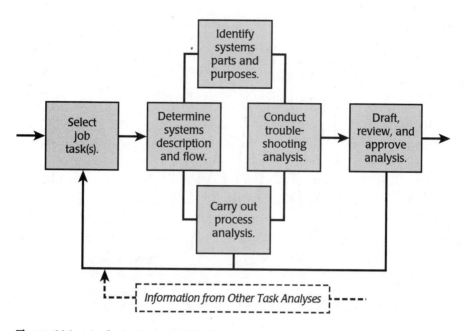

Figure 11.1   Analyzing Systems Tasks (*Source:* Swanson, 1994, p. 152)

analyzed their own work, became experts as a result of doing the analysis work, and the production problem went away (see Figure 11.2)! Even though the immediate problem disappeared through analysis of the work processes and documenting the required expertise, a training program was produced for other work groups and future workers.

Process-Referenced Training

Most T&D is organized in relation to a person's job. Job-referenced expertise is T&D connected to the work process instead of the job. Here is an example: Six people working in the organization make contributions to the successful execution of a sale. In the past, they viewed their work in terms of their individual jobs, such as office manager. The office manager job requires that person to support three different sales processes, sales marketing, and human resource management.

Instead of starting by analyzing the sales manager job, the starting point is to analyze the core processes and then see how the office manager fits into the process. Figure 11.3 is a conceptual illustration of an integrated flowchart that shows process activity steps 1 to 17 of one of the three sales processes and the fact that people holding six different jobs (A–F) contribute to the process. Imagine that job E in Figure 11.3 is the sales manager job. The office manager participates in selected activity steps and may be a contributor or the responsible person for that step. The activity steps are then classified into tasks by themselves or in clusters. These

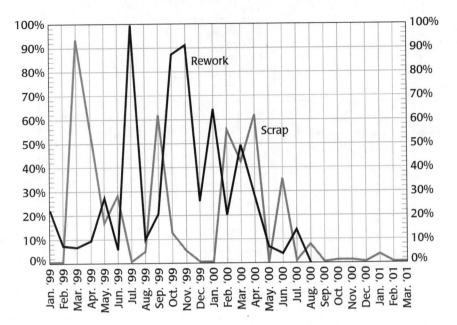

Figure 11.2 Scrap and Rework Chart for a Fortune 100 Food-Processing Company before and after Implementing the TPS

process-referenced tasks are then used as the unit of expertise analysis and training. This illustrates a fundamental reorientation of the isolated job to activity to a composite of activities directly connected into core organizational processes that are shared by others in the organization. It results, then, in process-referenced training (Swanson & Holton, 1998).

ORGANIZATION-FOCUSED T&D PRACTICES

As we have noted elsewhere, almost every sound T&D effort has an OD component, and almost every sound OD effort has a T&D component. Large system change nearly always requires T&D. The overall change effort will likely be classified as OD with a heavy dose of T&D. Organization-focused T&D can be thought of as being in two forms: one focused on core values and the other on core knowledge and expertise.

Core Values through T&D

Standard business vocabulary has come to include *vision* and *values*. T&D regularly gets called upon to engage personnel with understanding the company vision and values and with internalizing them for the purpose of harmonizing the workforce. Most such efforts require the changing of one value set for another

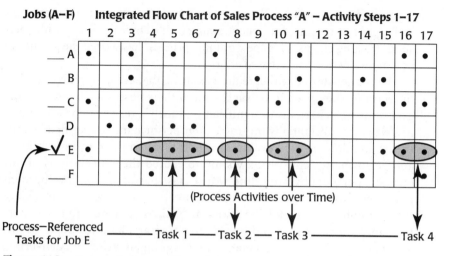

Figure 11.3 Process-Referenced Expertise

(one Gestalt for another). For example, companies that embraced the total quality movement engaged in up-front training at all levels in the organization to get their personnel to accept the paradigms of customer, process, and quality as being essential for sustainable performance. These were in place of short-term output and financial measures.

Rasmussen (1997, p. 132) proposes nine steps to establishing a total organization focused on values learning effort through T&D:

1. Survey internal customers to identify a need.
2. Form a partnership with senior management.
3. Form a vision team.
4. Communicate two-way with all employees.
5. Design/conduct the vision conference.
6. Design/conduct vision team training.
7. Design/conduct interdepartmental forum.
8. Design/conduct training for individuals.
9. Conduct ongoing vision process meetings.

System-wide Knowledge and Expertise through T&D

Sometimes T&D addresses an overarching system condition or state of affairs, not an individual contributor, work group, or work process problem. For example, in one Fortune 50 insurance organization, training efforts had been distributed across a number of different functions and levels. Uniformity was needed to ensure system-wide knowledge and expertise. Here is a portion of its T&D story:

A new team was formed to merge various training activities under one umbrella: product training with sales training with technical training with operations training efforts. This "new training process" has started the journey to becoming a performance-based effort.

The charter started with a request assuring that every employee receives the training they need to be successful in their position. In the sales organization, the charter is to significantly "touch" every person twice a year in a way that substantially improves their performance as verified by self-report and documented evaluation. This resulted in an overall training and performance consulting vision: to exceed the expectations of our business partners by providing world-class performance development processes, expertise, and tools driving superior performance. To achieve this vision by: (1) consulting with our business partners to assess performance gaps, recommend improvement strategies and shepherd ongoing performance improvement, (2) designing, developing, delivering, and producing HRD/performance improvement interventions for work processes and employees—new and old, (3) evaluating the impact of T&D/performance improvement interventions focused on the strategic imperatives of achieving customer/provider satisfaction, dominating market share, maximizing profitability, and promoting a culture of winning with highly motivated, well-informed, diverse associates.

Recognizing that this required a shift in internal functioning and a realignment of relationships with customers, training staff met as a team to consider what to rename what had been a training function. Based on the perceptions of a new role in the organization they selected "Training and Performance Consulting." Training provided a connection to the past and a framework for internal customers to engage in the shifts implied by performance consulting. The name illustrated the recognition of the need to redesign T&D efforts around performance improvement from the beginning of every intervention and not to justify programs based on participant satisfaction. (McClernon & Swanson, 1998, pp. 1–2)

Furthermore, a performance improvement roundtable of corporate stakeholders was established to guide the overall effort (see Figure 11.4).

CONCLUSION

Personnel training and development takes many forms. At the narrow and specific end of the spectrum there can be a very small training program that teaches employees how to use their electronic access card properly to enter the building. In fact, it may end up getting packaged as a self-instructional job aid that comes in the envelope with the access card. At the other end of the spec-

Figure 11.4 Performance Roundtable (*Source:* McClernon & Swanson, 1998)

trum, you could find employees self-directing their own learning under the auspices of a company-sponsored tuition reimbursement plan in conjunction with a systematic self-managed career planning and career development process.

The dominant practices in the middle of the T&D spectrum described in this chapter are focused on imparting the expertise required of personnel to perform their present work or to prepare for the new work required of their changing workplace.

REFLECTION QUESTIONS

1. Briefly describe an organization with which you are familiar. Speculate as to how that organization's mission would impact on the T&D practices.

2. What are two to four major implications of having one person needing training in an area versus two hundred people needing the same training?

3. When does team or group learning make sense and not make sense?

4. How does thinking about T&D at the work process level impact on the work of T&D professionals?

5. What does T&D need to do in order to be instrumental in organization-wide expertise issues?

Unleashing Human Expertise through Organization Development

This section captures the essence of organization development component of HRD as well as the nature of the change process. Illustrations of organization development practice that exist in host organizations are presented along with variations in core thinking, processes, interventions, and tools.

Overview of Organization Development

The central view of organization development (OD) is that OD has the capability of *unleashing human expertise,* resulting in improvements at the organization, process, work group, and individual levels. OD constitutes the smaller realm of HRD practitioner activity when compared to personnel training and development (T&D). Yet, it can be argued that OD has larger or more systemic influence on the organization. Within organization development, as much effort has been focused on studying individuals as it has on studying organizations. While this is the history of OD, it appears that there is a shift to an organizational system focus (vs. individual or group focus) in OD theory and practice.

Organization development practice is more likely to be focused on existing conditions that are not functioning well than on long-range improvement or holistic change efforts. In all cases, whether present performance issues related to system maintenance or system changes for the future, OD interventions deal with the *change process* for the purpose of improvement. Cummings and Worley (2001) provide an explanatory definition of organization development that begins to frame this chapter: "Organization development is a system-wide application of behavioral science knowledge to the planned development, improvement, and reinforcement of the strategies, structures, and processes that lead to organization effectiveness" (Cummings & Worley, 1997, p. 1).

In earlier chapters, we have identified three core theories that stand as the basis of HRD, T&D, and OD: psychological, system, and economic theories. Embracing the three necessarily causes us to revise this previous definition to go beyond the behavioral science base (psychological only) that has limited OD. It would read as follows:

> Organization development is a system-wide application of social science knowledge (primarily psychological, systems, and economic theories) to the planned development, improvement, and reinforcement of the strategies, structures, and processes that lead to organization performance.

Our concise definition of OD is as follows:

> OD is the process of systematically unleashing human expertise to implement organizational change for the purpose of improving performance.

Organizational leaders need help in their quest for sustainable performance. According to Beer and Nohria (2000), the mantra for the twenty-first century is to "lead change." They go on to report, "The results are not always encouraging, however. . . . The dramatic reduction in CEO tenure confirms that leaders do not have the knowledge and skills, or perhaps the will to transform their companies" (p. ix). Clearly, organizations need OD, and the OD needs to be good to help organizations achieve their performance goals.

VIEWS OF OD

Fortunately, there is not one view of OD. The nature of organizations, the conditions surrounding the need for system change, and the process of change all vary so greatly that one lens would be inadequate. Alternative views are useful. Three snapshots will be presented in this chapter to capture the range of thinking in OD. First is Egan's analysis of the outcomes and definitions of OD. Second, we will revisit early change models, including Lewin's classic unfreeze-move-refreeze change process, and, third, we will take a look at whole systems change such as the Rummler and Brache (1996) organization performance improvement process.

The Dependent Variable and Definitions of OD

A great deal of literature and practice is aimed at systematically implementing organizational change for the purpose of improving performance that does not formally call itself "OD." Starting with Beckhard's 1969 definition (being the first reported use of the term in the literature) to the latest Cummings and Worley (2001) definition reported at the beginning of this chapter, OD has been an evolutionary journey. Egan's (2000) review of this definitional history has produced a chronological report worth reviewing (see Figure 12.1).

Egan (2000) concludes from his analysis that ten key dependent variables are reported throughout the definitional literature (Figure 12.2). Reviewing these purported outcomes of OD highlights the range of thinking. For example, *Facilitate Learning and Development* as an outcome is very different from *Enhance Profitability and Competitiveness*. Egan's compilation of the definitions OD found in the OD literature also helps us understand the range of thinking in OD and its historical development.

Figure 12.1   Organization Development Definitions

Author	Date	Definitions (dependent elements bolded)	Dependent Variable
Beckhard	1969	Organization development is an effort (1) planned, (2) organization-wide, and (3) managed from the top, **to (4) increase organization effectiveness and health** through (5) planned interventions in the organization's "processes," using behavior-science knowledge.	Increase organization effectiveness and health
Bennis	1969	Organization development (OD) is a response to change, a complex educational strategy **intended to change the beliefs, attitudes, values, and structure of organizations so that they can better adapt to new technologies, markets, and challenges** and the dizzying rate of change itself.	Adapt to new technologies, markets, challenges and change

(Continued)

Figure 12.1   Continued

Author	Date	Definitions (dependent elements bolded)	Dependent Variable
Blake and Mouton	1969	Organization development emphasizes the "O" in every sense of the word. It means **development of the entire organization** or self-sustaining parts of an organization from top to bottom and throughout. True OD is theory based, team focused, and undertaken by means of self-help approaches that place a maximum reliance on internal skills and leadership for **development activities.** It is top led, line managed, and staff supported. **Development activities** focus on the "system," those traditions, precedents, and past practices that have become the culture of the organization. Therefore, **development must include individual, team, and other organization units** rather than concentrating on any one to the exclusion of others. OD is thus this comprehensive approach that integrates the management sciences, business logic, and behavioral systems of an organization into an organic, interdependent whole.	Development and development activities
French	1969	Organization development refers to **a long-range effort to improve an organization's problem-solving capabilities and its ability to cope with changes in its external environment** with the help of external or internal behavioral-scientists consultants, or change agents, as they are sometimes called.	Improve problem solving capabilities and ability to cope with environmental change
Golembiewski	1969	Organizational development implies a normative, reeducation strategy intended to affect systems of beliefs, values, and attitudes within the organization so that it can **adapt better to the accelerated rate of change in technology, in our industrial environment and society in general.** It also includes formal organizational restructuring that is frequently initiated, facilitated, and reinforced by the normative and behavioral changes.	Adapt better to change in technology, the industrial environment and society

Author	Date	Definitions (dependent elements bolded)	Dependent Variable
Lippit	1969	Organization development is the **strengthening of those human processes in organizations that improve the functioning of the organic system so as to achieve its objectives. Organization renewal** is the process of initiating, creating, and confronting needed changes so as to make it possible for organizations to become or remain viable, to adapt to new conditions, to solve problems, to learn from experiences, and to move toward greater **organizational maturity.**	Strengthening human processes; organizational renewal and maturity
Schmuck and Miles	1971	Organizational development can be defined as **a planned and sustained effort to apply behavior science for system improvement,** using reflexive, self-analytic methods.	System improvement
Burke and Hornstein	1972	Organization development is a process of planned change—change of an organization's culture **from one that avoids an examination of social process (especially decision making, planning, and communication) to one that institutionalizes and legitimizes this examination.**	Institutiona lization and legitimizing of the examination of social process
Hall	1977	Organizational development refers to **a long-range effort to improve an organization's problem-solving capabilities and its ability to cope with changes in its external environment** with the help of external or internal behavior-scientist consultants or change agents.	Improve problem-solving capabilities and ability to cope with changes in its external environment
French and Bell	1978	Organization development is **a long-range effort to improve an organization's problem-solving and renewal processes,** particularly through a more effective and collaborative management of organization culture—with special emphasis on the culture of formal work teams—with the assistance of a change agent, or catalyst, and the use of the theory and technology of applied behavioral science, including action research	Improve problem-solving and renewal processes

(Continued)

Figure 12.1 Continued

Author	Date	Definitions (dependent elements bolded)	Dependent Variable
Beer	1980	Organization development is **a system-wide process** of data collection, diagnosis, action, planning, intervention, and evaluation **aimed at (1) enhancing congruence between organizational structure, process, strategy, people, and culture; (2) developing new and creative organizational solutions; and (3) developing the organization's renewing capacity.** It occurs through collaboration of organizational members working with a change agent using behavioral science theory, research, and technology	Enhancing congruence; developing creative organizational solutions; developing renewing capacity
Beer	1980	Organizational development is **a process for diagnosing organization problems** by looking for incongruencies between environment, structures, processes, and people.	Problem diagnosis
Burke	1982	Organization development is a **planned process of change in an organization's culture** through the utilization of behavioral science technology, research, and theory.	Cultural change
Davis	1983	Organization development consists of a series of theory-based workshops, techniques, programs, systematic approaches, and individual consulting interventions **designed to assist people in organizations in their day-to-day organizational life and the complex processes this involves.** All of this is backed up with beliefs, biases, and values held by the organization development practitioner.	Assist people in organizations
Nielsen	1984	Organization development is the attempt **to influence the members of an organization to expand their candidness with each other** about their views of the organization and their experience in it, and **to take greater responsibility for their own actions** as organization members. The assumption behind OD is that when people pursue both of these objectives	Expand candidness; increase accountability; achieve individual and organizational goals

Author	Date	Definitions (dependent elements bolded)	Dependent Variable
		simultaneously, they are likely to discover new ways of working together that they experience as more effective for **achieving their own and their shared (organizational) goals.** And that when this does not happen, such activity helps them to understand why and to make meaningful choices about what to do in light of this understanding.	
Burke and Schmidt	1985	Organizational development is **a process that attempts to increase organizational effectiveness** by integrating individual desires for growth and development with organizational goals. Typically, this process is planned change effort that involves a total system over a period of time, and these change efforts are related to the organization's mission.	Increase organizational effectiveness
Beer and Walton	1987	Organization development comprises a set of actions undertaken to **improve organizational effectiveness and employees' well-being.**	Organizational effectiveness and employee well-being
French, Bell, and Zawacki	1989	Organizational development is **a process of planned system change that attempts to make organizations better able to attain their short- and long-term objectives.**	Obtain long- and short-term objectives
Vaill	1989	Organization development is **an organizational process for understanding and improving any and all substantive processes an organization may develop** for performing any task and pursuing any objectives. . . . A "process for improving process"—that is what OD has basically sought to be for approximately 25 years.	Improving processes
McLagan	1989	Organization development: Assuring healthy inter- and intraunit relationships and **helping groups initiate and manage change.** Organization development's primary emphasis is on relationships and processes between and among individuals and groups. Its primary intervention is influence on the relationship of individuals and **groups to effect and impact the organization** as a system.	Initiate and manage change to effect and impact the organization

(Continued)

Figure 12.1 Continued

Author	Date	Definitions (dependent elements bolded)	Dependent Variable
Porras and Robertson	1992	Organizational development is a set of behavioral science-based theories, values, strategies, and techniques aimed at the planned change of the organizational work setting **for the purpose of enhancing individual development and improving organizational performance,** through the alteration of organizational members' on-the-job behavior.	Enhancing individual development and organizational performance
Cummings and Worley	1993	Organization development is a systemwide application of behavioral science knowledge to the planned development and reinforcement of organizational strategies, structures, and processes **for improving an organization's effectiveness.**	Improving organizational effectiveness
Burke	1994	Organization development is **a planned process of change in an organization's culture** through the utilization of behavioral science technologies, research, and theory.	Culture change
Church, Waclawski, and Siegal	1996	Organization development is a field based on values—promoting positive humanistically oriented large-large system change in organizations—plain and simple. . . . If they are not morally bound to the core values of the field, then they simply are not doing OD. . . . OD is about **humanistic change on a systemwide level.** . . . It is about **improving the conditions of people's lives in organizations.** . . . OD is about helping people in organizations.	Humanistic change on a systemwide level; improving the conditions of people's lives
Dyer	1997	Organization development is a process whereby actions are taken to **release the creative and productive efforts of human beings** at the **same time achieving certain legitimate organizational goals such as being profitable, competitive, and sustainable.**	Release creative and productive efforts; profitability, competitiveness, and sustainability

Author	Date	Definitions (dependent elements bolded)	Dependent Variable
French and Bell	1999	Organization development is **a long-term effort,** led and supported by top management, **to improve an organization's visioning, empowerment, learning, and problem-solving processes,** through an ongoing, collaborative management of organization culture—with special emphasis on the culture of intact work teams and other team configurations—using the consultant–facilitator role and the theory and technology of applied behavioral science, including action research.	Improve visioning, empowerment, learning, and problem-solving processes

Source: Egan (2000, pp. 14–16). Used with permission.

Figure 12.2   Ten Key Dependent Variables from Definitions of Organization Development

Facilitate Learning and Development

Improve Problem-solving

Advance Organizational Renewal

Strengthen System and Process Improvement

Increase Effectiveness

Enhance Profitability and Competitiveness

Ensure Health and Well-being of Organizations and Employees

Initiate and/or Manage Change

Support Adaptation to Change

Engage Organization Culture Change

Source: Egan (2000). Used with permission.

Taxonomy of Performance

Once again, the taxonomy of performance (refer back to Figure 9.1) is one way of gaining perspective on OD. It poses the two challenges of "maintaining the system" and "changing the system." Both realms can demand OD interventions as the development of human expertise (T&D) may not be enough to advance the system. The "changing the system" portion of the taxonomy of performance—in the form of improvements or inventions of whole new systems—is where the most challenging and risky OD work takes place.

An organizational system that is mature, works well, and yields great returns will not necessarily remain in that state. A variety of forces cause organizations to deteriorate or disappear. Fundamental paradigm shifts in technology or customer demands are two examples. Thus, leaders and managers have the continuing pressure of changing their organizational systems to meet the new demands of the immediate and far future. Curiously, it gives rise to the motto "If it ain't broke, fix it!"

Early Change Models

The classic change model of "unfreezing, moving, and refreezing" is attributed to Kurt Lewin (1951). This simple and basic model still has utility today as a word picture of change. The unfortunate part of this view is its rigid beginning and end states. But the 1950s was a different time. Today's view of the world is closer to *continuous* change. As powerful as Lewin's frozen imagery remains to this day, it was refuted from the onset. General system theory (also developed in the early 1950s) informed us that all systems are open systems and therefore fluid and adapting. It is problematic that many easily understood metaphors in the organization development profession are simply inadequate or inaccurate, and Lewin's unfreeze-move-refreeze metaphor is one example.

Lewin's model declares that the *information* that highlights the discrepancy between the actual and desired behaviors among stakeholders will result in their willingness to engage in the change process—or to unfreeze. While this remains a basic tenet among many OD professionals, economic and system variables are now viewed as equally important. It is important to note that the focal point of Lewin's work was on individuals and groups within organizations.

Prior to Lewin's work, Gunnar Myrdal (1944/1996), the Swedish economist, in studying the white–black racial divide in the United States, proposed that in a democratic society the higher-order beliefs among its members would win out over unexamined illogical practices. This idea is fundamental to OD practice, and it is interesting to note that so many of the implicit values of OD coming out of the behavioral sciences are predicated on democracy. Myrdal was named Nobel laureate in 1974 for his pioneering and penetrating analysis of the interdependence of economic, social, and institutional phenomena.

Lewin's *moving* phase involves intervening in the organization through changes in the organizational processes and structures to develop a new set of values and behaviors. The *refreezing* phase is one that systemically installs and reinforces the new set of values and behaviors. Again, while the freeze-move-refreeze metaphor dominates the interpretation of Lewin, it is his reliance on information showcasing discrepancies between actual and desired states that is probably the greater contribution to OD.

The fact that Lewin was a scholar (not simply a problem solver) and experimented with the change process of individuals in the actual social situation, or the milieu of life, led to "field theory." *Field theory* is the proposition that human behavior is related to one's personal characteristics and the environment (Lewin, 1961). This view of OD—working through the individuals and groups from a psychologist's view—continues to resonate in OD theory and practice. The rival view is to study the organization's system and its connection with society.

Whole System Change

One of the key characteristics of substantive whole system change through OD is the commitment to carefully study the organizational system. This is in contrast to simply engaging groups in a generic problem-solving method along with a reliance on stakeholder perception data as a measure of results. Whole system change requires (1) careful study of the organization and (2) reliance on multiple types of data. There is a fair amount of shallow literature about whole system change that misses these two requirements. They often report cases of action-oriented problem solving on narrowly focused issues.

Two examples of whole system OD can be characterized by system-level performance improvement by Rummler and Brache (1995) and the scenario planning by Schwartz (1991). Schwartz advocates a scenario process of planning for an uncertain future and preparing for alternative futures. The goal of his whole future state whole systems planning is to provide paths to strategic insight for individuals and the company. Scenario planning can be seen as the expansive thinking that precedes traditional strategic planning.

The role of HRD and OD in strategic organizational planning is ill defined at best. One model for thinking about the theory and practice of strategic HRD combines scenario planning and strategic planning into strategic organizational planning (Swanson, Lynham, Ruona, & Provo, 1998). Central to this thinking are the three strategic roles of HRD and the inclusion of scenario building along with traditional strategic planning into an overall framework of strategic organizational planning (Figure 12.3).

HRD that is truly of strategic value to an organization is (1) *performance based*—it must contribute directly to important business goals and must be based on key business performance requirements; (2) *demonstrates its strategic capability*—provides strategic organizational planning education and learning, and actively participates in the strategic organizational planning process, and (3) is responsive to the emergent nature of strategy—assumes a deliberate role in the emergent nature of strategic organizational planning (Torraco & Swanson, 1995).

KEY OD TERMS

Beyond the definition of OD, key concepts and terms provide a basis of understanding the profession. The definitions provided in Figure 12.4 include basic OD terms as well as strategic OD and change role terms.

Figure 12.3 Strategic Organizational Planning (SOP) *(Source:* Swanson, Lynham, Ruona & Provo, 1998, p. 591).

Figure 12.4 Definitions of Key OD Terms

OD Term	Description/Definition of the Term
Change	A departure from the status quo and implies movement toward a goal, an idealized state, or a vision of what should be, and movement away from present conditions, beliefs, or attitudes.
Change agent	A person or team responsible for beginning and maintaining a change effort. May come from inside the organization (internal consultant) or from outside the organization (external consultant).
Choosing to participate	One of the six ethical dilemmas faced by the OD practitioner. Means that people should have the freedom to choose whether to participate in OD interventions if they are to gain self-reliance to solve their own problems. It implies knowledge about OD.
Client	The client is the organization, group, or individuals whose interests the change agent primarily serves. It is to the client that the consultant is responsible. On occasion the "client" may differ from those who originally sponsored, or participated, in the change effort.
Client-centered consultation	Using the client's knowledge and experience, by the OD practitioner, in delivery and conduct of the consulting process. Ensures consultant's views are not imposed on the client and that the client develops the expertise and knowledge to conduct and sustain the intervention.
Culture	The basic assumptions and beliefs that are shared by members of an organization, that operate unconsciously, and that define in a basic 'taken-for-granted'

fashion an organization's view of itself and its environment. These assumptions and beliefs are learned responses to a group's problems.

Empathy and support	The need to know how people are experiencing change. Can help identify those who are having trouble accepting the changes, the nature of their resistance, and possible ways to overcome it.
Entry	The need for change in an organization when a problem is discovered.
Environment	Those external elements and forces that can affect the attainment of strategic goals, including suppliers, customers, competitors, and regulators, as well as cultural, political, and economic forces.
Human process intervention	Intervention processes focuses on improving communication, problem solving, decision making, and leadership. Derive mainly from the disciplines of psychology and the applied fields of group dynamics and human relations. Are based on assumption/beliefs that value human fulfillment and expect that organizational effectiveness follows from improved functioning of people and organizational processes.
Intervention	A change effort or a change process. It implies an intentional entry into an ongoing system for the purpose of initiating or introducing change. The term *intervention* refers to a set of planned activities intended to help the organization increase its effectiveness.
Marginality	The ability to successfully straddle boundaries between two/more groups.
Mission	The organization's major strategic purpose or reason for existing. May include specification of target customers and markets, principal products or services, geographic domain, core technologies, strategic objectives, and desired public image.
Open system	A set of interdependent components having a purpose. Any organization is an open system: it takes in inputs, acts on them through a transformation process, and releases them into the environment as outputs.
Organization development	OD is the process of systematically unleashing human expertise to implement organizational change for the purpose of improving performance.
Performance norms	Implicit or explicit member beliefs about how the group should perform its task and include acceptable levels of performance. They derive from interactions among members and serve as guides to group behavior.
Process	Refers to "how" things are done. Is a key definitional component of OD and is dynamic in nature. Is often associated with the transformational component of an open system—for example, products or service delivery methods, referring to how inputs get converted to outputs in a(n open) system.
Separation	Usually the final step in the OD intervention, and where the change agent prepares to leave the change effort.
Sponsor	The one/s who underwrites, legitimizes, and champions a change effort or OD intervention.

(Continued)

Figure 12.4 Continued

OD Term	Description/Definition of the Term
Stakeholder	The one who has an interest in the change intervention. Includes such stakeholders as customers, suppliers, distributors, employees, and government regulators.
Startup	The point when the change agent enters the picture, working to clarify issues surrounding the problem and to gain commitment to the change effort.
Strategic intervention	Interventions that link the internal functioning of the organization to the larger environment and transform the organization to keep pace with changing conditions. They are organization-wide and bring about a fit among business strategy, structure, culture, and the larger environment. Are derived from the disciplines of strategic management, organizational theory, open systems theory, and cultural anthropology.
Subsystem	A part of a system. May include work units, departments, or divisions. May also cut across the organization to encompass activities, processes, or structures.
Survey feedback	A special version of data feedback that has arisen out of the wide use of questionnaires in OD work. A flexible and potentially powerful feedback technique.
System	A set of interdependent components. Any organization is an open system: it takes in inputs, acts on them through a transformation process, and releases them into the environment as outputs.
Technostructural intervention	Interventions focused on the technology and structure of organizations. Are rooted in the disciplines of systems engineering, sociology, and psychology and in the applied fields of sociotechnical systems and organization design.
Unobtrusive measures	Involves data not collected directly from respondents and from secondary sources, such as company records and archives. They are especially helpful in diagnosing the organization-, group-, and individual-level outputs.

THE GENERAL OD PROCESS

We have defined OD as a five-phase process that is essentially a problem-defining and problem-solving method related to the organization. For those who react negatively to the notion of problems, we suggest they use the positive word of their choice (e.g., *opportunity, change, improvement,* etc). In fact, there is an OD methodology called *appreciative inquiry* that demands a positive approach to change (Copperrider & Srivasta, 1987). This method only allows for the search and utilization of positive information in the OD process.

The general five-phase process that captures the essence of OD is as follows:

1. Analyze/contract
2. Diagnose/feedback
3. Plan/develop
4. Implement
5. Evaluate/institutionalize

You will recall that we identified the HRD phases as analyze, propose, create, implement, and assess and the T&D phases as analyze, design, develop, implement, and assess.

OD professionals within HRD usually do not talk about their work in universal terms, and many OD process models and rival terminology exist. Two models are overviewed here: action research and organization development for performance system.

ACTION RESEARCH (PROBLEM-SOLVING METHOD)

Cummings and Worley (2001) have summarized "action research" (actually a problem-solving method) in eight steps (Figure 12.5). Some claim that action research is the foundation for most OD interventions (Rothwell et al., 1995). The Cummings and Worley (2001) portrayal of the action research process and their description of each process step (pp. 24–26) follows:

1. *Problem identification.* This stage usually begins with a key executive in the organization or someone with power and influence who senses that the organization has one or more problems that might be solved with the help of an OD practitioner.

2. *Consultation with a behavioral science expert.* During the initial contact, the OD practitioner and the client carefully assess each other. The practitioner has his or her own normative, developmental theory or frame of reference and must be conscious of those assumptions and values. Sharing them with the client from the beginning establishes an open and collaborative atmosphere.

3. *Data gathering and preliminary diagnosis.* This step is usually completed by the OD practitioner, often in conjunction with organization members. It involves gathering appropriate information and analyzing it to determine the underlying causes of organizational problems. The four basic methods of gathering data are interviews, process observation, questionnaires, and organizational performance data (the latter, unfortunately, is often overlooked). One approach to diagnosis begins with a questionnaire to measure precisely the problems identified by the earlier steps. When gathering diagnostic

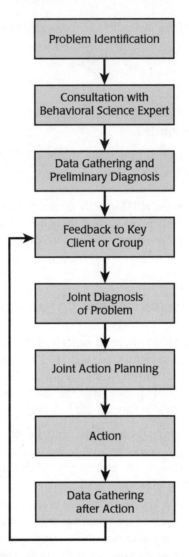

Figure 12.5   Action Research Model (*Source:* Adapted from Cummings and Worley, 2001.)

information, OD practitioners may influence members with whom they are collecting data. In OD, every action on the part of the consultant constitutes an intervention that will have some effect on the organization.

4. *Feedback to a key client or group.* Because action research is a collaborative activity, the diagnostic data are fed back to the client, usually in a group or work team meeting. The feedback step, in which members are given the information gathered by the OD practitioner, helps them determine the strengths and weaknesses of the organization or the department under study. The consultant provides the client with all relevant

and useful data. Obviously, the practitioner will protect confidential sources of information and, at times, may even withhold data. Defining what is relevant and useful involves considerable privacy and ethics as well as judgment about when the group is ready for the information or if the information would make the client overly defensive.

5. *Joint diagnosis of the problem.* At this point, members discuss the feedback and explore with the OD practitioner whether they want to work on identified problems. A close interrelationship exists among data gathering, feedback, and diagnosis because the consultant summarizes the basic data from the client members and presents the data to them for validation and further diagnosis. An important point to remember, as Schein (1970) suggests, is that the action research process is very different from the doctor–patient model, in which the consultant comes in, makes a diagnosis, and prescribes a solution. Schein notes that the failure to establish a common frame of reference in the client–consultant relationship may lead to faulty diagnosis or to a communications gap whereby the client is sometimes "unwilling to believe the diagnosis or accept the prescription." He believes "most companies have drawers full of reports by consultants, each loaded with diagnoses and recommendations which are either not understood or accepted by the 'patient'" (p. 78).

6. *Joint action planning.* Next, the OD practitioner and the client members jointly agree on further actions to be taken. This is the beginning of the moving process (described in Lewin's change model), as the organization decides how best to reach a different quasi-stationary equilibrium. At this stage, the specific action to be taken depends on the culture, technology, and environment of the organization, the diagnosis of the problem, and the time and expense of the intervention.

7. *Action.* This stage involves actual change from one organizational state to another. It may include installing new methods and procedures, reorganizing structures and work designs, and reinforcing new behaviors. Such actions typically cannot be implemented immediately but require a period as the organization moves from the present to a desired future state.

8. *Data gathering after action.* Because action research is a cyclical process, data must also be gathered after the action has been taken to measure and determine the effects of the action and to feed the results back to the organization. This, in turn, may lead to rediagnosis and new action.

ORGANIZATION DEVELOPMENT FOR PERFORMANCE SYSTEM

Organization development for performance system (ODPS) (Lynham, 2000c) represents a basic OD process highlighting performance improvement. The ODPS process focuses more on the conceptual phases of the work rather than on the profession activity of the OD consultant. This approach is counter to an unfortunate trend for many of those writing about change. They talk about change out of context of *needed* or *resulting* excellence, improvement, and performance. For example, a recent edited handbook that details eighteen change methods pays scant attention to the question of the resulting excellence, improvement, and performance from any of them (Holman & Devive, 1999). In contrast, ODPS is a process of planned, systemic change through the utilization of human expertise for the purpose of improving individual, group, process, and organization performance. This basic process is described as follows (Lynham, 2000c).

First, organization development involves planned and systemic change, as opposed to short-term, haphazard, and unintegrated change. Second, organization development is aimed at ensuring the development of the requisite human expertise necessary to initiate, implement, maintain, and sustain the targeted change. Third, organization development is guided by system theory, meaning that the planned change is understood and managed in terms of integrated inputs, processes, outputs, and feedback. Fourth, it is itself a process; that is, organization development involves a specific *way* of implementing change, which is informed by humanistic values and theories, techniques and tools primarily from the behavioral sciences. Fifth, organization development takes place within a performance system and for purposes of performance improvement within that performance system. Finally, organization development results in outputs in various domains of performance—for example, individual, group, process, and organization performance.

Notwithstanding these characteristics, the application of organization development is not always implemented in a manner that reflects these characteristics. Common criticisms of organization development include change interventions that are often fragmented and disconnected from the core business performance outcomes; interventions that build dependence on the external consultant for the expertise needed by the organization to maintain and sustain the change begun; change "cures" that are based more on the expertise of the change agent (usually external to the organization) than on the performance needs of the organization; a lack of ability and intent to show measurable, verifiable outcomes throughout and in conclusion of the change implemented; and the dilemma of short-term, high-turnover leadership in the context of long-term, large-scale change that depends on ongoing leadership support.

ODPS underscores the importance of system theory in organization development and frames organization development as a system of planned, systemic change, achieved through the development of related human expertise for the purpose of achieving specific and multiple performance domain outputs. ODPS embraces the above characteristics of traditional organization development as well as the titles of the traditional components of planned change presented in most models of organization development. These titles include (1) analyze and contract; (2) diagnose and feedback; (3) plan, design, and develop; (4) implement;

and (5) evaluate and institutionalize. This five-phase model is generally referred to as "the *generic change model*." In addition, the critical overarching task of "leading the organization development process" is added to the core change model.

The ODPS Model

The ODPS model is illustrated in Figure 12.6, which shows the five phases of the organization development for performance process being integrated and supported through leadership. Worthy of note is that the systematic process of the ODPS has integrity and can be maintained even in the simplest of situations (severe time, resource, and budget constraints) or can be violated in the most luxurious of situations (generous time, resource, and budget allocations). Professional expertise—organization development process knowledge and experience—is what is necessary to maintain organization development integrity.

Phases of ODPS

The five phases of the ODPS model are analyze and contract; diagnose and feedback; plan, design and develop; implement; and evaluate and institutionalize. It is assumed that there is a performance system with an apparent performance problem and need for change, and a recognized need to engage someone (either inside or outside the organization) to assist with the related problem solving and needed change.

Phase 1: Analyze and Contract
The first phase of the ODPS is composed of two steps. First, it is necessary to analyze the perceived performance problem and need for change. This first

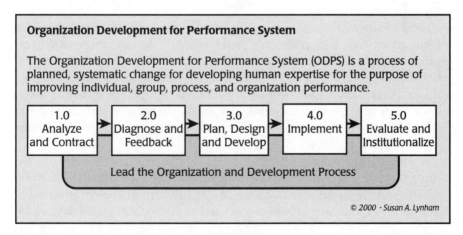

Figure 12.6   Organization Development for Performance System
(*Source:* Lynham 2000c).

step requires that an initial analysis be done of the performance requirements of the organization that can be improved through the documenting and development of planned, systemic change and the development of human expertise required to implement, maintain, and sustain workplace change and performance. Analysis therefore provides the initial documented evidence that the problem presented for resolution and change is indeed real. Furthermore, analysis helps initially clarify the issues surrounding the problem, establishes the organization's apparent commitment to problem resolution and change, and provides an opportunity to determine and optimize the "match" among the needs, values, and expertise of the organization and those of the change consultant or agent.

The second step in phase 1 involves the contract. Informed by the outcomes of step 1, the contract documents agreements about how the OD process will proceed. This includes specification of agreements in terms of mutual expectations, time, money, and other resources that will be made available during the change process, and the ground rules under which all involved parties will operate.

Phase 2: Diagnose and Feedback

The second phase of ODPS consists of two steps: diagnosing the performance and provide feedback to the performance system on the change needed and the accompanying human expertise required to address and advance performance. A thorough diagnosis of the performance problem is critical to successful organization development intervention, as this step ensures that the root cause(s) of the performance and need for change are uncovered and made explicit to the performance system. Diagnosis plays a critical role in informing the rest of the organization development process. It is intended to ensure that the actual, and not the presenting, performance problem that gave rise to the need for the change intervention is effectively addressed.

Multiple data collection methods are used to perform a thorough diagnosis of the performance. Four commonly used methods of data collection used to diagnose the performance problem and inform the change needed include questionnaires or surveys, interviews, direct observations, and unobtrusive data (e.g., organization records). Each method of data collection has strengths and weaknesses. As a result, it is important that triangulation be pursued and as many data collection methods as possible are used to conduct the diagnosis and inform the feedback steps in the ODPS.

Feedback, the second step in phase 2, involves the return of the data collected during the diagnostic step to the performance system for further verification, problem solving, decision making, and corrective action. The effectiveness of feedback varies according to both content and process—that is, *what* data are fed back and *how* data are fed back. Some criteria of good feedback data include relevance, appropriateness, timeliness, comparability, validity, clarity, and engagement. Criteria of a good feedback process includes an appropriate setting, structure, and selection of participants, as well as using the feedback data to facilitate the development of human expertise for further problem solving and decision making regarding the performance requirement and desired change.

Both steps in phase 2 of ODPS, diagnosis and feedback, are critical in harnessing and activating commitment and energy for the rest of the organization development process, namely, to plan, implement, and evaluate and institutionalize the desired and necessary change in the performance system.

Phase 3: Plan, Design, and Develop

Phase 3 of the ODPS involves three steps. First is that of compiling the plan required to ensure corrective action and development of the necessary human expertise to address the performance requirement in multiple performance domains (individual, group, process, and organization) and in an enduring way. During the development of the plan, the kind of planned change (or intervention) and human expertise needed to address the performance situation effectively are discussed and agreed upon. Numerous types of planned change processes (also referred to as *interventions*) can be selected from at this stage, and these vary according to the performance domain and corresponding human expertise development at which they are targeted (individual, group, process, and organization). Due to the systemic nature of organization development, the plan of action often spans multiple types of planned change. Also typically included in the plan for change is the recognition and initial consideration of the actions required to manage the changes that will likely accompany the change intervention(s).

A good intervention plan is specific, is clear about roles and desired outcomes, makes the resulting human expertise explicit in terms of knowledge and experience, includes an achievable time line, and is derived in a participative and commitment-seeking manner.

The second step of phase 3 is the design, through either creation and/or acquisition, of general and specific change strategies (or interventions) for people to develop the expertise to implement and sustain workplace change and performance. The third step involves the development, or acquisition, of specific participant and change agent materials needed to execute the planned change strategy(ies) and/or programs.

Phase 4: Implement

The fourth phase in the ODPS is to implement the planned change strategies selected, designed, and developed in phase 3 of the ODPS. This involves managing the individual change strategies and programs as well as their delivery to the participants of the performance system.

Phase 5: Evaluate and Institutionalize

To determine whether the planned change has been successfully implemented, the effectiveness of the planned change strategies/programs in terms of performance, learning, and satisfaction must be established. The first step in the fifth and final phase of the ODPS requires that one evaluate multiple aspects of the actual outcomes of the planned change strategies and compare these against the desired outcomes of the planned change strategies. Evaluation therefore requires the determining and reporting on change strategy/program effectiveness in terms of performance, learning, and satisfaction.

It is generally recognized that it is easier to initiate change than it is to maintain and sustain change. As a result, it is very important that the new behaviors, practices, and processes that accompany planned change strategies are embedded into the organization's culture and become part of the way business is done on a day-to-day basis in the organization. This embedding or stabilization of the new ways that accompany the planned change processes refers to the need to institutionalize the change strategies/programs, constituting the second step of phase 5. Institutionalizing the change strategies/programs for integrated and long-term performance requires both management of the institutionalization process and reinforcement of the changes through further feedback, rewards, and development of human expertise.

Leading the OD Process

The ODPS, like any performance system, requires leadership and management to maintain the integrity of the OD process in terms of inputs, processes, outputs, and feedback. Leading the ODPS requires, for example, championing the OD mission, values, and goals, as well as managing and improving the OD process.

COMPARISON OF CORE OD MODELS

While the literature describes numerous OD processes, five have been selected here for the purpose of illustration and comparison. For each, the main feature, strength, and weakness are identified.

Field Theory

by Lewin (1961)

Main Features

- Starts with the assumption that people get stuck in their thinking and that getting unstuck is the key to change.
- OD phases: freeze-unfreeze-refreeze

Strengths

- Simple process model designed to help change people's perception.
- Well grounded in psychological theory

Weakness

- Core method is narrowly focused on individual–group interactions.

General Model of Planned Change

by Cummings and Worley (2001)

Main Features

- Starts with assumption that change is needed.
- OD phases: entering and contracting; diagnosing; planning and interpreting change; evaluating and institutionalizing change

Strengths

- Well grounded in psychological theory and system theory
- Embraces broad OD thinking

Weaknesses

- Conceptual change model is too general.
- No integrated set of tools

Action Research

by Shani and Bushe (1978) and others

Main Feature

- Consultant role is primary, along with participants who are colearners in addressing an organizational problem.
- OD phases: problem identification; consultation with a behavioral science expert; data gathering and preliminary diagnosis; feedback to a key client or group; joint diagnosis of the problem; joint action planning; action; data gathering after action

Strengths

- Grounded heavily in psychological theory and some systems theory
- Provides a well-defined process

Weaknesses

- Does not explicitly study the organization and its core processes and their outputs
- Rarely reports results in terms of actual organization/business core measures

Improving Performance

by Rummler and Brache (1995)

Main Features

- Starts with assumption that organizations can be viewed and analyzed at the organization, process, and individual contributor levels

- OD phases: establish a clear strategy; document and analyze the current "is" organization system; document and analyze the "is" (current) processes; develop "should" process flows and measures; design the organization chart; develop function models for each department; develop job models for each job; structure the human performance system for each job; establish management processes.

Strengths

- Well grounded in psychological, economic, and system theory
- Has an integrated set of practical "tools"
- Demonstrates results in terms of core organization measures

Weakness

- Entire process is often viewed as too demanding of the organization.

Organization Development for Performance System (ODPS)

by Lynham (2000c)

Main Features

- Starts with assumption that performance improvement is the purpose and that unleashing human expertise is essential.
- OD phases: analyze and contract; diagnose and feedback; plan, design, and develop; implement; and evaluate and institutionalize

Strengths

- Well grounded in psychological, economic, and system theory
- Has a well defined process
- Focused on core organization performance outcomes

Weakness

- Does not have an integrated set of "tools"

CONCLUSION

Organization development is a process with the potential of unleashing the human expertise required to maintain and change organizations. As such, OD also has the potential of strategically aligning the organizational components of its host organization within the context in which it must function. It also has the potential of searching out and utilizing the expertise required to create new strategic directions for the host organization.

REFLECTION QUESTIONS

1. How would you define OD and describe its relationship to HRD?
2. What are the unique aspects of the OD component of HRD?
3. What is the role of the OD consultant in the OD process?
4. What is the purpose of each of the five phases of the general OD process and the relationship between the phases?
5. How does OD help with the organizational challenges of managing the system and changing the system?

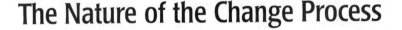

The Nature of the Change Process

CHAPTER OUTLINE

Change has been a central concept in human resource development since its origins. Thinking about change in HRD has emerged from two basic directions: individual development and organizational development. Individual change models focus on ways individuals change. While this may affect the organization, the primary emphasis is on the individual and helping the individual change him- or herself. Individual learning and skill development can be seen as a special type of change at the individual level, especially transformational learning. Career development specialists focus on helping people change their lives and jobs. Adult development theory focuses us on the many ways that adults change throughout their life span. While none of these is usually thought of as change theory, we suggest that change is the overarching construct that unites them within HRD.

Organization change models embrace the individual but within the context of changing the organization. Most of these models emerge from what is generically known as organization development. Organization development professionals specialize in change, usually at the group, work process, or organization level.

Thus, all HRD professionals can be seen as leading or facilitating change (Holton, 1997). Change is pervasive, powerful, and challenging. The purpose of this chapter is to examine change as an organizing construct for human resource development in its effort to contribute to the performance requirements. In this chapter we are not so interested in specific contexts of change but rather in core foundations of change that cut across all arenas of practice and research.

DEFINITIONS OF CHANGE IN HRD

Change is a familiar construct but one that is seldom explicitly defined. It is important to understand what is meant by change.

Change as Individual Development

A definition of change offered by Schein (1970) focuses first on the fact that change in organizations always involves changing individual people: "Induction of new patterns of action, belief, and attitudes among substantial segments of a population." From this view, organizational change is about getting people in organizations to do, believe, or feel something different. It is this view of change that has dominated training-oriented change interventions.

Change as Learning

Watkins and Marsick (1993) offer a different definition of change that speaks to the means by which change occurs: "Change is a cyclical process of creating knowledge (the change or innovation), disseminating it, implementing the change, and then institutionalizing what is learned by making it part of the organization's routines" (p. 21). This definition reminds us that change always involves learning. "Learning and change processes are part of each other. Change is a learning process and learning is a change process" (Beckhard & Pritchard, 1992). This fundamental relationship points out why change is one of the core constructs for the discipline of human resource development.

Change as Work and Life Roles

Within career development there is some disagreement about the exact definition of a career, but here are two leading definitions:

> "the evolving sequence of a person's work experiences over time" (Osipow & Fitzgerald, 1996, p. 51)

> "the combination and sequence of roles played by a person during the course of a lifetime" (Super, 1980, p. 282; Super & Sverko, 1995, p. 23)

The point of agreement is that a career is conceptualized as the sequence of roles a person fills. The point of disagreement is whether those changes include just work roles, or work and life roles. Regardless, career development is fundamentally concerned with change and evolution of a person's roles.

Change as Internal Adult Development

Another view of change comes from adult development theory, the now generally accepted notion that adults continue to develop throughout the life span—biologically, psychologically, cognitively, and socially. Merriam and Caffarella (1999) link adult development with change: "The concept of development, as with learning, is most often equated with change" (p. 93). Thus, adult development theory serves to define the types of internal changes that adults experience in their lives in contrast to career development theory, which defines the roles adults fill in society.

Change as Goal-Directed Activity

The previous definitions offer little guidance toward the purpose of change. Rothwell, Sullivan, and McLean (1995) suggest in their definition that change should have a purpose: "Change is a departure from the status quo. It implies movement toward a goal, an idealized state, or a vision of what should be and movement away from present conditions, beliefs, or attitudes" (p. 9). Change should therefore be directed at some goal or outcome that represents a vision of a more desirable end state. Thus, they remind us that not all change is good. Change can be in negative directions and can result in a less effective organization if it is not focused on desired outcomes.

Change as Innovation

Van de Ven, Polley, Garud, and Venkataraman (1999) are equally purposeful when they define innovation in organizations: "The innovation journey is defined as new ideas that are developed and implemented to achieve outcomes by people who engage in transactions (relationships) with others in changing institutional and organizational contexts" (p. 7). Change in their definition consists of new ideas implemented in a social process directed at achieving outcomes to change organizations.

CORE DIMENSIONS OF CHANGE

Two core dimensions of change are important to consider: the depth of change (incremental vs. transformational) and the tempo of change (continuous vs. episodic).

Incremental versus Transformational Change

The distinction between incremental and transformational change is concerned with the depth and scope of change. Incremental change deals with smaller, more adaptive changes while transformational change requires major shifts in direction or perspective. This distinction is found in both the organization development and adult learning literature. Not surprisingly, the two are closely aligned.

OD and Planned Incremental Change

A fundamental issue for OD has been the scope of change in which its tools are applied. The traditional focus of OD has been on planned incremental change. Cummings and Worley (2001) distinguish the OD approach from other organization change approaches in this way:

> OD and change management both address the effective implementation of planned change. They are concerned with the sequence of activities, processes and leadership issues that produce organizational improvements. They differ, however, in their underlying value orientation. OD's behavioral science foundation supports values of *human potential, participation, and development,* whereas change management is more focused on economic potential and the

creation of competitive advantage. As a result, OD's distinguishing feature is its concern with the transfer of knowledge and skill such that the system is more able to manage change in the future. Change management does not necessarily require the transfer of such skills. In short, all OD involves change management, but change management does not involve OD. (p. 3; emphasis added)

The change process that lends itself best to the values of human potential, participation, and development is incremental change. That is, change that "produces appreciable, not radical, change in individual employees' cognitions as well as behaviors" (Porras & Silvers, 1991).

Cummings and Worley (2001) go on to say:

Similarly, organization change is a broader concept than OD.... [O]rganization development can be applied to managing organizational change. However, it is primarily concerned with managing change in such a way that knowledge and skills are transferred to build the organization's capability to achieve goals and solve problems. It is intended to change the organization in a particular direction, toward improved problem solving, responsiveness, quality of work life, and effectiveness. Organization change, in contrast, is more broadly focused and can apply to any kind of change, including technical, managerial innovations, organization decline, and the evolution of a system over time. (p. 3)

The traditional emphasis on planned incremental change has limited OD's influence on organizational change. This presents a perplexing dilemma for HRD. On the one hand, the philosophical ideals of human potential, participation, and development embedded in OD approaches to change are also ones embraced by most HRD professionals. For that reason, these approaches are inherently attractive to HRD professionals. On the other hand, by definition they eliminate HRD from participating in more strategic organizational changes in which planned incremental approaches cannot be utilized. As noted by Cummings and Worley, these other approaches to organization change do not fit the traditional OD "toolbox" very well.

Transformational Change
The alternative model, transformational change, has increasingly moved to the forefront of organizational and individual change. French, Bell, and Zawacki (1999) define organization transformation as:

a recent extension of organization development that seeks to create massive changes in an organization's structures, processes, culture, and orientation to its environment. Organization transformation is the application of behavioral science theory and practice to large-scale, paradigm-shifting organizational change. An organization transformation usually results in totally new paradigms or models for organizing and performing work. (p. vii)

Thus, transformational change goes well beyond the incremental change characterized by traditional OD and is a fairly recent addition to OD practice, though not to organizational life.

Transformational change has five key characteristics (Cummings & Worley, 2001):

- *Triggered by environmental and internal disruptions*—Organizations must experience a severe threat to survival.

- *Systemic and revolutionary*—The entire nature of the organization must change, including its culture and design.

- *Demands a new organizing paradigm*—By definition it requires gamma change (discussed later).

- *Is driven by senior executives and line management*—Transformational change cannot be a "bottom-up" process because senior management is in charge of strategic change.

- *Continuous learning and change*—The learning process is likely to be substantial and require considerable unlearning and innovation.

Clearly this type of change does not lend itself to traditional OD methodologies. Sometimes transformational change threatens traditional OD values because it may entail layoffs or major restructurings. In addition, it is not always possible to have broad participation in planning transformational change, and it is often implemented in a top-down manner.

New methods have emerged in an attempt to expand OD's reach into large-scale whole systems change in a manner that is consistent with OD values (Bunker & Alban, 1997). These include techniques such as future search (Weisbord & Janoff, 1995), open space technology (Owen, 1992), preferred futuring (Lippitt, 1998), real-time strategic change (Jacobs, 1994), and the ICA Strategic Planning Process (Spencer, 1989).

Nadler, Shaw, and Walton (1995) remind us that incremental and transformational change can be implemented in reaction to events (reactive) or in a proactive way in anticipation of events that may occur (anticipatory). Thus, they suggest four types of change: tuning, adaptation, reorientation, and re-creation (see Figure 13.1). Adaptation, which is reactive incremental change, is probably the most common type of change and occurs constantly in organizations. Reorientation, which is anticipatory transformational change, is the hardest type to implement.

Continuous versus Episodic Change

Weick and Quinn (1999) suggest that another important dimension of change is the *tempo of change,* which they define as the rate, rhythm, or pattern of the change process. The first tempo, *continuous change,* is described as "a pattern of endless modifications in work processes and social practices.... Numerous small accommodations cumulate and amplify" (p. 366). Continuous change has historically been

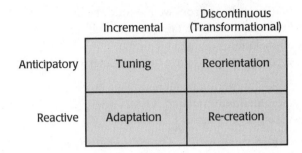

Figure 13.1   Types of Organizational Change

closely related to incremental change but is actually a different construct, which has an important implication in today's fast-changing world.

The second tempo, *episodic change,* is defined as "occasional interruption or divergence from equilibrium. . . . It is seen as a failure of the organization to adapt its deep structure to a changing environment" (p. 366). Episodic change tends to be infrequent and occurs in short-term episodes. In this view, organizations have a certain amount of change inertia until some force triggers them to change.

While Weick and Quinn's description is close to the definition of incremental versus transformational change, considering tempo of change (continuous vs. episodic) separately from scope of change (incremental vs. transformational) is useful. The problem is that deep change is defined as episodic. In today's world, companies such as Internet firms are finding themselves having to make continuous transformational change, which is not even contemplated in the original definitions. The notion that transformational change only occurs episodically has been true historically but is increasingly being challenged today. Furthermore, it is also possible for organizations to make episodic change that is actually only incremental rather than transformational. Christensen (1997) suggests that modern corporate management structures are most likely to lead to incremental change, even when attempting strategic changes, that ultimately cause them to overlook disruptive technological changes that threaten their business.

CHANGE OUTCOMES

When one considers the multitude of individual, process, group, and organizational constructs that can be affected by change, the possible outcomes from change are enormous and would fill a volume by themselves. We are more interested in searching for more fundamental ways to describe outcomes from change. In a landmark article, Golembiewski, Billingsley, and Yeager (1976) suggest that three basic types of change can occur: alpha, beta, and gamma change.

Porras and Silvers (1992) extend their classification by splitting gamma change into two types. They defined the four basic types of change as follows (p. 57):

■ *Alpha change*—change in the perceived levels of variables within a paradigm without altering their configuration (e.g., a perceived improvement in skills)

■ *Beta change*—change in people's view about the meaning of the value of any variable within an existing paradigm without altering their configuration (e.g., change in standards)

■ *Gamma(A) change*—change in the configuration of an existing paradigm without the addition of new variables (e.g., changing the central value of a "production-driven" paradigm from "cost containment" to "total quality focus"). This results in the reconfiguration of all variables within this paradigm.

■ *Gamma(B) change*—the replacement of one paradigm with another that contains some or all of new variables (e.g., replacing a "production-driven" paradigm with a "customer-responsive" paradigm).

For example, suppose you are dealing with an organization that has declining performance (e.g., profits) requiring some type of organizational change. An example of alpha change would be for the organization to focus on doing a better job at what it is already doing, perhaps by eliminating errors and waste. Beta change would result if the organization realized that the industry had become so competitive that its previous notions of what high performance meant had to be revised upward. An example of gamma(A) change might be the introduction of enterprise software (e.g., SAP) to run its business more effectively but requiring a reorganization of their work processes. Gamma(B) change would result if it discarded its old business model of selling through retail stores and replaced it with one of selling through the Internet.

This conceptualization is extremely powerful because these different types of outcomes clearly would require different change strategies. Porras and Silvers (1991) portray this in the model shown in Figure 13.2. Note they start with two basic types of change interventions discussed earlier: organization development (incremental) and organization transformation. The target variables are those at which interventions are aimed. As a result of the interventions on these target variables, alpha, beta, or gamma cognitive change results in individual members, leading to enhanced individual development and improved organizational performance.

OVERARCHING PERSPECTIVES ON CHANGE

In this section, three metatheories of change are discussed. Most other theories or models of change processes can be located within these three basic frameworks.

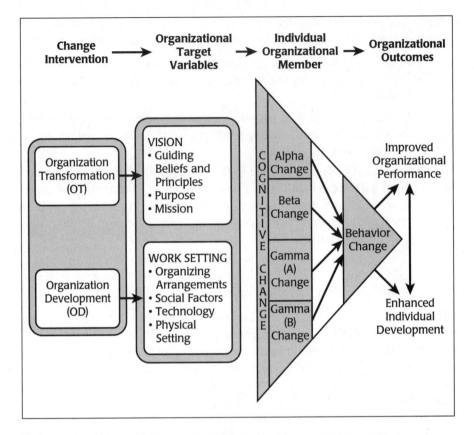

Figure 13.2   Porras and Silvers's Model of Change Outcomes   (*Source:* Porras and Silvers (1991, p. 53). Used with permission.)

Lewin's Field Theory

The classic metatheory of change is Kurt Lewin's (1951) field theory. This theory remains at the core of most change theories. The essence of field theory is deceptively simple but extraordinarily powerful. Let's examine the core components of Lewin's field theory.

The most fundamental construct in Lewin's theory is the *field*. According to Lewin, "all behavior is conceived of as a change of some state of a field in a given unit of time" (p. xi). For individuals, he says this "is the 'life space' of the individual. This life space consists of the person and the psychological environment as it exists for him" (p. xi). It is important to realize that a field also exists for any unit of social structure or organization. Thus, a field can be defined for a team, a department, or an organization.

The field or life space includes "all facts that have existence and excludes those that do not have existence for the individual or group under study" (p. xi).

This is vitally important in considering change because individuals or groups may have distorted views of reality or may not see certain aspects of reality. What matters to the person or group, and what shapes their behavior, is only what they see as existing.

Finally, Lewin believes that behavior is not dependent on what happened in the past or what is expected to happen in the future, but rather on the field as it exists in the present. He did not ignore the effects of history or anticipated events. Instead, he says that it is how those past or anticipated events manifest themselves in the present that affects behavior. In other words, it is how those events are perceived today that is part of a person's field and influences the person's behavior today.

Change, according to Lewin, is the result of a constellation of psychological forces in a person's field at a given point in time. *Driving* forces are those that push a person toward a positive outcome; *restraining* forces are those that represent barriers. Driving forces push a person toward locomotion (movement), while restraining forces may inhibit locomotion. Forces in a person's field create tension. If the driving and restraining forces are equal and in opposite directions, conflict results and no locomotion is likely to result. Thus, to understand a person or group's likelihood of changing, driving forces have to be stronger than restraining forces. A field in which the forces are approximately in balance results in a quasi-equilibrium state in which no change is likely.

Perhaps the best-known part of Lewin's theory is his three-step change process: *unfreezing, movement,* and *refreezing.* However, it is rarely discussed in the context of field theory, which is the most useful way to understand it.

From the preceding discussion, it would appear that all one has to do to invoke change is to increase driving forces or decrease restraining forces and a proportional change would result. According to Lewin, this is not the case. Social systems that are in a quasi-equilibrium develop an inner resistance to change, which he calls a *social habit* or *custom.* In force terms, the equilibrium level acquires a value itself, becoming a force working to maintain that equilibrium. Furthermore, "the greater the social value of a group standard the greater is the resistance of the individual group member to move away from this level" (p. 227).

To overcome this inner resistance, Lewin says that "an additional force seems to be required, a force sufficient to 'break the habit,' to 'unfreeze' the custom" (p. 225). In other words, to begin the change process, some larger force is necessary to break the inherent resistance to change. The unfreezing force will result in a less than proportional movement, but it will begin the movement toward a new equilibrium. Lewin also notes that this is one reason group methods are so powerful in leading change. Because the inner resistance is often group norms, change is more likely to happen if the group can be encouraged to change those norms themselves.

Lewin goes on to note that change is often short-lived. After exerting the effort to unfreeze a group, change may occur but then people revert to the previous level. Therefore, equal attention must be paid to what he called *freezing*, usually referred to today as *refreezing*, rather than just moving people to a new level. Lewin defines freezing as that point when "the new force field is made secure against change" (p. 229). Freezing involves harnessing the same power of the social field that acted to prevent change in the beginning by creating new group norms that reinforce the changes.

Sociotechnical Systems

Sociotechnical system theory was developed by Eric Trist, based on work he did with the British coal mining industry while at the Tavistock Institute (Fox, 1995). First presented in the early 1950s (Trist & Bamforth, 1951), it, too, has stood the test of time and remains at the core of most organizational development change efforts. Trist and Bamforth were studying a successful British coal mine at a time when most of the industry was having a great deal of difficulty, despite large investments to improve mining technology. They observed that this particular mine had made improvements in the social structure of work (to autonomous work teams), not just to the technology. They realized that the cause of much of the industry's problems was a failure to consider changes in the social structure of work to accompany the technical changes being made. While this may sound obvious, the same mistake is still being made today. For example, many organizations have struggled while trying to implement SAP enterprise software, largely because they have approached it as a technology problem without considering the people aspects of the change.

From that work emerged the relatively simple but powerful concept that work consists of two interdependent systems that have to be jointly optimized. The *technical system* consists of the materials, machines, processes, and systems that produce the outputs of the organization. The *social system* is the system that relates the workers to the technical system and to each other (Cooper & Foster, 1971). Usually, organizational change initiatives emphasize one more than the other. Typically the technical system is emphasized more than the social system because it is easy to change computers, machines, or buildings and ignore the effect of the change on people.

Unfortunately, sociotechnical systems has remained a loosely defined metatheory without careful explication like Lewin's field theory. However, elements of sociotechnical systems theory are present in many modern change initiatives such as TQM and reengineering (Shani & Mitki, 1996). Thus, it continues to provide a very useful framework for organizational change.

Typology of Change

More recently, Van de Ven and Poole (1995) have identified four basic process theories of change that they say underlie change in the social, biological, and physical sciences. They contend that these four schools of thought about change are distinctly different and that all specific theories of organizational and individual change can be built from one or a combination of these four. As a result, these four offer a more parsimonious explanation of organization change and development. "In each theory: a) process is viewed as a different cycle of change events, b) which is governed by a different "motor" or generating mechanism that c) operates on a different unit of analysis, and d) represents a different mode of change" (p. 520).

Life Cycle Theory
The first model depicts change as progressing through some sequence of stages that are governed by some natural or logical "law" that prescribes the stages. This theory operates on single entities with certain prescribed stages. For example, life cycle theories of organizations (Adizes, 1988) project certain critical stages that every firm experiences as it grows from a small company to a larger, more complex organization. Life cycle theories of adult development portray predictable stages of adult life that occur at certain ages.

Teleological Theory
This theory also operates within a single entity but is one that offers constructive rather than prescribed stages of change. Teleological theory views development as a cycle of goal formulation and implementation. These goals are constructed by individuals within the entity. Strategic planning could be a classic example of this theory whereby an organization sets goals for its future and works to implement them. Career planning might be an individual level teleological theory.

Evolutionary Theory
This theory differs from the previous two in that it operates on multiple entities. This model views change as occurring out of competition for scarce resources within the environment in which the entity operates. As a result, entities within the population go through cycles of variation, selection, and retention. That is, some grow and thrive; some decline or die. These cycles are somewhat predictable so the change process is prescribed in these theories. Theories of organization development that focus on external competitive forces and how firms thrive or die within competitive environments fall within this theory.

Dialectic Theory
The last theory also operates on multiple entities, but with constructed change processes. In this model, change arises out of conflict between entities espousing opposing thesis and antithesis. Change occurs through the confrontation and conflict that results. Many instances of organizational change that occur due to changes in societal norms fit within this framework. For example, changes in the workplace reflecting racial, gender, and ethnic diversity often arise out of dialectical tensions.

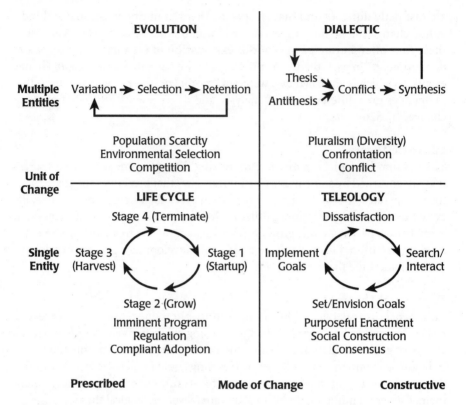

Figure 13.3 Process Theories of Organizational Development and Change (*Source:* Van de Ven and Poole (1995, p. 520). Used with permission.)

Conclusion

This four-part framework is particularly useful for understanding the variety of change theories in the literature (summarized in Figure 13.3). Using these four general theories, one can find the commonalities among diverse theories. It is helpful in practice because it enables one to understand the multiple forces for change that occur. Van de Ven and Poole (1995) also identify sixteen possible combinations of these four theories that represent logically possible composite theories.

FUNDAMENTAL STEPS OF CHANGE

Tichy (1983) reminds us that "all change requires exchanging something old for something new. . . . People have to unlearn and relearn, exchange power and status, and exchange old norms and values for new norms and values. These changes are often frightening and threatening while at the same time potentially stimulating and providers of new hope" (p. 332). The notion of exchange is particularly important because there are costs and benefits to each side of the exchange. Ultimately, the benefits have to outweigh the costs for change to succeed.

Given that there is some exchange of old for new taking place, then it is instructive to look at models of fundamental steps of change. Earlier you were introduced to Lewin's classic three-stage model: unfreezing, movement, and refreezing. This is a very useful model for change agents whose lens is thinking about how to get people to change.

Bridges (1991) offers a parallel model that he calls the *transition model* and we call the *internal psychological view*. Bridges maintains that alongside every organizational change event is an internal process people undergo called transition. Ironically, the psychological experience of transition starts with some *ending*. Whether it is a job, a phase of life, a house being given up, or a project, the transition starts by letting go of something old and familiar. This is vitally important for change agents to understand because it creates feelings of loss, not unlike the grieving process after a death. The stages a person undergoes during organizational or personal change are conceptually similar to those identified by Kubler-Ross (1969) in terminally ill patients. In a sense, people experience the "death" of something important to them when change occurs. This stage is roughly parallel to Lewin's unfreezing stage in that the endings begin to occur when the change agent starts "unfreezing."

This stage is followed by a *wilderness* phase, which is a time of confusion, lack of trust, and trying to find a new path through the changed world. During this period, the ending is less salient to people, but neither have they committed to the new way. This stage is roughly parallel to Lewin's movement stage.

Following this stage, individuals enter the *new beginning* phase where they begin to understand the new vision and commit to it. From Lewin's perspective, this is parallel to his refreezing stage. It is only at this point that the change will be successful.

Figure 13.4 summarizes these models. The models are rich with implications that are beyond the scope of this book. What is important is that the conception of change occurring in three basic phases is fundamental to most change theories. The three stages, or something close to them, occur again and again in the literature. For example, the Armenakis, Harris, and Field (1999) model is shown in Figure 13.4 for comparison purposes. Their stage model is conceptually similar to Lewin's, despite being formulated almost fifty years later.

RESISTANCE TO CHANGE

Resistance to change is a universal phenomenon whether one is implementing a new strategy in an organization or helping individuals lose weight. In fact, without resistance, change would not be difficult, and many change interventions and models would be greatly simplified. It is resistance that shapes most change strategies and makes effective change leaders so valuable.

There are more suggestions for overcoming resistance than can possibly be covered in this chapter. Of interest here is the more fundamental question of

Figure 13.4 Three-Step Model Comparison

Change Agent View (Lewin, 1951)	Internal Psychological View (Bridges, 1991)	Behavioral View (Armenakis et al., 1999)
Unfreezing	Ending	Readiness
Movement	Wilderness	Adoption
Refreezing	New Beginning	Institutionalization

what causes resistance. If the causes of resistance are understood, then strategies to overcome it become clearer.

Resistance has been shown to be a multidimensional phenomenon. Piderit (2000) summarizes the resistance to change literature and proposes that resistance to change consists of three dimensions:

- Cognitive—beliefs about the change
- Emotional (affective)—feelings in response to change
- Behavioral—actions in response to change

This three-part view of resistance is particularly important because a person may not be consistent on all three dimensions. Clearly, if a person is negative on all three dimensions, resistance occurs, or, if positive on all three dimensions, support for change occurs. However, it is not uncommon for a person to be conflicted. For example, a person may believe change is needed (cognitive) but still fear it (affective). Or, a person may not believe in it and fear it, but act as if in support of the change. Piderit (2000) calls this *ambivalence*, defined as the state where two alternative perspectives are both strongly experienced (p. 787). She also suggests that this phenomenon may be more widespread during change than is acknowledged.

Tichy (1983) approaches organizational change from three aspects of organizational reality: technical, political, and cultural. The *technical* view focuses on organizing to get the work accomplished most effectively. The *political* view focuses on power and the allocation of rewards. The *cultural* view focuses on the norms and values in the organization. He then defines a useful framework of possible causes of resistance at the individual and organizational levels for each view (see Figure 13.5).

Probably the most vexing question in the literature is why resistance to change occurs. King and Anderson (1995) suggest that there are four fundamentally different views of causes of resistance in the literature, each of which we will explore in the following sections.

Resistance as Unavoidable Behavioral Response

This is probably the dominant view of resistance to change. In this view, individuals resist change simply because it represents a move into the unknown.

Figure 13.5   Possible Causes of Resistance to Change

View	Individual	Organizational
Technical	• Resistance due to habit • Resistance due to fear of the unknown • Resistance due to absence of skills	• Organization predictability • Resistance due to sunk costs
Political	• Resistance due to need for power • Resistance due to overdependence on others • Resistance due to competition for power	• Resistance due to threats to powerful coalitions • Resistance due to resource limitations • Resistance due to sunk costs
Cultural	(none)	• Resistance due to selective perception (cultural filters) • Resistance due to values and beliefs • Resistance due to security by regression to past • Resistance due to conformity to norms • Resistance due to climate for change

Therefore, resistance is a natural and unavoidable response. The fact that individuals have a strong need to hold onto what is familiar is a powerful force, a point that has been neglected in the change literature (Bridges, 1991; Tannenbaum & Hanna, 1985). This deep-seated need to hold on may be the root cause of much resistance to change. Tannenbaum and Hanna (1985) suggest that there are four primary reasons for this need:

- Change is *loss*, requiring us to let go of something familiar and predictable.
- Change is *uncertainty*, requiring us to move from the known to the unknown.
- Change *dissolves meaning*, which in turn affects our identity.
- Change *violates scripts*, disrupting our unconscious life plans.

Change leaders who understand the natural psychological process individuals undergo are able to facilitate the letting go and moving on process. Those who ignore it encounter resistance to change that may seem insurmountable.

Resistance as Politically Motivated Insurrection and Class Struggle

The most radical of the four views, this view holds that resistance stems from the fundamentally inequitable relationship between workers and the organization.

Because workers often feel alienated and exploited, they resist change that bene-fits the organization. King and Anderson (1995) suggest this type of resistance may be more prevalent among labor groups who feel most alienated from man-agement and the organization. For example, some unions have been known to resist change because it is perceived to exploit workers. Also, one of the chief crit-icisms of the corporate restructurings that occurred in the late 1980s and early 1990s is that it exploited employees in organizations. As a result, many employees were reluctant to embrace other changes proposed in those organizations.

Resistance as Constructive Counterbalance

From this view, resistance may not always be a bad thing but rather acts as a counterbalance to change that is ill conceived, poorly implemented, or viewed as detrimental to the organization. Resistance to change has most often been dis-cussed from a managerial point of view whereby resistance is viewed as a barrier employees present to management's change initiatives and something that must be overcome. However, implicit in that traditional view is that management is "right" and employees are "wrong" when it comes to change. Yet, frequently man-agement's change initiatives may not be the right course of action, and resistance is a healthy response by the organization to ill-conceived change. Thus, resistance may not be bad but instead serves as part of a check-and-balance system to pre-vent poorly conceived change from destroying the organization.

This perspective is supported by evidence that employees are increasingly cyni-cal about change (Reichers, Wanous, & Austin, 1997). According to these researchers, cynicism about change is different than resistance in that it involves a loss of faith in leaders of change due to a history of failed attempts at change. It has been shown to be related to poorer job attitudes and motivation. A common cause of this is "pro-gram of the month" types of change efforts. Cynicism may in turn lead to resistance, which is usually viewed negatively. However, if an organization has a history of "pro-gram of the month" change efforts, then resistance may be a useful counterbalance to force management to think more carefully before proposing new change.

Resistance as Cognitive and Cultural Restructuring

In this perspective, resistance is conceived as a by-product of restructuring cognitive schemas at the individual level and as recasting of organizational culture and climate at the organizational level. The paradox is that individuals and organizations seek both change and stability (Leana & Barry, 2000). Individual schemas help people maintain a sense of identity and meaning in their day-to-day activities. Yet, change is also necessary to prevent boredom. Organizational schemas are necessary for effi-cient day-to-day operation and help perpetuate successful practices. Yet, continuous change is necessary to adapt to fast-changing environments. Thus, there is always a tension between maintaining schemas and changing them when necessary.

The focus on individual schema has increased in recent years, due in part to Senge's (1990) popular work on the learning organization in which he cites mental models (a closely related term) as one of his five disciplines. He defines mental models as "deeply held internal images of how the world works, images that limit us to familiar ways of thinking and acting" (p. 174). In other words, mental models are the cognitive structures that arise from an individual's experiences. While they help employees be more efficient, they also impede change because many people resist changes that do not fit their mental model, particularly if change involves restructuring long- or deeply held schema.

Senge based his work on that of Argyris (1982, 1999), who had described two basic theories-in-use (mental models) that people use to guide action in organizations. Model I, as he calls it, has four governing values: (1) achieve your intended purpose, (2) maximize winning and minimize losing, (3) suppress negative feelings, and (4) behave according to what you consider rational. This theory in use leads people to advocate their positions, and cover up mistakes, which he calls *defensive routines*. Defensive routines are blocks to individual and organizational learning. Model II, on the other hand, is predicated on open sharing of information and detecting and correcting mistakes. As a result, defensive routines are minimized and genuine learning is facilitated. The ability to change schema or mental models has been linked to a firm's ability to engage in strategic change and renewal (Barr, Stimpert, & Huff, 1992). Unfortunately, Model I is predominant in most organizations, serving as a fundamental source of resistance to change. Conversion to Model II usually requires double-loop learning.

Similarly, the role of organization culture in blocking or facilitating change is widely recognized. In fact, changing culture remains as one of the most difficult challenges in organizational change. Organizational culture, which is usually deeply rooted in an organization, can be a tremendous source of resistance to change. It represents organizational mental models of shared assumptions about how the organization should function.

As Schein (1999) points out, "changing something implies not just learning something new but unlearning something that is already there and possibly in the way" (p. 116). He equates the unlearning process to overcoming resistance to change. In the case of major change, such as changing culture, change has to begin with some disconfirmation such that survival anxiety exceeds learning anxiety. If so, then cognitive redefinition results for the learner.

In summary, resistance to change is a complex but vitally important change construct. Whether viewed from the individual, group, or organizational level, addressing resistance to change is a central concern for theory and practice.

FOCUSED THEORETICAL PERSPECTIVES ON CHANGE

Alongside the metatheories of change have arisen numerous middle-range theories that describe change from a particular perspective or lens. Each lens is instructive and useful for understanding change in more depth. This section is not intended to be a comprehensive review but rather to present several focused theories representative of major perspectives.

Organizational Theories

Four theories are presented here: organizations as performance systems, the Burke–Litwin model, innovation diffusion theory, and the organizational communications approach.

Organizations as Performance Systems

Thinking about the organization as a performance system functioning within the larger environment and as a collection of subsystems has been the work of numerous organizational scholars, including Senge's (1990) *The Fifth Discipline: The Art and Practice of the Learning Organization* and Wheatley's (1992) *Leadership and the New Science: Learning about Organization from an Orderly Universe.* Both influential pieces have minimal direct connection of their theories to the substantive work of change.

In contrast, Rummler and Brache's (1995) holistic and systemic view of the organization as performance system intricately bridges the theory–practice gap from much of the literature (discussed in more detail in Chapter 8). They begin by viewing organizations as adaptive systems. A relationship map of a hypothetical computer company is presented in Figure 13.6 to illustrate an early step of their change process.

As the Rummler and Brache inquiry model unfolds, the organization, work process, and individual contributor performance levels are laid out. In addition, the three performance needs of goals, design, and management are specified. The resulting 3×3 matrix creates nine performance cells (see Figure 2.4). Together they create a framework for thinking about the performance variables that impinge upon change. Their overall methodology is portrayed in Figure 13.7.

The Rummler and Brache change process is aimed at organizational performance, and it has been shown to be both a theoretically sound organization development change process (see Wimbiscus, 1995) and one that has been proven in practice. It combines thinking models, systemic relationships, tools, and metrics to guide the change effort. More than most change models, Rummler and Brache require the OD consultant and the improvement team to be serious students of the organization, its larger environment, and the inner working of the organization's processes and people.

Burke–Litwin Model of Organizational Performance and Change

One of the more complex but also more comprehensive models of organization change is the Burke–Litwin (1992) model. Burke and Litwin attempted to capture the interrelationships of complex organizational variables and distinguish between transformational and transactional dynamics in organizational change (Burke, 1994). Furthermore, the model portrays how the primary variables or

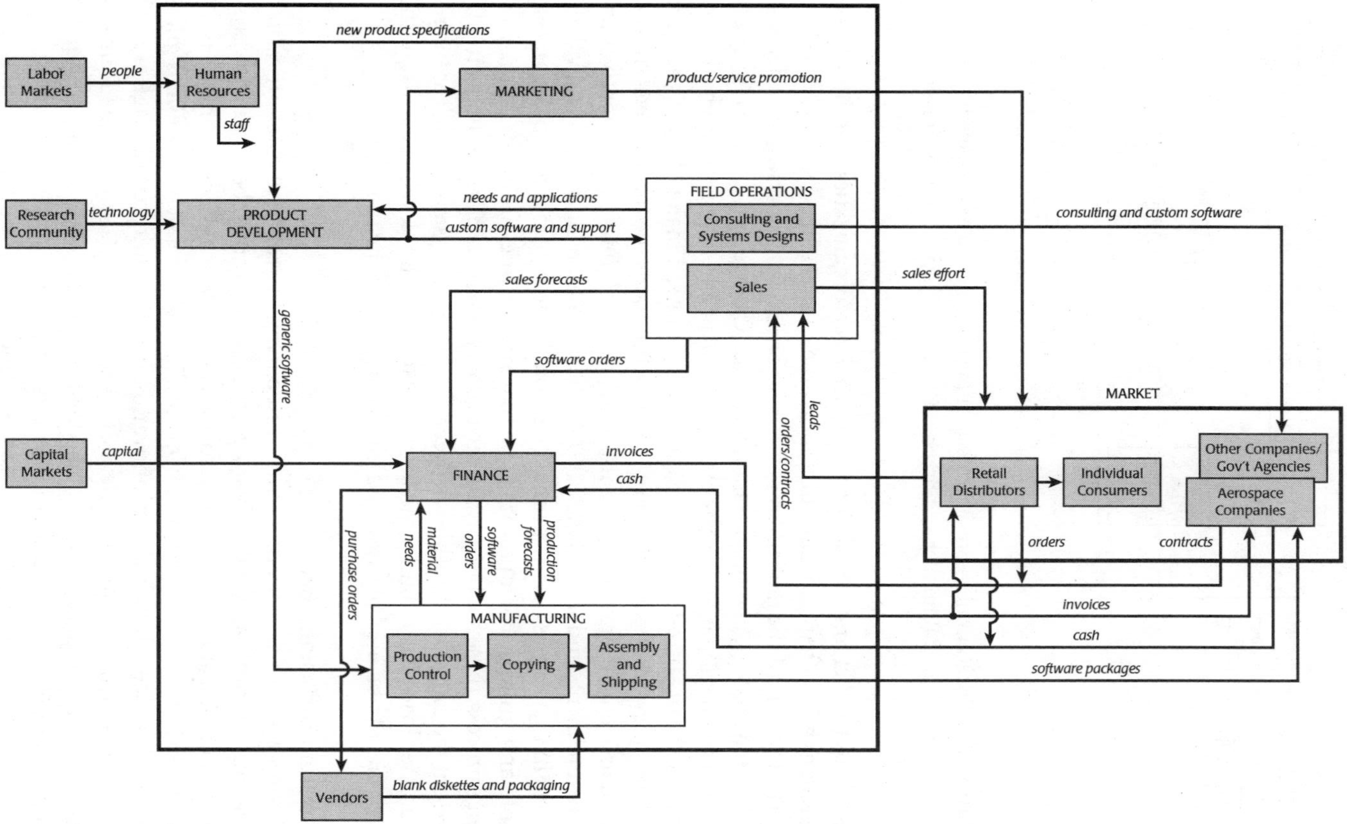

Figure 13.6 Relationship Map for Computec, Inc. (*Source:* Rummler & Brache (1995, p. 38) Used with permission.

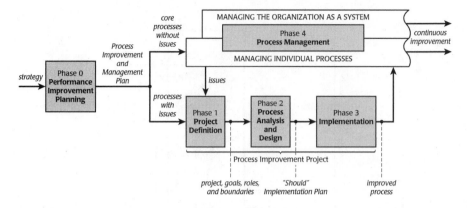

Figure 13.7 The Rummler–Brache Process Improvement and Management Methodology (*Source:* Rummler and Brache (1995, p. 117). Used with permission.)

subsystems predict and explain performance in an organization and how those subsystems affect change. Figure 13.8 shows the complete model.

The top part of the model shows the *transformational* subsystems: leadership, mission and strategy, and organizational culture. Change in these areas is usually caused by interaction with the external environment and requires entirely new behavior by the organization. For organizations that need major change, these are the primary levers. The lower part of the model contains the *transactional* subsystems: management practices, systems, structure, work unit climate, motivation, task requirements and individual skills/abilities, and individual needs and values. Change in these areas occurs primarily through short-term reciprocity among people and groups. For organizations that need a fine-tuning or improving change process, these subsystems are the primary levers. The arrows in the model represent the causal relationships between the major subsystems as well as the reciprocal feedback loops. Burke and his associates have also developed a diagnostic survey that can be used to assess and plan change using the model.

Innovation Diffusion Theory

Diffusion research focuses on factors influencing the rate and extent to which change and innovation is spread among and adopted by members of a social system (e.g., organization, community, society, etc.). Rogers (1995) offers the most comprehensive and authoritative review of diffusion research. He defines *diffusion* as "the process by which an innovation is communicated through certain channels over time among members of a social system" (p. 10). The four key components of a diffusion system embedded in this definition are an innovation, communication channels, time, and the social system.

The body of research on diffusion is immense and is often overlooked by HRD professionals. An extremely useful part of this research is the work on the rate at which change is adopted in social systems. It turns out that the rate is rea-

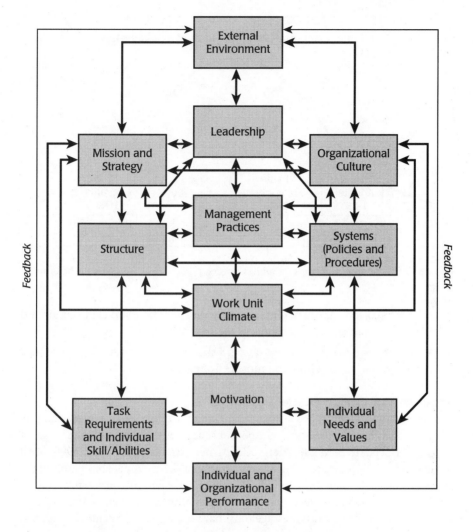

Figure 13.8 Burke–Litwin Model of Organizational Performance and Change
(*Source:* Burke and Litwin, 1992, p. 528. Used with permission.)

sonably predictable and almost always follows a normal distribution, as shown in
Figure 13.9.

Rogers defines five categories of adopters (of change or innovation):

- *Innovators*—venturesome with a desire for the rash, daring, and risky

- *Early adopters*—are respected by peers and embody the successful, discrete
  use of new ideas; often the opinion leader

- *Early majority*—tend to deliberate for some time before completely adopting a new idea but still adopt before the average person

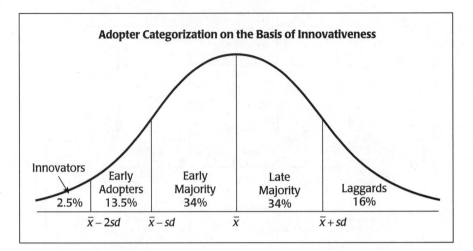

Figure 13.9 Adopter Categories (*Source:* Rogers, 1995, p. 262. Used with permission.)

- *Late majority*—approach innovation with a skeptical and cautious air and do not adopt until most others in the system have
- *Laggards*—tend to be suspicious and skeptical of innovations and change agents; the last to adopt and most resistant to change

Organizational Communications Approach

Communication is central to any successful change effort. Surprisingly, few OD change models have focused on this aspect of change. Armenakis and his colleagues (Armenakis, Harris, & Mossholder, 1993; Armenakis, Harris, & Field, 1999) are a notable exception to this, offering an organizational change model built around the change message. In their view, "all efforts to introduce and institutionalize change can be thought of as sending a message to organizational members" (Armenakis et al., 1999, p. 103). The change message must have five key components that address five core questions organizational members have about the change:

Message Element	Question Answered
Discrepancy	Is the change really necessary?
Appropriateness	Is the specific change being introduced an appropriate reaction to the discrepancy?
Efficacy	Can I/we successfully implement the change?
Principal support	Are formal and informal leaders committed to successful implementation and institutionalization of the change?
Personal valence	What is in it (the change) for me?

Their model is considerably more complex than this, but the change message is the most unique component. Also included in the model are seven generic strategies used to transmit and reinforce the message: active participation, management of external and internal information, formalization activities, diffusion practices, persuasive communication, human resource management practices, and rites and ceremonies. These strategies and the message combine to move people in the organization through stages of readiness, change adoption, commitment to the change, and institutionalization.

Work Process Theories

The quality improvement revolution of the 1980s was led by two elderly scholar-practitioners: Dr. Joseph M. Juran and Dr. W. Edwards Deming. Both had been called upon to help rebuild the Japanese economy after World War II and were asked again by the captains of American industry in the 1980s to help save its faltering economy. Their basic thesis is that producing quality goods and services ends up costing less money, increases profits, delights customers who then return, and provides satisfying work to people at all levels in the organization.

Both of these men began their journey in the realm of change at the work process level. In addition, they began it at a time when the rate of change was much slower. Over the years, they expanded their process improvement models—up to the leadership level and down to the individual worker level. Even so, the core of their work has been anchored at the work process level. A few defining features from each are highlighted here.

Juran's Quality by Design

At the process level, Juran (1992) defines *process control* and *process design* as follows: "Process control is the systematic evaluation of performance of a process, and taking of corrective action in the vent of nonconformance" (p. 509), and "[p]rocess design is the activity of defining the specific means to be used by the operating forces for meeting product quality goals" (p. 221).

At the overall level, Juran identifies three universal processes of managing for quality: quality planning, quality control, and quality improvement (Figure 13.10).

Deming's Fourteen Points for Management

Like Juran, Deming was a statistician and relied heavily on hard data to make decisions about process improvement. He believed in documenting processes to the point that many of the flaws in the work process would simply reveal themselves. While he generally distrusted work processes that informally emerge and evolve in the workplace, he trusted numbers from good measures of those processes as the basis of improving them. He also trusted human beings and human nature—the people that work in the processes. Over time, Deming became better known for his fourteen points for management, which he believed would produce saner and more productive workplaces. They are as follows:

Figure 13.10   The Three Universal Processes of Managing for Quality

Managing for Quality		
QUALITY PLANNING	**QUALITY CONTROL**	**QUALITY IMPROVEMENT**

• Establish quality goals
• Identify who are the customers
• Determine the needs of the customers
• Develop product features that respond to customers' needs
• Develop processes able to produce the product features
• Establish process controls; transfer the plans to the operating forces
	• Evaluate actual performance
	• Compare actual performance to quality goals
	• Act on the difference
		• Prove the need
		• Establish the infrastructure
		• Identify the improvement projects
		• Establish project teams
		• Provide the teams with resources, training, and motivation to:
		  – Diagnose the causes
		  – Stimulate remedies
		• Establish control to hold the gains

Source: Juran (1992, p. 16). Used with permission.

1. Create constancy of purpose for improvement of product and service.

2. Adopt a new philosophy.

3. Cease dependence on inspection to achieve quality.

4. End the practice of awarding business on price tag alone. Instead, minimize total cost by working with a single supplier.

5. Improve constantly and forever every process for planning, production, and service.

6. Institute training on the job.

7. Adopt and institute leadership.

8. Drive out fear.

9. Break down barriers between staff areas.

10. Eliminate slogans, exhortations, and targets for the workforce.

11. Eliminate numerical quotas for the workforce and numerical goals for management.

12. Remove barriers that rob people of pride of workmanship. Eliminate the annual rating or merit system.

13. Institute a vigorous program of and self-improvement for everyone.

14. Put everybody in the company to work to accomplish the transformation (Deming, 1982).

Group Theories

Group dynamics researchers have long had an interest in how groups change and evolve over time. The result has been a plethora of sequential stage theories describing predictable stages groups move through as they grow and develop. While they appear different on the surface, there is more agreement than disagreement in them.

Tuckman (1965) has put forth what is probably the best-known theory. He reviewed over fifty studies conducted in a variety of settings and identifies four stages. Later (Tuckman & Jensen, 1977), updated the model to include a fifth stage, though it is usually ignored in the popular literature. The five stages he identifies are as follows:

- *Forming*—As the group comes together, a period of uncertainty prevails as members try to find their place in the group and the rules of the group are worked out.
- *Storming*—Conflicts begin to arise as members confront and work out their differences.
- *Norming*—The group reaches some consensus regarding the structure and norms for the group.
- *Performing*—Group members become proficient at working together.
- *Adjourning*—The group disbands.

These theories collectively represent another important example of midrange change theory in HRD. Groups are a fundamental part of organizational life and therefore a primary client of HRD. Group change theories of this type help explain critical features of group dynamics and help practitioners work effectively with groups.

Individual Theories

Two groups of theories, adult development theory and career development theory, represent significant change theories at the individual level.

Adult Development Theory

Adults do not become adults in an instant—it is a developmental process. Researchers now understand that development does not end when adulthood is reached but rather continues to progress in a variety of ways. Adult development theories are having a profound influence on thinking about learning and change because adults' learning behavior varies considerably due to developmental influences. What is not clear is exactly how it changes, largely because adult development theory is still mostly an array of untested models. This section provides only a brief overview of adult development theory. Readers seeking a more complete discussion of adult development should consult Knowles et al. (1998), Bee (1996), Tennant and Pogson (1995), Knox (1977), or Merriam and Cafferella (1991).

Overview of Adult Development Theories

Adult development theories are generally divided into three types: physical changes; personality and life span role development; and cognitive or intellectual development (Merriam & Cafferella, 1991; Tennant, 1997). Life-span role development theory's, primary contribution is to help explain how adults change in life roles. Cognitive development theories help explain key ways adults' thinking changes over their life.

Bee (1996) characterizes development theories as varying along two dimensions. First, theories vary as to whether they include defined *stages* or *no stages*. Stage theories imply fixed sequences of sequentially occurring stages over time. Stage theories are quite common, while others offer no such fixed sequence of events.

Second, some theories focus on *development,* while some focus on change during adult life. *Change theories* are merely descriptive of typical changes experienced by adults. There is no normative hierarchy intended, so one phase is not better than another is. They merely seek to describe typical or expected changes. Many of the life span role development theories fit into this category. The premise of these theories is that certain predictable types of changes occur throughout an adult's life. Here are some examples of these:

- Levinson's (1978, 1990) life stage theory, which divides adult life into three eras with alternating period's stability and transitions. Each era brings with it certain predictable tasks, and each transition between eras certain predictable challenges.

- Erikson's (1959) theory of identity development, which proposes that an adult's identity develops through resolution of eight crises or dilemmas

- Loevinger's (1976) ten-stage model of ego development progressing from infancy to adulthood

The contribution of all life span theories to HRD is similar. First, they say that adult life is a series of stages and transitions, each of which pushes the adult into unfamiliar territory. Second, each transition to a new stage creates a motivation to learn.

Development theories imply a hierarchical ordering of developmental sequences, with higher levels being better than lower levels. They include a normative component, which suggests that adults should progress to higher levels of development. Many of the cognitive development theories fit into this category. The core premise of cognitive development theories is that changes occur in a person's thinking process over time. The foundation of most adult cognitive development theories is the work of Swiss psychologist Jean Piaget (Merriam & Cafferella, 1991). Piaget hypothesized that children move through four stages of thinking: *sensory motor, preoperational, concrete operational,* and *formal operations.* Formal operations, at which a person reaches the ability to reason hypothetically and abstractly, is considered the stage at which mature adult thought begins, though many adults never reach it. Because Piaget was a child development specialist, his model implies that cognitive development stops upon reaching adulthood. Adult development theorists dispute that idea, focusing on various ways that cognitive development continues beyond formal operations. Following are some selected examples.

Dialectic Thinking

Dialectic thinking is a level of thinking at which a person comes to see, understand, and accept alternate views and truths about the world, and the inherent contradictions in adult life. It enables adults to make peace with the complexity of life in which few truths exist and in which numerous contradictions and compromises are confronted daily. Kramer (1989), Riegel (1976), Pascual-Leone (1983), and Benack and Basseches (1989) have all proposed models of postformal operations that embrace dialectic thinking.

Other Postformal Operations

Other theorists have recognized that thinking develops beyond formal operations, but propose different types of postformal operations. For example, Arlin (1984) proposes a fifth stage of development, the problem-finding stage. Labouvie-Vief (1990) suggests that the hallmark of mature adult thought was the ability to make a commitment to a position or life course, despite recognizing the many different possibilities.

Relativistic Thinking

Closely related to dialectic thinking is relativistic thinking. Perry (1970) proposes a nine-stage model of cognitive development based on his research with college students. These stages describe change from dualistic, right-wrong, black-and-white type thinking to more complex relativistic thinking.

Selective Optimization with Compensation

Baltes and colleagues (Baltes, 1997; Baltes, Dittman-Kohli, & Dixon, 1984) have developed a model of development that accounts for the general finding that adults maintain high levels of performance and functioning, despite apparent losses in some physical capacities. Their theory has three core components: selection, optimization, and compensation. From this perspective, as adults age and recognize limits to their capacity, they first become more selective about tasks (both life and cognitive tasks) to which they devote their energy. As aging-related losses continue, adults seek to optimize the use of their cognitive resources to those areas in which they are most efficient. For example, adults may decide to focus their work on fewer activities that are most meaningful to them or at which they are most successful. Finally, as age-related losses occur more frequently, they find means to compensate for those losses. These may be as common as using aids (hearing, sight, memory, etc.) or devoting more time and attention to certain tasks.

Implications from Developmental Theories

Though few of the theories about adult development have been thoroughly tested, they have persisted because most adults intuitively recognize that change and development continues throughout adult life. The implications of the adult development perspective for HRD are immense because adult learning is inextricably intertwined with adult development. We tend to agree with the prevailing thinking today that there is no one theory that is "best." Rather, adult development should be viewed as consisting of multiple pathways and multiple dimensions (Daloz, 1986; Merriam & Cafferella, (1991).

Career Development Theory

While McLagan (1989) defines career development as one of the three areas of practice for HRD (see Chapter 2), it has had declining influence in HRD in recent years. HRD has increasingly coalesced around personnel training and development and organization development as the primary fields of practice. Career development functions as an extension of the development component of T&D.

This shift in responsibility for career development is due to the changes that have occurred in the workplace where the notion of long-term careers with single organizations is mostly gone. Individuals have taken control of their own career development where organizations once had prevailed.

We tend to think that career development is being overlooked as a contributor to HRD. Career development theories pertaining to career choice among young people are less important to HRD because they do not fit traditional venues for HRD practice. However, career development theories that describe adult career development are important contributors to HRD practice because they describe adult progression through work roles—a primary venue for HRD practice. Fundamentally, these theories are a special type of change theory at the individual level. Two streams of research are particularly useful to HRD: Super's life span, life space approach to careers, and Dawis and Lofquist's theory of work adjustment. Readers wishing more information on these theories are encouraged to consult Brown and Brooks (1996), Osipow and Fitzgerald (1996), Super and Sverko (1995), and Dawis and Lofquist (1984).

Super's Life Span, Life Space Approach

Super's theory developed over a lifetime of research. Currently, the theory consists of fourteen basic propositions (Super et al., 1996). Because it is the most complex career development theory, many elements are included in the propositions. Fundamentally, it includes these basic components:

- *Self-concept*—Development through life is a process of defining, developing, and implementing one's self-concept, which will change over time.
- *Life space*—A person's life is comprised of a constellation of work and non-work roles, the balance of which change over life.

- *Life span*—Life also consists of a macrostructure of developmental stages as described in adult development theory.
- *Role changes in life*—A person's self-concept changes as life roles change, in turn resulting in career changes as a person fits work to their changes in life roles and self-concept.

Unlike more traditional trait approaches to career choice and development, Super's theory is focused on change. Super sees adult life as built upon change and development (the adult development perspective), which in turn changes a person's self-concept. A person's work and career are then places where the self-concept is acted out.

The power of this theory for HRD is that it directly explains many of the work-related changes adults undergo. A large portion of the demand for HRD in organizations is influenced by adults in the workplace changing roles and acting out their changing needs at work. Furthermore, adults often turn to HRD to help them make career changes outlined in this theory. Thus, because this theory is change oriented, it is a powerful career development theory for HRD.

Theory of Work Adjustment

This theory is built upon the process of individuals and organizations adjusting to fit each other (Dawis & Lofquist, 1984). According to this theory, individuals and organizations have needs, and they interact in order to meet these needs through the other. When the interaction is mutually satisfying, the person and environment are said to be in correspondence with each other. Correspondence will mean that workers are *satisfied,* and they are *satisfactory* to the organization because they possess the necessary skills and expertise. This is now called *person–environment correspondence* (PEC).

What makes this a change-oriented theory is that correspondence rarely lasts because the needs of the worker and of the organization are constantly changing. Thus, work and a career is an ongoing process of the organization and the worker providing feedback to each other. Both may attempt to make changes to accommodate the other, called *adjustment behaviors.* A person's perceptions of needed adjustments is influenced by his or her self-concept. This adjustment often takes the form of development as capabilities are expanded to meet organizational requirements.

Like most good theories, the theory of work adjustment is deceptively simple to describe, but powerful in practice. It describes the fundamental systemic dynamics underlying much of the employee–organization interaction. Again, many of the adjustments made as a result of the interactions lead directly to HRD interventions. For example, changes in skills needed by the organization will result in developmental opportunities for employees. Similarly, changes in individual employee needs will often lead to HRD assistance for changing work roles. When combined with Super's work, these theories provide valuable insights to change dynamics at the individual level in organizations.

Figure 13.11   Cummings and Worley's Five Stages of Change

Motivating Change
- Creating readiness for change
- Overcoming resistance to change

Creating a Vision
- Describing the core ideology
- Constructing the envisioned future

Developing Political Support
- Assessing change agent power
- Identifying key stakeholders
- Influencing stakeholders

Managing the Transition
- Activity planning
- Commitment planning
- Management structures

Sustaining Momentum
- Providing resources for change
- Building a support system for change agents
- Developing new competencies and skills
- Reinforcing new behaviors

Source: Cummings and Worley (2001, p. 154). Used with permission.

STAGES OF THE ORGANIZATION CHANGE LEADERSHIP PROCESS

Of primary interest to the study of change has been development of prescriptive process models to help change agents understand the best approach to leading change. These models provide specific tasks that change agents must accomplish in order to lead change successfully. Many different process models have been developed, and, while each has its different nuances, at the core most are really quite similar. In this chapter, we review two representative ones from Cummings and Worley (2001) and Kotter (1996).

Cummings and Worley's Model

Cummings and Worley (2001) suggest that there are five key activities for effective change management. Although not a strict stage model, the five activities comprise something of an action plan (see Figure 13.11).

Kotter's Eight-Stage Model

Kotter (1996) proposes an eight-stage model for creating major change. The steps are shown in Figure 13.12.

These models provide change agents with a normative framework useful to guide change management programs. If one thinks deeply about them, it is easy

Figure 13.12   Kotter's Eight Stages of Change

1. **Establishing a Sense of Urgency**
    - Examining the market and competitive realities
    - Identifying and discussing crises, potential crises, or major opportunities

2. **Creating the Guiding Coalition**
    - Putting together a group with enough power to lead the change
    - Getting the group to work together like a team

3. **Developing a Vision and Strategy**
    - Creating a vision to help direct the change effort
    - Developing strategies for achieving that vision

4. **Communicating the Change Vision**
    - Using every vehicle possible to constantly communicate the new vision and strategies
    - Having the guiding coalition role model the behavior expected of employees

5. **Empowering Broad-Based Action**
    - Getting rid of obstacles
    - Changing systems or structures that undermine the change vision
    - Encouraging risk taking and nontraditional ideas, activities, and actions

6. **Generating Short-term Wins**
    - Planning for visible improvements in performance, or "wins"
    - Creating those wins
    - Visibly recognizing and rewarding people who made the wins possible

7. **Consolidating Gains and Producing More Change**
    - Using increased credibility to change all systems, structures, and policies that don't fit together and don't fit the transformation vision
    - Hiring, promoting, and developing people who can implement the change vision
    - Reinvigorating the process with new projects, themes, and change agents

8. **Anchoring New Approaches in the Culture**
    - Creating better performance through customer- and productivity-oriented behavior, more and better leadership, and more effective management
    - Articulating the connections between new behaviors and organizational success
    - Developing means to ensure leadership development and succession

Source: Kotter (1996, p. 21). Used with permission.

to see how metatheories of change (e.g., Lewin's) result in middle-range theories that in turn lead to these change leadership models.

CONCLUSION

It is only by understanding the complexities of change that HRD professionals can be effective in organizations. It may be that the characteristic that distinguishes HRD from training is that HRD focuses on change as well as learning. The integration of learning, performance, and change under one umbrella discipline makes HRD unique and powerful. These three constructs are central to organizational effectiveness and are likely to become even more important in the future.

REFLECTION QUESTIONS

1. Do you agree or disagree that change is an organizing construct for HRD? Explain your answer.

2. How can HRD become more of a change leader in organizations, rather than a change facilitator?

3. What similarities and differences do you see among the organization, work process, group, and individual change theories?

4. Can all theories of change be captured in one type or a combination of types within Van de Ven and Poole's typology?

5. What is the responsible connection between change and performance?

Organization Development Practices: From Organizations to Individuals

CHAPTER OUTLINE

Part Five of this book has dealt with organization development (OD). Chapter 12 captured the essence of the OD component of HRD, and Chapter 13 delved deeper into the nature of change, the focal point of OD. This third and final chapter in this part of the book provides illustrations of OD practice as it exists in host organizations along with variations in core thinking that guides OD practices, interventions, and tool selection.

VARIATIONS IN OD PRACTICES

OD is the process of systematically unleashing human expertise to implement organizational change for the purpose of improving performance. Under this definition, and others, there are variations in OD practice. Practices in OD have historically been rooted in the psychological realm, with intervention outcomes being human perceptions and the spirit of the organization versus hard business measures. This remains a fundamental problem for OD as the field seems to value its OD processes more than its results. Even to this day, a recent scholarly review of the organization change and development literature pays scant attention to verified outcomes (Weick & Quinn, 1999). The authors spend large amounts of time talking about the inner workings change process—adaptation, learning, intervention, and transformation—with scant connection to success or failure. In contrast, Church and McMahan (1996) studied the perceptions of OD practitioner leaders in top U.S. firms as to the purpose of OD. When asked to react to the statement "Practitioners should focus more on effectiveness, efficiency, and competitive advantage to remain viable organizations for the future," 53 percent strongly agreed, 29 percent moderately agreed, 12 percent slightly agreed, 6 percent slightly disagreed, and none strongly disagreed.

Expected Results from OD Interventions

Expected outcomes from OD interventions have shifted so that the new emphasis is on organization results. This coincides with the inclusion of economic and systems principles and tools increasingly being utilized in OD practice. Historically, OD has been noted for its focus on process and tools. "The OD Cube" (Schmuck & Miles, 1971) with its axes of (1) diagnosed problems, (2) focus of attention, and (3) mode of interventions illustrates this point (Figure 14.1). The list of diagnosed problems does not include any mission-level outcomes or financial measures as a focus of problems. Instead, the cube offers *solutions* to unidentified mission-level organization problems. For example, an organizational problem would be in closing sales, not the quality of the communication during the sales process. The up-front analysis and diagnosis may suggest that having an improved understanding of communication and better communication in the sales transaction will result in increasing sales. Thus, improving the sales is the performance focus and business problem.

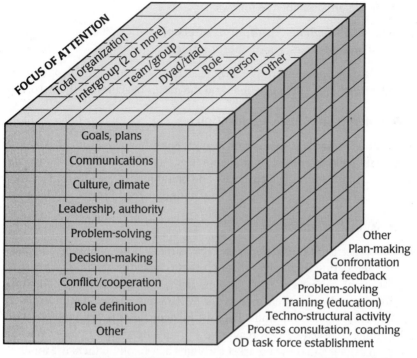

DIAGNOSED PROBLEMS   **MODE OF INTERVENTIONS**

Figure 14.1   The OD Cube: A Scheme for Classifying OD Interventions
(*Source:* Schmuck and Miles, 1971, p. 5. Used with permission.)

Thinking more clearly about the anticipated results from the onset of any OD effort fundamentally affects the process. For example, the assessment domains of performance, learning, and perceptions from the *Results Assessment System* (Swanson & Holton, 1999) help frame the anticipated results. *Performance results* are defined as follows:

> *System:* The units of mission-related outputs in the form of goods and/or services having value to the customer and that are related to the core organizational, work processes, group/individual contributors in the organization.

> *Financial:* The conversion of the output units of goods and/or services attributable to the intervention into money and financial interpretation. (p. 14)

Learning results are defined as follows:

> *Knowledge:* Mental achievement acquired through study and experience.

> *Expertise:* Human behaviors, having effective results and optimal efficiency, acquired through study and experience within a specialized domain. (p. 17)

Perception results are described as follows:

> *Participant Perceptions:* Perceptions of people with first-hand experience with systems, processes, goods and/or services.
>
> *Stakeholder Perceptions:* Perceptions of leaders of systems and/or people with a vested interest in the desired results and the means of achieving them. (p. 18)

OD in Relation to the Host Organization

The range of OD providers spans from a single consultant (internal or external), to consultant firms larger than their clients (e.g., Accenture), to guru status consultants (e.g., Tom Peters). The authority and credibility of the OD organization and the OD person leading the process have a fundamental impact on OD work.

OD Professional Expertise

OD process expertise is considered a strategic variable. Consultants and consultant firms often define themselves through their particular method of up-front analysis or by their means of entry into the firm. For example, large consulting firms pride themselves on their industry-level data (e.g., banking or auto industry) and holistic analysis methods. High-profile consultants (e.g., Nadler et al., 1992; Rummler & Brache, 1995) may have a unique up-front organizational diagnosis methodology that they market through their books. Others use an inviting planning or diagnostic tool (e.g., future search or 360-degree assessment) for entry into organizations.

CORE OD PRACTICES

OD does not employ a large number of standard practices; rather, practices *issues* are fairly standard. Three of these standard practice *issues* are presented here.

OD Revolves around the Change Process

OD is committed to change and to guiding the change process. With all the evidence of the constancy of change and the increasing rate of change, OD is eager to assist and to help organizations and individuals to drive change not for the sake of change but for the attainment of worthy goals.

Trust and Integrity in OD

OD processes rely on information from stakeholders and ultimately provide information back to those stakeholders. This information is often very uncomfortable, even threatening. Information confidentiality is an overriding practice issue with OD. Intelligent synthesis and sensitive presentation of information to clients build both trust and integrity. The trust in the OD process itself and the process leader depends on the essential fairness of the OD consultant.

OD Dynamics

The analogy of the card game and the challenge of knowing when to play, hold, or fold the cards are useful in thinking about the OD process dynamics. Practitioners know that once the OD practitioner is engaged in an intervention, he or she becomes part of the ongoing organization. Change is a dynamic process that stretches out over time. It may be that this dynamic is the most challenging part of OD and why some people enjoy the process. The threat to an OD consultant, as with most helping professions, is in overrating one's importance in the process. Consultant humility and the use of sources of authority beyond the consultant are essential in managing the dynamics of the OD process.

ORGANIZATION-FOCUSED OD PRACTICES

As we have noted elsewhere in discussions about HRD, almost every sound OD effort has a T&D component, and almost every sound T&D effort has an OD component. The overall change effort will likely be classified as an OD intervention or carry a mission-focused title such as the Ford Motor Company mantra of "Quality Is Job 1." Organization-wide OD practice is often focused on *organization culture* or a *future state* to ensure the existence of the organization as well as its advancement.

Organization Strategy and Culture

Given shifts in the environment (economic, political, and cultural forces) and the organization itself (mission/strategy, organizational structure, technology, and human resources), an organization can find itself in or on the cusp of mission erosion, cultural disarray, and system disconnects. Let's consider the following example.

In a three-phase change effort, OD experts led the management team of a small manufacturer through a strategic planning process including strategic planning, culture assessment and realignment, and quality improvement. A refocused vision and mission of the firm was produced by the top management team after careful and deliberate analysis. It was painfully apparent that the existing state of the firm was far from this new vision and that all employees in the firm needed to be informed of and seriously consider the implications of the change required. It was decided to use external OD consultants to oversee a process of culture assessment and realignment before moving on to the quality improvement phase. This cultural assessment phase was seen as critical in moving from strategic planning to issues of quality improvement. Culture surveys have become an important tool for managers in business and industry in heading off cultural problems and facilitating the change journey. What is done with the survey data is critical in getting the full benefit. The following discussion is a closer look at the use of culture surveys.

Culture Surveys

Culture surveys can be used to gather information directly from all employees that are not quickly available from other sources. For example, managers experiencing problems in operations often use production reports to get information about the status of operation, but production reports are insufficient for guiding any organization-wide change effort.

A culture survey, by its nature, is participatory and highly visible. Management can use a culture survey to communicate its vision to the organization's culture and the performance expectations and operationalize the vision. For example, if management's vision of the organization culture emphasizes employee participation in decision making for the purpose of improvements, items on the culture survey could measure employees' perceptions of their involvement in specific decision-making processes.

Some principles that have proven useful in successfully implementing a cultural survey include the following (Sleezer & Swanson, 1992):

- Analyze the situation before developing the survey.
- Design the survey instrument to collect specific information.
- Administer the survey consistently.
- Take care not to overreact to the data.
- Act on the results of a survey.

Sleezer and Swanson (1992) describe a company-wide change effort that was driven by the use of culture surveys that were filled out by all employees every six months. The survey was first organized around dimensions of the strategic plan of the company. Those dimensions were then used as means of selecting the general cultural variables and the specific survey questions. McLean's (1988) bank of culture climate questions framed the categories and specific questions for the culture survey. The first survey provided baseline information that management and employees reviewed and reacted to. The consultants identified the key issues related to the purpose of this survey and suggested specific actions in sharing the data with all employees through group meetings. Employees became trusting when they discovered that their responses had been accurately reported and confidentiality had been maintained.

When the second survey was implemented six months later, the trust of the survey process and follow-up meetings allowed for much more open and honest discussion and planning. When management examined the report from the second survey, they were surprised that the intensity of the employees' feelings and the specificity of their concerns.

The culture survey results caused managers to look closer at its reorganization plan and to reexamine their vision. Workers and managers then decided that they needed to focus on quality, be a more participative organization, and execute an open-door policy. They also supported a six-point action plan with such items as (1) changing the structure of the workforce and (2) insisting that managers and supervisors work participatively with employees.

By the time the third survey was implemented, management had begun to see changes in the way workers were talking about their company and responding to issues throughout the company. Employees were beginning to contribute toward product quality and quantity. The culture survey process forced management to listen to employees, and their listening began to payoff in increased productivity and employee satisfaction measures—a new company culture was emerging, and they began to engage in full-blown quality improvement efforts.

Planning for the Future

As more organizations face continuous change, OD practitioners have developed expertise and tools to operate successfully in such an environment. In an environment of constant change and challenge, nontraditional tools for anticipating and planning for change are being used, such as future search conferences, large-scale interventions, and scenario building.

Organization development for a future state of an organization is the purpose of the scenario-planning process. A scenario is "a tool for ordering one's perceptions about alternative future environments in which decisions might be played out" (Schwartz, 1996, p. 4). The process of scenario planning generally involves development of several plots and supporting narratives that illustrate primary forces driving change within a system, their interrelationships, and uncertainties in the environment (Wack, 1985b). Scenarios help decision makers structure and think about uncertainty, test their assumptions about how critical driving forces will interact, and reorganize their mental model of reality (Wack, 1985a).

Many think of scenario development as an art rather than a science (Schwartz, 1996). The process provides safe and often engaging opportunities to explore the implications of uncertainty and to think through ways of responding to it. Scenarios enable planners to deal more confidently in the midst of uncertainty (Schwartz, 1996; van der Heijden, 1996).

Van der Heijden (1996) characterizes the individual and organizational learning process of scenario building: by organizing complex information on future trends and possibilities into a series of plausible stories, scenarios are seen as interpretive tools that create meaning and thereby guide action. The use of multiple plausible futures helps decision makers think more expansively about change and to adopt multiple perspectives for the purpose of understanding future events. In the end, scenarios offer entrepreneurial and protective benefits to organizations (Wack, 1985b).

The Centre for Innovative Leadership (van der Merwe, 1997) describes the scenario development process as follows:

1. Identification of a strategic organizational agenda, including assumptions and concerns about current strategic thinking and vision.

2. Challenging of existing assumptions of organizational decision makers by questioning current mental models about the external environment.

3. Systematically examining the organization's external environment to improve understanding of the structure of the key forces driving change.

4. Synthesis of information about possible future events into three or four alternative plots or story lines about possible futures.

5. Development of narratives around the story lines to make the stories relevant and compelling to decision makers.

6. Use of the stories to help decision makers "re-view" their strategic thinking.

Chapter 15 deals with strategies for advancing HRD and contains a discussion of the integration of scenario building and strategic planning into a strategic organizational planning process.

WORK PROCESS–FOCUSED OD

W. Edwards Deming (1982) believed that 90 percent of the problems in organizations were the result of bad systems, not bad people. Nevin (1992) went on to say, "If you want to drive a person crazy, give them [*sic*] a great sense of responsibility and no authority." The picture is that there are good people working in bad processes over which they have no authority. The great advantage of studying work processes is that they are "out there," something apart from individual perceptions and emotions.

While work systems and work processes are inventions of individuals, they end up taking on a life of their own. When work processes are used as the point of OD entry into the organization, they simply represent the way things get done, apart from managers and workers. So many of the OD models and methods start with people and finger pointing (usually an exercise in power). When an OD practitioner asks would-be finger pointers to review the actual way things get done (the work processes that are regularly carried out), the present work process becomes more of a matter of fact versus blame—"it is simply the way it is."

We believe that engaging people in studying work processes is one of the most underused OD strategies. Two specific practices are *process improvement* and *benchmarking*.

Process Improvement

Numerous strategies are available for improving work processes. Process reengineering as proposed by Hammer and Champy (1992) is the most radical and unacceptable methodology because of its disregard for people. It fails in most cases and causes systemic havoc (Swanson, 1993). Shewhart's classic "plan-do-check-act" cycle (Shultz & Parker, 1988) is a sound method of studying processes (Figure 14.2). Rummler and Brache (1995) have a very practical tool in their larger organization development methodology for producing "is" and "should" process flow charts. The act of documenting things just as they are produces a

Cycles of Transformation Efforts

Though no hard and fast rules exist, there seems to be adequate testimony and experience to roughly describe the first "cycles of transformation" for a typical organization. We have chosen "cycles of transformation" as the descriptive phrase because transformation is an iterative process and the Shewhart cycle is an elegant model. Each iteration of the cycle includes:

ACT: Does the data confirm the "plan"? Are other "causes" operating? Are the "risks" of proceeding to further change necessary and worthwhile?

PLAN: What could be? What changes are needed? What obstacles need to be overcome? What are the most important results needed? etc. Are data available? What new information is needed?

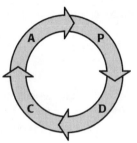

CHECK: Measure and observe "effects" of change or test.

DO: Small scale implementation of change or test to provide data for answers.

Figure 14.2   Shewart's Plan-Do-Check-Act Cycle *(Source:* Schultz and Parker, 1988, p. 53. Used with permission.)

pragmatic and objective view of reality. This strategy is in contrast to the accumulation of people's feelings and perceptions that is the focus of many OD methods. In both process improvement models noted, the gap between the existing process and the redesigned process represents the improvement focus that can be easily understood and pursued.

Another plan for process improvement has been put forward by Davenport (1993). It is conceptually between the incremental process improvement and radical reengineering (see Figure 14.3). Calling it *process innovation,* he believes it "encompasses the envisioning of new work strategies, the actual process design activity, and the implementation of the change in all its complex technological, human, and organizational dimensions" (p. 2). Figure 14.4 illustrates the general five-step process. Work process expertise is required to engage in process innovation. It is much more focused than many of the general problem-solving methods used by OD practitioners.

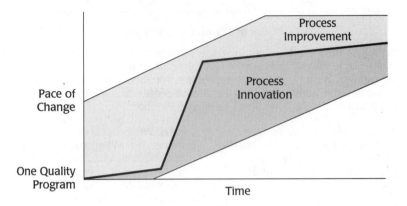
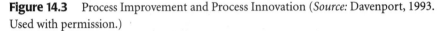

Figure 14.3 Process Improvement and Process Innovation (*Source:* Davenport, 1993. Used with permission.)

Benchmarking

Benchmarking is the search for and implementation of the best practices (Camp, 1995, p. 15). It is a process of learning from the best of the best and emulating those best practices. As such, it is best suited to analyzing work processes aimed at defined organization goals. The five phases of the benchmarking process include planning, analysis, integration, action, and maturity (see Figure 14.5).

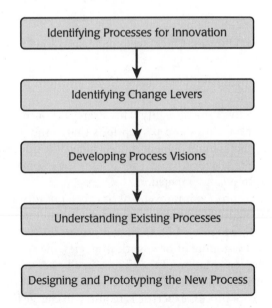

Figure 14.4 High-Level Depiction of the Process Innovation

- **Planning:** Identify what to benchmark, identify whom to benchmark, and gather data.
- **Analysis:** Examine the performance gap and project future performance.
- **Integration:** Communicate the findings and develop new goals.
- **Action:** Take actions, monitor progress, and recalibrate measures as needed.
- **Maturity:** Achieve the desired state.

Phase 1: Planning

A plan for benchmarking is prepared.

- Decide: What to benchmark
- Identify: Whom to benchmark
- Plan: The investigation and conduct it
  - Gather necessary information and data
  - Observe the best practices

Phase 2: Analysis

The gap is examined and the performance is assessed against best practices.

- Determine: The current performance gap
- Project: Future performance levels

Phase 3: Integration

The goals are redefined and incorporated into the planning process.

- Communicate: Benchmark findings and gain acceptance
- Revise: Performance goals

Phase 4: Action

Best practices are implemented and periodically recalibrated as needed.

- Develop: Action plans
- Implement: Actions and monitor progress
- Recalibrate: The benchmarks

Phase 5: Maturity

Leadership may be achieved.

- Determine: When leadership position is attained
- Assess: Benchmarking as an ongoing process

Figure 14.5   The Five Phases of the Benchmarking Process (Camp, 1995. Used with persmission.)

GROUP-FOCUSED OD

Group-focused OD has been the mainstay of organization development practice. More OD discussions and tools are aimed at this level than any other. Two examples highlighted here are team building and group conflict.

Cross-Cultural Team Building

Team building is "the process of helping a work group become more effective in accomplishing its tasks and satisfying the needs of group members" (Cummings & Worley, 2001, p. 676). The Web site of Personnel Decisions International (1996) describes a cross-cultural team-building challenge it addressed:

> *The Challenge:* Copenhagen-based Oresund Tunnel Contractors was formed in 1995 to build a tunnel that will connect Copenhagen, Denmark and Malmo, Sweden. Oresund's parent companies—NCC (Sweden), John Laing (United Kingdom), Dumez GTM (France), Boskalis (Netherlands), and Phil & Soen (Denmark)—challenged the company's new management team, which included 45 representatives from each of the founding companies, to create a cohesive culture that would benefit from the leadership of a diverse management team and communicate clear goals and consistent strategies.
>
> *The Solution:* Early in 1996, the consultants from each of the parent companies' countries administered a questionnaire to Oresund's management team that examined the impact of cultural differences on their success. The consultants also interviewed certain members of the team about the effectiveness of the group's new working relationships. Using the results of their research, the consultants designed and facilitated workshops that addressed how cultural differences affect corporate culture. The program culminated in a three-day team-building event consisting of exercises that developed the communications skills and trust levels between Oresund management team members.
>
> *The Result:* Members of Oresund's management team have reported that their new understanding of how cultural differences impact working behavior has reduced the potential for misunderstanding and conflicts between colleagues. They've also said that the positive relationships that now exist between key managers have improved the consistency and flow of information. The consultants planned a follow-up session to track how the management team has progressed against a "change" questionnaire.

Group Conflict

OD is often called upon to intervene when group conflict arises. OD practitioners employ any number of diagnostic and communication techniques to analyze and resolve the problems. While differences in perceptions can vary between any two people, the situation is heightened when there are age differences, ethnic differences, gender differences, educational differences, and national differences. OD practitioners must be sensitive to those differences and fair in their transactions.

Hofstede's (2001) helps us to understand cultural differences at a national level highlights both the differences and the challenge to OD practitioners (Figure 14.6). The ideal situation would be that the potential for conflict would be anticipated and that interventions would be carried out to ward off conflict rather than react to conflict.

INDIVIDUAL-FOCUSED OD

Much of OD's history has been focused on the development of individuals (primarily the process of changing a person's gestalt from one pattern to another) and the expectation that such a transformation would result in organization development. The highly criticized T-groups developed in the 1950s are the most vivid example. The avenue to organization development through individual development and the unleashing of human expertise remains. Two OD practices focused at the individual include 360-degree feedback and career assessment centers.

360-Degree Feedback

Individual contributors in organizations almost universally desire to be effective. Even so, individuals nearly always function in their environments with limited feedback as to how well they are functioning in the eyes of those around them. Addressing this need is 360-degree feedback, sometimes referred to as *multirater appraisals, multisource feedback,* or *360-degree profiling.* It is essentially a process that enables a person to receive feedback from a number of people, usually entailing developmental feedback relating to behaviors, skills, and competencies. Typically, in a 360-degree feedback scenario, an individual would receive feedback from their peers, direct reports, and manager. Sometimes other stakeholders such as clients, professional associates, and friends are polled.

Feedback can include ratings against questions or statements as well as comments and suggestions. The purpose of the feedback is usually to help individuals determine areas they need to develop. In some organizations it is also used to determine performance increases as part of a performance appraisal process. The question of whether 360-degree feedback should be used to determine performance increases is the cause of debate, however, and the misuses of this tool have been cited (McLean, 1997). In other contexts, this approach could be part of an ongoing leadership development process.

Suggestions for making 360-degree feedback work include the following:

- Enable participants to contribute to the design of the 360-degree feedback system.
- Develop a competency standard with careful consideration and much feedback from the people who will use it and from experts in the field.

Figure 14.6 Cultural Values and Organization Customs

Value	Definition	Organization Customs When the Value is at One Extreme	Representative Countries
Context	The extent to which words carry the meaning of a message; how time is viewed	Ceremony and routines are common. Structure is less formal; fewer written policies exist. People are often late for appointments	*High:* Asian and Latin American countries *Low:* Scandinavian countries, United States
Power distance	The extent to which members of a society accept that power is distributed unequally in an organization	Decision making is autocratic. Superiors consider subordinates as part of a different class. Subordinates are closely supervised Employees are not likely to disagree. Powerful people are entitled to privileges.	*High:* Latin American and Eastern European countries *Low:* Scandinavian countries
Uncertainty avoidance	The extent to which members of an organization tolerate the unfamiliar and unpredictable	Experts have status/authority. Clear roles are preferred. Conflict is undesirable. Change is resisted. Conservative practices are preferred.	*High:* Asian countries *Low:* European countries
Achievement orientation	The extent to which organization members value assertiveness and the acquisition of material goods	Achievement is reflected in wealth and recognition. Decisiveness is valued. Larger and faster are better. Gender roles are clearly differentiated.	*High:* Asian and Latin American countries, South Africa *Low:* Scandinavian countries
Individualism	The extent to which people believe they should be responsible for themselves and their immediate families	Personal initiative is encouraged. Time is valuable to individuals. Competitiveness is accepted. Autonomy is highly valued.	*High:* United States *Low:* Latin American and Eastern European countries

Source: Based on Hofstede, 2001. Used with permission.

- Develop a system that will not require employees to spend excessive time learning and then using.
- Run a small trial before implementing across the organization.
- Make changes to the system based on the feedback from the trial.
- Educate everyone in the organization before implementing the system.
- Ensure confidentiality is maintained.
- Monitor the success of the system and modify appropriately.

Career Development Assessment Center

Assessment centers within organizations or external consulting firms provide in-depth information about individual contributors. They are used for selection, individual development, and organization development purposes. Assessment centers engage people in high-fidelity simulations, role plays, and in-basket exercises. The military has done a great deal of work with the assessment center approach, and in recent years it has been used for upper management and executive-level career development.

Career development assessment centers sponsored by large organizations are often part of the career development assistance they provide to benefit individual and organization objectives. Responsible assessment centers do both.

Centers gain a large amount of information on individuals that can be used as a basis for advancing individual career development and actual careers in the sponsoring firm. When this is not feasible, assessment centers help individuals get to new employment that offers a better fit. With this level of integrity being known to company personnel, there is a willingness to "risk the growth."

Overview of an assessment process as reported on Personnel Decision International's (1999) Web site is as follows:

1. Understand the company's business strategies, context, and requirements of the role.
   - Review documentation.
   - Interview those knowledgeable about the role.

2. Determine the purpose of the assessment.
   - Needs that drive the assessment
   - How the results will be used
   - Key questions to be addressed

3. Design the assessment to meet organizational requirements.
   - Ensure the content of the assessment matches the content and requirements of the target role.
   - Use multiple, valid measurement techniques (e.g., could include tests of thinking ability and work style, structured interviews, work simulations) to assess the needed capabilities.

- Use measures that are appropriate for the person's culture and language.
- Tailor the output to meet the organization's needs.
- Communicate clearly to all stakeholders about the purpose, process, and outcomes.

4. Conduct the assessment.
- Provide a standardized setting.
- Create a supportive environment.
- Use well-trained staff.

5. Provide feedback/results.
- Address the company's needs and questions.
- Address the needed capabilities.
- Provide input on how to develop the person's potential.
- Protect confidentiality.

6. Use the results to align people with the business requirements.
- Review the fit between people's capabilities and the needs of the business.
- Advise on how to optimize allocation and development of competencies.

CONCLUSION

Organization development takes many forms. At the narrow and specific end of the spectrum, it can be focused on one person having difficulty fitting in and contributing to their organization. At the other end of the spectrum, it can emphasize shaping the future state of the organization, through whole systems analysis, alignment, and improvement or through guided future search or scenario building. The dominant OD practices in the middle of the OD spectrum are centered on improving existing work processes and work group conditions in a changing work environment.

REFLECTION QUESTIONS

1. What are three principles of good OD practice?
2. Identify an organization with which you are familiar and briefly describe it. Speculate as to how that organization's mission would impact the OD practices.
3. What are two to four major implications of having an OD effort in a single site location versus ten sites across the nation?
4. When does work process- versus group-focused OD make sense?
5. How do career development and OD connect?

Human Resource Development in the Twenty-first Century

The sixth and final part is a springboard into the twenty-first century based on best practices, strategies for advancement, and identification of the twenty-first century challenges to HRD, with a focus on globalization and technology. In addition, two major issues for HRD, strategic roles of HRD and accountability, are carefully explained.

Strategies for Advancing HRD

CHAPTER OUTLINE

Viewing human resource development as a strategic partner is a relatively new perspective (Wognum & Mulder, 1999). Walton's (1999) recent text is dedicated to increasing such strategic awareness and effectiveness among HRD professionals. The systems view of organizations, with HRD as a process within the organization and the organization functioning within the larger environment, provides the big-picture framework to begin thinking about the strategic roles of HRD (see Figure 2.1).

This chapter discusses the issues surrounding the role of HRD in organizational strategic planning as originally proposed by Torraco and Swanson (1995) and expanded upon by Swanson et al. (1998). Two factors have influenced the evolution of HRD toward a more active role as a key determinant of business strategy: (1) the centrality of information technology to business success and (2) the sustainable competitive advantage offered by workforce knowledge and expertise. These factors work together in such a way that the competitive advantages they offer are nearly impossible to achieve without developing and maintaining a highly competent workforce. They go on to build the case for a view of HRD that truly holds strategic value to an organization.

The major sections to this chapter include the schools of strategic thinking, the strategic roles of HRD, adopting a strategic HRD perspective, and scenario planning plus strategic planning.

SCHOOLS OF STRATEGIC THINKING

Mintzberg, Ahlstrand, and Lampel (1999) have summarized ten schools of strategic thinking. They argue that having a wider picture allows managers, consultants, and academics to better understand and pursue strategy. The schools are summarized through comparison of their features, including sources, base discipline, champions, intended messages, realized messages, school category, and an associated homily (see Figure 15.1).

Figure 15.1   Ten Schools of Strategic Thinking

1. **Design School**
   - Sources   P. Selznick
   - Base discipline   None (architecture as a metaphor)
   - Champions   Case study teachers (e.g., Harvard) leadership aficionados, especially in the United States
   - Intended messages   Fit
   - Realized messages   Think (strategy making as case study)
   - School category   Prescriptive
   - Associated homily   "Look before you leap."

2. **Planning School**
   - Sources   H. I. Ansoff
   - Base discipline   Some links to urban planning, systems theory, and cybernetics
   - Champions   Professional managers, MBAs, staff experts, consultants, and government controllers
   - Intended messages   Formalize
   - Realized messages   Program (rather than formulate)
   - School category   Prescriptive
   - Associated homily   "A stitch in time save nine."

3. Positioning School

• Sources	Purdue University work (D. Schendell and K. Hatten), then notably M. E. Porter
• Base discipline	Economics (industrial organization) and military history
• Champions	Analytical staff types, consultants, and military writers
• Intended messages	Analyze
• Realized messages	Calculate (rather than create or commit)
• School category	Prescriptive
• Associated homily	"Nothing but the facts, ma'am."

4. Entrepreneurial School

• Sources	J. A. Schumpeter, A. H. Cole, and others in economics
• Base discipline	None (although early writings came from economics)
• Champions	Popular business press, individuals, small-business people everywhere
• Intended messages	Envision
• Realized messages	Centralize (then hope)
• School category	Descriptive (some prescriptive)
• Associated homily	"Take us to your leader."

5. Cognitive School

• Sources	H. A. Simon and J. G. March
• Base discipline	Psychology (cognitive)
• Champions	Those with a psychological bent—pessimists in one wing and optimists in the other
• Intended messages	Cope or create
• Realized messages	Worry (being unable to cope in either case)
• School category	Descriptive
• Associated homily	"I'll see it when I believe it."

6. Learning School

• Sources	G. Lindboim, R. Cyert, J. March, K. Weick, J. Quinn, C. Prahalad, and G. Hamel
• Base discipline	None (perhaps links to learning theory in psychology and education; chaos theory)
• Champions	People inclined to experimentation, ambiguity, and adaptability
• Intended messages	Learn
• Realized messages	Play rather than pursue
• School category	Descriptive
• Associated homily	"If at first you don't succeed, try, try again."

(Continued)

Figure 15.1 Continued

7. **Power School**

• Sources	G. Allison (micro), J. Pfeffer and G. Salancik, and W. Astley (macro)
• Base discipline	Political science
• Champions	People who like power, politics, and conspiracy
• Intended messages	Promote
• Realized messages	Hoard (rather than share)
• School category	Descriptive
• Associated homily	"Look out for number one."

8. **Cultural School**

• Sources	E. Rhenman and R. Normann
• Base discipline	Anthropology
• Champions	People who like the social, the spiritual, and the collective
• Intended messages	Coalesce
• Realized messages	Perpetuate (rather than change)
• School category	Descriptive
• Associated homily	"An apple never falls far from the tree."

9. **Environmental School**

• Sources	M. Hannan and J. Freeman; contingency theorists
• Base discipline	Biology
• Champions	Population ecologists, some organization theorists, and positivists in general
• Intended messages	React
• Realized messages	Capitulate (rather than confront)
• School category	Descriptive
• Associated homily	"It all depends."

10. **Configuration School**

• Sources	A. Chandler, H. Minzberg, D. Miller, R. Miles, and C. Snow
• Base discipline	History
• Champions	Lumpers and integrators in general, as well as change agents
• Intended messages	Integrate, transform
• Realized messages	Lump (rather than split, adapt)
• School category	Descriptive and prescriptive
• Associated homily	"To everything there is a season."

The profiles of the strategic thinking schools depicted in Figure 15.1 help stake out the range and variation in thinking in general in this realm. They can also be used to examine one's own dominant strategic thinking model as well as to classify the strategic approaches being taken by partners and competitors. This level of strategic consciousness is an important ingredient in strategic positioning.

THE STRATEGIC ROLES OF HUMAN RESOURCE DEVELOPMENT
Contributed by Richard J. Torraco and Richard A. Swanson

HRD has served the needs of organizations to provide employees with up-to-date expertise. Here *expertise* is defined as the optimal level at which a person is able and/or expected to perform within a specialized realm of human activity (Swanson, 1996a).

Advances in HRD models and processes have kept pace with the increasingly sophisticated information and production technologies that continue to spread throughout our nation's most vital industries (Swanson & Torraco, 1994). During this period of rapid technological development, the HRD function can be relied on to support a broad range of business initiatives that require a competent workforce. Critical business issues, from new marketing strategies to innovations in production methods, are based on, among other factors, the performance capabilities of those expected to use these new work systems. As a factor integral to business success, employee competence itself has been expanded through effective programs of development. In short, the development and unleashing of workplace expertise through training has been vital to optimal business performance.

Yet, today's business environment requires that training not only *support* the business strategies of organizations but assume a pivotal role in *shaping* business strategy. Business success increasingly hinges on an organization's ability to use employee expertise as a major force in the shaping of business strategy.

As a primary means of sustaining an organization's competitive edge, HRD serves a strategic role by assuring the competence of employees to meet the organization's present performance demands. Concurrent with meeting present organizational needs, HRD also contributes to shaping strategy and enabling organizations to take full advantage of emergent business strategies. Both the strategy-supporting and strategy-shaping roles of HRD have distinctive features that are evident in business practices of successful companies. This article examines the origins and features of the strategic roles of HRD and illustrates these roles with examples from today's most innovative organizations.

HRD to Support Business Objectives

The HRD function has long been relied on to support a broad range of business objectives that require competent employees. Business objectives themselves are almost as diverse in nature as the wide range of organizations that articulate them. They can span long- or short-term time frames and can focus on broad business issues (e.g., diversification in the defense industry in the post–cold war era) or relatively narrow issues (e.g., reduction of employee turnover in company field offices). The rationale for using HRD interventions to support business objectives is quite straightforward: enhancing or unleashing needed employee expertise through HRD increases the likelihood that business objectives will be achieved (Jacobs & Jones, 1995; Swanson, 1995).

Examples abound of HRD used to support business objectives. Indeed, most HRD programs referred to as somehow having "strategic" value assume roles that are supportive of a given business strategy or set of objectives. The education and training used to support business objectives at Motorola, for example, is typical of the challenges and opportunities faced by many organizations in today's business environment. What Motorola discovered earlier than most organizations that began introducing new, sophisticated technologies into the workplace was that their employees did not have the skills to make full use of the technologies (Agrawal, 1994). Companies that compete in the fast-paced communications market where customers are particularly innovation-conscious must deliver high-quality, reliable products despite short product development cycles. Motorola sought production advantages through both the integration of new technology and the development of employee expertise. The company offers on- and off-site classroom education and training, laboratory training, and structured training in the workplace for employees at all levels of the organization. In addition to supporting Motorola's successful pursuit of its business objectives, many of their education and training initiatives serve as best-practices examples against which other organizations' training functions benchmark their performance. These examples from Motorola provide an example of the use of HRD to *support* business objectives.

Numerous additional examples of HRD serving in roles supportive to the implementation of strategy can be cited. Training and other initiatives associated with total quality management have been critical in transforming marginal manufacturing plants into successful facilities (Sullivan, 1994). HRD continues to be a primary vehicle for assuring mandated levels of employee competence and public safety in highly regulated sectors like the nuclear power industry (Paquin, 1994). Several leading corporations consider the value added through state-of-the-art employee expertise so important to their operations that they have created extensive internal systems for providing education and training, such as the Texas Instruments Learning Institute (Mancuso, 1994).

HRD, Expertise, and Strategy

The influence of HRD on strategic planning is moving from being exclusively in a role supportive of business strategy to becoming a major force in the shaping of business strategy. However, present conceptions of the strategic role of HRD, if training is even thought of in a strategic context at all, still view training in a supportive role. Strategies for product innovation or cost leadership, for example, are usually conceived and adopted by the organization, and when implementation constraints surface, only then is formal consideration given to employee expertise and the training implications of the strategy. Although the role HRD serves in support of strategy is necessary and important to operational success, HRD can offer an organization even greater strategic value.

Although not always obvious, there is a natural fit between initiatives for developing employee expertise and the organization's strategic direction. This "HRD–business strategy linkage" is the basis for HRD's influential role as shaper of strategy. Jacobs and Jones (1995) posit the argument as follows: "Organizations in the new economy have come to realize that employee expertise is a vital and dynamic living treasure. The desire for employee expertise is meaningless unless an organization can develop it in ways that respond to the business needs" (p. 178).

The Strategic Value of HRD

Two factors have influenced the evolution of HRD toward a more active role as a key determinant of business strategy: (1) the centrality of information technology to business success and (2) the sustainable competitive advantage offered by workforce expertise. These two factors work together in such a way that the competitive advantages they offer are nearly impossible to achieve without developing and maintaining a highly competent workforce.

Organizations have rushed to embrace information technology as a way to improve overall efficiency and reduce costs. Yet, it is not the information technology itself but the way it is thoroughly integrated into major business processes that represents the greatest opportunity for the successful transformation of outdated business processes (Davenport, 1993). Information technology is being applied across industries in virtually every major service and manufacturing process as a way of rapidly transmitting data to crucial process decision points, integrating component functions that were formerly isolated, and improving the overall quality and timeliness of key business processes. However, those who have successfully used information technology to improve business performance will quickly point out that these advantages will not materialize without highly competent people to both implement and utilize these innovative work systems. The human expertise must exist to use information technology to maximize performance. HRD is then in a strategic position to assure that the required expertise is available and effectively utilized.

Once competitive advantage is attained and begins to attract the attention of other key players in the marketplace, an organization's premier market position can quickly erode unless the organization finds ways to sustain its present advantage or generate new ones. Organizations in market leadership positions realize sooner or later that human resources are ultimately the only business resource with the creativity and adaptive power to sustain and renew an organization's success despite changing market conditions. The development and unleashing of employee expertise provides a potentially inexhaustible source of ideas for further innovation and increased productivity because the most basic output of highly competent employee—knowledge—is not used up in the process of producing it. Investments in employee education and training increasingly fund the development of an infrastructure to support the sustainable competitive advantage that a highly trained workforce provides. Developing employee expertise at all levels of the organization and using knowledge as a catalyst for growth and competitive advantage represent a major frontier in organizational performance that is only now beginning to be fully appreciated.

The Nature of the HRD–Business Strategy Linkage

The influential role of HRD as a shaper of strategy is premised on a clear understanding of the relationship between the development of employee expertise and the ways in which strategy emerges. This section describes both traditional and contemporary notions of strategy and examines the relationship between strategy and HRD.

A straightforward definition of *business strategy* is given by Tichy, Fombrun, and Devanna (1982): "strategy is the process by which the basic mission and objectives of the organization are set, and the process by which the organization uses its resources to achieve those objectives" (p. 47). HRD becomes a critical component in this view of strategy as the developer of key resources—the human resources—needed to achieve business objectives. Setting strategy itself may involve using a broad range of analytical and decision-making techniques that assist strategists in determining the present status and future direction of their organizations. *Strategy* has been traditionally described as a deliberate process of planning in which data are collected and analyzed using prescribed techniques (e.g., environmental scanning, competitive benchmarking, analysis of strengths, weaknesses, opportunities, and threats [SWOTs analysis], and portfolio analyses) through which informed judgments are then made about the organization's future plans and objectives.

Yet, business strategy is more than a plan of action for addressing business conditions anticipated in the future. Strategy is a dynamic phenomenon that necessarily unfolds over a period of time in a business environment that is inherently unstable. While strategies may be based on structured planning and analysis, they also emerge out of the many business opportunities and constraints that continually challenge organizations. That is, strategies may be deliberate, but they may also emerge from events. As expressed by strategy theorist Henry Mintzberg (1987), "strategy can *form* as well as be *formulated*. A realized strategy can emerge in response to an evolving situation, or it can be brought about deliberately, through a process of formulation followed by implementation" (p. 68). While we may be capable of even more clever strategies, enlightened strategists also allow strategy to develop out of the organization's action and experiences. They acknowledge that decision makers cannot possibly think through all possible events and contingencies in advance. Indeed, as longitudinal research on strategy has shown, strategy that has materialized through actual events has both *deliberate* and *emergent* components. As will be demonstrated in the sections that follow, the emergent properties of strategy allow the HRD function to exercise considerable strategic leverage in shaping the future direction of the organization. This influential role of HRD is made possible because high levels of employee expertise are inevitably required if organizations are to capitalize fully and quickly on *emergent opportunities* for business growth as strategy unfolds within a broader context of business developments.

HRD as a Shaper of Strategy

Thus far we have examined the strategic role that HRD plays in *supporting* strategies to achieve the goals of the organization. Next, a more influential role of HRD is examined—that of a major force in *shaping* emergent strategy.

The expanding influence of HRD can be seen in patterns of business development both from within organizations and from a more global perspective. Both views of the strategic role of HRD are examined in this section. First, strategic initiatives based on employee expertise are briefly illustrated in successful manufacturing and service organizations where they have become firmly established. Then, the business planning and relocation strategies of multinational corporations are examined. These strategies are increasingly based on the availability of a competent workforce and reflect changing patterns of workforce skill development at the global level.

HRD and Strategy in Organizations

Successful companies advance from a solid base of proven competence within distinctive market niches to exploit emerging business opportunities in related areas. For general direction, the guidance offered by deliberate, purposeful strategy is useful and relevant for organizations operating in familiar markets where they possess a distinctive competence. By continuously developing employee expertise in key domains of product and market expertise, competitive advantage is achieved and expanded. The nature of this strategy is closer to the deliberate than the emergent end of the strategy continuum as organizations use existing patterns of strategy to expand in areas where they already enjoy sales leadership or other measures of market success. While employee expertise is developed to maintain present advantages, HRD also serves as a key enabler of strategy for expanding growth. Examples of the strategic role of HRD from companies that rely on employee expertise to capitalize on business opportunities are described next.

L. M. Ericsson Corporation is a Swedish telecommunications equipment manufacturer that reconfigured its sprawling international operations to streamline its design and product development functions (Flynn, 1994). What to outsiders appeared as a major corporate restructuring was in fact a fundamental reconception of how work was accomplished based on expanding the breadth and depth of employee expertise across previously inviolable divisional and functional boundaries. Using recommendations offered by design and production technicians themselves, the wholesale renovation of major processes was undertaken, and a matrix system for production and information sharing emerged among the forty labs of this research-intensive organization. Based on newly acquired expertise in systems thinking, business processes, and key technical skills, employees have, since 1990, been able to design telecommunications equipment and set up manufacturing and service networks simultaneously. Once an organization that behaved like seven different companies and was slow in bringing new products to an innovation-conscious market, Ericsson is now a leader in lightweight, digital mobile phones and asynchronous switching, surpassing $10 billion in annual sales.

Home Depot has become a dominant force in the home improvement business in part by making a conscious effort to learn from every aspect of its business (McGill & Slocum, 1994). It continues to achieve a phenomenal annual growth rate within the industry by dedicating its people, policies, and practices to developing expertise and learning through every dimension of its business. Home Depot explicitly pursues objectives to ensure a long-term, competitive advantage through learning from experience and maintaining employee expertise at state-of-the-art levels. Company interactions with employees, customers, vendors, suppliers, and competitors are constantly analyzed to reap value-added lessons from a variety of business experiences, whether they involve a sales transaction, a delivery, a management meeting, or an unhappy customer or employee. On one hand, Home Depot invests in developing employees at all levels of the organization. Entry-level employees receive nearly four weeks of training and participate in periodic conferences and training sessions at the store and company-wide levels. On the other hand, Home Depot values learning from customers in any way it can. It allows building contractors to use its makeshift classrooms in each store to share their needs and expertise with employees and other customers. It has added contractor check-out areas and new products for first-time home buyers in response to suggestions from both its own employees and customers. Home Depot demonstrates a recent and compelling example of the growth that can be achieved when organizations make a conscious effort to learn and develop new expertise from every aspect of their business.

HRD and Expertise from a Global Perspective

HRD as a major force in the shaping and emergence of business strategy can also be seen from a global perspective. Levels of education and expertise among populations of geographic regions in the world vary widely when viewed from a global perspective. But the traditional view that the most educated and most *educable* people are predominantly in the Western industrialized nations is changing rapidly. In some regions, the levels of education, particularly in technical and scientific areas, and the readiness of the population to acquire even higher levels of training are at least as favorable as it is in the United States. Singapore and Malaysia, for example, have invested heavily in an infrastructure for developing targeted industry-specific expertise and have attracted export-oriented manufacturers and advance technology from abroad. China and India are rapidly developing workers capable of absorbing new technologies and direct a large proportion of their top students into elite technical institutes.

Just as we witnessed a recent shift in domestic manufacturing offshore to take advantage of lower labor costs for unskilled workers, the planning and location strategies of large corporations increasingly target countries other than the United States for business development based largely on the availability of a technically competent workforce. Rather than the offshore relocation of manufacturing based on *unskilled* labor, today's relocation patterns are increasingly based on the need for more *skilled* labor. Business strategies are increasingly predicated on the availability and sustainability of state-of-the-art expertise.

As HRD efforts and worker expertise in less developed countries rapidly improve, corporations are shifting their locations and centers of expansion away from the West to countries like Malaysia, Taiwan, and Singapore. Recent examples of relocation strategies based on the availability of highly skilled workers include Hewlett-Packard's design center for advanced "personal digital assistants" and new portable ink-jet printers in Singapore; Intel Corporation's product development and manufacturing center in Penang, Malaysia; Motorola's new semiconductor and telecom equipment plant in Taiwan, China; and Robert Bosch's (the German engine and automotive parts firm) new manufacturing operations in the Czech Republic (*Business Week* Staff, 1994).

HRD and the Shaping of Business Strategy

Instability and change continue to dominate the landscape in many of our domestic industries. Witness the volatility in health care systems, upheaval and corporate transformations in the vast defense industry, the productivity growth afforded through information technology, and continued turnover among successful and failed business ventures. On a global scale, political and economic instability underlies much of the social turbulence that confounds business development planning in many regions of the world. Yet, at the same time, social and economic change abroad creates vast opportunities for new business development for enterprising firms around the globe. As ripple effects occur throughout all of our domestic industries, few organizations remain untouched by recent economic and technological change.

Always an uncertain undertaking, devising strategy is a particularly precarious process under such volatile circumstances. Pursuing deliberate strategy, although systematic and goal oriented, is certainly less fruitful during periods of business instability. Direction from present plans can be quickly lost as the need for strategic adjustments and new business directions emerge. It is during such periods that the emergent nature of strategy offers the most promise that future business growth can evolve from quite uncertain origins.

While the emergent properties of strategy seem elusive, some organizations appear to be prepositioned to capitalize on emerging opportunities in the marketplace. By fostering cultures of innovation and flexibility, these organizations are capable of rapid adaptation to changing events and emerging business opportunities. The development of employee expertise now represents a critical strategic imperative for organizations wishing both to create new opportunities for growth and to take advantage of the opportunities that inevitably unfold in a rapidly changing business environment. Only through the explicit adoption of policies for advancing employee expertise can organizations fully capitalize on the emergent properties of strategy. As business conditions force the reshaping of strategy, competence and flexibility at all levels of the organization become more critical to business success. In the midst of emergent strategies, planners and decision makers with HRD backgrounds are in the best position to examine business opportunities, determine the key performance requirements of new business objectives, and position highly competent people within state-of-the-art work systems to achieve those objectives. The emergent properties of strategy inevitably require high levels of employee expertise to capitalize fully and quickly on opportunities for growth as they become available.

Yet, how does HRD assume such a strategic role in actively shaping the direction of the firm? HRD that is truly of strategic value to an organization has three important attributes: (1) it is rooted in needs and outcomes that are performance based; (2) it has earned credibility and respect among key stakeholders by demonstrating its *strategic capability,* and (3) its role as shaper of strategy arises as organizational leaders acknowledge the importance of strategy's emergent properties, for only emergent strategy can be actively shaped by influential forces such as HRD. Each of these strategic attributes of HRD are examined next.

ADOPTING A STRATEGIC HRD PERSPECTIVE

HRD that is truly of strategic value to an organization (1) is performance based, (2) demonstrates its strategic capability, and (3) is responsive to the emergent nature of strategy.

The first two of these are attributes of HRD itself, whereas the third element is dependent on the nature of the strategy with which HRD interacts. All three of these features taken together determine HRD's strategic value and must be attended to if it is to adopt a strategic perspective.

Strategic Role 1: Performance-Based HRD

HRD serves a broad range of interests and outcomes in organizations. The primary purposes to be served by HRD can range from programs intended to meet the personal development needs of individuals (e.g., identifying personal learning styles or family financial planning) to HRD efforts that involve everyone in the organization (e.g., programs addressing a new performance appraisal method or structural reorganization). Although HRD can potentially address many personal interests of employees and can serve a variety of organizational needs, HRD that purports to be of strategic value has stepped forward onto hallowed ground. For HRD that offers real strategic value to the organization must contribute directly to important business goals and must be based on key business performance requirements (Swanson, 1994).

Viable organizations continuously encounter new performance requirements in their efforts to adapt successfully to changing market demands. Although these performance needs may exist at the organizational, group, or individual levels, true performance needs are ultimately rooted in the core processes that constitute the distinctive competencies for which customers rely on the organization (e.g., providing premium quality, innovative products, high value-added service, etc.). HRD functions that adopt a systems perspective of the organization and its environment and that recognize the centrality of employee expertise to optimal business performance are in the best position to provide the performance-based interventions needed by organizations for continued growth and success. Performance-oriented HRD also distinguishes itself through consistently offering high-leverage interventions based on critical insights gained from performance analysis.

Performance-based HRD must be based on a clear definition of the performance problem through accurate identification of actual and desired performance requirements at the organization, process, and individual levels (Swanson, 1994). Up-front analysis that acknowledges the multiple determinants of performance provides a reliable framework that leads to improvement. None of the strategic roles of HRD discussed in this chapter can be assumed unless HRD is first based on an analysis of key performance needs and directed at meeting important business outcomes. Even HRD that simply supports the execution of a given business strategy must be, first and foremost, performance based. The future business direction that strategy hopes to clarify for the organization is based on its core strengths and competencies, and ultimately, it is the organization's *performance* in the marketplace that determines success.

Strategic Role 2: Demonstrating the Strategic Capability of HRD

Being performance based is not enough to demonstrate fully the strategic importance of HRD. HRD will only be perceived as having strategic value if it also demonstrates genuine *strategic capability*. As HRD demonstrates strategic capability, it earns respect and credibility as a full partner in forging the organization's future direction.

HRD's demonstration of strategic capability goes beyond simply being able to provide interventions that support a given strategic initiative. Strategic capability is based on a HRD philosophy that reflects the unique value of human resources to pursue long-range business goals flexibly and the conviction that people are the only organizational resource that can shape and re-create the ways in which all other business resources are used. HRD demonstrates its strategic capability as it adds two important dimensions to the organization's business-planning process: (1) HRD provides education and learning in the concepts and methods of strategic planning and systems thinking to those responsible for setting the strategic direction for the organization; and (2) the HRD function itself plays an active role in strategic planning through direct participation of HRD professionals in the business-planning process. Together these two features dramatically emphasize HRD's value to the business planning process and distinguish HRD that has strategic capability from traditional HRD functions that can only offer marginal benefits to the organization.

Education and Training in Strategic Planning
The first of these capabilities, providing education and training in business planning and systems thinking to those responsible for setting the strategic direction for the organization, is needed because many of those who participate in business planning may not possess a broad perspective on the business or may not be able to apply readily the perspectives they have to the planning issues at hand. Presumably, those who participate in strategic planning possess the business acumen and understanding needed for meaningful contributions to long-term planning. However, strategic planning requires a sophisticated array of conceptual, analytical, and interpersonal skills. Business planning involves strategic decisions that are frequently group decisions. Planners, therefore, need skills in problem definition, facilitating analysis by the group, resolving communication breakdowns, reaching consensus, and building commitment. Important analytical and visioning skills needed by business planners include performing environmental scanning, analyzing industries and competition, conducting organizational analysis (SWOTs), employing competitive benchmarking, using systems frameworks to identify inconsistencies and threats to business development, and clarifying and articulating a unified organizational mission.

Those who participate in business planning are often strong in some of these planning skills but not in others (Catalanello & Redding, 1989). And even those who seem to have a more complete picture of the business-planning scenario often fail to account fully for the *emergent* properties of strategy. The training function can take the initiative by ensuring that business planning is not a process that is entered into blindly by some who will inevitably lack a few of these important skills and perspectives.

Active Participation in Strategic Planning
The second capability that demonstrates HRD's strategic value is the active participation of HRD professionals in the business-planning process. The importance of HRD to strategic planning is reflected in the centrality of developing employee ex-

pertise to maintaining competitive advantage in today's business environment. As emphasized earlier in this chapter, even well-planned strategies cannot stand up to the uncertainties of the marketplace. However, human competence is a stable and renewable resource on which today's organizational strategies must be based if they are to remain viable. HRD professionals add a valuable dimension to the strategic planning process by ensuring that planning is based on an accurate assessment of current and achievable levels of employee expertise. In addition, HRD professionals represent unique perspectives on the workforce when answering the following questions that are central to the strategic planning process:

- Given critical success factors in the organization's market niche or industry, what domains of employee expertise are crucial to achieving key business objectives in each operational area? That is, what skills must the organization make the most of to succeed?

- What are the capabilities of the HRD function (in terms of its strengths and weaknesses) to provide state-of-the-art development of workforce skills?

- How do the organization's HRD systems, methods, and technologies stand up against the best practices in the HRD profession?

The proactive use of data in these and other areas provided by the HRD function is indispensable to effective business planning. Like those who lead other functions considered crucial to the business, HRD professionals must communicate to the organization that, in response to even the most pressing business demands, the HRD function can be relied on to deliver and support key expertise when and where it is needed by the workforce. Ultimately, this is the most visible and valuable measure of strategic capability.

HRD that is directed at business performance requirements and that demonstrates strategic capability will not need elaborate promotional measures to be widely recognized as offering strategic value to the organization. But HRD cannot consistently represent these attributes without a close partnership with planners and the planning process itself. That is, in addition to being performance-based and demonstrating strategic capability, strategic HRD is also dependent on the nature of the strategy with which HRD interacts. Treating strategy as an *emergent* process is an important prerequisite for HRD that consistently offers strategic value. This determinant of HRD's strategic role is considered next.

Strategic Role 3: Emergent Strategy and HRD

At present, HRD serves a role that is predominantly supportive to strategy. HRD that primarily serves to support the execution of a given strategy fills an adjunctive role to strategy that is clearly more deliberate than emergent. Unfortunately, a majority of today's HRD that purports to be of strategic value may provide the workforce with important expertise, but it does so after the formulation and adoption of strategy. *HRD cannot add value to the shaping of strategy if the strategy is already fully formulated.*

While HRD can improve operational performance by providing skills in areas such as process improvement and customer sensitivity, HRD is inhibited from making truly formative contributions to strategic innovation and performance if deliberate strategic plans are handed down from a small group of management elite to the rest of the organization in prepackaged form. HRD and other functions critical to organizational performance cannot actively shape strategy if strategy is already structured and positioned in the organization as a given.

The benefits of developing and using employee expertise to capitalize on evolving business opportunities can only be fully realized if strategy is treated as both a deliberate and emergent phenomenon. The potential for HRD's strategic leverage must exist by treating strategic planning as an emergent process. Further prescriptions for advancing the strategic contributions of HRD are of little value if strategy is fully formulated and adopted without the performance perspectives that HRD offers.

Examples of Active Participation

The following examples are of deliberative strategic planning involving HRD. The first example is from a medical high-technology corporation that produces artificial body organs. The firm's core expertise has been a creative integration of multidisciplinary theory and practice in a technological context.

The general strategic business goal is to keep the company on the cutting edge of an intense and competitive industry through an expert workforce. HRD, as a part of the top management team, works to determine the workforce expertise required by the firm to invent and produce products that do *not* yet exist and that most likely require expertise in theoretical and technical areas that are often viewed separately.

The HRD strategic contribution is in (1) systematically guiding the process of visioning the technological future through the eyes of the technological and business leaders of the firm and (2) determining the workforce knowledge and expertise required to perform in those "future states." The outputs of this ongoing strategic analysis process serve as primary input to the overall strategic business planning process, thus influencing the business direction of the firm and the plans to meets the corresponding workforce expertise and development requirements.

The second example of *deliberative* strategic planning involving HRD is a large health care insurance provider organization. The traditional core expertise of the insurance firm had been defined by a conservative culture. Furthermore, the culture was built on power relationships among an uneasy mix of underwriting and sales personnel. The changing conditions of regulations, increased costs, competition, and new technology have shaken the organization to the core. The old power relationship model was filled with ineffective methods of achieving goals in the new business environment.

HRD, revitalized through an infusion of new leadership and a new perform-ance consulting model (Robinson & Robinson, 1995), took on the role of im-proving performance rather than simply providing training events. In this new role, the analysis of performance gaps within and between the individual, process, and organization levels yields broad base participation in performance diagnosis, systemic understanding, and strategic goal setting that shape the firm.

HRD regularly engages top management as diagnosis partners and provides critical core information to the top management team about performance dis-connects that exist in present strategies and developing strategies. For example, it is common that systemic performance issues that are initially viewed as job-level concerns may turn into process-level mapping at the job level. From that level of analysis major business process redesign and redefinition of performance goals often emerge as the strategic mandate.

These two illustrations highlight the potential of HRD as a partial determi-nant of the organization's strategic and operational direction. Each example clearly demonstrates that expertise at the three levels of performance—individual, process, and organization—can be aligned for the purpose of shaping strategy.

SCENARIO BUILDING PLUS STRATEGIC PLANNING

Parallel to the concept of traditional strategic planning is the idea of scenario build-ing. Schwartz (1996) defines a scenario as "a tool for ordering one's perceptions about the future environments in which decisions might be played out" (p. 4). This tool is most often in the form of a story or plot line that allows the organization members to explore fully a rich story of possible future events. These scenarios are stories describing the current and future states of the business environment, and they become stories about alternative possible futures (van der Heijden, 1996).

"Scenarios deal with two worlds: the world of facts and the world of percep-tions. They explore for facts but they aim at perceptions inside the heads of deci-sion-makers. Their purpose is to gather and transform information of strategic significance into fresh perceptions" (Wack, 1985b, p. 140). Used in this way, scenario planning presents "an efficient approach to strategic business planning, focusing on business ideas in an uncertain world" (van der Heijden, 1996, p. 2). The problem is one of not knowing the fit between strategic planning and scenario building along with the role of HRD in shaping and supporting strategic organizational planning.

Miller, Lynham, Provo, and St. Claire (1997) have provided a useful overview of scenario building for the HRD profession. The following summary mirrors their analysis of the scenario-building component of strategic organizational planning along with the traditional strategic planning component.

As more organizations face continuous change as the order of the day, organi-zational professionals have developed expertise and tools to operate successfully in such an environment. The traditional tools of strategic planning, which are commonly extrapolations of the past to determine the future, are not effective when future forces do not mirror past forces . In an environment of constant change and challenge, nontraditional tools for anticipating and planning for change are needed. One such tool is scenario building.

A scenario is "a tool for ordering one's perceptions about alternative future environments in which decisions might be played out" (Schwartz, 1996, p. 4). The process of scenario planning generally involves development of several plots and supporting narratives that illustrate primary forces driving change within a system, their interrelationships, and uncertainties in the environment (Wack, 1985b). Scenarios help decision makers structure and think about uncertainty, test their assumptions about how critical driving forces will interact, and reorganize their mental model of reality .

Scenario development is described as an art rather than a science (Schwartz, 1996). By providing safe and often engaging opportunities to explore the implications of uncertainty and to think through ways of responding to it, scenarios enable planners to deal more confidently in the midst of uncertainty (Schwartz, 1996; van der Heijden, 1996).

Van der Heijden (1996) characterizes the individual and organizational learning process of scenario building like so: By organizing complex information on future trends and possibilities into a series of plausible stories, scenarios are seen as interpretive tools that create meaning and thereby guide action. The use of multiple plausible futures helps decision makers think more expansively about change and to adopt multiple perspectives for the purpose of understanding future events. In the end, scenarios offer entrepreneurial and protective benefits to organizations (Wack, 1985b). The Centre for Innovative Leadership (van der Merwe, 1997) describes the scenario development process as follows:

1. Identification of a strategic organizational agenda (including assumptions and concerns about current strategic thinking and vision)

2. Challenging of existing assumptions of organizational decision makers by questioning current mental models about the external environment

3. Systematically examining the organization's external environment to improve understanding of the structure of the key forces driving change

4. Synthesis of information about possible future events into three or four alternative plots or story lines about possible futures

5. Development of narratives around the story lines to make the stories relevant and compelling to decision makers

6. Use of the stories to help decision-makers "review" their strategic thinking

Traditional *strategic planning* refers to the business planning and systems thinking required of those responsible for setting the strategic direction for the organization (Mintzberg, 1994). Presumably, those who participate in strategic planning possess the business acumen and understanding needed for meaningful contributions to long-term planning. However, strategic planning by itself requires a sophisticated array of conceptual, analytical, and interpersonal skills. Business planning involves strategic decisions that are frequently group decisions. Planners, therefore, need skills in problem definition, facilitating analysis by the group, resolving communication breakdowns, reaching consensus, and building commitment. Skills associated with strategic planning include environmental scanning, analyses of industries and competition, organizational analysis (e.g., SWOTs), competitive benchmarking, using systems frameworks to identify inconsistencies and threats to business development, and clarifying and articulating a unified organizational mission.

Together, *scenario building* and *strategic planning* are proposed as a holistic view of strategic organizational planning (SOP). Figure 15.2 illustrates the SOP components and their relationships. The SOP "double funnel" graphically contrasts the roles and relationships between scenario building and strategic planning in the SOP process. Scenario building flares out the thinking in its expansiveness, and strategic planning reins in the thinking into an action plan. All the while, both SOP phases are operating in the complex environment, and SOP is viewed as a continuing process. HRD engages in supporting and shaping the entire process.

Contributions of HRD to Strategic Organizational Planning

What, then, are the potential contributions of HRD to SOP? To explore this question, a matrix of the three HRD strategic roles in context of the two SOP components, scenario building and strategic planning, is proposed in Figure 15.3. It is important to highlight the definitions of scenario building as an expansive process and strategic planning as a reductionist process as being crucial to the exploration of the interpretation of HRD contributions to SOP.

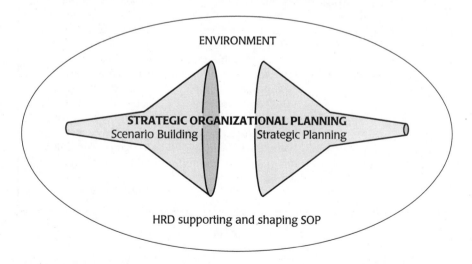

Figure 15.2 Strategic Organizational Planning (SOP) (*Source:* Swanson, Lynham, Ruona, & Provo, 1998, p. 591. Used with permission.

Figure 15.3 Human Resource Development's Contribution in Supporting and Shaping Strategic Organizational Planning

	Strategic Organizational Planning	
HRD STRATEGIC ROLES		
	SCENARIO BUILDING *Defined:* SB is a process for ordering perceptions about the future environments in which decisions might be played out (Schwartz, 1996, p. 4).	STRATEGIC PLANNING *Defined:* SP is a process for developing a comprehensive statement of the organization's mission, objectives, and strategy
PERFORMANCE BASED *Defined:* HRD must contribute directly to important business goals and must be based on key business performance requirements (Torraco & Swanson, 1995, p. 17).	*Contribution:* • HRD provides critical judgements as to the organization's probability of being able to develop and/or unleash the human expertise required of the various scenarios being proposed and what each would require.	*Contribution:* • HRD provides a road map for developing and/or unleashing the human expertise required to achieve the strategic plan and commitment to execute related SP action plans.
STRATEGIC CAPABILITY *Defined:* To demonstrate genuine strategic capability, HRD (1) provides SOP education and learning, and (2) actively participates in the SOP process (Torraco & Swanson, 1995).	*Contribution:* • HRD oversees the SB education and learning required of personnel for building "shared, integrated mental models of multiple plausible futures" (Lynham, Provo, & Ruona, 1998, p. 6). • HRD experts serve as contributors of key human resource information and value all information being considered during the SB process.	*Contribution:* • HRD oversees the SP education and learning required of personnel for planning strategy, including the analysis and synthesis of internal and external conditions. • HRD experts participate on the SP team and act as a catalyst to create new business based on the strategic development and/or unleashing of human expertise (see Mintzberg, 1994).

	Strategic Organizational Planning	
HRD STRATEGIC ROLES		
EMERGENT STRATEGY *Defined:* HRD assumes a deliberate role in the emergent nature of SOP (Torraco & Swanson, 1995).	*Contribution:* • HRD creates and maintains "an institutional learning and memory system . . . and helps an organization avoid repeating mistakes" (van der Heijden, 1996, p. 2) within the realm of core expertise and new learning requirements. • HRD assumes itself critical to the ongoing strategic SB conversations of the organization. SB makes "discussing strategy a natural part of any [HRD] management task and not the exclusive domain of specialist" (van der Heijden, 1996, p. 22).	*Contribution:* • HRD creates and maintains a system for ongoing learning (in the forms of internalization, comprehension, and synthesis) from its own SP effort. • HRD assumes itself critical in the catalytic information sharing, strategic partnering, and strategy finding SP challenge facing its host organization. (see Mintzberg, 1994).

Source: Swanson, Lynham, Ruona, & Provo (1998, p. 592. Used with permission.)

The Strategic Agenda Facing HRD

The following research agenda is based on the contribution cells of the supporting and shaping of strategic organization planning matrix (Figure 15.3). The three strategic roles of HRD are used as the major organizers of the proposed action agenda.

Performance Based

1. From a *strategic planning* perspective, the profession needs to learn more as to why HRD is not able to consistently provide a road map for developing and/or unleashing the human expertise required of an organization to achieve its strategic plan and is not able to consistently fulfill its commitment to execute its related strategic planning action plans.

2. From a *scenario-building* perspective, the HRD profession needs to cull valid tools for making critical judgments as to an organization's probability of being able to develop and/or unleash the human expertise required of the various scenarios.

Strategic Capability

3. From a *strategic planning* perspective, the HRD profession needs to develop and validate a core strategy for overseeing the strategic planning education and learning required of personnel for planning strategy (including the analysis and synthesis of internal and external conditions).

4. From a *strategic planning* perspective, the HRD profession needs to develop and validate a process (grounded in performance-based strategic contributions) for legitimizing their role as experts on the strategic planning team in creating new business based on the strategic development and/or unleashing of human expertise.

5. From a *scenario-building* perspective, the HRD profession needs to develop and validate a core strategy for overseeing the scenario-building education and learning required of personnel for building shared, integrated mental models of multiple plausible futures.

6. From a *scenario-building* perspective, the HRD profession needs to develop and validate a process (grounded in performance-based strategic contributions) for legitimizing their role as experts on the SB team in contributing key human resource information and valuing all information being considered during scenario building.

Emergent Strategy

7. From a *strategic planning* perspective, the HRD profession needs to develop and validate a system for creating and maintaining ongoing learning and systems thinking (in the forms of internalization, comprehension, and synthesis) from its own strategic planning effort.

8. From a *strategic planning* perspective, the HRD profession needs to develop and validate a strategic planning process of information-sharing, strategic partnering, and strategy finding critical to its host organization.

9. From a *scenario-building* perspective, the HRD profession needs to develop and validate an institutional learning and memory system that helps an organization avoid repeating mistakes within the realm of core expertise and new learning requirements.

10. From a *scenario-building* perspective, the HRD profession needs to develop and validate a process of engaging in ongoing strategic conversations of the organization from the HRD perspective.

CONCLUSION

This chapter has examined the strategic roles assumed by HRD functions that offer a key contribution to their organizations—the development of employee expertise that is vital to optimal business performance. HRD has been traditionally served in roles that are supportive of the strategies chosen to guide organizations. Although the supporting role of HRD is important for operational success in assuring the employee competence to meet present performance demands, HRD offers even greater strategic value as a major force in the shaping of business strategy. This strategic role will most likely be achieved through a purposeful connection of sound theory and practice.

REFLECTION QUESTIONS

1. How is strategic planning different from planning?
2. Select the strategic thinking school you believe to be the best for HRD and explain why.
3. What are the three strategic roles of HRD? Describe each and give an example of each.
4. Illustrate *strategic* from *nonstrategic* personnel training and development practices.
5. Illustrate *strategic* from *nonstrategic* organization development practices.
6. Describe a major strategy for advancing the human resource development profession.

Accountability in HRD

CHAPTER OUTLINE

Perhaps one of the toughest issues in HRD today is how HRD and its organizational sponsors can structure an effective accountability system. Such a system must meet sponsors' need to know that HRD resources are being deployed effectively and HRD's need to have measures that indicate whether desired results are being achieved efficiently. Organizations are increasingly demanding that HRD develop effectiveness and efficiency measures as a result of the increasing importance of HRD interventions for organizational effectiveness.

A chapter such as this would usually be titled "Evaluation in HRD," but we wanted to take a fresh approach. The core issue is accountability, not evaluation. Traditionally, HRD professionals have relied on variations of program evaluation models derived from educational evaluation approaches. As will be discussed, this approach has largely failed because it has not been widely adopted despite forty years of promotion.

Development defies measurement in many ways. Unlike staffing or other HR activities, development is a virtual kaleidoscope of activities, only a portion of which is under the control of the organization. Development ranges from the informal and nearly impossible to measure (e.g., when one employee teaches another how to do something) to the formal and easily measured (e.g., employees attending formal training). It would be easy to throw up our hands and say, "It can't be done." But organizations demand accountability, so it is necessary to think creatively to produce approaches that advance accountability for development, even if they are still imperfect.

In this chapter we review the two primary approaches to accountability, the program evaluation approach and the HRD metrics approach. We conclude with our insights about the future of accountability.

THE PROGRAM EVALUATION APPROACH TO ACCOUNTABILITY

Evaluation in HRD is a subset of the broader field of evaluation literature with a greater emphasis on summative measures than formative measures. The focus of most evaluations in business and industry is on measuring a program's effect on (1) the participants, (2) the participant's work, and (3) the organization (Brinkerhoff, 1991; Broad & Newstrom, 1992; Dixon, 1990; Kirkpatrick, 1998; Phillips, 1997a; Swanson & Holton, 1999).

The Kirkpatrick Model

The Kirkpatrick model (1998) model of training evaluation has dominated training evaluation discussion since it was first published more than forty years ago (Kirkpatrick, 1959a, 1959b, 1960a, 1960b). It suggests that training should be evaluated at four "levels": 1—participant reactions, 2—learning, 3—on-the-job behaviors, and 4—results from behavior change. The American Society for Training and Development (ASTD) has embraced this framework in its learning outcomes report (Bassi & Ahlstrand, 2000). As part of its benchmarking service, participants provided data on standardized measures of level 1 and level 3 outcomes.

Despite its popularity, "it's probably fair to say that the bulk of all employee training programs conducted in the United States are evaluated only at level 1 [reaction], if at all. Of the rest, the majority measured only at level 2 [learning]" (Gordon, 1991, p. 21). Very little comprehensive training evaluation is accomplished across American industry (Dixon, 1987; Phillips, 1997a; Robinson & Robinson, 1989). Dixon (1987) observes that when evaluation is done, the participant reaction form is the most frequently used vehicle. This observation has been confirmed for management training as well (Saari, Johnson, McLaughlin, & Zimmerle, 1988).

Criticisms of the Kirkpatrick Model

Despite its popularity with practitioners, in recent years the four-level taxonomy has come under increasingly intense criticism (Alliger, Tannenbaum, Bennett, Trave, & Shotland, 1997; Alliger & Janak, 1989; Holton, 1996b; Swanson & Holton, 1999). The chief criticisms are as follows:

- *Not supported by research*—Research has consistently shown that the levels within the taxonomy are not related, or only correlated at a low level.

- *Emphasis on reaction measures*—Research has shown that reaction measures have nearly a zero correlation with learning or performance outcome measures.

- *Failure to update the model*—The model has remained the same for the last forty years with little effort to update or revise it.

- *Not used*—As will be discussed in the next section, the model is not widely used. Despite decades of urging people to use it, most do not find it a useful approach.

- *Can lead to incorrect decisions*—The model leaves out so many important variables that four-level data alone are insufficient to make correct and informed decisions about training program effectiveness.

To What Extent Is Program Evaluation Conducted in Practice?

One stream of research in training evaluation has been to document the extent to which methods are used in practice. This research is important because it shows to what extent prescriptive models and methods are actually utilized in practice, which in turn should inform development of new models and methods. Despite efforts to build new evaluation models, most surveys of evaluation practices use the Kirkpatrick framework as the frame for survey questions because it is the most widely recognized.

Surveys have reported use in one of two ways. One approach has been to report the *percentage of organizations* that are conducting evaluations at each level. It is important to realize that this approach says nothing about the extent to which they are using it, but just that they are using a certain evaluation level in some number of their courses greater than zero. Thus, the actual use level could be quite low (e.g., one course), but an organization would be reported as using that level. The alternative approach is to report the *percentage of programs* an organization is evaluating at each level. This approach captures the intensity of use but does not conveniently show how widespread use is across organizations.

The most current and valid information on evaluation practices comes from two sources: the *Training* magazine annual training practices survey and the

ASTD. Both organizations have only recently begun tracking evaluation use. *Training* magazine now includes evaluation practices as part of its annual training *Industry Report* that surveys United States organizations with one hundred or more employees. The ASTD primarily uses its Benchmarking Service to collect data. Its sample had slightly more small firms (i.e., fewer than five hundred employees, 39 percent of sample vs. 24 percent for *Training* magazine). In addition, over a third of the ASTD sample is from outside the United States. It has also reported data from its Benchmarking Forum, a more select group of companies, and its "Leading Edge" subset of the Benchmarking Service.

Historical data are more difficult to locate. One twelve-year-old benchmark is found in Robinson and Robinson (1989). They report data from the 1987 Training Director's Forum that was attended by 150 people, most of whom were training managers and directors. While less scientific, it does provide a measure of practice in the late 1980s, so it is useful. Another historical benchmark comes from a survey conducted more than thirty years ago (Catalanello & Kirkpatrick, 1968) that reports results of a survey sent to 154 firms who had used Kirkpatrick's Supervisory Inventory on Human Relations to evaluate training. Respondents ($n = 110$) reported that 77 percent used level 1, 51 percent used level 2, 54 percent used level 3, and 45 percent had attempted level 4.

Data for technical training evaluation are almost nonexistent. Twitchell, Holton, and Trott (2000) conducted the only known broad study of technical trainers' evaluation practices. Another benchmark comes from Hill's (1999) study of health care trainers using the same instrument as Twitchell et al. Much of the training that occurs in the health care industry might be regarded as technical because of the measurable objective outcomes.

Finally, Moller and Mallin (1996) surveyed a random sample of three hundred International Society for Performance Improvement (ISPI) and one hundred American Communication Technology Society (ACTS) members who identified themselves as instructional designers. This study is of particular interest because presumably the participants would be most aware of the importance of evaluation and perhaps most skilled at conducting them. However, 40 percent indicated that evaluation was not part of their job description. Respondents were asked to indicate whether they "routinely" use each level of evaluation.

A comparison of all the known benchmarks of evaluation use is shown in Figure 16.1. All surveys show a declining degree of use from level 1 through level 4. The top half of Figure 16.1 shows surveys dating from 1987 to present. For level 1, the findings are tightly clustered from 72 to 83 percent. For level 2, all but the ASTD Benchmarking Service data were between 40 and 53 percent.

Level 3 indicates more variability. Three studies are between 25 and 31 percent (Hill, 1999; Robinson & Robinson, 1989; Twitchell et al., 2000). The two ASTD benchmarks were substantially lower (11–12 percent), while the 1996 *Training* magazine study was substantially higher (51 percent). For level 4, the

Figure 16.1   Percentage of Programs and Organizations Using Each Level of Evaluation

Where reported	Level 1 (%)	Level 2 (%)	Level 3 (%)	Level 4 (%)
PERCENTAGE OF *PROGRAMS* USING EACH LEVEL (AVERAGE PERCENTAGE USING)				
Technical trainers (Twitchell et al., 2000)	73	47	31	21
Training magazine (1996)	83	51	51	44
ASTD Benchmarking Service (1999)	72	32	12	7
ASTD "Leading Edge" (1999)	81	40	11	6
Health care trainers (Hill, 1999)	81	53	31	17
Training Directors Forum—1987 (est.) (Robinson & Robinson, 1989)	72	46	25	14
PERCENTAGE OF *ORGANIZATIONS* (ANY PERCENTAGE OF PROGRAMS > 0)				
Technical trainers (Twitchell et al., 2000)	92	84	65	53
ASTD Benchmarking Forum (1995) (in Bassi, Gallagher, & Schroer, 1996)	100	90	83	40
Training magazine (1996)	86	71	65	49
Instructional designers (Moller & Mallin, 1996)[1]	90	71	43	21
Training Directors Forum—1987 (Robinson & Robinson, 1989)	97	90	69	41
Catalanello & Kirkpatrick (1968)	77	51	54	45

[1]Question asked if they "routinely" used a level.

two ASTD benchmarks were the lowest (6 and 7 percent), two other studies were in the teens (14 and 17 percent), and one study found 21 percent. The odd number is the 44 percent finding from *Training* magazine. Because it is totally inconsistent with all other data, one has to question the validity of this finding.

The bottom portion of Figure 16.1 compares five more recent studies and one older study reporting the percentage of organizations using each level. Looking first at the three more recent studies, the findings are remarkably similar with only a few small differences. The highest use at levels 1, 2, and 3 was reported by ASTD Benchmarking Forum organizations, which is understandable because they are a rather select group of organizations with a special interest in best practices. Even including that study, levels 1 and 2 were all reported to be used by a large majority of organizations.

Level 3 was used by 83 percent of Benchmarking Forum members, more than three of the other more recent studies that found essentially the same percentage (65–69 percent) of organizations using level 3. Instructional designers (Moller & Mallin, 1996) report the lowest use of level 3 with only 43 percent, which could be partially explained by the fact the question asked if they "routinely" used each level. At level 4, Twitchell et al. found 53 percent of organizations, which is similar to the *Training* magazine survey (49 percent) but somewhat above the other two benchmarks (which found about 40 percent of organizations using it) and well above the study of instructional designers (which reported only 21 percent). Taken together, though, the same picture emerges: organizations do not appear to be using evaluation practices much differently for technical training than other training.

The other benchmark study is the only older survey, done by Catalanello and Kirkpatrick in 1968, that examined evaluation practices of supervisory training. Results from this study are somewhat higher for levels 1 (92 vs. 78 percent) and 2 (81 vs. 50 percent), but only slightly higher at levels 3 (65 vs. 54 percent) and 4 (53 vs. 45 percent). Thus, it would appear that evaluation practices today are not much more widespread than thirty years ago, except at level 2.

The ASTD Learning Outcomes report results reflect the scope of the problem. The data reported for level 1 outcomes are very rich, representing 375,704 learners and 7,917 courses. However, for level 3 outcomes, data were submitted for only 3.8 percent (14,386) of the original learners, representing 21.4 percent (1,695) of the original courses. Furthermore, 2,118 organizations provided descriptive data on their training programs, but only 12.4 percent of those organizations provided any outcomes data.

The overall conclusions from these surveys are (1) many organizations use levels 1 and 2 evaluation for at least some programs, (2) fewer than half the organizations even try level 4, and (3) only a small percentage of programs receive level 3 and 4 evaluation. Overall, these findings present a very disappointing view of evaluation practices.

Furthermore, when following the literature back to the development of the four levels forty years ago, there seems to have been little change in the amount of evaluation conducted within business and industry. As early as 1953 (Wallace & Twitchell, 1953), researchers were discussing the need for and lack of training evaluation. Today's literature contains parallel comments, and the lack of training evaluation still exists. While caution must be exercised in drawing conclusions about trends based on limited historical data, the trend they suggest is quite striking: only modest gains have been made in the number of organizations using these evaluation practices. More specifically, it would appear that modest gains were made in levels 1 and 2 from 1968 to 1989 but little gain in the last twelve years. Even more troubling is that very little gain has occurred at levels 3 and 4, which are the most important levels for demonstrating training's effect on organizational performance.

The main reason that training is not evaluated is usually the same for *all* levels: it is not required by the organization. The usual interpretation of this is that it continues to raise serious questions about whether training is valued by organizations as a core business process. An alternative interpretation is that level 3 and 4 evaluation does not provide organizations with information they consider valuable. Yet another possibility is that organizations simply are not aware that evaluation of performance improvement from training is even possible.

The second most important reason for not doing levels 3 and 4 is usually lack of time, with lack of training close behind. Evaluation continues to be seen as something harder to do than it should be. Perhaps it is time to ask whether our models and methods simply have not been sufficiently clear to assist the average practitioner. What is unknown is the causal sequence: Do organizations not require evaluation because trainers do not know how to do it efficiently, or do trainers not learn how to do it because organizations do not require it?

New Approaches to Program Evaluation

It would be easy at this point to lament the lack of training evaluation yet again encourage practitioners to make use of evaluation methodologies. Instead, it may be time to ask new questions about the use of training evaluation. Popular press and business leaders all discuss the need to increase the rate of growth in productivity in the face of ever-increasing competition. Furthermore, increasing research evidence indicates that human resource practices contribute significantly to organizational outcomes (Huselid, 1995; Lau & May, 1998; Wellbourne & Andrews, 1996). The training literature presents evaluation as a necessary component in providing training that can help organizations increase these outcomes. There are numerous case studies of effective evaluation (e.g., Hartz, Niemiec, & Walberg, 1993; Sleezer, Cipicchio, & Pitonyak, 1992; Smith, 1993). Even estimating financial return, which is often presumed to be the hardest part of evaluation, has been widely demonstrated to be very feasible (e.g., Kaufman et al., 1997; Lyau & Pucel, 1995; Swanson, 1998a; Swanson & Sleezer, 1989).

Yet, all the literature on how much evaluation is used by business and industry suggests that only about half of the training programs are evaluated for objective performance outcomes. Additionally, less than one-third of training programs are evaluated in any way that measure changes in organizational goals or profitability. After at least forty years of bemoaning the lack of evaluation, promoting the value of evaluation, developing methods of evaluation, and pushing the evaluation cause, only modest changes seem to have been made in the amount, types, or quality of evaluation in business and industry. Even instructional designers, who arguably should be among the most sophisticated training practitioners with regard to evaluation, do not use evaluation to any greater extent than anyone else.

A variety of HRD researchers have offered elaborations, updates, and variations in an attempt to improve the taxonomy. For example, Phillips (1997a, 1997b) and Swanson (2001) have stressed the addition of return on investment to the analysis. Kaufman and Keller (1994) propose the addition of societal impact as a fifth level. Lewis (1996) has offered an expanded model that captures context, process, and outcome factors. Brinkerhoff (1991) offers a six-level system to blend formative and summative evaluation. Others have observed that some organizations are suggesting that completely new approaches are needed (Abernathy, 1999). Preskill and Torres (1999) offer evaluative inquiry as a different approach that emphasizes evaluation as a learning process.

Swanson and Holton (1999) created the Results Assessment System (www.ResultsAssessment.com) in an effort to provide practitioners a systematic and theoretically sound process for assessing learning, performance, and perceptions. They suggest abandoning the use of the term *evaluation* because it is essentially unknown outside educational arenas. They adopt *results assessment* instead as a term more descriptive of the business process they propose for making outcome assessment an integral part of organizational HRD. Their system suggests three domains with two options in each domain for results assessment:

Performance Results

- System—the units of mission-related outputs in the form of goods and services having value to the customer and that are related to core organizational outputs, work processes, and group or individual contributors in the organization
- Financial—the conversion of the output units of goods and/or services attributable to the intervention into money and financial interpretation

Learning Results

- Expertise—human behaviors having effective results and optimal efficiency, acquired through study and experience within a specialized domain
- Knowledge—mental achievement acquired through study and experience

Perception Results

- Stakeholders—perceptions of leaders of systems and/or people with a vested interest in the desired results and the means of achieving them
- Participants—perceptions of people with firsthand experience with systems, processes, goods, and/or services

In addition to these domains, the system includes three other components: a process for results assessment, a plan for designing results assessment, and tools for measuring outcomes. The process begins with front-end analysis and includes the following five steps:

1. Specify expected results.
2. Plan assessment of results.
3. Develop measures of results.
4. Collect and analyze results data.
5. Interpret and report results assessment.

The outcome of the process is organizational decisions about HRD effectiveness. This is quite different than research outcomes because the emphasis is on organizational decisions. It turns out that decision making leads to different data collection strategies and makes the results assessment process much more manageable. However, it also requires more complete consideration of system variables that affect outcomes.

Summary

The persistent low levels of training evaluation, particularly at the more sophisticated levels 3 and 4, raises serious questions about the state of training evaluation research as well as whether currently used models will enable trainers to achieve higher levels of program evaluation. Simply, if forty years of promoting its use has not changed the overall picture, something else must be needed. Clearly the Kirkpatrick model of training evaluation has *not* been effective in making evaluation an integral part of HRD practice. It does not matter if you examine practitioners more highly trained in evaluation (instructional designers), those that have more well-defined outcomes (technical trainers, health care), those in more sophisticated organizations (ASTD benchmarking group) or simply average training practitioners; the level of evaluation use is about the same and is not changing much.

In training evaluation, the prescriptive frameworks have generally failed to be confirmed by practice. The usual interpretation has been that practitioners aren't doing what they should. An alternate interpretation may be that the models and methods are not correct. The endorsement of participant reactions in the Kirkpatrick model is particularly troubling given research that clearly shows they are not related to meaningful outcomes.

Because most descriptive training evaluation research has used the Kirkpatrick four-level framework as a lens through which to assess evaluation of training, it all suffers from what may be the same "fatal flaw." The Kirkpatrick framework was not one derived from studies of evaluation practices. It was originally offered as a prescriptive evaluation framework. Thus, it is important to recognize it represents a *trainer's* notion of what constitutes effective evaluation, not a business manager's.

In the face of business and industry's apparent resistance to formal evaluation, those in the training field must ask, "Is it truly possible that business and industry spend billions of dollars without verifying the value of what they purchase?" This is highly unlikely. Thus, it may be time to more deliberately revisit the question "How are business and industry placing value on training?" instead of lamenting that they do not evaluate training by the accepted methods reported in the literature. A more intensive examination of organizational decision-making processes about human resource development may reveal fundamentally different notions of what evaluation means from a business perspective.

Additionally, it is worth asking why evaluations are not more recognized as a management tool. Recent research in the use of utility analysis reinforces the need to reexamine this question. Utility analysis is a sophisticated technique to determine the dollar value (i.e., utility) of interventions that affect human performance (Cascio, 1999). In two experimental studies, managers were shown data on a new human resource practice (Latham & Wythe, 1994; Wythe & Latham, 1997). Some managers were taught how to interpret the utility analysis, which provided the best cost–benefit data. Control group managers were given other data that were less complete. Based on rational economic theory, it was expected that managers would seek and use the best cost–benefit data available to make the decision. In both studies, exactly the opposite occurred! After learning about utility analysis, fewer managers preferred to use that data. For some reason, managers moved away from the more sophisticated tools once they learned about them. Statistical techniques such as statistical process control have also struggled to gain widespread utilization, perhaps because they are not strategic in their application (Hoerl, 1995).

This research raises puzzling questions and offers few answers. However, one cannot help but wonder whether something similar could be happening with training evaluation. Researchers interested in evaluation practices have typically started with some framework or lens that is presumed to be "correct" practice and then investigated the extent to which that framework is being used in practice. In training evaluation, the prescriptive frameworks have generally failed to be confirmed by practice. The usual interpretation has been that practitioners are not doing what they should. An alternate interpretation may be that the models and methods are not correct.

It would seem pointless to simply spend another ten to twenty years pushing practitioners to use a taxonomy and methods that they continue to resist after forty years of effort. New research is needed that takes a more exploratory look at the decision and influence processes that managers use to make decisions about training. Such research should *not* start with a prescriptive framework but rather study actual decision processes in action. In addition, HRD researchers must take responsibility to examine existing models more critically. It may well be that fundamentally new models and methods would lead to more widespread acceptance of training evaluation. Such research might ask questions such as these:

- How are decisions made about
  whether training should be initiated?
  whether training was effective?
  whether training changed performance?
  whether to continue using a form of training?
  whether to adopt a different method?
  whether to spend money on training?
- How are best practices determined?
- Who are the opinion leaders that most influence training decisions?
- What are the actual decision steps used?
- What factors or events lead to changes in training practices?

THE METRICS APPROACH TO ACCOUNTABILITY
Contributed by Elwood F. Holton III and Sharon S. Naquin

An alternate approach to accountability is called the *metrics approach*. Metrics have become more popular in recent years thanks to the popularity of Kaplan and Norton's (1996) balanced scorecard approach to accountability. The balanced scorecard suggests that no one measure or metric is sufficient. Instead, a set of key measures is advocated that together provide a more complete picture of performance. Think of driving a car and looking at multiple gauges: any one alone would be inadequate, but together they enable you to drive safely.

Metrics are typically high-level measures that provide an indicator of success. If program-level evaluation is a micro approach, then the metrics approach is a macro approach. For many organizations, metrics is an easier approach and one more likely to be used. Metrics can also be used to establish benchmarks across organizations for comparison purposes because they are standardized measures.

Program-level results assessment is very useful for diagnosis of programs. It has clearly shown that development works (Swanson, 1998a), but it is more difficult to implement organization-wide. A comprehensive approach would include both program-level results assessment and organization unit-level metrics.

In this section, four approaches to metrics are examined: the ASTD, financial, intellectual capital, and human resource approaches (Holton & Naquin, 2001).

The ASTD Approach

Each year the American Society of Training and Development prepares a state of the industry report (ASTD, 2000) that provides a comprehensive overview of employer-provided training in the United States. This report provides organizations with important benchmarking information for training, learning, and performance improvement processes, practices, and services. In short, it is a snapshot of investments and expenditures made in training across organizations. Figure 16.2

Figure 16.2 ASTD Training Metrics

Total training expenditures per training eligible employee
Total training expenditures as percentage of payroll
Percentage of training eligible employees trained
Training eligible employees to trainer ratio
Percentage of training time via classroom
Percentage of training time via learning technologies
Payment to outside companies as percentage of expenditures
Total training hours per training eligible employee
Total training expenditures
Wages and salaries of full- and part-time training staff as percentage of expenditures
Payments to outside companies as percentage of expenditures
Tuition reimbursements as percentage of expenditures
Percentage of expenditures on learning technologies
Other expenses as percentage of expenditures
Return on expectations
Knowledge- or skill-based pay
Individual development plans
Skill certification
Documentation of individual competencies

---

lists some of the key metrics provided. The ASTD also publishes an annual learning outcomes report using different measures that will be discussed in the next section.

Unquestionably, these key metrics (e.g., total training expenditures as a percentage of payroll, percentage of training eligible employees trained, training ratio of eligible employees to trainer, etc.) provide interesting training-related information. Another significant benefit of these measures is that they are based on readily available data. For instance, the calculation of total training expenditures per training eligible employee can be quick and easy since both figures are usually readily available in most organizations. It is hard to imagine a scenario in which an extensive data collection effort would be required to obtain the figures necessary to make any calculation in the ASTD metrics.

However, in many ways the shortcomings of these measures mirror the problems with other more traditional metrics that are devised because they are easy to measure. Consider *training as a percentage of payroll,* which has traditionally been used as the key metric. What does it really mean? Is any manager using it to decide how much training to offer employees? Is any organization making strategic training decisions using it? While it is an interesting benchmark, it does not seem to be one that has led to increases in training budgets within organizations, even though training investments have increased.

Furthermore, because these measures focus solely on *training,* their scope is entirely too limited to be considered *development* metrics. Other developmental programs and initiatives (i.e., on-the-job training [OJT], coaching, mentoring, etc.) are not included, thereby leaving a tremendous void in their usefulness as developmental metrics. As noted earlier, development, unlike training, is not limited to structured learning activities designed to help employees fulfill job duties. It extends past training to include short- and long-term activities. Unless an organization has an extraordinarily good human resource accounting system, these activities are not likely to be included in training expenditures. The general trend in organizations today is to use more nontraining initiatives, making these metrics even less useful. By omitting or overlooking developmental efforts that extend beyond training initiatives, the ASTD metrics are somewhat incomplete.

The Financial Approach

Human resources has not usually looked to finance and accounting to create metrics. While it will become clear that metrics other than financial ones will be needed, this separation between human resources and finance is unnecessary and counterproductive. The financial approach represents selected financial metrics related to development that have arisen from human capital economics, utility analysis from industrial-organizational psychologists, intellectual capital, and financial analysis. It uses existing financial measures to place a value on human capital.

Intellectual capital theory posits that some employees are more productive than others due in large part to their acquired knowledge, skills, and abilities. The presumption is that returns from human capital are represented by the difference between the worth of a firm's assets, and the value placed on it by the stock market.

Intellectual capital theory has attempted to use financial measures to determine the return from human capital. One key metric for human capital is the following:

$$\text{Human Capital Return} = \text{Market Value} - \text{Book Value}$$

From this perspective, all returns over the book value of the firm are attributable to returns from human capital development. However, book value is often too conservative, so another approach is to use Tobin's Q, which is

$$\text{Human Capital Return} = \frac{\text{Market Value}}{\text{Replacement Cost of Assets}}$$

This ratio controls for different depreciation policies that affect book value. Values greater than one indicate returns from intellectual capital.

Intellectual capital theory is fundamental to any attempt to create development metrics. However, the use of market value to calculate human capital returns is problematic except in the long run. We need only look to the stock market in the late 1990s (particularly Internet stocks) to see how market valuations can become disconnected from real firm performance. Thus, linking development metrics to stock market valuations could create tremendous short-term volatility in the metric, rendering it unusable.

Financial analysts have used a different measure called *economic value added* (EVA) (Stewart, 1999). EVA has replaced traditional notions of net present value, internal rate of return, and return on investment in many firms. The basic notion of EVA is that an organization, or a unit within an organization, must return more profit than the cost of the capital it employs. Thus:

Economic Value Added　　=　　Operating Profit – Cost of Capital

EVA has had only limited application in HR metrics to date. Its most notable contribution is that it does not depend on the firm's market value as represented by stock price. EVA attempts to capture the intrinsic value of the company. It also introduces the notion that operating profit must exceed the cost of capital employed. However, EVA only considers compensation as an expense, not as representing the cost of human capital. The returns are actually a composite of returns from financial and human capital.

Another key metric comes from human capital economists (Cascio, 2000). They consider tenure in the organization as an indicator of accumulated competence. Human capital theory makes a sharp distinction between general training and specific training. General training offers no unique contribution because it is applicable in any organization. Specific training offers unique value to the organization and is not easily transferred to other organizations.

Thus, tenure in the organization is a proxy for accumulated firm-specific expertise, encompassing both knowledge and experience. Both human capital economics and utility analysis (Cascio, 2000) consider an employee's wages and salaries to represent the economic value of the employee. Analyses of returns on development thus begin with an assumption that compensation reflects the cost of human capital.

The metric that is quite useful is tenure in the organization as a proxy for accumulated expertise. It is certainly reasonable to expect that employees with longer tenure will, on average, have greater expertise than those with less tenure. However, it must be noted that there are instances in which newcomers with less tenure might bring new expertise into the organization.

The notion of using compensation as the cost of human capital is an appealing one when considered along with the EVA model. That is, another view of compensation is that it should be considered the cost of human capital just as interest would be considered the cost of debt capital. This suggests that the EVA model might be useful for valuing the contribution of human capital.

The Intellectual Capital Approach

In recent years, the concept of knowledge or intellectual capital has received increasing attention. This movement has been driven largely by the recognition that traditional accounting systems failed to capture the value of an organization's human capital. In a knowledge economy, the contribution of human capital is likely to meet or exceed the value of financial capital. What has been missing are metrics to measure and manage human capital. Thus, the intellectual capital strategy has been to create new measurement systems.

In 1995, Skandia Corp. released what is believed to be the world's first Intellectual Capital Annual Report (Edvinsson & Malone, 1997). Since then, more and more organizations have tackled the difficult task of measuring their intellectual capital, spawning several approaches to measurement.

Skandia Corp. made some contributions by offering definitions that are also useful to us. First, they defined the total value of the organization as

Market Value = Financial Capital + Intellectual Capital

This is a fundamentally different view of an organization because it suggests that value results from employing two forms of capital, not just financial capital that traditional accounting and financial systems do.

Intellectual capital was then defined simply as

Intellectual Capital = Human Capital + Structural Capital

Structural capital was defined as all those things left behind when the employees went home. In the old industrial economy, it was the structural capital that created the greatest competitive advantage. In the knowledge economy it is the human capital that creates competitive advantage, but accounting systems do not adequately account for its value. Thus, Skandia and others are forced to create new metrics. The metrics created at Skandia that could be used to measure intellectual capital development are shown in Figure 16.3.

Sveiby (1997) has created what he calls the Intangible Asset Monitor (IAM). It considers three groups of measures: internal structure, external structure, and competence indicators. Figure 16.4 shows his competence indicators, which are of primary interest here as they speak to development activities. Many of Sveiby's metrics assume that knowledge professionals in an organization are the primary revenue-generating employees.

The intellectual capital approach has gone farther than any other approach in measuring and valuing human capital development in organizations. As such, it has made an enormous contribution to human resource metrics.

Unfortunately, the primary focus of the metrics has been on organizations that are predominantly knowledge driven. The metrics are not as appropriate for organizations that have huge investments in plants and equipment. These organizations carry a huge cost of financial capital that must be accounted for. While human capital is still a vital source of competitive advantage in these companies, it is not the only source as financial capital plays a large role as well. For a metric

Figure 16.3   Skandia Corp. Development Metrics

Training Focus
Training expense/employee (dollars)
Time in training (days/year) (number)
Per capita annual cost of training, communication, and support programs for full-
time permanent employees

Renewal and Development Focus
Competence development expense/employee (dollars)
Share of training hours (percentage)
Share of development hours (percentage)
Training expense/employee (dollars)
Training expense/administrative expense (percentage)

Growth/Renewal
Total competence of experts in years
Value added per employee

More information can be found at www.icvisions.com.

Figure 16.4   Development Metrics from the Intangible Asset Monitor

Indicators of Growth and Renewal
Number of years in the profession
Level of education
Training and education costs
Marking
Competence turnover
Competence-enhancing customer

Indicators of Efficiency
Proportion of professionals
Leverage effect
Value added per employee
Value added per professional
Profit per employee
Profit per professional

Indicators of Stability
Professionals turnover
Relative pay
Seniority

For more information, see www.sveiby.com.au.

to be widely used, it must be applicable in *any* type of organization and account for the contributions of financial and human capital.

In addition, their standard advice is that each organization should create its own measure that represents the key drivers of performance. While this recommendation is very sound, it almost guarantees that cross-company comparisons will be difficult at best.

The Human Resource Metrics Approach

Others have attempted to develop HRD organizational level metrics. We will call this the human resource metrics approach, which includes work by Fitz-enz (2000), Ulrich, Zenger, and Smallwood (1999), and Kaplan and Norton (1996). These researchers have attempted to define key organizational-level indicators that provide a picture of development effectiveness across a broad sample of companies. Figure 16.5 illustrates some of the metrics that they espouse.

These metrics demonstrate the value of organization-level metrics used in a balanced scorecard approach to HR accountability. Together they provide a useful starting point. However, there are two primary flaws:

1. They still tend to rely heavily on training as a key indicator, not our broader conception of development.

2. Some are too complex to collect in large-scale surveys. For example, establishing employees' reputation with headhunters would be very difficult to do.

New Horizons in Metrics

A new independent nonprofit organization, Staffing.org (www.staffing.org), has taken on the challenge of creating new international standard metrics for staffing, development, and retention. Backed by the Employment Management Association and the Society for Human Resource Management, this organization is attempting to improve on existing metrics so they are useful to management for internal controls and externally for benchmarking. Holton and Naquin (2000) used these key criteria for establishing development metrics:

- *Parsimonious*—Development metrics should be a limited number of key criteria, not a lengthy scorecard.

- *Usable by all companies*—While they endorse creating company specific metrics and scorecards, for their purposes the metrics had to be applicable to all companies.

- *Provide leading and lag indicators*—Leading indicators predict future performance, while lag indicators report on past performance. Leading indicators are important because they provide management early warning signs of future problems with time to intervene.

Figure 16.5 Human Resource Development Metrics

BECKER, B., HUSELID, M. A., & ULRICH, D. (2001)

High-Performance Work System Measures (for development):
Backup talent ratio
Competency development expense per employee
Percentage of employees with development plans

HR Efficiency Measures (for development):
Cost per trainee hour
Number of safety training and awareness activities
Number of training days and programs per year
Percentage of and number of employees involved in training
Percentage of employee development plans completed
Percentage of employees with access to appropriate training and development opportunities
Percentage of new material in training programs each year
Percentage of payroll spent on training
Time needed to orient new employees

HR Performance-Driver Measures (for development):
Extent of organizational learning
Extent to which employees have ready access to the information and knowledge they need
Extent to which HR is helping to develop necessary leadership competencies
Percentage of workforce that is promotable
Percentage of employees with experience outside their current job responsibility or function
Planned development opportunities accomplished
Success rates of external hires

ULRICH, ZENGER, AND SMALLWOOD (1999)

Collective Assessment: Quantitative Collective Measures
Employee training and development expenses as percentage of total expenses
Reputation of company employees with headhunters
Years of experience in profession
The proportion of employees suggesting new ideas, including the proportion implemented
Position backup ratio: percentage of key jobs for which backup is ready and available
Overall backup ratio: number of people qualified to move into key jobs
Ratio of offers to acceptances overall and in key positions

Competence
Vertical boundary: employees at each level have the talent and skills they need to do their jobs
Horizontal boundary: talent moves from one unit to the other as needed
External boundary: talent inside the organization meets the requirements of the value chain
Global boundary: organization's talent can compete globally

KAPLAN AND NORTON (1996)

Learning and Growth Perspective—Employee Capabilities
Employee satisfaction
Employee retention
Employee productivity
Strategic skills
Training levels
Skill leverage

- *Balance new data with existing data*—It is easy to create metrics that require creating entirely new information systems, but it is not very practical. They try to create effective metrics that incorporate some existing and easily accessible data along with new data.

- *Useful to management*—As seen from the program evaluation approach to measurement, metrics that are not useful to management are not likely to be completed. Thus, the organization looked for metrics that would provide new and useful information that management would not know without the metric.

- *Correlated with performance*—The metrics should have a reasonable chance of predicting performance.

- *Not easily manipulated*—The metrics need to be credible and not easily manipulated.

- *Based on systematic rather than anecdotal information*—Too many development metrics are based on anecdotal information. This group wanted metrics that provide hard data.

- *Minimally impacted by extraneous factors*—The metric must reasonably represent organizational factors without incorporating unrelated extraneous factors.

Holton and Naquin proposed five key development metrics (complete details can be found on the Staffing.org Web site) (Holton & Naquin, 2000):

- *Development quality*—One of the fundamental purposes of development is to have people ready to fill vacant positions when needed. Thus, an appropriate metric of development quality is the percentage of vacancies that the organization was able to fill internally.

- *Capacity to meet potential needs*—Two metrics were proposed. First, there must be some "bench strength" of competency in the organization. That is, it is possible for an organization to have just enough competency to meet current needs, but no excess competency that could be called upon if needed. Thus, Holton and Naquin proposes a metric based on the number of job openings that could be filled internally if desired. Second, capacity is also dependent on employee's motivation to use learning and development to enhance performance. Traditionally this has been stated as motivation to learn. However, given that the primary desired outcome of organizational development programs is *improvement in work outcomes,* an exclusive focus on motivation to learn or train is too limiting. A new metric is recommended: Employee Motivation to Improve Work through Learning (MTIWL), which posits that an individual's motivation to improve work through learning is a function of his or her motivation to train *and* motivation to transfer (Naquin & Holton, in press).

- *Development of customer satisfaction*—The new metrics break rank with most development satisfaction data by adopting the Results Assessment System's (Swanson & Holton, 1999) approach in two ways. First, it focuses on collecting perceptual data from a key stakeholder, managers of development participants, rather than participants themselves. While participants may be consumers of development, it is their managers who are the real customers. Second, the perceptual data to be collected focus on *utility* of development for improving performance.

- *Formal development investment per employee*—Traditionally, training investments have been measured by training expense as a percentage of payroll. As discussed earlier, this measure is flawed. In its place is proposed the Formal Development Investment per Employee metric. This measure improves on the old by (1) expanding beyond training cost to include other formal development, (2) including the hidden cost of participant's salary, and (3) converting to a per-person ratio so it is more usable my management.

- *Human capital development contribution (HCDC)*—Some claim that the value of development cannot be calculated. A new measure that comes closest to anything we have seen is proposed. As stated earlier, in the financial world, economic value added or EVA has become a popular way to value business units. EVA is simply the profit attributable to a business unit less the cost of capital employed in that unit. This group suggests an EVA-type measure to estimate the economic value of each dollar of compensation to reflect the economic value added of development.

MEETING THE ACCOUNTABILITY CHALLENGE

While not everyone in the HRD profession is convinced, we see accountability as a challenge that HRD must find a way to meet. Critics of accountability and measurement in HRD maintain that development is impossible to measure and that learning should not be evaluated by external means. This argument is grounded mostly in the humanistic perspective from adult education that views the learner as the primary evaluator of learning outcomes.

Organizations, on the other hand, are asking questions such as these:

- Are employees developing the expertise necessary to achieve organizational goals?
- Are scarce HRD resources being utilized most effectively?
- Is HRD adding value to the organization?
- Is the learning necessary to drive organizational effectiveness readily available?

The good news is that many organizations today *really* care about HRD, but they care because it is central to organizational success to a greater extent than in recent history. Along with increased status comes increased accountability. Our argument is a pragmatic one: It is not a question of *whether* HRD will be held accountable but rather *how*. And, if HRD does not define approaches to accountability, someone else will. We think it best if HRD defines appropriate approaches to accountability rather than allowing accountants to do it.

Accountability is also healthy for the profession. Being accountable only to learners is not sufficient for HRD to be a strategic partner. Accountability forces HRD to reassess its practices and pushes the field to learn how to focus its resources. We see no reason that HRD should not be held accountable just as marketing, production, engineering, or any other department would be. In the end, such an approach will advance the profession.

REFLECTION QUESTIONS

1. If the Kirkpatrick model of evaluation is so flawed, why does it continue to have such a strong following in HRD?

2. Why do you think there is such resistance to evaluating results of HRD interventions?

3. Are metrics a viable approach to HRD accountability?

4. Which metrics listed in this chapter could be used to build an effective balanced scorecard for HRD accountability?

5. How can the field overcome what seems to be a persistent fear of accountability?

Globalization and Technology Challenges to HRD

CHAPTER OUTLINE
Globalization Challenge to HRD
 Economics of Globalization
 Globalization of HRD Systems
Technology Challenge to HRD
 Definitions
 Technology and Touch
 Sources of HRD Expertise
Conclusion
Reflection Questions

We opened this book with the following sentences:

> Human resource development (HRD) is a relatively young academic disci-
> pline, but an old, well-established field of practice. The idea of human beings
> purposefully developing, in anticipation of being able to improve conditions,
> seems almost part of human nature. HRD theory and practice are deeply
> rooted in this developing and advancing perspective.

Clearly, the role and practices of HRD ring true for both individuals and organizations. Even so, they may not always be in sync. The evolution of people and systems is a complex matter and they are rarely, if ever, moving at the same rate and
in the same direction. If they were in sync, the need for HRD would be radically
diminished.

 The fundamental ideas valued in HRD are the development and improvement agendas of individuals, organizations, and governments. As we enter the
twenty-first century, two overriding phenomena rise to the top of the list of challenges facing HRD: globalization and technology. These two highly interrelated
phenomena are explored in this concluding chapter.

While we will discuss these two forces, we do not pretend to understand their full implications. The are pervasive and dynamic. We sense that we have not seen anything yet! Having said this, we are excited about the future and the challenges they pose for HRD.

GLOBALIZATION CHALLENGE TO HRD

The globalization of the world economy is challenging the core values, theories, and tools of the HRD profession. Globalization is so fundamental that most people are probably viewing only fragments or the tip of the iceberg. Those who look below the surface do not all agree as to its goodness or badness. However, they all agree the full realization of globalization will make for a very different world and life experience.

The economic and systems perspectives on globalization are worth noting. First and foremost, globalization and the change it represents are being driven by economics. It is important to recognize that economics has always been the fundamental driving force behind globalization, the change it provokes, and the entrée of HRD into the movement. It requires a systematic and systemic response. This globalization perspective transcends the "we need to understand your culture" perspective most HRD professionals think about when they think of globalization.

Economics of Globalization

HRD professionals should be knowledgeable about the global economy and the underlying philosophical struggle beneath a free market economy. Adam Smith (1723–1790) provided us a watershed treatise on economics. In 1776, he published *An Inquiry into the Nature and Causes of the Wealth of Nations,* arguing that people ought to be left to follow their own inclinations of sustaining life and acquiring goods. He believed that government should not interfere with free enterprise and should resist temptations to interfere. He had great faith in individuals and believed that given the freedom to pursue their own interests, they would ultimately serve the common good. Thus, he hypothesized that all people will gain and prosper. Most scholars believe that Smith's *Wealth of Nations* is the definitive defense of capitalistic economics.

Looking more closely at the individual as an economic entity, Gunnar Myrdal (1944/1996), the Swedish economist, concluded that you are not free until you are economically free. His concern for allowing individuals the opportunity for economic freedom was a journey toward intellectual freedom.

The mantra of leaving people alone (freedom)—to work hard and as smart as they can to make money (wealth)—is not supported by everyone. Korten (1995) warns that "an unregulated global economy dominated by corporations that recognize money as their only value is inherently unstable, egregiously unequal, destructive of markets, democracy, and life, and is impoverishing humanity." We are reminded that globalization does not affect all countries or people alike. They are winners and losers. (Hansen & Headley, 1998; Marquardt, 1999). Combine this with the shift from manual to knowledge work, and the issue is compounded. The cognitive elite in the new global economy "are centered outside a geographic community; their professional associates and friends may be scattered over miles of suburbs, or for that matter across the nation and around the world" (Herrnstein & Murray, 1996, p. 539). Cognitive-economic elite world citizens have been accused of making life more difficult for everybody else as they create rules in society that work for them. Herrnstein and Murray (1996) call for action that lets people find valued places in society and for simplifying the rules that control their lives.

Globalization of HRD Systems

HRD practitioners are active partners in the globalization of their employing organization—profit and nonprofit organizations and government agencies. Fortunately, reports of HRD practice within nations are on the increase. For example, Nijhof and Streumer (1998) report on the new roles and training models for managers in the printing and communications industry in the Netherlands, while Mulder and Tjepkema (1999) provide an international briefing on T&D in the Netherlands. These industry-level reports of practices as well as reports on national HRD norms are important for developing a basic understanding of global variations. Osman-Gani and Tan (2000) have produced a similar overview on T&D in Singapore, and Odenthal and Nijhof (1996) look closer at the HRD roles in Germany. Briefings like these make it clear that sophisticated economies, like those in the Netherlands, Germany, and Singapore, have many commonalties when it comes to HRD. Understanding cultural norms and natural links only increase the potential of global partnering and globalization.

Information sharing on national HRD practices in multinational companies is also essential in building practical global practices models. The literature is beginning to report explicit models for HRD in response to the globalization of business. Krempl and Pace (2001) believe that not doing so "creates a risk of failing to reach mission-critical goals of managing knowledge in multiple locations, supporting diverse cultures, and enhancing performance across geographic and national boundaries" (p. 16).

Researchers in HRD are beginning to function globally as a worldwide community of scholars. Scholars distinguish themselves through the generation of new knowledge and in giving that knowledge back to the world. The Academy of Human Resource Development (AHRD) is the exemplar in functioning as the global community of HRD scholars. Compared with practitioner organizations, it has a small membership, and all members communicate via Internet technology. Even so, it is the shared vision among members for leading the profession through research, respect for inquiry, and openness in participation that has resulted in a global presence. The most visible AHRD contribution is in sponsoring four journals: *Advances in Developing Human Resources* (topical issues; theory and practice), *Human Resource Development Quarterly* (research), *Human Resource Development International* (international research forum), and *Human Resource Development Review* (theory research).

In summary, the ethical challenge that globalization presents to HRD is eloquently summarized by Marquardt (1999): "Political and economic freedom have proven to be essential to the development of any society, but human resource development is critical in building on these opportunities" (p. vi).

TECHNOLOGY CHALLENGE TO HRD

Given the forces of knowledge creation, technology, democratization, information technology, and the sheer rate and magnitude of change, it is only rational that HRD will be very different in the twenty-first century. To say so sounds almost trite. Pushing the twenty-first-century view to the limit, here is a mind-stretching question for HRD professionals:

"What is the role of HRD in a virtual organization?"

We could venture an answer to this challenging question but instead leave it to you to formulate a scenario response. It is worth thinking about and discussing with other HRD professionals.

We have selected three variables to consider in thinking about technology and HRD in the twenty-first century. They include *technology* versus touch, *sources* of HRD expertise, and *ownership* of HRD. Individually, these variables constitute challenges to the existing mental models and professional practices of HRD. Together the have the potential of fundamentally changing HRD.

Definitions

Before considering these three variables, take a look at the word *technology*. *Technology* is one of those sloppily used words in our vocabulary. Most people think they know what it means—however, the word's meanings and their surrounding values vary greatly. Here are some definitions that illustrate our point about confusion surrounding the term technology.

Technology (in general): Technology is the application of the sciences to the objectives of industry, business, government systems, and human endeavors in general.

Technology (as a process): As a process, technology is a sociotechnical means of defining and solving problems.

Technology definitions from the popular literature:

Any sufficiently advanced technology is indistinguishable from magic.
—Arthur C. Clarke, *The Lost Worlds of 2001*

Technology, when misused, poisons air, soil, water and lives. But a world without technology would be prey to something worse: the impersonal ruthlessness of the natural order, in which the health of a species depends on relentless sacrifice of the weak.

—*New York Times* editorial, August 29, 1986

Technology was developed to prevent exhausting labor. It is now dedicated to trivial conveniences.

—B. F. Skinner

That great, growling engine of change—technology.

—Alvin Toffler, *Future Shock* (1970)

Technology shapes society and society shapes technology.

—Robert W. White, *Environmental Science and Technology* (1990)

Here are some technology definitions used in HRD:

Open space technology: A self-organizing approach to meetings of people

—Owen (1997)

Human performance technology: A set of methods and procedures, and a strategy for solving problems for realizing opportunities related to the performance of people. It can be applied to individuals, small groups, and large organizations. It is, in reality, a systematic combination of three fundamental processes: performance analysis, cause analysis, and intervention selection.

—International Society for Performance Improvement (2000)

Technology-based training: Uses of technology to deliver training and education materials . . . mainframe computers, floppy diskettes, multimedia CD-ROMs, and interactive video disks. Most recently, internet and intranet delivery has become the preferred delivery method.

—Kruse and Keil (2000, p. 8)

Technology and Touch

The mode in which HRD should exist is a variable that will be fully explored in the twenty-first century. This exploration, we believe, will be a continuing journey in terms of the mission of HRD and HRD strategies. The discussion on the role of technology in HRD can be thought of in terms of strategies in the full use of technology (or high-tech) and the human need for personal connection (or high-touch).

For the most part, HRD has functioned at a low-tech level throughout its history. The twenty-first-century challenge for HRD is to be engaged in high-tech means of developing and unleashing human expertise coming from the demand to do HRD work better, faster, and cheaper. It is easy to imagine computers, the Internet, information technology, and artificial intelligence at the center of this high-tech challenge (Rossett & Sheldon, 2001).

Apart from its own technology, the HRD profession has prided itself in terms of its sensitive engagement of client and participant high-touch. The twenty-first century challenge for HRD will be retain this core value of connecting with human beings and in connecting human beings in a meaningful way. This will need to be accomplished in light of the rate of change and the intrusion of technology. The human need of high-touch will not likely diminish, yet the organization—the virtual office—may diminish the organization's capability to provide this essential work ingredient (which it never consciously planned for in the past). One challenge to the HRD profession is to learn more about the effective application and appropriate use of high-tech, high-touch, and *integrated* high-touch plus high-tech interventions.

We know of one major communication corporation that made an across-the-board switch from three hundred high-touch, facilitator-led programs to three hundred high-tech, media-based programs in less than a year. In our professional assessment, both options were wrong. A careful analysis of the desired outcomes and the appropriateness of the strategies (along with the stability of the content and numbers of participants) made it clear that some interventions should be high-tech, some high-touch, and some combined high-tech plus high-touch. This group was so committed to the technology that it was unable to question its limitations in the context of its desired goals.

Sources of HRD Expertise

The source, or home-base operations, of HRD is a variable that will be explored in the twenty-first century. Competitiveness in general, and technology specifically, has opened up this option. Globalization is another driving force.

The discussion on the sourcing of HRD expertise can be thought of in terms of internal providers (HRD professionals within a host organization), external providers (providers of off-the-shelf or custom services and goods), and partnerships between internal and external providers.

- Midsize companies in the same city that need first-class, but only part-time OD expertise, hire a local OD expert who has four clients that he or she works with on a continuing basis (e.g., one day each per week for a year or more).

- A Fortune 50 insurance company needs to continually train its sales force and chooses to create core learning via the company's intranet system that salespeople can access seven days a week, twenty-four hours a day. The proprietary programs are developed in-house, and an external-consulting firm develops the nonproprietary programs.

The sources of HRD expertise are increasing, and the HRD profession is challenged as to how to effectively and efficiently access and use available resources. The first step is to determine what high-quality internal and external resources are actually available. The next step is to determine how they might best complement one another. Information technology is an efficient asset in searching out the options. That is the good news. Assessing the *quality* of the information at hand and potential providers, however, is another story. The HRD profession is challenged to establish standards for providers and consumers in this realm in order to sort out the HRD charlatans.

CONCLUSION

Given the forces of globalization and technology, the ownership, or primary stakeholder, of HRD will emerge as a variable to be explored in the twenty-first century. Our primary definition of HRD as *a process of developing and unleashing human expertise for the purpose of improving performance* does not inform us as to who owns HRD. Thus, the discussion of ownership and responsibility will be a debatable issue. Some of the options include governments, individual organizations and their management, the HRD profession itself, organizations providing off-the-shelf or custom HRD services and goods, individual workers, or some combination of these options.

Our conclusion is that HRD is so important to individuals, organizations, and society that there will be an ongoing struggle globally and locally as to the ownership and purposes of HRD. We also believe that this struggle over the role of HRD and who participates in HRD decisions will ensure the continued advancement of the profession.

REFLECTION QUESTIONS

1. Articulate your personal view of the global economy. (Write seventy-five to one hundred words.)

2. What specific activities would help you to be more informed of globalization? List five specific activities and describe their benefits.

3. Articulate your personal view of technology. (Write seventy-five to one hundred words.)

4. What is the role of HRD in a virtual organization? (Write 100 to 125 words.)

5. What is your "best-case" scenario for HRD in the twenty-first century? (Write a 250- to 300-word essay.)

References

Abernathy, D. J. (1999). Thinking outside the evaluation box. *Training and Development, 53*(2), 19–23.

Academy of Human Resource Development. (1999). *Standards on Ethics and Integrity.* Baton Rouge, LA: Author.

Adizes, I. (1988). *Corporate Lifecycles: How and Why Corporations Grow and Die and What to Do about It.* Englewood Cliffs, NJ: Prentice Hall.

Agrawal, A. (1994). Technology learning laboratories. In L. Kelly (Ed.), *The ASTD Technical and Skills Training Handbook.* New York: McGraw-Hill.

Alliger, G. M., & Janak, E. A. (1989). Kirkpatrick's levels of training criteria: Thirty years later. *Personnel Psychology, 42,* 331–342.

Alliger, G. M., Tannenbaum, S. I., Bennett, W., Trave, H., & Shotland, A. (1997). A meta-analysis of the relations among training criteria. *Personnel Psychology, 50,* 341–358.

American Heritage Dictionary (3rd ed.). (1993). Boston: Houghton Mifflin

American Society for Training and Development. (2000). *The 2000 State of the Industry Report.* Alexandria, VA: Author.

Apps, J. W. (1985). *Improving Practice in Continuing Education.* San Francisco: Jossey-Bass.

Aragon, S. R., & Hatcher, T. (Eds.). (2001). Ethics and integrity in HRD: Case studies in research and practice. *Advances in Developing Human Resources, 3*(1).

Argyris, C. (1952). *An Introduction to Field Theory and Interaction Theory.* New Haven, CT: Yale University Labor and Management Center.

Argyris, C. (1970). *Intervention Theory and Method.* Reading, MA: Addison-Wesley.

Argyris, C. (1977). Double-loop learning in organizations. *Harvard Business Review, 55,* 115–125.

Argyris, C. (1982). *Reasoning, Learning, and Action.* San Francisco: Jossey-Bass.

Argyris, C. (1993). *Knowledge for Action.* San Francisco: Jossey-Bass.

Argyris, C. (1999). *On Organizational Learning.* Malden, MA: Blackwell.

Argyris, C., Putnam, R., & Smith, S. (1985). *Action Science.* San Francisco: Jossey-Bass.

Argyris, C., & Schon, D. (1978). *Organizational Learning: A Theory of Action Perspective.* Reading, MA: Addison-Wesley.

Argyris, C., Schon, D. (1982). *Theory in Practice: Increasing Professional Effectiveness.* San Francisco: Jossey-Bass.

Arlin, P. K. (1984). Adolescent and adult thought: A structural interpretation. Reprinted in M. L. Commons, F. A. Richards, & C. Armos (Eds.), *Wisdom: Its Nature, Origins, and Development.* Cambridge: Cambridge University Press, 1990.

Armenakis, A. A., & Bedeian, A. G. (1999). Organizational change: A review of theory and research in the 1990s. *Journal of Management, 25,* 292–215.

Armenakis, A. A., Harris, S. G., & Field, H. S. (1999). Making change permanent: A model for institutionalizing change. In W. Pasmore & R. Woodman (Eds.), *Research in Organization Change and Development* (Vol. XII, pp. 97–128). Greenwich, CT: JAI.

Armenakis, A. A., Harris, S. G., & Mossholder, K. W. (1993). Creating readiness for organizational change. *Human Relations, 46*(3), 1–23.

Baldwin, T. T., & Ford, J. K. (1988). Transfer of training: A review and directions for future research. *Personnel Psychology, 41,* 63–105.

Baltes, P. (1997). On the incomplete architecture of human ontogeny: Selection, optimization, and compensation as foundations of developmental theory. *American Psychologist, 52*(4), 366–380.

Baltes, P. B., Dittman-Kohli, F., & Dixon, R. (1984). New perspectives on the development of intelligence in adulthood: Toward a dual process conception and a model of selective optimization with compensation. In P. B. Baltes & O. G. Brim, Jr. (Eds.), *Life-Span Development and Behavior* (Vol. 6, pp. 33–76). New York: Academic Press.

Barlow, M. L. (1967). *History of Industrial Education in the United States.* Peoria, IL: Bennett.

Barney, J. (1991). Firm resources and sustained competitive advantage. *Journal of Management, 17,* 99–120.

Barr, P. S., Stimpert, J. L., & Huff, A. S. (1992). Cognitive change, strategic action, and organization renewal. *Strategic Management Journal, 13,* 15–36.

Barrick, M. R., & Mount, M. K. (1991). The Big Five personality dimensions and job performance: A meta-analysis. *Personnel Psychology, 44,* 1–26.

Barrie, J., & Pace, R. W. (1997). Competence, efficiency, and organizational learning. *Human Resource Development Quarterly, 8*(4), 335–342.

Barrie, J., & Pace, R. W. (1998). Learning for organizational effectiveness: Philosophy of education and human resource development. *Human Resource Development Quarterly, 9,* 39–54.

Barrie, J., & Pace, R. W. (1999). Learning and performance: Just the end of the beginning—A rejoinder to Kuchinke. *Human Resource Development Quarterly, 10,* 293–296.

Bartlett, K. R. (2001). The relationship between training and organizational commitment: A study in the health care field. *Human Resource Development Quarterly, 12*(4).

Bassi, L., & Ahlstrand, A. (2000). *The 2000 ASTD Learning Outcomes Report.* Alexandria, VA: American Society for Training and Development.

Bassi, L. J., & Van Buren, M. E. (1999). *The 1999 ASTD State of the Industry Report.* Alexandria, VA: American Society for Training and Development.

Bates, R., Holton E., & Seyler D. (1997). Factors affecting transfer of training in an industrial setting. In R. Torraco (Ed.), *Academy of Human Resource Development 1997 Conference Proceedings.* Baton Rouge, LA: Academy of Human Resource Development.

Bates, R. A., Holton, E. F., III, & Seyler, D. L. (2000). The role of interpersonal factors in the application of computer-based training in an industrial setting. *Human Resource Development International, 3,* 19–42.

Beatty, A. J. (1918). *Corporation Schools.* Bloomington, IL: Public School Publishing.

Becker, B. E., Huselid, M. A., & Ulrich, D. (2001). *The HRD Scorecard: Linking People, Strategy, and Performance.* Boston: Harvard Business School Press.

Becker, G. S. (1993). *Human Capital: A Theoretical and Empirical Analysis with Special Reference to Education* (3rd ed.). Chicago: University of Chicago Press.

Beckhard, R., & Pritchard, W. (1992). *Changing the Essence: The Art of Creating and Leading Fundamental Change in Organizations.* San Francisco: Jossey-Bass.

Beder, H. (1989). Purposes and philosophies of adult education. In S. B. Merriam & P. M. Cunningham (Eds.), *Handbook of Adult and Continuing Education* (pp. 37–50). San Francisco: Jossey-Bass.

Bee, H. L. (1996). *The Journey of Adulthood* (3rd ed.). Upper Saddle River, NJ: Prentice Hall.

Beer, M., & Nohria, N. (Eds.). (2000). *Breaking the Code of Change.* Boston: Harvard Business School Press.

Benack, S., & Basseches, M. A. (1989). Dialectical thinking and relativistic epistemology: Their relation in adult development. In M. L. Commons, J. D. Sinnott, F. A. Richards, & C. Armon (Eds.), *Adult Development.* New York: Praeger.

Bennett, C. A. (1926). *History of Manual and Industrial Education Up to 1870.* Peoria, IL: Manual Arts Press.

Bennett, C. A. (1937). *History of Manual and Industrial Education 1870 to 1917.* Peoria, IL: Bennett.

Bereiter, C., & Scardamalia, M. (1993). *Surpassing Ourselves: An Inquiry into the Nature and Implications of Expertise.* Chicago: Open Court.

Bierema, L. L. (1996). Development of the individual leads to a more productive workplace. In R. Rowden (Ed.), *Workplace Learning: Debating Five Critical Questions of Theory and Practice* (pp. 21–28). San Francisco: Jossey-Bass.

Bierema, L. L. (1997). The development of the individual leads to more productive workplaces. In R. J. Torraco (Ed.), *Academy of Human Resource Development* (pp. 652–659). Baton Rouge, LA: Academy of Human Resource Development.

Bierema, L. L. (2000). Moving beyond performance paradigms in human resource development. In A. L. Wilson & E. R. Hayes (Eds.), *Handbook of Adult and Continuing Education* (pp. 278–293). San Francisco: Jossey-Bass.

Black, G. (1979). *Trends in Management Development and Education: An Economic Study.* White Plains, NY: Knowledge Industry Publications.

Boone, E. J. (1985). *Developing Programs in Adult Education.* Englewood Cliffs, NJ: Prentice Hall.

Bossard, J. H. S., & Dewhurst, J. F. (1931). *University Education for Business.* Philadelphia: University of Pennsylvania Press.

Boulding, K. E. (1956a). General systems theory—The skeleton of science. *Management Science, 2,* 197–208.

Boulding, K. E. (1956b). Toward a general theory of growth. *General Systems, 66–75.*

Boyd, W. (1962). *The EMILE of Jean-Jacques Rousseau.* New York: Columbia University, Teachers College.

Brennan, J. F. (1994). *History and Systems of Psychology.* Englewood Cliffs, NJ: Prentice Hall.

Brethower, D. M. (1995). Specifying a human performance technology knowledge base. *Performance Improvement Quarterly, 8*(2), 17–39.

Brethower, D., & Smalley, K. (1998). *Performance-Based Instruction: Linking Training to Business Results.* San Francisco: Jossey-Bass.

Bridges, W. (1991). *Managing Transitions: Making the Most of Change.* Reading, MA: Addison-Wesley.

Briggs, L. J., Gustafson, K. L., & Tillman, M. H. (Eds.). (1991). *Instructional Design Principles and Applications* (2nd ed.). Englewood Cliffs, NJ: Educational Technology Publications.

Brinkerhoff, R. O. (1991). *Achieving Results from Training.* San Francisco: Jossey-Bass.

Broad, M. L. (2000). Managing the organizational learning transfer systems: A model and case study. In E. F. Holton III, T. T. Baldwin, & S. S. Naquin (Eds.), *Managing and Changing Learning Transfer Systems, Advances in Developing Human Resources, 8,* 75–94.

Broad, M. L., & Newstrom, J. W. (1992). *Transfer of Training: Action-Packed Strategies to Ensure High Payoff from Training Investments.* Reading, MA.: Addison-Wesley.

Brookfield, S. D. (1984). The contribution of Eduard Lindeman to the development of theory and philosophy in adult education. *Adult Education Quarterly, 34,* 185–196.

Brookfield, S. D. (1986). *Understanding and Facilitating Adult Learning.* San Francisco: Jossey-Bass.

Brookfield, S. D. (1987). *Developing Critical Thinkers.* San Francisco: Jossey-Bass.

Brooks, A. K. (1992). Building learning organizations: The individual-culture interaction. *Human Resource Development Quarterly, 3*(4), 323–335.

Brown, D., & Brooks, L. (Eds.). (1996). *Career Choice and Development* (3rd ed.). San Francisco: Jossey-Bass.

Brown, J., & Duguid, P. (1991). Organizational learning and communities-of-practice: Toward a unified view of working, learning, and innovation. *Organization Science, 2*(1), 40–57.

Bruning, R. H., Schraw, G. J., & Ronning, R. R. (1999). *Cognitive Psychology and Instruction* (3rd ed.). Upper Saddle River, NJ: Simon & Schuster.

Bryson, L. (1936). *Adult Education.* New York: American Book.

Buckley, W. (Ed.). (1968). *Modern Systems Research for the Behavioral Scientist.* Chicago: Aldine.

Bunker, B. B., & Alban, B. T. (1997). *Large Group Interventions: Engaging the Whole System for Rapid Change.* San Francisco: Jossey-Bass.

Burke, W. W. (1994). Diagnostic models for organization development. In A. Howard (Ed.), *Diagnosis for Organizational Change.* New York: Guilford. Burke, W. W., & Litwin, G. H. (1992). A causal model of organizational performance and change. *Journal of Management, 18*(3), 523–545.

Business Week Staff. (1994, December). The new global workforce. *Business Week* (Special Issue: 21st Century Capitalism), 110–132.

Callahan, J. L. (2000). Emotion management and organizational functions: A case study of patterns in a not-for-profit organization. *Human Resource Development Quarterly, 11*(3), 245–267.

Camp, R. C. (1995). *Business Process Benchmarking.* New York: McGraw-Hill.

Campbell, C. P. (1984). Procedures for developing and validating vocational training programs. *Journal of Industrial Teacher Education, 21*(4), 31–42.

Campbell, J. P. (1990). Modeling the performance prediction problem in industrial and organizational psychology. In M. Dunnette (Ed.), *Handbook of Industrial and Organizational Psychology* (pp. 678–732). Palo Alto, CA: Consulting Psychologists Press.

Carnevale, A. (1984). *Jobs for the Nation: Challenges for a Society Based on Work.* Alexandria, VA: American Society for Training and Development.

Cascio, W. F. (1999). *Costing Human Resources: The Financial Impact of Behavior in Organizations.* Cincinatti, OH: Southwestern.

Case, K. E., & Fair, R. C. (1996). *Principles of Microeconomics* (4th ed.). Upper Saddle River, NJ: Prentice Hall.

Catalanello, R., & Redding, J. (1989). Three strategic training roles. *Training and Development Journal, 73*(12), 51–54.

Chalofsky, N. (1990). Professionalization comes from theory and research: The why instead of the how to. In R. W. Rowden (Ed.), *Workplace Learning: Debating Five Critical Questions of Theory and Practice* (pp. 51–56). New Directions for Adult and Continuing Education 72. San Francisco: Jossey-Bass.

Chandler, A. D., Jr. The beginnings of "big business." American industry. *Business History Review* (1959, Spring). Reprinted in J. P. Baughman (Ed.) (1969), *The History of American Management.* Englewood Cliffs: Prentice Hall.

Chi, M. T. H., Glaser, R., & Farr, M. J. (1988). *The Nature of Expertise.* Hillsdale, NJ: Erlbaum.

Chin, R., & Benne, W. G. (1976). General strategies for effecting changes in human systems. In *The Planning of Change* (3rd ed.). New York: Holt, Rinehart, & Winston.

Christensen, C. M. (1997). *The Innovator's Dilemma: When New Technologies Cause Great Firms to Fail.* Boston: Harvard Business School Press.

Church, A. H., & McMahan, G. C. (1996). The practice of organization and human resource development in America's fastest growing firms. *Leadership and Organization Development Journal, 17*(2), 17–33.

Churchman, C. W. (1971). *The Design of Inquiring Systems: Basic Concepts of Systems and Organizations.* New York: Basic Books.

Clark, H. F., & Sloan, H. S. (1958). *Classrooms in the Factories: An Account of Educational Activities Conducted by American Industry.* Teaneck, NJ: Institute of Research, Farleigh Dickinson University.

Cohen, B. P. (1991). *Developing Sociological Knowledge: Theory and Method* (2nd ed.). Chicago: Nelson Hall.

Confessore, S. J., & Kops, W. J. (1998). Self-directed learning and the learning organization: Examining the connection between the individual and the learning environment. *Human Resource Development Quarterly, 9*(4), 365–375.

Cooper, R., & Foster, M. (1971). Sociotechnical systems. *American Psychologist, 26,* 467–474.

Cooperrider, D. L., & Srivastva, R. (1987). Appreciative inquiry in organizational life. In R. Woodman & W. Passmore (Eds.), *Research in Organizational Change and Development* (pp. 129–169). Greenwich, CT: JAI.

Cornwell, J. M., & Manfredo, P. A. (1994). Kolb's learning style theory revisited. *Educational and Psychological Measurement, 54,* 317–327.

Cseh, M., Watkins, K. E., & Marsick, V. J. (1998). Informal and incidental learning in the workplace. In R. Torraco (Ed.), *Proceedings of the Annual Conference of the Academy of Human Resource Development.* Baton Rouge, LA: AHRD.

Cseh, M., Watkins, K. E., & Marsick, V. J. (1999). Re-conceptualizing Marsick and Watkins's Model of Informal and Incidental Learning in the workplace. In K. P. Kuchinke (Ed.), *1999 Academy of Human Resource Development Conference Proceedings.* Baton Rouge, LA: Academy of Human Resource Development.

Cummings, T. G., & Worley, C. G. (1993). *Organizational Development and Change* (5th ed.). St. Paul, MN: West.

Cummings, T. G., & Worley, C. G. (1997). *Organization Development and Change* (6th ed.). Cincinnati, OH: Southwestern.

Cummings, T. G., & Worley, C. G. (2001). *Organization Development and Change* (7th ed.). Cincinnati, OH: Southwestern College Publishing.

Current Practice in the Development of Management Personnel. (1955). American Management Association, Research Report Number 26.

Dahl, H. L. (1984). Human resource development needs a unifying theory. In D. B. Gradous (Ed.), *Systems Theory Applied to Human Resource Development* (pp. 7–11). Alexandria, VA: ASTD Press.

Daloz, L. A. (1986). *Effective Teaching and Mentoring.* San Francisco: Jossey-Bass.

Damanpour, F. (1991). Organizational innovation: A meta-analysis of effects and determinants and moderators. *Academy of Management Journal, 34*(3), 555–590.

Damanpour, F., & Evan, W. (1984). Organizational innovation and performance: The problem of organizational lag. *Administrative Science Quarterly, 29,* 392–409.

Darkenwald, G. G., & Merriam, S. B. (1982). *Adult Education: Foundations of Practice.* New York: HarperCollins.

Dash, D. P. (1995). Systems practice challenges. In K. Ellis, A. Gregory, B. R. Mears-Young, & G. Ragsdell (Eds.), *Critical Issues in Systems Theory and Practice* (pp. 453–457). New York: Plenum.

Davenport, J. (1987). Is there a way out of the andragogy morass? *Lifelong Learning, 11,* 17–20.

Davenport, J., & Davenport, J. A. (1985). A chronology and analysis of the andragogy debate. *Adult Education Quarterly, 35,* 152–159.

Davenport, T. H. (1993). *Process Innovation: Reengineering Work through Information Technology.* Cambridge, MA: Harvard Business School Press.

Davidson, T. (1900). *A History of Education.* New York: Scribner's.

Davies, I. K. (1994). Process re-design for enhanced human performance. *Performance Improvement Quarterly, 7*(3), 103–113.

Davis, E. G. (1978). Education in industry: A historical overview. *Education Canada,* Spring, 40–46.

Davis, J. R., & Davis, A. B. (1998). *Effective Training Strategies: A Comprehensive Guide to Maximizing Learning in Organizations.* San Francisco: Berrett-Koehler.

Davis, L. E., & Taylor, J. C. (Eds.). (1972). *The Design of Jobs.* Baltimore: Penguin.

Dawis, R. V., & Lofquist, L. H. (1984). *A Psychological Theory of Work Adjustment.* Minneapolis: University of Minnesota Press.

Day, C., & Baskett, H. K. (1982). Discrepancies between intentions and practice: Re-examining some basic assumptions about adult and continuing professional education. *International Journal of Lifelong Education,* 143–156.

Dean, P. J. (1993). A selected review of the underpinnings of ethics for human performance technology professionals: Part 1. Key ethical theories and research. *Performance Improvement Quarterly, 6*(4), 3–32.

Dean, P. J. (1997). Social systems science and the practice of performance improvement. *Performance Improvement Quarterly, 10*(3), 3–6.

Dean, P. J., & Ripley, D. E. (Eds.). (1997). *Performance Improvement Pathfinders: Models for Organizational Learning Systems.* Washington, DC.: International Society for Performance Improvement.

Deming, W. E. (1986). *Out of the Crisis.* Cambridge, MA: MIT Press.

Deming, W. E. (1993). *The New Economics for Industry, Government, Education.* Cambridge: Massachusetts Institute of Technology.

Dewey, J. (1938). *Experience and Education.* New York: Collier McMillan.

Dibella, A. J., & Nevis, E. C. (1998). *How Organizations Learn: An Integrated Strategy for Building Learning Capability.* San Francisco: Jossey-Bass.

Dierkes, M., & Coppocks, R. (1975). Human resources accounting: A tool for measuring and monitoring manpower utilization in a business environment. In W. T. Singleton & P. Sturgeon (Eds.), *Measurement of Human Resources.* New York: Halsted.

Dirkx, J. (1996). Human resource development as adult education: Fostering the educative workplace. In R. Rowden (Ed.), *Workplace Learning: Debating Five Critical Questions of Theory and Practice.* San Francisco: Jossey-Bass.

Dirkx, J. M. (1997). Human resource development as adult education: Fostering the educative workplace. In R. Rowden (Ed.), *Workplace Learning: Debating Five Critical Questions of Theory and Practice* (pp. 41–47). San Francisco: Jossey-Bass.

Dirkx, J. M., & Prenger, S. M. (1997). *A Guide for Planning and Implementing Instruction for Adults: A Theme-based Approach.* San Francisco: Jossey-Bass.

Dixon, N. (1992). Organizational learning: A review of the literature with implications for HRD professionals. *Human Resource Development Quarterly, 3,* 29–49.

Dixon, N. (1994). *The Organizational Learning Cycle: How We Can Learn Collectively.* New York: McGraw-Hill.

Dixon, N. M. (1987). Meeting training's goals without reaction forms. *Personnel Journal, 66*(8) 108–115.

Dixon, N. M. (1990a). *Evaluation: A Tool for Improving Quality.* San Diego: University Associates.

Dixon, N. M. (1990b). The relationship between trainee responses on participation reaction forms and posttest scores. *Human Resource Development Quarterly, 1,* 129–137.

Dodgson, M. (1993). Organizational learning: A review of some literatures. *Organization Studies, 14*(3), 375–394.

Dooley, C. R. (1945). *The Training within Industry Report, 1910–1945.* Washington, DC: War Manpower Commission Bureau of Training, Training within Industry Service.

Dooley, K. J. (1995). *Complex, Adaptive Systems.* Unpublished manuscript.

Dooley, K. J. (1996). A complex adaptive systems model of organization change. In *Nonlinear Dynamics, Psychology and Life Sciences.* Unknown publication data.

Drucker, P. F. (1964). *Managing for Results: Economic Tasks and Risk-Taking Decisions.* New York: Harper & Row.

Dubin, R. (Ed.). (1976). *Handbook of Work, Organization, and Society.* Chicago: Rand McNally.

Dubin, R. (1978). *Theory Building* (rev. ed.). New York: Free Press.

Ebenstein, W. (1969). *Great Political Thinkers: Plato to the Present.* Hinsdale, IL: Dryden.

Edvinsson, L., & Malone, M. S. (1997). *Intellectual Capital: Realizing Your Company's True Value by Finding Its Hidden Brainpower.* New York: Harper Business.

Egan, T. M. (2001). *Organization Development: An Examination of Definitions and Dependent Variables.* St. Paul: Human Resource Development Research Center, University of Minnesota.

Elias, J. L. (1979). Andragogy revisited. *Adult Education, 29,* 252–255.

Elias, J. L., & Merriam, S. B. (1995). *Philosophical Foundations of Adult Education* (2nd ed.). Malabar, FL: Krieger.

Ellinger, A. D., Ellinger, A. E., Yang, B., & Howton, S. W. (2000). An empirical assessment of the relationship between the learning organization and financial performance. In K. P. Kuchinke (Ed.), *1999 Academy of Human Resource Development Conference Proceedings.* Baton Rouge, LA: Academy of Human Resource Development.

Ericcson, K. A., & Smith, J. (1991). Prospects and limits of the empirical study expertise: An introduction. In K. A. Ericcson & J. Smith (Eds.), *Towards a General Theory of Expertise: Prospects and Limits* (pp. 1–38). Cambridge: Cambridge University Press.

Erikson, E. H. (1959). *Identity and the Life Cycle.* New York: International Universities Press.

Feur, D., & Gerber, B. (1988). Uh-oh . . . Second thoughts about adult learning theory. *Training, 25*(12), 125–149.

Fifty years of management education bring "organized body of knowledge" to managers in a galaxy of forms. (1973, February). *Management Review.*

Fitz-enz, J. (2000). *ROI of Human Capital: Measuring Economic Value of Employee Performance.* New York: AMACOM.

FitzGerald, J. M., & FitzGerald, A. F. (1973). *Fundamentals of Systems Theory.* New York: Wiley.

Flamholtz, E. (1985). *Human Resource Accounting* (2nd ed.). New York: Wiley.

Flynn, J. (1994, December). An ever-quicker trip from R&D to customer. *Business Week* (Special Issue: 21st Century Capitalism), 88.

Ford, J. K. (Ed.). (1997). *Improving Training Effectiveness in Work Organizations.* Mahwah, NJ: Erlbaum.

Ford, J. K., & Weissbein, D. A. (1997). Transfer of training: An update review and analysis. *Performance Improvement Quarterly, 10,* 22–41.

Fox, W. M. (1995). Sociotechnical system principles and guidelines: Past and present. *Journal of Applied Behavioral Science, 31,* 91–105.

Freedman, R. D., & Stumpf, S. A. (1980). Learning style theory: Less than meets the eye. *Academy of Management Review, 5,* 445–447.

Freire, P. (1970). *Pedagogy of the Oppressed.* New York: Herder & Herder.

French, W. L., Bell, C., & Zawacki, R. A. (Eds.). (1999). *Organization Development and Transformation: Managing Effective Change* (5th ed.). New York: McGraw-Hill.

Friedman, T. L. (2000). *The Lexus and the Olive Tree.* New York: Anchor.

Gagne, R. M. (1965). *The Conditions of Learning.* New York: Holt, Rinehart & Winston.

Gagne, R. M., Briggs, L. J., & Wager, W. (1988). *Principles of Instructional Design* (3rd ed.). Fort Worth, TX: Holt, Rinehart & Winston.

Gagne, R. M., & Medsker, K. L. (1996). *The Conditions of Learning: Training Applications.* Fort Worth, TX: Harcourt Brace.

Galbraith, J. (1974, May). Organization design: An information processing view. *Interfaces, 4,* 28–36.

Galbraith, J. (1982). Designing the innovating organization. *Organizational Dynamics, 10*(3), 5–25.

Gephart, M., Marsick, V., Van Buren, M., & Spiro, M. (1996). Learning organizations come alive. *Training & Development, 50*(12), 35–45.

Geroy, G. D., Jankovich, J., & Wright, P. C. (1997). Research design: An integrated quantitative and qualitative model for decision-making researchers. *Performance Improvement Quarterly, 10*(3), 23–36.

Geuss, R. (1981). *The Idea of a Critical Theory.* New York: Cambridge University Press.

Gilbert, T. F. (1978). *Human Competence: Engineering Worthy Performance.* New York: McGraw-Hill.

Gilbert, T. F. (1996). *Human competence: Engineering Worthy Performance* (tribute ed.). Amherst, MA: International Society for Performance, HRD Press.

Gilley, J. W., & Maycunich, A. (2000). *Organizational Learning, Performance, and Change.* Cambridge, MA: Perseus.

Gioia, D. A., & Pitre, E. (1990). Multiparadigm perspectives on theory building. *Academy of Management Review, 15,* 584–602.

Glaser, R. (1985). *The Nature of Expertise.* Occasional Paper No. 107, National Center for Research in Vocational Education. Columbus: Ohio State University.

Glaser, R., & Chi, M. T. H. (1988). Overview. In M. T. H. Chi, R. Glaser, & M. J. Farr (Eds.), *The Nature of Expertise* (pp. xv–xxviii). Hillsdale, NJ: Erlbaum.

Gleespen, A. V. (1996). How individual expertise may be socially constructed: A literature review. In E. F. Holton (Ed.), *1996 AHRD Conference Proceedings* (pp. 497–504). Austin, TX: Academy of Human Resources Development.

Gleick, J. (1987). *Chaos: Making a New Science.* New York: Penguin.

Glynn, M. A. (1996). Innovative genius: A framework for relating individual and organizational intelligences to innovation. *Academy of Management Review, 21*(4), 1081–1111.

Goldstein, T. L. (1993). *Training in Organizations* (3rd ed.). Pacific Grove, CA: Brooks/Cole.

Goldstein, T. L., Ford, K., & Goldstein, D. (2001). *Training in Organizations: Needs Assessment, Development, and Evaluation* (4th ed.). Belmont, CA: Wadsworth.

Golembiewski, R. T., Billingsley, K., & Yeager, S. (1976). Measuring change and persistence in human affairs: Types of change generated by OD designs. *Journal of Applied Behavioral Science, 12,* 133–157.

Gordon, J. (1991, August). Measuring the goodness of training. *Training, 30*(8), 19–25.

Grace, A. P. (1996). Striking a critical pose: Andragogy-missing links, missing values. *International Journal of Lifelong Education, 15,* 382–392.

Gradous, D. B. (Ed.). (1989). *Systems Theory Applied to Human Resource Development.* Alexandria, VA: ASTD Press.

Grattan, C. H. (1955). *In Quest of Knowledge: A Historical Perspective on Adult Education.* New York: Association Press.

Greenman, J. (Ed.). (1978). *Applied General Systems Theory.* New York: Harper & Row.

Grow, G. (1991). Teaching learners to be self-directed: A stage approach. *Adult Education Quarterly, 41.*

Guastello, S. J. (1995). *Chaos, Catastrophe, and Human Affairs.* Mahwah, NJ: Erlbaum.

Guns, B. (1996). *The Learning Organization: Gain and Sustain the Competitive Edge.* San Diego, CA: Pfeiffer.

Gutek, G. L. (1998). *Philosophical and Ideological Perspectives on Education.* Boston: Allyn & Bacon.

Hackman, J. R., & Oldham, G. R. (1980). *Work Redesign.* Reading, MA: Addison-Wesley.

Hall, C., & Lindzey, G. (1970). *Theories of Personality* (2nd ed.). New York: Wiley.

Hammer, M., & Champy, J. (1994). *Reengineering the Corporation.* New York: HarperCollins.

Hanson, C. D., & Headley, J. (1998). HRD in West Africa: Cultural constraints to organizational productivity. *Human Resource Development International, 1*(1), 19–34.

Harless, J. (1970). *An Ounce of Analysis (Is Worth a Pound of Objectives).* Newnan, GA: Guild V.

Harris, L. (2000). A theory of intellectual capital. In R. W. Herling & J. M. Provo (Eds.), *Strategic Perspectives on Knowledge, Competence, and Expertise* (pp. 22–37). San Francisco: Berrett-Koehler.

Hartree, A. (1984). Malcolm Knowles' theory of andragogy: A critique. *International Journal of Lifelong Education, 3,* 203–210.

Hartz, R., Niemiec, R. P., & Walberg, H. J. (1993). The impact of management education. *Performance Improvement Quarterly, 6*(1), 67–76.

Hatcher, T. G., & Ward, S. (1997). Framing: A method to improve performance analysis. *Performance Improvement Quarterly, 10*(3), 84–103

Haynes, B. R., & Jackson, H. P. (1935). *A History of Business Education in the United States.* Cincinatti: Southwestern.

Hearn, G. (1958). *Theory Building in Social Work.* Toronto: University of Toronto Press.

Hellriegel, D., Slocum, J. W., & Woodman, R. W. (1986). *Organizational Behavior* (4th ed.). New York: West.

Henschke, J. A. (1998). *Historical Antecedents Shaping Conceptions of Andragogy: A Comparison of Sources and Roots.* Paper presented at the International Conference on Research in Comparative Andragogy, September 1998, Radovljica, Slovenia.

Hergenhahn, B. R., & Olson, M. H. (1993). *An Introduction to Theories of Learning* (4th ed.). Englewood Cliffs, NJ: Prentice Hall.

Herling, R. W. (2000). Operational definitions of expertise and competence. In R. W. Herling & J. M. Provo (Eds.), *Strategic Perspectives on Knowledge, Competence, and Expertise* (pp. 8–21). San Francisco: Berrett-Koehler.

Herrnstein, R. J., & Murray, C. (1996). *The Bell Curve: Intelligence and Class Structure in American Life.* New York: Free Press.

Herrscher, E. G. (1995). Why is systemic thinking "difficult to sell"? In K. Ellis, A. Gregory, B. R. Mears-Young, & G. Ragsdell (Eds.), *Critical Issues in Systems Theory and Practice* (pp. 45–49). New York: Plenum.

Hewitt, D., & Mather, K. F. (1937). *Adult Education: A Dynamic for Democracy.* New York: Appleton-Century.

Heylighten, F. (1996). *Complex Adaptive Systems.* (On-line.) Available: http://www.pespmc1.vub.ac.be/CAS.html (1998, January 1).

Heylighten, F., & Joslyn, C. (1992). *What Is Systems Theory?* (On-line.) Available: http://www.pespmc1.vub.ac.be/systheor.html (1997, October 21).

Hill, D. R. (1999). *Evaluation of Formal, Employer-Sponsored Training in the U.S. Healthcare Industry.* Unpublished doctoral dissertation, University of Texas at Austin.

Hill, W. F. (1971). *Learning: A Survey of Psychological Interpretations* (rev. ed.). Scranton, OH: Chandler.

Hitt, M. A., Ireland, R. D., & Hoskisson, R. E. (1997). *Strategic Management: Competitiveness and Globalization.* St. Paul, MN: West.

Hoerl, R. W. (1995, Summer). Enhancing the bottom-line impact of statistical methods. *Quality Management Journal,* 58–69.

Hoffman, R. R., Shadbolt, N. R., Burton, A. M., & Klein, G. (1995, May). Eliciting knowledge from experts: A methodological analysis. *Rational Behavior and Human Decision Processes, 62*(2), 129–158.

Hofstede, G. (2001). *Culture's Consequences: Comparing Values, Behaviors, Institutions, and Organizations across Nations.* Thousand Oaks, CA: Sage.

Holding, D. H. (1981). *Human Skills.* New York: Wiley.

Holman, P., & Devane, T. (Eds.). (1999). *The Change Handbook: Group Methods for Shaping the Future.* San Francisco: Berrett-Koehler.

Holton, E. F. (Ed.). (1996a). *Academy of Human Resource Development 1996 Conference Proceedings.* Austin, TX: AHRD.

Holton, E. F. (1996b). The flawed 4-level evaluation model. *Human Resource Development Quarterly, 7*(1), 5–21.

Holton, E. F., III. (1996c). New employee development: A review and reconceptualization. *Human Resource Development Quarterly, 7*, 233–252.

Holton, E. F., III. (Ed.). (1997). *In Action: Leading Organizational Change.* Alexandria, VA: American Society for Training and Development.

Holton, E. F. III. (1998). What is performance? Levels of performance revisited. In R. Torraco (Ed.), *The Research Agenda for Improving Performance.* Washington, DC: ISPI Press.

Holton, E. F., III. (1999). An integrated model of performance: Bounding the theory and practice. *Advances in Developing Human Resource Development, 1*, 26–46.

Holton, E. F., III. (2000). On the nature of performance and learning in human resource development. In R. A. Swanson (Series Ed.), W. E. A. Ruona & G. A. Roth (Issue Eds.), *Advances in Developing Human Resources: Philosophical Foundations of Human Resource Development Practice.* San Francisco: Berrett-Koehler.

Holton, E. F., III. (in press-a). Theoretical Assumptions Underlying the Performance Paradigm of Human Resource Development. *Human Resource Development International.*

Holton, E. F., III. (in press-b). What is performance? Levels of performance revisited. In R. Torraco (Ed.), *The Research Agenda for Improving Performance.* Washington, DC: ISPI Press.

Holton, E. F., III, & Baldwin, T. T. (2000). Making transfer happen: An action perspective on learning transfer systems. In E. F. Holton III & T. T. Baldwin (Eds.), *Managing and Changing Learning Transfer Systems, Advances in Developing Human Resources, 2*(4), 1–6.

Holton, E. F., III, Bates, R. A., & Ruona, W. E. A. (2000). Development of a Learning Transfer System Inventory. *Human Resource Development Quarterly, 11.*

Holton, E. F., III, Bates, R. A., Seyler, D., & Carvalho, M. (1997). Toward construct validation of a transfer climate instrument. *Human Resource Development Quarterly, 8.*

Holton, E. F., III, & Kaiser, S. M. (2000). Relationship between learning organization strategies and performance driver outcomes. In *Proceedings of the 2000 Academy of Human Resource Development Annual Meeting, Raleigh, NC.* Baton Rouge, LA: AHRD.

Holton, E. F., III, & Naquin, S. S. (2000). Proposed Development and Retention Metrics. *Staffing 2000: HR Performance and Measurement Toolkit.* (On-line.) Available: Staffing.org.

Holton, E. F., III, & Naquin, S. S. (2001). *Accountability Systems in Human Resource Development.* Unpublished manuscript.

Holton, E. F., III, & Russell, Craig J. (1999). Organizational entry and exit: An exploratory longitudinal examination of early careers. *Human Performance, 12*(3), 311–341.

Holton, E. F., III., Swanson, R. A., & Naquin, S. S. (2001). Andragogy in practice: Clarifying the andragogical model of adult learning. *Performance Improvement Quarterly, 14*(1), 118–143.

Horton, W. (2000). *Designing Web-based Training: How to Teach Anyone Anything Anywhere Anytime.* New York: Wiley.

Houle, C. O. (1972). *The Design of Education.* San Francisco: Jossey-Bass.

Hronec, S. M. (1993). *Vital Signs: Using Quality Time and Cost Performance Measurements to Chart Your Company's Future.* New York: American Management Association.

Hunt, M. (1993). *The Story of Psychology.* New York: Doubleday.

Huselid, M. A. (1995). The impact of human resource management practices on turnover, productivity, and corporate financial performance. *Academy of Management Journal, 38,* 635–672.

International Institute for Management. (1996). *World Competitiveness Yearbook, 1996.* Lausanne: IMD Press.

Jackson, M. C. (1995). Beyond the fads: Systems thinking for managers. *Systems Research, 12*(1), 25–42.

Jacobs, R. L. (1989). Systems theory applied to human resource development. In D. Gradous (Ed.), *Systems Theory Applied to Human Resource Development* (pp. 27–60). Alexandria, VA: ASTD Press.

Jacobs, R. L. (1996). Human resource development with integrity. In E. F. Holton (Ed.), *Academy of Human Resource Development 1996 Conference Proceedings.* Austin, TX: AHRD.

Jacobs, R. L. (1997a). A proposed domain of human performance technology: Implications for theory and practice. *Performance Improvement Quarterly, 1*(2), 2–12.

Jacobs, R. L. (1997b). The taxonomy of employee development: Toward an organizational culture of expertise. In R. J. Torraco (Ed.), *1997 AHRD Conference Proceedings* (pp. 278–283). Baton Rouge, LA: Academy of Human Resources Development.

Jacobs, R. L., & Jones, M. J. (1995). *Structured On-the-Job Training: Unleashing Employee Expertise in the Workplace.* San Francisco: Berrett-Koehler.

Jacobs, R. W. (1994). *Real Time Strategic Change.* San Francisco: Berrett-Koehler.

Jaques, E. (1985, March 3). His brilliant theory scares management. *Sunday Express News,* San Antonio, TX.

Jaros, G. G., & Dostal, E. (1995). The organization as a doublet. *Systems Practice, 8*(1), 69–83.

Jarvis, P. (1987). *Adult Learning in the Social Context.* London: Croon-Helm.

Johnson, T. R., McLaughlin, S. D., Snari, L. M., & Zimmerle, D. M. *The Demand and Supply of University-Based Executive Education.* Los Angeles: Graduate Management Admission Council.

Jonassen, D. H., & Grabowski, B. L. (1993). *Handbook of Individual Differences, Learning, and Instruction.* Hillsdale, NJ: Erlbaum.

Joslyn, C. (1992). *The Nature of Cybernetic Systems.* Available: http://www.pespmc1.vub.ac.be/systheor.html (1998, January 1).

Juran, J. M. (1992). *Juran on Quality by Design: The New Steps for Planning Quality into Goods and Services.* New York: Free Press.

Kammeyer, K. C. W., Ritzer, G., & Yetman, N. R. (1997). *Sociology: Experiencing Changing Societies* (7th ed.). Boston: Allyn & Bacon.

Kaplan, R. S., & Norton, D. P. (1996). *The Balanced Scorecard.* Boston: Harvard Business School Press.

Kast, F. E., & Rosenweig, J. E. (1972). General systems theory: Applications for organization and management. *Academy of Management Journal, 447–465.*

Katz, D., & Kahn, R. L. (1966). *The Social Psychology of Organizations.* New York: Wiley.

Katzell, R. A., & Thompson, D. E. (1990) Work motivation: Theory and practice. *American Psychologist, 42*(2), 144–153.

Katzell, R. A., Thompson, D. E., & Guzzo, R. A. (1992). How job satisfaction and job performance are and are not linked. In C. J. Cranny, P. C. Smith, & E. F. Stone (Eds.), *Job Satisfaction: How People Feel about Their Jobs and How It Affects Their Performance.* New York: Lexington.

Kaufmann, R. (1997). A strategic planning framework: Mega planning. In R. Kaufman, S. Thiagarajan, & P. MacGillis (Eds.), *The Guidebook for Performance Improvement: Working with Individuals and Organizations* (pp. 61–91). San Francisco: Jossey-Bass.

Kaufmann, R., & Keller, J. M. (1994). Levels of evaluation: Beyond Kirkpatrick. *Human Resource Development Quarterly, 5,* 371–380.

Kaufmann, R., Rojas, A. M., & Mayer, H. (1993). *Needs Assessment: A User's Guide.* Englewood Cliffs, NJ: Educational Technologies.

Kaufmann, R., Watkins, R., Sims, L., Crispo, N. S., Hall, J. C., & Sprague, D. E. (1997). Cost-consequence analysis: A case study. *Performance Improvement Quarterly, 10*(3), 7–21.

Kaufmann, R., Watkins, R., Triner, D., & Smith, M. (1998). The changing corporate mind: Organizations, visions, mission, purposes, and indicators on the move toward societal payoff. *Performance Improvement Quarterly, 11*(3), 32–44.

Kellert, S. H. (1993). *In the Wake of Chaos: Unpredictable Order in Dynamical Systems.* Chicago: University of Chicago.

Kessels, J. W. (1993). *Towards design standards for curriculum consistency in corporate education.* Ecschede, The Netherlands: Twente University Press.

Kidd, J. R. (1978). *How Adults Learn.* Englewood Cliffs, NJ: Prentice Hall.

King, N., & Anderson, N. (1995). *Innovation and Change in Organizations.* London: Routledge.

Kirkpatrick, D. L. (1959a). Techniques for evaluating training programs: Part 1. Reactions. *Journal of the American Society for Training and Development, 13*(11), 3–9.

Kirkpatrick, D. L. (1959b). Techniques for evaluating training programs: Part 2. Learning. *Journal of the American Society for Training and Development, 13*(12), 21–26.

Kirkpatrick, D. L. (1960a). Techniques for evaluating training programs: Part 3. Behavior. *Journal of the American Society for Training and Development, 14*(1), 13–18.

Kirkpatrick, D. L. (1960b). Techniques for evaluating training programs: Part 4. Results. *Journal of the American Society for Training and Development, 14*(2), 28–32.

Kirkpatrick, D. L. (1998). *Evaluating Training Programs: The Four Levels* (2nd ed.). San Francisco: Berrett-Koehler.

Klein, K. J., Tosi, H., & Cannella, A. A., Jr. (1999). Multilevel theory building: Benefits, barriers, and new developments. *Academy of Management Review, 2,* 243–248.

Kline, P., & Saunders, B. (1993). *Ten Steps to a Learning Organization.* Arlington, VA: Great Ocean.

Knowles, M. S. (1970). *The Modern Practice of Adult Education: Andragogy versus Pedagogy.* Chicago: Follett.

Knowles, M. S. (1977). *A History of the Adult Education Movement in the United States.* Malabar, FL: Krieger.

Knowles, M. S. (1980). *The Modern Practice of Adult Education: From Pedagogy to Andragogy* (2nd ed.). Chicago: Follett.

Knowles, M. S. (1984). *The Adult Learner: A Neglected Species* (3rd ed.). Houston: Gulf.

Knowles, M. S. (1990). *The Adult Learner: A Neglected Species* (4th ed.). Houston: Gulf.

Knowles, M. S. (1995). *Designs for Adult Learning.* Alexandria, VA: American Society for Training and Development.

Knowles, M. S., Holton, E. F., & Swanson, R. A. (1998). *The Adult Learner: The Definitive Classic in Adult Education and Human Resource Development.* (5th ed.) Houston: Gulf.

Knox, A. B. (1986a). *Adult Development and Learning.* San Francisco: Jossey-Bass.

Knox, A. B. (1986b). *Helping Adults Learn.* San Francisco: Jossey-Bass.

Kolb, D. A. (1981). Experiential learning theory and the learning style inventory: A reply to Freedman and Stumpf. *Academy of Management Review, 6,* 289–296.

Kolb, D. A. (1984). *Experiential Learning: Experience as the Source of Learning and Development.* Englewood Cliffs, NJ: Prentice Hall.

Korten, D. C. (1995). *When Corporations Rule the World.* San Francisco: Berrett-Koehler.

Kotter, J. P. (1996). *Leading Change.* Boston: Harvard Business School Press.

Kramer, D. A. (1989). Development of an awareness of contradiction across the life span and the question of postformal operations. In M. L. Commons, J. D. Sinnott, F. A. Richards, & C. Armon, *Adult Development* (pp. 133–157). New York: Praeger and the Dare Association.

Krempl, S. F., & Pace, R. W. (2001). *Training across Multiple Locations: Developing a System That Works.* San Francisco: Berrett-Koehler.

Kruse, K., & Keil, J. (2000). *Technology-based Training.* San Francisco: Jossey-Bass.

Kubler-Ross, E. (1969). *On Death and Dying.* New York: Macmillan.

Kuchinke, K. P. (1997). Employee expertise: The status of the theory and the literature. *Performance Improvement Quarterly, 10*(4), 72–77.

Kuchinke, K. P. (1998). Moving beyond the dualism of performance and learning: A response to Barrie and Pace. *Human Resource Development Quarterly, 9,* 377–384.

Kuhn, T. (1970). *The Structure of Scientific Revolutions* (2nd ed.). Chicago: University of Chicago Press.

Kuhn, T. S. (1996). *The Structure of Scientific Revolutions* (3rd ed.). Chicago: University of Chicago Press.

Kusy, M. (1988). The effects of types of training evaluation on support of training among corporate managers. *Performance Improvement Quarterly, 1*(2), 23–30.

LaBelle, T. (1988, September). Nonformal education for industrialization in Latin America: The human capital approach. *Albeta Journal of Educational Research, 34*(3), 203–214.

Labouvie-Vief, G. Models of cognitive functioning in the older adult: Research need in educational gerontology. Reprinted in R. H. Sherron & D. B. Lumsden, *Introduction to Educational Gerontology* (3rd ed., pp. 243–263). New York: Hemisphere, 1990.

Lam, L. W., & White, L. P. (1998). Human resource orientation and corporate performance. *Human Resource Development Quarterly, 9,* 351–364.

Langdon, D. G. (1995). *The New Language of Work.* Amherst, MA: HRD Press.

Laszlo, E., & Laszlo, A. (1997). The contribution of the systems sciences to the humanities. *Systems Research in the Behavioral Sciences, 14*(1), 5–19.

Latham, G., & Wythe, G. (1994). The futility of utility analysis. *Personnel Psychology, 47,* 31–46.

Lau, R. S. M., & May, B. E. (1998). A win-win paradigm for quality of work life and business performance. *Human Resource Development Quarterly, 9,* 211–226.

Laird, D. (1978). *Approaches to Training and Development.* Reading, MA: Addison-Wesley.

Laird, D., & Schleger, P. R. (1985). *Approaches to Training and Development* (2nd ed.). Cambridge: Perseus.

Latham, G., & Wythe, G. (1994). The futility of utility analysis. *Personnel Psychology, 47,* 31–46.

Leana, C. R., & Barry, B. (2000). Stability and change as simultaneous experiences in organizational life. *Academy of Management Review, 25,* 753–759.

Lee, M. (2001). A refusal to define HRD. *Human Resource Development International,* 4(3).

Levinson, D. J. (1978). *The Season's of a Man's Life.* New York: Knopf.

Levinson, D. J. (1990). A theory of life structure development in adulthood. In C. N. Alexander & E. J. Langer (Eds.), *Higher Stages of Human Development* (pp. 35–54). New York: Oxford University Press.

Levinthal, D. (1988). A survey of agency models of organizations. *Journal of Economic Behavior and Organization, 9,* 153–185.

Lewin, D., & Mitchell, D. J. B. (1995). *Human Resource Management: An Economic Approach* (2nd ed.). Cincinnati, OH: South-Western.

Lewin, K. (1951). *Field Theory in Social Science: Selected Theoretical Papers.* New York: Harper.

Lewis, D. R. (1977). An introduction to the economics of education. In W. G. Meyer (Ed.), *Vocational Education and the Nation's Economy.* Washington, DC: American Vocational Association.

Lindeman, E. (1926). *The Meaning of Adult Education.* New York: New Republic.

Lippitt, L. L. (1998). *Preferred Futuring: Envision the Future You Want and Unleash the Energy to Get There.* San Francisco: Berrett-Koehler.

Liveright, A. A. (1968). *A Study of Adult Education in the United States.* Boston: Center for the Study of Liberal Arts.

Loevinger, J. (1976). *Ego Development.* San Francisco: Jossey-Bass.

Lorsch, J. (1997, Autumn). Organization design: A situational perspective. In *Organizational Dynamics.* New York: American Management Association.

Lundin, R. W. (1991). *Theories and Systems of Psychology.* Lexington, MA: Heath.

Lyau, A., & Pucel, D. (1995). *Performance Improvement Quarterly.*

Lynham, S. A. (2000a). *The Development and Validation of a Model of Responsible Leadership for Performance.* St. Paul: University of Minnesota Human Resource Development Research Center.

Lynham, S. A. (2000b). Theory building in the human resource development profession. *Human Resource Development Quarterly, 11*(2), 159–178.

Lynham, S. A. (2000c). Organization Development for Performance System. St. Paul: University of Minnesota Human Resource Development Research Center.

Mager, R. F. (1997). *Preparing Instructional Objectives* (3rd ed.). Atlanta: Center for Effective Performance.

Mancuso, J. C. (1994). Anatomy of a training program: A start-to-finish look. In L. Kelly (Ed.), *The ASTD Technical and Skills Training Handbook.* New York: McGraw-Hill.

Marquardt, M. J. (1995). *Building the Learning Organization: A Systems Approach to Quantum Improvement and Global Success.* New York: McGraw-Hill.

Marquardt, M. J. (1996). *Building the Learning Organization.* New York: McGraw-Hill.

Marshall, A. (1949). *Principles of Economics* (8th ed.). New York.

Marsick, V. J., & Neaman, P. G. (1997). Individuals who learn create organizations that learn. In R. Rowden (Ed.), *Workplace learning: Debating Five Critical Questions of Theory and Practice* (pp. 21–28). San Francisco: Jossey-Bass.

Marsick, V. J., & Watkins, K. (1990). *Informal and Incidental Learning in the Workplace.* London: Routledge.

Marsick, V. J., & Watkins, K. E. (1997). Lessons from informal and incidental learning. In J. Burgoyne & M. Reynolds (Eds.), *Management Learning: Integrating Perspectives in Theory and Practice* (pp. 295–311). Thousand Oaks, CA: Sage.

Martelli, J. (1998). Training for new technology: Midwest steel company. In W. Rothwell (Ed.), *Linking HRD Programs with Organizational Strategy.* Alexandria, VA: ASTD.

Maslow, A. H. (1968). *Toward a Psychology of Being* (2nd ed.). Princeton, NJ: Princeton University Press.

Maslow, A. H. (1970). *Motivation and Personality* (2nd ed.). New York: Harper & Row.

Mattson, B. W. (2000). Development and validation of the critical outcome technique. *Human Resource Development International, 3*(4), 465–487.

Mattson, B. W. (2001). *The Effects of Alternative Reports of Human Resource Development Results on Managerial Support.* Unpublished doctoral dissertation, University of Minnesota, St. Paul.

McClelland, D. C. (1965). Toward a theory of motive acquisition. *American Psychologist, 20,* 29–47.

McGehee, W., & Thayer, P. W. (1961). *Training in Business and Industry.* New York: Wiley.

McGill, M. E., & Slocum, J. W. (1994). Unlearning the organization. *Organizational Dynamics,* 67–79.

McGoldrick, J., Stewart, J., & Watson, S. (2001), Theorizing human resource development. *Human Resource Development International, 4*(3).

McIntyre, R. M., & Salas, E. (1995). Measuring and managing for team performance: Emerging principles from complex environments. In R. A. Guzzo, E. Salas, & Associates (Eds.), *Team Effectiveness and Decision Making in Organizations* (pp. 9–45). San Francisco: Jossey-Bass.

McLagan, P. A. (1989). Systems Model 2000: Matching Systems Theory to Future HRD Issues. In D. B. Gradous, (Ed.) *Systems Theory Applied to Human Resource Development.* Alexandria, VA: ASTD Press. p. 61–90.

McLagan, P. A. (1989). *The Models.* A volume in Models for HRD Practice. Alexandria, VA: American Society for Training and Development.

McLagan, P. A. (1997). Competencies: The next generation. *Training & Development, 51*(5), 40–47.

McLean, G. N., & McLean, L. (2001). If we can't define HRD in one country, how can we define it in another? *Human Resource Development International, 4*(3).

McLean, G. N. (1988). *Construction and analysis of organization climate surveys.* St. Paul: University of Minnesota HRD Research Center.

McLean, G. N. (1997). Multirater 360 feedback. In L. J. Bassi & D. Russ-Eft (Eds.), *What Works: Assessment, Development, and Measurement* (pp. 87–108). Alexandria, VA: American Society for Training and Development.

McLean, G. N. (1998). HRD: A three legged stool, an octopus, or a centipede? *Human Resource Development International, 1*(4), 6–7.

Merriam, S. B. (1993). *Adult Learning: Where Have We Come From? Where Are We Headed?* New Directions for Adult and Continuing Education, No. 57. San Francisco: Jossey-Bass.

Merriam, S. B., & Brockett, R. G. (1997). *The Profession and Practice of Adult Education: An Introduction.* San Francisco: Jossey-Bass.

Merriam, S. B., & Caffarella, R. S. (1999). *Learning in Adulthood: A Comprehensive Guide.* San Francisco: Jossey-Bass.

Mezirow, J. (1981). A critical theory of adult learning and education. *Adult Education*, 3–24.

Mezirow, J. (1991). *Transformative Dimensions of Adult Learning.* San Francisco: Jossey-Bass.

Mezirow, J. (1996). Contemporary paradigms of learning. *Adult Education Quarterly, 46*, 158–173.

Mezirow, J., & Associates. (2000). *Learning as Transformation: Critical Perspectives on a Theory in Progress.* San Francisco: Jossey-Bass.

Micklethwait, J., & Wooldridge, A. (1996). *The Witch Doctors: Making Sense of the Management Gurus.* New York: Times Books.

Milgrom, P., & John, R. (1992). *Economics, Organization and Management.* Englewood Cliffs, NJ: Prentice Hall.

Miller, J. G. (1978). *Living Systems.* New York: McGraw-Hill.

Miller, R. F., Lynham, S. A., Provo, J., & St. Claire, J. M. (1997). Examination of the use of scenarios as learning and decision-making tools for human resource development. In R. Torraco (Ed.), *Academy of Human Resource Development 1997 Conference Proceedings* (pp. 80–91). Baton Rouge, LA: AHRD.

Mincer, J. (1989). Human capital and the labor market: A review of current research. *Educational Researcher, 37*, 27–34.

Mink, O., & Watkins, K. (1981). Implementing a competency-based program. In *Models and Concepts for T&D/HRD Academic Programs.* Washington, DC: American Society for Training and Development.

Mintzberg, H. (1987, July–August). Crafting strategy. *Harvard Business Review,* 66–75.

Mintzberg, H. (1994). *The Rise and Fall of Strategic Planning.* New York: Free Press.

Mintzberg, H., Ashstrand, B., & Lampel, J. (1999, September 27). Strategy, blind men and the elephant. In *Mastering Strategy* (pp. 6–7). London: Financial Times.

Moller, L., & Mallin, P. (1996). Evaluation practices of instructional designers and organizational supports and barriers. *Performance Improvement Quarterly, 9*(4), 82–92.

Moore, E. C. (1936). *The Story of Instruction: The Beginnings.* New York: Macmillan.

Moore, M. L., & Dutton, P. (1978). Training needs analysis: Review and critique. *Academy of Management Review,* 532–545.

Morf, M. (1986). *Optimizing Work Performance: A Look beyond the Bottom Line* (pp. 107–119). New York: Quorum.

Mosier, N. R. (1990). Financial analysis: The methods and their application to employee training. *Human Resource Development Quarterly, 1*(1), 45–63.

Mulder, M., & Tjepkema, S. (1999). International briefing 1: Training and development in the Netherlands. *International Journal of Training and Development, 3*(1), 62–73.

Myrdak, G. (1996). *An American Dilemma: The Negro Problem and American Democracy.* New York: Transaction. (Originally published 1944.)

Nadler, D. A., Gerstein, M., & Shaw, R. (1992). *Organizational Architecture: Designs for Changing Organizations.* San Francisco: Jossey-Bass.

Nadler, D. A., Shaw, R. B., & Walton, A. E. (1995). *Discontinuous Change: Leading Organizational Transformation.* San Francisco: Jossey-Bass.

Nadler, L., & Nadler, Z. (1989). *Developing Human Resources.* San Francisco: Jossey-Bass.

Naquin, S. S., & Holton, E. F., III (in press). The effects of personality, affectivity, and work commitment on motivation to improve work through learning. *Human Resource Development Quarterly.*

Nevin, C. (1992). *Time.* New York: Time-Warner.

Nijhof, W. J., & Jager, A. (1999). Reliability testing of multi-rater feedback. *International Journal of Training and Development, 3*(4), 292–300.

Nijhof, W. J., & Streumer, J. N. (1998). New roles and training models for managers in the printing and communications industry in the Netherlands. *International Journal of Training and Development, 2*(3), 215–232.

Noe, R. A. (1999). *Employee Training and Development.* New York: McGraw-Hill.

Odenthal, L. E., & Nijhof, W. J. (1996). *HRD Roles in Germany.* De Lier, The Netherlands: Academisch Boeken Centrum.

Ormond, J. E. (1999). *Human Learning* (3rd ed.). Upper Saddle River, NJ: Merrill/Prentice Hall.

Osipow, S. H., & Fitzgerald, L. F. (1996). *Theories of Career Development* (4th ed.). Boston: Allyn & Bacon.

Osman-Gani, A. A. M., & Tan, W. (2000). International briefing 7: Training and development in Singapore. *International Journal of Training and Development, 4*(4), 305–323.

Ostroff, C., & Ford, J. K. (1989). Assessing training needs: Critical levels of analysis. In I. Goldstein & Associates, *Training and Development in Organizations.* San Francisco: Jossey-Bass.

Owen, H. (1996). *Open Space Technology: A User's Guide.* San Francisco: Berrett-Koehler.

Paquin, D. C. (1994). Skilled trades programs: Apprentice to master. In L. Kelly (Ed.), *The ASTD Technical and Skills Training Handbook.* New York: McGraw-Hill.

Parnes, H. (1986). *Developing Human Capital.* Columbus, OH: National Center for Research in Vocational Education.

Passmore, D. L. (1997). Ways of seeing: Disciplinary bases of research in HRD. In R. Swanson & E. Holton (Eds.), *Human Resource Development Research Handbook: Linking Research and Practice* (pp. 199–214). San Francisco: Berrett-Koehler.

Patterson, C. H. (1983). *Theories of Counseling and Psychotherapy.* Chicago: University of Chicago Press.

Pearlin, L. I. (1980). Life strains and psychological distress among adults. In N. J. Smesler & E. H. Erikson (Eds.), *Themes of Work and Love in Adulthood* (pp. 174–192). Cambridge, MA: Harvard University Press.

Pedler, M., Bourgoyne, J., & Boydell, T. (1991). *The Learning Company: A Strategy for Sustainable Development.* London: McGraw-Hill.

Perelman, L. (1984). *The Learning Enterprise: Adult Learning, Human Capital, and Economic Development.* Washington, DC: Council of State Planning Agencies.

Perry, W. (1970). Cognitive and ethnical growth: The making of meaning. In *Forms of Intellectual and Ethnical Developments with the College Years: A Scheme* (pp. 76–116). New York: Holt, Rinehart & Winston.

Personnel Decisions International. (1996). (On-line.) Available: http://ww.pdi-corp.com (2001, April 28).

Personnel Decisions International. (1999). (On-line.) Available: http://www.pdi-corp.com/ei/success_defined/success97bx1.html (2001, May 2).

Pestalozzi, J. H. (1898). *Life, Educational Principles and Methods.* Bardeen, Switzerland: N.p.

Peterson, S. L., & Provo, J. (1999). *A Case Study of Academic Program Integration in the United States: Andragogical, Philosophical, Theoretical and Practical Perspectives.* Unpublished manuscript.

Pfeffer, J. (1994). *Competitive Advantage through People: Unleashing the Power of the Work Force.* Boston: Harvard Business School Press.

Pfeiffer, J., & Jones, J. (1973). Design considerations in laboratory education. In *1973 Annual Handbook for Group Facilitators.* San Diego, CA: University Associates.

Phelan, S. E. (1995). *From Chaos to Complexity in Strategic Planning.* (On-line.) Available: http://comsp.com.latrobe.edu.au/Papers/chaos.html (1997, October 21).

Phillips, J. J. (1997a). *Handbook of Training Evaluation and Measurement Methods* (3rd ed.). Houston: Gulf.

Phillips, J. J. (1997b). *Return on Investment in Training and Performance Improvement.* Houston: Gulf.

Piderit, S. K. (2000). Rethinking resistance and recognizing ambivalence: A multi-dimensional view of attitudes toward an organizational change. *Academy of Management Review, 25,* 783–794.

Pirsig, R. M. (1991). *Lila: An Inquiry into Morals.* New York: Bantam.

Piskurich, G. M. (1993). *Self-directed Learning: A Practical Guide to Design, Development and Implementation.* San Francisco: Jossey-Bass.

Poell, R. F., Van der Krogt, F. J., & Wildemeersch. D. (1999). Strategies in organizing work-related learning projects. *Human Resource Development Quarterly, 10*(1), 43–61.

Porras, J. I., & Silvers, R. C. (1991). Organization development and transformation. *Annual Review of Psychology, 42,* 51–78.

Porter, L. W., & McGibbon, L. E. (1988). *Management Education and Development: Drift or Thrust into the Twenty-first Century.* New York: McGraw-Hill.

Porter, M. E. (1980). *Competitive Strategy: Techniques for Analyzing Industries and Competitors.* New York: Free Press.

Posner, M. I. (1988). Introduction: What is it like to be an expert. In M. T. H. Chi, R. Glaser, & M. J. Farr (Eds.), *The Nature of Expertise* (pp. xxix–xxxvi). Hillsdale, NJ: Erlbaum.

Pratt, D. D. (1988). Andragogy as a relational construct. *Adult Education Quarterly, 38,* 160–181.

Pratt, D. D. (1993). Andragogy after twenty-five years. In S. B. Merriam (Ed.), *An Update on Adult Learning Theory.* New Directions for Adult and Continuing Education, No. 57. San Francisco: Jossey-Bass.

Preskill, H. S., & Torres, R. (1999). *Evaluative Inquiry for Learning Organizations.* Thousand Oaks, CA: Sage.

Prigogine, I., & Stengers, I. (1984). *Order Out of Chaos.* New York: Bantam.

Rachal, J. R. (1988). Taxonomies and typologies of adult education. *Lifelong Learning: An Omnibus of Practice and Research, 12*(2), 20–23.

Raelin, J. A. (2000). *Work-based Learning: The New Frontier of Management Development.* Upper Saddle River, NJ: Prentice Hall.

Rashford, N. S., & Coghlan, D. (1994). *The Dynamics of Organizational Levels: A Change Framework for Managers and Consultants.* Reading, MA: Addison-Wesley.

Rassmussen, T. (1997). VisionLink: A participative process to clarify and act on a vision and values. In E. F. Holton III (Ed.), *Leading Organizational Change* (pp. 125–143). Alexandria, VA: American Society for Training and Development.

Reichers, A. E., Wanous, J. P., & Austin, J. T. (1997). Understanding and managing cynicism about organizational change. *Academy of Management Executive, 11*(1), 48–59.

Reichheld, F. F. (1996). *The Loyalty Effect: The Hidden Force behind Growth, Profits, and Lasting Value.* Boston: Harvard Business School Press.

Reynolds, P. D. (1971). *A Primer in Theory Construction.* New York: Macmillan.

Rhinesmith, S. H. (1995). Open the door to a global mindset. *Training & Development, 495,* 34–44.

Riegel, K. F. (1976). The dialectics of human development. *American Psychologist, 31,* 689–700.

Robinson, D. G., & Robinson, J. C (1995). *Performance Consulting: Moving beyond Training.* San Francisco: Berrett-Koehler.

Rogers, C. (1983). *Freedom to Learn for the 80s.* Columbus, OH: Merrill.

Rogers, C. R. (1961). *On Becoming a Person: A Therapist's View of Psychotherapy.* Boston: Houghton Mifflin.

Rogers, C. R. (1980). *A Way of Being.* Boston: Houghton Mifflin.

Rogers, E. M. (1995). *Diffusion of Innovations* (4th ed.). New York: Free Press.

Rosenberg, M., Coscarelli, W., & Hutchinson, C. (1992). The origins and evolution of the field. In H. Stolovich & E. Keeps (Eds.), *Handbook of Human Performance Technology* (pp. 14–31). San Francisco: Jossey-Bass.

Rossett, A., & Sheldon, K. (2001). *Beyond the Podium: Delivering Training and Performance to a Digital World.* San Francisco: Pfeiffer.

Rothwell, W. J., & Kasanas, H. C. (1994). *Improving On-the-Job training: How to Establish and Operate a Comprehensive OJT Program.* San Francisco: Jossey-Bass.

Rothwell, W. J., Sullivan, R., & McLean, G. N. (1995). *Practicing Organization Development: A Guide for Consultants.* San Diego: Pfieffer.

Rouillier, J. Z., & Goldstein, I. L. (1993). The relationship between organizational transfer climate and positive transfer of training. *Human Resource Development Quarterly, 4,* 377–390.

Rowden, R. W. (Ed.). (1990). *Workplace Learning: Debating Five Critical Questions of Theory and Practice.* New Directions for Adult and Continuing Education, 72. San Francisco: Jossey-Bass.

Rummelhart, D. E., & Norman, D. A. (1978). Accretion, tuning, and restructuring: Three models of learning. In J. W. Cotton & R. L. Klatzky (Eds.), *Semantic Factors in Cognition.* Hillsdale, NJ: Erlbaum.

Rummler, G. A., & Brache, A. P. (1992). *Improving Performance: How to Manage the White Space on the Organization Chart.* San Francisco: Jossey-Bass.

Rummler, G. A., & Brache, A. P. (1995). *Improving Performance: How to Manage the White Space on the Organization Chart* (2nd ed.). San Francisco: Jossey-Bass.

Ruona, W. E. A. (1998). Systems theory as a foundation for HRD. In R. Torraco (Ed.), *Proceedings of the 1998 Academy of Human Resource Development Conference.* Baton Rouge, LA: Academy of Human Resource Development.

Ruona, W. E. A. (1999). *An Investigation into Core Beliefs Underlying the Profession of Human Resource Development.* Unpublished doctoral dissertation, University of Minnesota, St. Paul.

Ruona, W. E. A. (2000). Core beliefs in human resource development. In W. E. A. Ruona, & G. A. Roth (Issue Eds.), *Advances in Developing Human Resources: Philosophical Foundations of Human Resource Development Practice.* San Francisco: Berrett-Koehler.

Ruona, W. E. A., & Lyford-Nojima, E. (1997). Performance diagnosis matrix: A discussion of human resource development scholarship. *Performance Improvement Quarterly, 10*(4), 87–118.

Ruona, W. E. A., & Roth, G. (Eds.). (2000). Philosophical foundations of human resource development practice. *Advances in Developing Human Resources, 2*(3).

Ruona, W. E. A., & Swanson, R. A. (1997). *Foundations of Human Resource Development.* St. Paul: Human Resource Development Research Center, University of Minnesota.

Ruona, W. E., & Swanson, R. A. (1998). Foundation of human resource development. In H. C. Hall (Ed.), *Human Resource Development.* Columbia, MO: University Council for Research in Vocational Education.

Ryan, R. M., & Deci, E. L. (2000). Self-determination theory and the facilitation of intrinsic motivation, social development, and well-being. *American Psychologist, 55,* 68–78.

Saari, L. M., Johnson, T. R., McLaughlin, S. D., & Zimmerle, D. M. (1988). A survey of management training and education practices in U.S. companies. *Personnel Psychology, 41,* 731–743.

Samuelson, P. A. (1980). *Economics* (10th ed.). New York: McGraw-Hill.

Schein, E. (1970). *Organizational Psychology* (2nd ed.). Englewood Cliffs, NJ: Prentice Hall.

Schmuck, R., & Miles, M. (1971). Organization development in schools. In M. Miles & R. Schmuck (Eds.), *Improving Schools through OD: An Overview* (pp. 1–28). Palo Alto, CA: National Press Books.

Schneir, C. E. (1995). Linking business strategy, unit goals, and performance management systems. In H. Fisher & C. Fay (Eds.), *The Performance Imperative: Strategies for Enhancing Workforce Effectiveness* (pp. 239–255). San Francisco: Jossey-Bass.

Scholtes, P. R. (1988). *The Team Handbook.* Madison, WI: Joiner and Associates.

Schon, D. (1983). *The Reflective Practitioner: How Professionals Think in Action.* New York: Basic Books.

Schon, D. A. (1987). *Educating the Reflective Practitioner.* San Francisco: Jossey-Bass.

Schultz, L., & Parker, B. (1988). Visioning the future. In G. McLean & S. DeVogel (Eds.), *The Role of Organization Development in Quality Management and Productivity Improvement* (pp. 47–67). Alexandria, VA: American Society for Training and Development.

Schultz, T. W. (1961). Investment in human capital. *American Economic Review, 51*(1), 1–17.

Schwartz, P. (1996). *The Art of the Long View: Planning for the Future in an Uncertain World.* New York: Doubleday.

Scott, J. F. (1914). *Historical Essays on Apprenticeship and Vocational Education.* Ann Arbor, MI: Ann Arbor Press.

Senge, P. (1987). Catalyzing systems thinking within organizations. In F. Masarik (Ed.), *Advances in Organization Development.* Norwood, NJ: Ablex.

Senge, P. (1992, March). Building the learning organization. *Journal for Quality and Participation,* 30–38.

Senge, P. (1993). Building the learning organization. In R. Frantzreb (Ed.), *Training & Development Yearbook, 1993/1994 Edition* (pp. 3.67–3.74). Englewood Cliffs, NJ: Prentice Hall.

Senge, P. (Ed.) (1994). *The Fifth Discipline Fieldbook.* New York: Doubleday.

Senge, P. M. (1990). *The Fifth Discipline: The Art and Practice of the Learning Organization.* New York: Doubleday/Currency.

Seybolt, R. F. (1917). *Apprenticeship and Apprenticeship Education in Colonial New England and New York.* New York: Columbia University, Teachers College.

Seyler D., Holton E., & Bates, R. (1997). Factors affecting motivation to use computer-based training. In R. J. Toracco (Ed.), *The Academy of Human Resource Development 1997 Conference Proceedings.* Baton Rouge, LA: Academy of Human Resource Development.

Shani, A., & Bushe, G. (1987, Spring). Visionary action research: A consultation process perspective. *Consultation, 6,* 22–33.

Shani, A. B., & Mitki, Y. (1996). Reengineering, total quality management and sociotechnical systems approaches to organizational change: Towards and eclectic approach? *Journal of Quality Management, 1,* 131–145.

Short, D. (Issue Ed.). (2001). Metaphor in human resource development. *Advances in Developing Human Resources, 3*(3).

Shughart, W. F., Chappell, W. F., & Cottle, R. L. (1994). *Modern Managerial Economics: Economic Theory for Business Decisions.* Cincinnati: South-Western.

Silber, K. H. (1992). Intervening at different levels in organizations. In H. Stolovich (Ed.), *Handbook of Human Performance Technology* (pp. 50–65). San Francisco: Jossey-Bass.

Simon, H. (1965, March). Administrative decision making. *Public Administration Review,* 31–37.

Sink, D. S., Tuttle, T. C., & DeVries, S. J. (1984). Productivity measurement and evaluation: What is available? *National Productivity Review.*

Sisson, G. R. (2001). *Hands-on Training: Low-Cost, High-Return Training.* San Francisco: Berrett-Koehler.

Slatter, P. E. (1990). Models of expertise in knowledge engineering. In H. Adeli (Ed.), *Knowledge Engineering: Vol. 1. Fundamentals* (pp. 130–154). New York: McGraw-Hill.

Sleezer, C. M. (1991). Developing and validating the performance analysis for training model. *Human Resource Development Quarterly, 2*(4), 355–372.

Sleezer, C. M., Cipicchio, D., & Pitonyak, D. (1992). Customizing and implementing training evaluation. *Performance Improvement Quarterly, 5*(4), 55–75.

Sleezer, C. M., Hough, J. R., & Gradous, D. B. (1998). Measurement challenges in evaluation and performance improvement. *Performance Improvement Quarterly, 11*(4), 62–75.

Sleezer, C. M., & Sleezer, J. H. (1997). Finding and using HRD research. In R. A. Swanson & E. F. Holton III (Eds.), *Human Resource Development Research Handbook: Linking Research and Practice* (pp. 183–198). San Francisco: Berrett-Koehler.

Sleezer, C. M., & Swanson, R. A. (1992). Culture surveys: A tool for improving organization performance. *Management Decision, 30*(2), 22–29.

Slife, B. D., & Williams, R. N. (1997). Toward a theoretical psychology: Should a sub-discipline be formally recognized? *American Psychologist, 52,* 117–129.

Smirich, L. (1983). Implications for management theory. In C. C. Putnam & M. E. Pecanowskey (Eds.), *Communications and Organizations: An Interpretive Approach.* Beverly Hills, CA: Sage.

Smith, M. (1993). Evaluation of executive development: A case study. *Performance Improvement Quarterly, 6,* 26–42.

Smith, M. C., & Pourchot, T. (Eds.). (1998). *Adult Learning and Development: Perspectives from Educational Psychology.* Mahwah, NJ: Erlbaum.

Snyder, E. E. (1985). The Chautauqua movement in popular culture: A sociological analysis. *Journal of American Culture, 8*(3), 79–90.

Spector, P. E. (1997). *Job Satisfaction: Application, Assessment, Causes, and Consequences.* Thousand Oaks, CA: Sage.

Spencer, L. J. (1989). *Winning through Participation.* Dubuque, IA: Kendall/Hunt.

Stacey, R. D. (1992). *Managing the Unknowable: Strategic Boundaries between Order and Chaos in Organizations.* San Francisco: Jossey-Bass.

Stata, R. (1989, Spring). Organizational learning—The key to management innovation. *Sloan Management Review,* 63–74.

Steinmetz, C. S. (1976). The history of training. In R. L. Craig (Ed.), *Training and Development Handbook* (2nd ed., pp. 1-3–1-14). New York: McGraw-Hill.

Stern, S. (1992). The relationship between human resource development and corporate creativity in Japan. *Human Resource Development Quarterly, 3*(3), 215–238.

Stewart, G. B. (1999). *The Quest for Value: The EVA Management Guide.* New York: HarperBusiness.

Stiglitz, J. E. (1975, June). The theory of "screening" education and the distribution of income. *American Economic Review, 3,* 283–300.

Stolovich, H. D., & Keeps, E. J. (1992). What is human performance technology? In H. Stolovich & E. Keeps (Eds.), *Handbook of Human Performance Technology* (pp. 3–13). San Francisco: Jossey-Bass.

Stolovich, H. D., & Keeps, E. J. (Eds.). (1999). *Handbook of Human Performance Technology* (2nd ed.). San Francisco: Jossey-Bass.

Stolovich, H. D., Keeps E. J., & Rodrigue, D. (1995). Skill sets for the human performance technologist. *Performance Improvement Quarterly, 8*(2), 40–67.

Strauss, A. S., & Corbin, J. (1998). *Basics of Qualitative Research: Techniques and Procedures for Developing Grounded Theory.* Thousand Oaks, CA: Sage.

Stumpf, S. A., & Freedman, R. D. (1981). The learning style inventory: Still less than meets the eye. *Academy of Management Review, 6,* 297–299.

Sullivan, M. A. (1994). Installation of total quality management in a high-tech environment: The Plant 16 Experience. In L. Kelly (Ed.), *The ASTD Technical and Skills Training Handbook.* New York: McGraw-Hill.

Super, D. E (1980). A life-span, life-space approach to career development. *Journal of Vocational Behavior, 16,* 282–298.

Super, D. E., Savickas, M. L., & Super, C. M. (1996). The life-span, life-space approach to careers. In D. Brown, L. Brooks, & Associates (Eds.), *Career Choice and Development* (3rd ed.). San Francisco: Jossey-Bass.

Super, D. E., & Sverko, B. (1995). *Life Roles, Values, and Careers: International Findings of the Work Importance Study.* San Francisco: Jossey-Bass.

Sveiby, K. E. (1997). *The New Organizational Wealth: Managing and Measuring Intangible Assets.* San Francisco: Berrett-Koehler.

Swanson, D. L. (1995). Addressing a theoretical problem by reorienting the corporate social responsibility performance model. *Academy of Management Review, 20,* 43–64.

Swanson, R. A. (1980). Training technology: The system and the course. *Journal of Epsilon Pi Tau, 6*(2), 9–52.

Swanson, R. A. (1982). Industrial training. In W. H. Mitzel (Ed.), *5th Encyclopedia of Educational Research* (pp. 864–870). New York: Macmillan.

Swanson, R. A. (1993). Scientific management is a Sunday school picnic compared to reengineering. *Human Resource Development Quarterly, 4*(3), 219–221.

Swanson, R. A. (1994). *Analysis for Improving Performance: Tools for Diagnosing Organizations and Documenting Workplace Expertise.* San Francisco: Berrett-Koehler.

Swanson, R. A. (1995). Human resource development: Performance is the key. *Human Resource Development Quarterly, 62*(2), 207–213.

Swanson, R. A. (1996a). In praise of the dependent variable. *Human Resource Development Quarterly, 7*(3), 203–207.

Swanson, R. A. (1996b). *Training for Performance System: Field Handbook.* St. Paul, MN: Swanson & Associates.

Swanson, R. A. (1997a). HRD Research: Don't go to work without it! In R. A. Swanson & E. F. Holton (Eds.), *Human Resource Development Research Handbook: Linking Research and Practice* (pp. 3–20). San Francisco: Berrett-Koehler.

Swanson, R. A. (1997b). TADDS short (Theory application deficit disorder). *Human Resource Development Quarterly, 8*(3), 1–3.

Swanson, R. A. (1998a). Demonstrating the financial benefit of HRD: Status and update on the theory and practice. *Human Resource Development Quarterly, 9,* 285–295.

Swanson, R. A. (1998b). The discipline of human resource development. In R. J. Torraco (Ed.), *Academy of Human Resource Development 1998 Annual Proceedings* (pp. 880–887). Baton Rouge, LA: AHRD.

Swanson, R. A. (1998c). The witch doctor's pharmacist. *Human Resource Development International, 1*(1), 7–8.

Swanson, R. A. (1999). The foundations of performance improvement and implications for practice. In R. Torraco (Ed.), *Performance Improvement Theory and Practice: Advances in Developing Human Resources* (pp. 1–25). Thousand Oaks, CA: Sage.

Swanson, R. A. (2001a). *Assessing the Financial Benefits of Human Resource Development.* Cambridge, MA: Perseus.

Swanson, R. A. (Ed.). (2001b). Origins of contemporary human resource development. *Advances in Developing Human Resources, 3*(2). Thousand Oaks, CA: Sage.

Swanson, R. A., & Arnold, D. E. (1997). The purpose of HRD is to improve performance. In R. Rowden (Ed.), *Workplace Learning: Debating Five Critical Questions of Theory and Practice* (pp. 13–19). San Francisco: Jossey-Bass.

Swanson, R. A., & Falkman, S. K. (1997). A survey of beginning trainer development problems and expert solutions: An analysis of novice and expert trainers. *Human Resource Development Quarterly, 8*(4), 305–314.

Swanson, R. A., & Gradous, D. (1986). *Performance at Work.* New York: Wiley.

Swanson, R. A., & Gradous, D. (1988). *Forecasting Financial Benefits of Human Resource Development.* San Francisco: Jossey-Bass.

Swanson, R. A., & Holton, E. F., III. (1997). *Human Resource Development Research Handbook: Linking Research and Practice.* San Francisco: Berrett-Koehler.

Swanson, R. A., & Holton, E. F., III. (1998). Process-referenced expertise: Developing and maintaining core expertise in the midst of change. *National Productivity Review, 17*(2), 29–38.

Swanson, R. A., & Holton, E. F., III. (1999). *Results: How to Assess Performance, Learning and Perceptions in Organizations.* San Francisco: Berrett-Koehler.

Swanson, R. A., Horton, G. R., & Kelly, V. (1986). Exploitation: One view of industry and business. *Journal of Industrial Teacher Education, 25*(1), 12–22.

Swanson, R. A., & Law, B. (1993). Whole-part–whole learning model. *Performance Improvement Quarterly, 6*(1), 43–53.

Swanson, R. A., Lynham, S., Ruona, W. E., & Provo. J. M. (1998). Human resource development's role in supporting and shaping strategic organizational planning. In R. Torraco (Ed.), *Academy of Human Resource Development 1998 Annual Proceedings* (pp. 589–594). Baton Rouge, LA: AHRD.

Swanson, R. A., & Sawzin, S. A. (1975). *Industrial Training Research Project.* Bowling Green, OH: Bowling Green State University.

Swanson, R. A., & Sleezer, C. M. (1989). Determining financial benefits of an organization development program. *Performance Improvement Quarterly, 2*(1), 55–65.

Swanson, R. A., & Torraco, R. J. (1994). The history of technical training. In L. Kelly (Ed.), *The ASTD Technical Skills Training Handbook.* New York: McGraw-Hill.

Tannenbaum, R., & Hanna, R. W. (1985). Holding on, letting go, and moving on: Understanding a neglected perspective on change. In R. Tannenbaum, N. Marguiles, F. Massarick, & Associates (Eds.), *Human Systems Development.* San Francisco: Jossey-Bass.

Taylor, F. W. (1912). *The Principles of Scientific Management.* New York: Harper's.

Tennant, M. (1986). An evaluation of Knowles' theory of adult learning. *International Journal of Lifelong Education, 5,* 113–122.

Tennant, M. (1997). *Psychology and Adult Learning.* London: Routledge.

Tennant, M., & Pogson, P. (1995). *Learning and Change in the Adult Years: A Developmental Perspective.* San Francisco: Jossey-Bass.

Thijssen, J. G. L. (1992). The meaning of an HRD department. *Opleiding & Ontwikkeling, 5,* 29–32.

Thurow, L. (1993). *Head to Head: The Coming Economic Battle among Japan, Europe, and America.* New York: Warner.

Tichy, N. M. (1983). *Managing Strategic Change: Technical, Political, and Cultural Dynamics.* New York: Wiley.

Tichy, N. M., Fombrun, C. J., & Devanna, M. A. (1982). Strategic human resource management. *Sloan Management Review, 22,* 47–60.

Tolman, E. C. (1932). *Purposive Behavior in Animals and Men.* New York: Naiburg.

Torraco, R. J. (1992). Accelerated training 1992: Buyer beware. *Human Resource Development Quarterly, 3*(2), 183–186.

Torraco, R. J. (1997). Theory building research methods. In R. A. Swanson & E. F. Holton (Eds.), *Human Resource Development Research Handbook* (pp. 114–137). San Francisco: Berrett-Koehler.

Torraco, R. J. (1998). Economics as a foundation for HRD. In R. Torraco (Ed.), *Proceedings of the 1998 Academy of Human Resource Development Conference.* Baton Rouge, LA: Academy of Human Resource Development.

Torraco, R. J. (2000). A theory of knowledge management. In R. W. Herling & J. M. Provo (Eds.), *Strategic Perspectives on Knowledge, Competence, and Expertise* (pp. 38–62). San Francisco: Berrett-Koehler.

Torraco, R. A., & Swanson, R. A. (1995). The strategic roles of human resource development. *Human Resource Planning, 18*(4), 10–21.

Tracey, J. B., Tannenbaum, S. I., & Kavanaugh, M. J. (1995). Applying trained skills on the job: The importance of the work environment. *Journal of Applied Psychology, 80,* 239–252.

Trist, E. L., & Bamforth, K. (1951). Social and psychological consequences of longwall coal mining. *Human Relations, 4,* 3–38.

Tuckman, B. (1965). Developmental sequence in small groups. *Psychological Bulletin, 63,* 384–399.

Tuckman, B., & Jensen, M. (1977). Stages of small group development revisited. *Group and Organizational Studies, 2,* 419–427.

Twitchell, S., Holton, E. F., III, & Trott, J. W., Jr. (2000). Technical training evaluation practices in the United States. *Performance Improvement Quarterly.*

Ulrich, D., Zenger, J., & Smallwood, N. (1999). *Results-Based Leadership.* Boston: Harvard Business School Press.

U.S. Civil Service Commission, Bureau of Training. (1969). *Application of a Systems Approach to Training: A Case Study.* Training Systems and Technology Series. No. 11. Washington, DC: Government Printing Office.

University of Minnesota HRD Faculty (1994). *Human Resource Development Definition.* St. Paul, MN: Author.

Van de Ven, A. (1986). Central problems in the management of innovation. *Management Science, 32,* 590–607.

Van de Ven, A. H., Polley, D. E., Garud, R., & Venkataraman, S. (1999). *The Innovation Journey.* New York: Oxford University Press.

Van de Ven, A. H., & Poole, M. S. (1995). Explaining development and change in organizations. *Academy of Management Review, 20,* 51–54.

Van de Ven, A., & Rogers, E. (1988). Innovations and organizations: Critical perspectives. *Communication Research, 15*(5), 632–651.

Van der Heijden, K. (1996). *Scenarios: The Art of Strategic Conversation.* New York: Wiley.

Van der Krogt, F. J. (1998). Learning network theory: The tension between learning systems and works systems in organizations. *Human Resource Development Quarterly, 9,* 157–177.

Van der Merwe, L. (1997). *Scenario Building: Keynote Address for the 1997 AHRD Annual Conference.* Johannesburg, South Africa: Centre for Innovative Leadership.

VanLehn, K. (1989). Problem solving and cognitive skill acquisition. In M. Posner (Ed.), *Foundations of Cognitive Science* (pp. 560–569). Cambridge, MA: MIT Press.

von Bertalanffy, L. (1962). General system theory: A critical review. *General Systems* (Yearbook of the Society for General Systems Research), *7,* 1–20.

von Bertalanffy, L. (1968). *General Systems Theory: Foundations, Development, Applications.* New York: Braziller.

Wack, P. (1985a). Scenarios: Shooting the rapids. *Harvard Business Review, 63*(6), 139–150.

Wack, P. (1985b). Scenarios: Uncharted waters ahead. *Harvard Business Review, 63*(5), 73–89.

Wallace, S. R., Jr., & Twitchell, C. M. (1953). *Evaluation of a training course for life insurance agents. Personnel Psychology, 6*(1) 25–43.

Walton, J. (1999). *Strategic Human Resource Development.* London: Financial Times.

Warfield, J. N. (1995). Demands imposed on systems science by complexity. In K. Ellis, A. Gregory, B. R. Mears-Young, & G. Ragsdell (Eds.), *Critical Issues in Systems Theory and Practice* (pp. 81–88). New York: Plenum.

Watkins, K. E. (1990). Tacit beliefs of human resource developers: Producing unintended consequences. *Human Resource Development Quarterly, 1*(3).

Watkins K. E., & Marsick, V. J. (1992). Towards a theory of informal and incidental learning in organizations. *International Journal of Lifelong Education, 11*(2), 287–300.

Watkins, K. E. (1989). Five metaphors: Alternative theories for human resource development. In D. Gradous (Ed.), *Systems Theory Applied to Human Resource Development* (pp. 167–184). Alexandria, VA: ASTD Press.

Watkins, K. E., & Marsick, V. J. (1993). *Sculpting the Learning Organization: Lessons in the Art and Science of Systematic Change.* San Francisco: Jossey-Bass.

Watkins, K. E., & Marsick, V. J. (1995). The case for learning. In E. F. Holton III (Ed.), *Proceedings of the 1995 Academy of Human Resource Development Annual Conference.* Baton Rouge, LA: Academy of Human Resource Development.

Watson, R. I., & Evans, R. B. (1991). *The Great Psychologists: A History of Psychological Thought.* New York: HarperCollins.

Weick, K. E. (1976). Educational organizations as loosely coupled systems. *Administrative Science Quarterly, 21,* 1–19.

Weick, K. E., & Quinn, R. E. (1999). Organization development and change. *Annual Review of Psychology, 50,* 361–386.

Weinberger, L. A. (1998). Commonly held theories of human resource development. *Human Resource Development International, 1,* 75–93.

Weisbord, M. R. (1987). *Productive Workplaces: Organizing and Managing for Dignity, Meaning, and Community.* San Francisco: Jossey-Bass.

Weisbord, M. R., & Janoff, S. (1995). *Future Search: An Action Guide to Finding Common Ground in Organizations and Communities.* San Francisco: Berrett-Koehler.

Wellbourne, T. M., & Andrews, A. O. (1996). Predicting the performance of initial public offerings: Should human resource management be in the equation? *Academy of Management Journal, 39,* 891–919.

Wellman, H. M., & Gellman, S. A. (1992). Cognitive development: Foundational theories of core domains. In M. R. Rosenzweig & L. W. Porter (Eds.), *Annual Review of Psychology* (Vol. 43, pp. 337–375). Stanford, CA: Annual Reviews.

Whitbourne, S. K. (1986). *Adult Identity and Work.* New York: Praeger.

Wiggins, J. A., Wiggins, B. B., & Vander Zanden, J. (1994). *Social Psychology* (5th ed.). New York: McGraw-Hill.

Wimbiscus, J. J. (1995). A classification and description of human resource development scholars. *Human Resource Development Quarterly, 6,* 5–38.

Wiswell, B., & Ward, S. (1997). Combining constructivism and andragogy in computer software training. In R. Torraco (Ed.), *Proceedings of the 1997 Academy of Human Resource Development Annual Conference.* Baton Rouge, LA: Academy of Human Resource Development.

Wognum, A. A. M., & Mulder, M. M. (1999). Strategic HRD within companies. *International Journal of Training and Development, 3*(1), 2–13.

Wood, R., & Bandura, A. (1989). Social cognitive theory of organizational management. *Academy of Management Review, 14,* 361–384.

Woodall, J. (2000). Management and leadership: Issues for integration in the emergent economy. *Human Resource Development International, 3*(1), 122–127.

Wren, D. A. (1979). *The Evolution of Management Thought* (2nd ed.). New York: Wiley.

Wright, P. M., McMahan, G. C., & McWilliams, A. (1994). Human resources and sustained competitive advantage. *International Journal of Human Resource Management, 5,* 301–326.

Wythe, G., & Latham, G. (1997). The futility of utility analysis revisited: when even an expert fails. *Personnel Psychology, 50,* 601–610.

Yorks, L., O'Neil, J, & Marsick, V. (Eds.). (1999). *Action Learning.* San Francisco: Berrett-Koehler.

Zuboff, S. (1988). *In the Age of the Smart Machine.* New York: Basic Books.

Name Index

Subject Index

About the Authors

Richard A. Swanson is professor of human resource development at the University of Minnesota. He is an internationally recognized authority on the strategic roles of human resource development, organizational change, performance improvement, adult learning, the analysis and evaluation of work behavior, and the financial analysis of human capital investments. He received his doctoral degree from the University of Illinois. His undergraduate and master's degrees are from the College of New Jersey.

During Swanson's thirty years of experience, he has performed consulting work for several of the largest corporations in the United States in the areas of performance improvement, strategic human resource planning, personnel training, organization development, and quality improvement. He has documented core business processes, designed management development programs, produced self-instructional technical training materials, guided organizational change efforts, and determined the return on investment of human capital investments. Some of the firms he has consulted with include Arthur Andersen Consulting, AT&T, 3M, Liquid Carbonic, PEMEX, Champion International, CIGNA, Citicorp, Ford, General Motors, Honeywell, Marathon Oil, Medtronic, and Sprint. He has conducted study trips to Great Britain, Japan, Germany, Netherlands, and South Africa for the purpose of studying their performance improvement, organization development, and personnel training practices.

Swanson has written or cowritten more than two hundred publications on the subjects of performance and human resource development. He is coauthor of *Performance At Work: A Systematic Program for Analyzing Work Behavior* (Wiley, 1986), the award-winning book *Forecasting Financial Benefits of Human Resource Development* (Jossey-Bass, 1988), and the 1990 ASTD monograph *Performance Appraisal: Perspectives on a Quality Management Approach*. His book *Analysis for Improving Performance: Tools for Diagnosing Organizations & Documenting Workplace Expertise* (Berrett-Koehler, 1994), received the outstanding book awards from the International Society for Performance Improvement and the Society for Human Resource Management. His coedited book, *Human Resource Development Research Handbook: Linking Research and Practice,* was released by Berrett-Koehler in 1997. Other books include *The Adult Learner* (5th ed.), with Malcolm Knowles, Elwood Holton III, and Swanson (Gulf, 1998) and *Results: How to Assess Performance, Learning, and Perceptions in Organizations* by Swanson and Holton (Berrett-Koehler, 1999), which is the main selection by the Executive Program Book Club. Books released in 2001 include *Assessing the Financial Benefits of Human Resource Development* (Perseus) and *Foundations of Human Resource Development*. Swanson has also served as editor of the *Journal of Industrial Teacher Education*, the *Performance and Instruction Journal*, founding editor of the *Human Resource Development Quarterly*, and founding editor of *Advances in Developing Human Resources*.

Swanson is presently on the boards of directors for LifeFormations, Inc., The Rite Stuff, Inc., and the Minnesota Business Academy and is past president of the Academy of Human Resource Development (AHRD). He also served on the Edison Welding Institute board of directors, was director of Graduate Studies in Industrial Technology (University of Northern Iowa), and was director of Graduate Studies in Career Education and Technology (Bowling Green State University). In 1993, he received the American Society for Training and Development (ASTD) professors' network national award for his Outstanding Contribution to the Academic Advancement of Human Resource Development. In 1995, ASTD/AHRD established the Richard A. Swanson Award for Excellence in Research. Swanson received the Outstanding HRD Scholar Award in 2000 from the AHRD and was inducted into the International Adult and Continuing Education Hall of Fame in 2001.

Elwood F. "Ed" Holton III is professor of human resource development in the School of Human Resource Education and Workforce Development at Louisiana State University, where he coordinates the B.S., M.S., and Ph.D. degree programs in HRD. He is also the founder and executive director of the Center for Leadership Development at LSU. He is immediate past president of the Academy of Human Resource Development. His research focuses on analysis and evaluation of organizational learning and performance systems, improving learning transfer systems, new employee development and retention, management and leadership development, and HRD policy and strategy. His research has won numerous awards, including the Richard A. Swanson Research Excellence Award from the Academy of Human Resource Development and six Citations of Excellence from ANBAR Management Intelligence. He teaches many different courses, including Fundamentals of Human Resource Development, Principles of Adult Education, Needs Assessment in Training and Development, Advanced Training Design and Methods, HRD Evaluation, Leadership in Organizations, Consulting in Organizations, Advanced HRD Theory, and Managing Change in Organizational Systems.

He is the author or editor of fifteen books, including coeditor of *Improving Learning Transfer Systems in Organizations* (Jossey-Bass, forthcoming); coeditor of *Costing, Monitoring, and Managing Employee Turnover* (ASTD Press, forthcoming); coauthor of *Approaches to Training and Development* (Perseus, forthcoming); coauthor of *How to Succeed in Your First Job: Tips for New College Graduates, So You Are New Again: How to Succeed When You Change Jobs,* and *Helping Your New Employee Succeed: Tips for Managers of New College Graduates* (Berrett-Koehler, 2001); coauthor of *The Adult Learner* (Gulf, 1998); co-author of *Results: How to Assess Performance, Learning, and Perceptions in Organizations* (Berrett-Koehler, 1999), which is the main selection of the Executive Program Book Club; author of *The Ultimate New Employee Survival Guide.* (Petersons, 1998); coeditor of the *HRD Research Handbook* (Berrett-Koehler, 1997); editor of the case book *Leading Change in Organizations* (ASTD, 1997); and coeditor of *Conducting Needs Assessment* (ASTD Press, 1995). Holton has also authored more than two hundred additional publications including academic and professional articles in journals such as *Advances in Developing Human Resources, Human Resource Development Quarterly, Human Resource Development International,* andb *Performance Improvement Quarterly.*

In addition, he is the founding editor of *Human Resource Development Review,* a new quarterly refereed journal devoted to theory and theory building in human resource development. He has also on the editorial board of *HRD Quarterly, Human Resource Development International,* and *Advances in Developing Human Resources* and is a reviewer for *Performance Improvement Quarterly, Personnel Psychology, Human Performance,* and the *International Journal of Training and Development.*

Holton has over seventeen years of experience consulting with a wide variety of private, public, and nonprofit organizations on human resource development and performance improvement issues. Some of the organizations he has consulted with include Formosa Plastics Corp., Baton Rouge City Police, J. P. Morgan, Cigna Corp., Enterprise Rent-a-Car, Ford Motor Company, Honeywell, U.S. Department of Energy, U.S. General Services Administration, eleven Louisiana state government departments, the Multiple Sclerosis Society, and Louisiana Workers Compensation Corp. He has personally designed and delivered programs to thousands of people during the last fifteen years. His many workshops and training programs include such diverse topics as new employee adaptation and socialization, training evaluation, training design and methods, adult learning principles, performance analysis, data collection methods in HRD, enhancing employee retention, assessing learning outcomes from training, managing the transition from college to work, needs assessment, management development, leadership, MBTI-based interpersonal skills, change and transition management, and career development. He is also trained in organizational development and consults on issues such as organizational climate and culture, organizational change, team building and organizational design.

Holton received his B.S. in business, an M.B.A., and an Ed.D. in human resource development, all from Virginia Tech. His other career positions include being president of his own human resource and organizational development consulting firm; director of Virginia Tech's Northern Virginia MBA program and directing its MBA career planning and placement services; and an analyst in international finance with the DuPont Co.